STRATEGIC COUNTRYSIDE MANAGEMENT

Related books

Countryside Stewardship: Policies, Farmers and Markets
1999, by G. van Huylenbroeck
ISBN: 0-08-043587-4

Adventure Tourism
Book, 2003, by John Swarbrooke
ISBN: 0-7506-5186-5

Related books

Land Use Policy
ISSN: 0264-8377

Journal of Rural Studies
ISSN: 0743-0167

Progress in Planning
ISSN: 0305-9006

Applied Geography
ISSN: 0143-6228

STRATEGIC COUNTRYSIDE MANAGEMENT

BY

Guy Garrod
University of Newcastle upon Tyne, UK

and

Martin Whitby
University of Newcastle upon Tyne, UK

2005

ELSEVIER

Amsterdam – Boston – Heidelberg – London – New York – Oxford
Paris – San Diego – San Francisco – Singapore – Sydney – Tokyo

ELSEVIER B.V.	ELSEVIER Inc.	**ELSEVIER Ltd**	ELSEVIER Ltd
Radarweg 29	525 B Street, Suite 1900	**The Boulevard, Langford**	84 Theobalds Road
P.O. Box 211	San Diego	**Lane, Kidlington**	London
1000 AE Amsterdam	CA 92101-4495	**Oxford OX5 1GB**	WC1X 8RR
The Netherlands	USA	**UK**	UK

© 2005 Elsevier Ltd. All rights reserved.

This work is protected under copyright by Elsevier Ltd, and the following terms and conditions apply to its use:

Photocopying
Single photocopies of single chapters may be made for personal use as allowed by national copyright laws. Permission of the Publisher and payment of a fee is required for all other photocopying, including multiple or systematic copying, copying for advertising or promotional purposes, resale, and all forms of document delivery. Special rates are available for educational institutions that wish to make photocopies for non-profit educational classroom use.

Permissions may be sought directly from Elsevier's Rights Department in Oxford, UK; phone: (+44) 1865 843830, fax: (+44) 1865 853333, e-mail: permissions@elsevier.com. Requests may also be completed on-line via the Elsevier homepage (http://www.elsevier.com/locate/permissions).

In the USA, users may clear permissions and make payments through the Copyright Clearance Center, Inc., 222 Rosewood Drive, Danvers, MA 01923, USA; phone: (+1) (978) 7508400, fax: (+1) (978) 7504744, and in the UK through the Copyright Licensing Agency Rapid Clearance Service (CLARCS), 90 Tottenham Court Road, London W1P 0LP, UK; phone: (+44) 20 7631 5555; fax: (+44) 20 7631 5500. Other countries may have a local reprographic rights agency for payments.

Derivative Works
Tables of contents may be reproduced for internal circulation, but permission of the Publisher is required for external resale or distribution of such material. Permission of the Publisher is required for all other derivative works, including compilations and translations.

Electronic Storage or Usage
Permission of the Publisher is required to store or use electronically any material contained in this work, including any chapter or part of a chapter.

Except as outlined above, no part of this work may be reproduced, stored in a retrieval system or transmitted in any form or by any means, electronic, mechanical, photocopying, recording or otherwise, without prior written permission of the Publisher.
Address permissions requests to: Elsevier's Rights Department, at the fax and e-mail addresses noted above.

Notice
No responsibility is assumed by the Publisher for any injury and/or damage to persons or property as a matter of products liability, negligence or otherwise, or from any use or operation of any methods, products, instructions or ideas contained in the material herein. Because of rapid advances in the medical sciences, in particular, independent verification of diagnoses and drug dosages should be made.

First edition 2005

British Library Cataloguing in Publication Data
A catalogue record is available from the British Library.

ISBN: 0-08-043889-X

∞ The paper used in this publication meets the requirements of ANSI/NISO Z39.48-1992 (Permanence of Paper). Printed in The Netherlands.

Contents

1. What is the Countryside? — 1
2. The Land Resource — 21
3. The Policy Machine — 37
4. Organisations and Management — 51
5. Planning for the Future — 75
6. Managing Information in the Countryside — 99
7. Accounting for the Countryside — 119
8. Financing the Countryside — 133
9. Allocating Funds — 149
10. Assessing the Impacts of Development — 163
11. Country Sports and Other Private Goods — 181
12. Public Goods and Property Rights — 195
13. Protecting the Countryside — 213
14. Incentives for Countryside Management — 241
15. Managing Access to the Countryside — 261
16. The Demand for Countryside Recreation — 281
17. Visitor Management — 295
18. A Future for Strategic Countryside Management — 315

Author Index 327

Subject Index 331

Chapter 1

What is the Countryside?

1. Introduction

Although built on natural foundations, the countryside remains very much a human construct. In developed countries, especially those with a mainly urban population, the key actors in debates about the countryside include those who live in and perhaps "own" parts of it, those whose livings depend upon it, those who visit, and those who care about it. There are many overlaps between these groups and the interactions between them provide much of the justification for countryside management. Our definition of this activity, given later in this chapter, is based on the need to manage countryside resources in ways that meet the sometimes conflicting needs of each of these groups.

We begin, however, by exploring the basic question: what is the countryside? There has been considerable debate among academics and politicians as to when an area of land should be classified as "rural." The resulting definitions are often based on population densities, and vary across different countries (Roberts & Hall 2001). Similarly, arguments arise when attempting to decide what is meant when we use the word "countryside" and whether or not this is the same as "rural." It is our contention that, in practice, such definitions are redundant and the important focus should be what individuals think of as countryside. Perceptions of what constitutes countryside inform a variety of sources, including the regular Great Britain Leisure Day Visits Survey (e.g. TNS Travel and Tourism 2004) an important source of information on how many people visit the countryside. For many of us whether or not we perceive an area of land as "countryside" will depend to a great extent on how that land is used and the values and ideas that we associate with those uses. On this basis, land use may be a sensible starting point in any text attempting to take a strategic approach to the management of the countryside.

Despite the importance of this issue, many texts on the countryside report only primary land use. This term describes the single dominant activity on an area of land, generally agriculture, forestry or urban use. Such simple descriptions can conceal as much as they reveal and hide the important fact that in most cases land has a number of secondary uses. Thus, agricultural land may be a valuable water catchment, provide habitats for non-agricultural plants and animals, store or recycle various substances (for example the greenhouse gases associated with global warming), and help to determine the landscape which is the key input for a range of recreational and cultural activities. Furthermore, any such definition of land use is static, ignoring the movement of land between different uses, a point we return to in Chapter 2.

Not surprisingly, when a change in land use is proposed, many people with an interest in the issue may attempt to influence events. This may be achieved by purchasing the land, thus acquiring some of the necessary rights to determine how it is used. A more common approach is to dispute the proposed change in use, either through the political process, or through the planning system (see Chapter 13). It is important to note that many of those participating in such debates have no claim to the ownership of the land but may legitimately assert some rights when change of use is under consideration. Legitimacy here would include what is politically acceptable as well as what is consistent with the law.

Many of the major items on the countryside management agenda are generated by the conflicting or competing demands over land. Such pressures have developed over long periods, so it is appropriate to begin this account with a review of the historical development of the countryside. Before attempting a more precise definition of countryside management, we briefly examine some of the major issues facing modern countryside managers and argue that a strategic approach is required in order to deal with them effectively.

2. The Evolution of the Countryside

To understand the modern countryside it is not necessary to go back to the earliest human occupation of the land that we now call the United Kingdom. The human relics of those periods form an important cultural element of the countryside and provide a potential attraction for visitors; however, the landscape in which our earliest predecessors lived differed in many important ways from what we know today. Indeed, it was not until the end of the first millennium AD, that the patterns of human settlement and agriculture that would provide the basis of the modern countryside became widely established.

Limitations in transport and communications at that time prevented any regional specialisation of agricultural production and the maintenance of law and order was also largely a local matter. Following the Norman Conquest in 1066, the system of land use was codified and rural occupation was standardised at the level of the manor. During much of the first half of the last millennium, land which was not held in manors was usually either owned by the crown or by the church; indeed, many Lords of the Manor held their land in the gift of the crown on condition of accepting certain military obligations.

Postan (1972) suggests that before the Norman Conquest "*the church had acquired a large part, perhaps as much as one third, of all England's occupied surface. The possessions were, as a rule, also held in large units.*" Following the Conquest, the Normans re-assigned the ownership of estate properties either to William the Conqueror or to those accompanying him. "*The superior ownership of land was vested in the Crown from whom all other titles now derived.*" Below the Crown, a systematic framework of land ownership and occupation, consisting of a hierarchy of owners, tenants and sub-tenants, covered the whole of England.

In the absence of a cash economy, or any system of written enforceable contracts, the rights to use land had to be assigned on the basis of commonly accepted custom. This "custom of the manor" defined for villagers their individual obligations to and rights in the collective economy (Dahlman 1980). Under this custom, rights to the use of land were carefully specified, differentiating between the rights of private cultivation of land in the few major arable fields and the rights to the key communal resource. The latter included the rights to graze green lanes and tracks, the gleaning and grazing of stubbles, as well as the use of commons and the wastes surrounding the arable fields. Various classes of tenure existed for villagers and this would entitle some to the right of private cultivation on strips in the arable fields. These strips were scattered through the fields in a seemingly random fashion, an apparently inefficient system of land use, the long survival of which is still debated by historians.

The significant contrast within this system was between the allocation of exclusive cultivation rights on the strips in the period between ploughing and harvest, and their use for communal purposes during the rest of the year. The common resources of the manor were extensive and important to all tenants. Decisions were therefore required at various points in the year to determine when land would move from private use to common, and back again.

These decisions were made by the manorial court, which, according to the custom of the manor, managed the collective resources and established the dates of cultivation, sowing, and harvest. Law and order and defence were also regulated by the custom of the manor (Dahlman 1980). Obligations to the manor, in return for the use of land and the provision of defense and law and order, were paid for by labour or through military duties.

It is not necessary to rhapsodise about the manorial system as a model of land management, but in the context of the last millennium, where nation states were just coming into existence in these islands and the technology of agricultural production was primitive, it can be seen as a notable success. Its role in establishing a settled agricultural system which persisted for several hundred years is not in dispute and its contribution to the early stages of economic growth was vital. Its particular interest to countryside managers comes from its ability to provide an effective means of delivering certain goods, such as law and order and defence, that provided common benefits to all members of society. The provision of such "public goods" (see Chapter 12) is, as we shall see, a central role of current countryside management systems.

The eventual demise of the manorial system was brought about by a changing economic and social situation to which other systems were better suited. One important change was the increased use of cash in the economy, a factor which made it possible for labour dues to be converted to wages. At the same time labour costs increased, due to a combination of the early development of urban centres and periodic reductions in the working population through disease (in particular the Black Death, which reached England in 1348). In addition, the developing legal framework led to the increasing use of written contracts and a more specialised economy began to provide inputs for more effective agricultural production.

As well as the manorial system, the Normans also introduced the concept of forests to the British Isles. Initially these had little to do with trees but were areas that certain superior landowners, usually the Crown or the monasteries, defined as forest. Forests might comprise a large area, perhaps several villages and manors, with their associated waste. Initially their main purpose was to provide an area for hunting and the sovereign retained all rights to the chase within them, controlling all activities which might influence the quality of the sport (James 1981). The sovereign might also make concessions regarding use of the forest to those he wished to reward. Such concessions could be very valuable, including the rights to take venison or timber, and possibly including rights of conversion of forest land to cropping (assart). As well as their use as gifts, these rights could also be sold if the monarch needed money. Wild boar were also hunted in the forest and, together with venison, these two species provided an important source of meat: this was highly significant given that cattle and sheep were not much eaten, providing mainly draught power, wool and tallow.

An important related form of land use in that period which, according to Rackham (1986), reached its peak towards the beginning of the fourteenth century, was the deer park. These parks were created by enclosing areas of forest and woodland with fences, high stone walls and banks, so that the deer (mainly fallow deer) within them were easily accessible for harvesting as venison. Rackham estimates that there were some 3,200 parks in England by 1300, averaging about 100 hectares in size and covered some 2% of the country.

The development of Scotland for human use and habitation was different from that experienced in England and Wales. In Scotland the early land owning system was essentially tribal and based on the clans. As the manors were being established in England the agricultural land use evolving in Scotland was based on a dichotomy of cultivation of separate plots or "riggs" on the lower lying inbye land, contrasting with the outbye, used for extensive grazing and hunting, on the slopes of hills and mountains (Bedford Franklin 1952). This inbye system of cultivation was known as run-rigg and the scattered strips or riggs are reminiscent of the manorial system further south, except that the riggs were ridges separated by furrows. It also differed from the English manors in that it was based on one field only, with subsequent weed infestations occasionally obliging the occupants to let the field lie fallow for a year. A further disadvantage of the system was that the riggs might become high enough to make ploughing difficult and to ensure that the furrows in between them became waterlogged. Occasional shifting cultivation might also be practised on the outbye.

The relationship between the Normans and the Scots was different from that in England where they took the role of conquerors. In Scotland, Norman knights helped settle some areas, bringing them under consolidated rule, and in some cases were rewarded with gifts of land. The Norman landlords had much fuller rights over their land than the tribal owners and used these to change the conditions of tenure for their tenants, although they did not succeed in changing their mode of cultivation. In Scotland, as in England and Wales, ownership by the church was very important, with the monasteries often playing a key role in civil administration and economic development. By the late thirteenth century the church had acquired much of the best land in Scotland (Callander 1987).

In England and Wales, the move from the manorial system to one of enclosed agriculture, took several hundred years to complete and two separate phases of enclosure can usefully be differentiated. The first phase, sometimes referred to as the Tudor enclosures, proceeded mainly by adding the waste surrounding the manors to the cultivated area. These areas had traditionally been used as extensive grazing for pigs or for hunting, and could be brought into the manorial cultivated area comparatively easily. In the process of enclosure, traditional common rights were diminished and some communal obligations lapsed. This phase was also affected by the rise of the wool trade with The Netherlands, which led to demands for extensive areas of grazing. Following the Act for Dissolution of the Monasteries of 1536 in England and later legislation in Scotland, large areas of land were transferred to the ownership of the Crown. However, this was passed on by the monarch to other owners, by sale or gift, within a short space of time.

The second phase of enclosure involved a more rigorous Parliamentary process of passing an Enclosure Act for each village. This process, although piecemeal, village by village, was nevertheless radical. Enclosure Commissioners were appointed by the Act of Parliament and would conduct hearings in the village where claims to land rights could be heard. The commissioners would then determine the apportionment of land amongst claimants. Historians debate whether this process seriously disadvantaged the poor, mainly through arguments about how many people were displaced from the countryside and lost their rights to cultivate land. It seems unlikely that the smallest landowners, especially those who had only common rights, will have benefited directly from enclosure. Certainly the main opponents of enclosure during this phase emphasise the appearance of a class of landless labourers, which, more recently, has made it easier for agriculture to reduce its labour force rapidly, as the industry has modernised its production processes. Nevertheless it is not appropriate to assert that all of those displaced from agriculture by enclosure will have lost as a result. As with any migration from one activity to another, many movers will have significantly improved their situation and enhanced their prospects.

Parliamentary enclosure in England was concentrated in the period from the mid-eighteenth to the early nineteenth centuries. In arable areas it produced the countryside with which we are now familiar, typified by regular rectangular fields and scattered farmsteads (Hoskins 1988). Strong opposition to enclosure came from early defenders of the countryside, such as the poets John Clare and William Wordsworth, who particularly attacked the disappearance of extensive public rights of access under the process. The debate about access in England and Wales (see Chapter 15) thus has strong roots in agricultural history, in that enclosure, by creating a more efficient agricultural system also removed many important public rights of access from the countryside.

In Scotland, the transition from tribal to modern land occupation was achieved through a process of feu-ing (Callander 1987), whereby landowners converted traditional tenancies to a fixed rent basis. This differed from the English enclosures in that change could take place on a small scale, driven rapidly by market forces. The resulting land ownership structure is more concentrated, with far fewer landowners than in the rest of the U.K. and consequently offers potential for more rapid change, as proposed in the Land Reform (Scotland) Bill 2003. In the Highlands of Scotland the situation was different in that the land was poorer and was only able to support part-time farming. Other significant activities in the highlands were cattle droving and professional soldiering, often as mercenaries. Haldane (1968) explains how the practice of rieving, which was an activity on the Borders between Scotland and England involving frequent raids across the border to steal cattle, was a natural precursor of the more civilised droving of cattle and sheep from Scottish producing areas to the growing English towns and cities further South. Before the advent of railways, such trade depended on the availability of a group of people able and willing to drive the cattle the substantial distances to market.

The development of the Highlands has not been without substantial problems. For example the Highland Clearances, which spanned the eighteenth and nineteenth centuries, and the rapid establishment of deer forests at the end of the nineteenth century. The Clearances were made by landowners restructuring their estates rapidly to facilitate the introduction of extensively grazed sheep, to meet the demand for wool. Controversy still continues, regarding the rights and wrongs of these events. It was an early major example of the conflict between highlands and lowlands within Scotland, with the highlanders seeing themselves as losing out to the southern landowners who took away their livelihoods. However, it has also been argued that the Highland form of land use, based on what crops could be grown, some droving and military service, had reached the end of its capacity to support the rural population. The potato famine (1846–1848) in Ireland had its counterpart in Scotland and many families left the land and emigrated for that reason. Others were moved to new settlements by landlords and had to find new ways of supporting themselves.

Later in the nineteenth century, another rapid change of land use was introduced in the Highlands with the rapid adoption of deer forests. This was brought about by several factors in combination (Orr 1982). First, economic growth elsewhere, notably in England, the United States and some European countries, generated a wealthy leisured class who were able to spend large sums in providing for their relaxation. Second, the spread of railways made it possible to travel significant distances in pursuit of recreational opportunities. Third, towards the end of the nineteenth century, the production of sheep for meat became uneconomic as refrigerated shipping brought New Zealand and Australian lamb to the British market which had traditionally been supplied partly from the Highlands.

According to Orr, these forces combined to bring significant numbers of wealthy people to Scotland in search of sporting opportunities. The main sport was deer stalking, but grouse shooting was also a significant interest. The new population of sportsmen visited on a seasonal basis, mainly coming by rail to the Highlands. Some of the wealthier sportsmen bought estates and reorganised them round the creation of deer forests, often quite drastically and with little attention to the interests of local people. The introduction of rail also allowed Scotch beef to be delivered to its traditional markets in the South more quickly and cheaply. This was another blow to the Highland working population as it removed the need for cattle droving, an important source of occasional employment in rural areas.

The full impact of these developments can be seen in Orr's estimate that more than one million hectares, nearly a quarter of the agricultural area, were diverted to deer forest management in the Highlands during this period. This implies a significant reduction in agricultural production and, more importantly, the loss of livelihood of many crofters. This very significant change in land use involved an important shift of emphasis from the production of one private good (food) to another (game) and in that sense it is perhaps untypical of the problems confronting countryside managers today. Nevertheless there is an important group of issues surrounding the pursuit of game in the countryside and their impact on many other types of activity. The developmental impact of such switches of activity may be crucial to the continued provision of countryside goods of all kinds.

3. Demographic Development

The *demand* for countryside is expressed by people and their geographical location will influence which areas of countryside they use. Therefore the demographic development of this country has been a key element in the evolution of the countryside. In this section we first report the broad facts of population growth over recent centuries and then seek to establish its distribution on either side of the urban-rural boundary.

3.1. Total Population

Deane & Cole (1967) present a useful summary of the historic evolution of the population of these islands based on an array of sources. They estimate that the population of Britain grew from 6.8 to 10.8 million in the century from 1701 to 1801, when the first Census was taken in Britain. However, Ireland diverged from England and Wales during the nineteenth century. The Irish potato famine in the 1840s, followed by high rates of emigration, reduced the population by 3.5 million, by the end of that century (Deane & Cole 1967). Scotland fared somewhat better in the nineteenth century, although it, too, suffered rural poverty and depopulation during the second half of the century.

The U.K. population as a whole grew threefold between 1851 and 2001. Although, rates of growth were different between its constituent parts. Whilst the population grew least in Northern Ireland, it trebled in England and roughly doubled in Wales and Scotland. The Government publication *Social Trends 2001* (Central Statistical Office 2001) includes a graph projecting population change to 2021, suggesting that an additional four million will be added to the U.K. population over the next 20 years, most of it in England, with a small decline in Scotland.

3.2. Rural Population

The internal distribution of population between urban and rural areas evolved over the eighteenth and nineteenth centuries, as can be seen in Table 1.1.

Comparing the agricultural counties with the industrial/commercial ones, we see roughly double the growth rate in the latter group. So what was the source of these differences in growth rate? It is tempting to argue that agricultural counties could be taken as synonymous with rural and industrial/commercial as approximating the urban situation. However, that is not strictly appropriate in the eighteenth century during which there was still substantial industrial activity in rural areas. Nevertheless, we may say that the industrial and commercial counties include most of the future urban areas in England and Wales. It is in the urbanising counties that we would expect the emergence of an interest in the countryside as a desirable location for recreation.

Table 1.1: Estimated population of England and Wales by type of county, 1701–1831 (millions).

County Type	1701	1751	1781a	1781b	1801	1831
Agricultural	1.95	1.96	2.38	2.33	2.61	3.69
Mixed	1.92	1.93	2.33	2.33	2.79	4.04
Industrial/commercial	1.95	2.25	2.82	2.87	3.76	6.32
Total	5.83	6.14	7.53	7.53	9.16	14.05

Source: Deane & Cole (1967).

8 Strategic Countryside Management

3.3. Urban and Rural Populations

Although there are no time series data for the rural population before 1851, from 1801 population censuses where conducted every ten years and these made a crude division between urban and rural, based essentially, on an administrative classification of what was urban and what was rural. In 1851 it was found that the balance of population between urban and rural had shifted so that England and Wales had become urban dominant, that is the urban population exceeded the rural population. We can see that Figure 1.1. presents a rather complex story, reflecting both a shifting boundary and the fact that people are migrating across it in both directions.

Following the enclosures, the agricultural population had reached its maximum at about 2.1 million, in 1851. After this high point in agricultural employment, technological advances led to new and more efficient farming systems that did not employ so many workers. Pressure on the agricultural workforce was compounded by the great Agricultural Depression of the 1870s and the last quarter of the nineteenth century saw rural poverty on a major scale in the arable districts and to a lesser extent in the livestock areas. From this time agriculture lost its traditional position as a monopoly supplier of the British market in one commodity after another, as other countries began to export large quantities of cheap food.

From the latter half of the nineteenth century we see considerable growth in urban populations, while their rural counterparts remained at much the same levels. Figure 1.1 shows a sharp decline in rural populations between 1951 and 1961: but this is an artifact of changes in the way that rural populations were classified after this date. Rural population increases after 1961 are a product of net out-migration from towns into rural areas. Growth in population has not been equal across all areas and population densities have continued to decline in some remoter rural areas.

The urban-rural dichotomy that now underlies all aspects of the countryside only became important when urban populations became large in comparison with rural ones. The importance of urban dominance is perhaps more symbolic than substantive, but it did signal the very definite arrival of an urban majority in this country. From then on, two distinct interest groups can be identified in the countryside. On one hand are those who live in rural

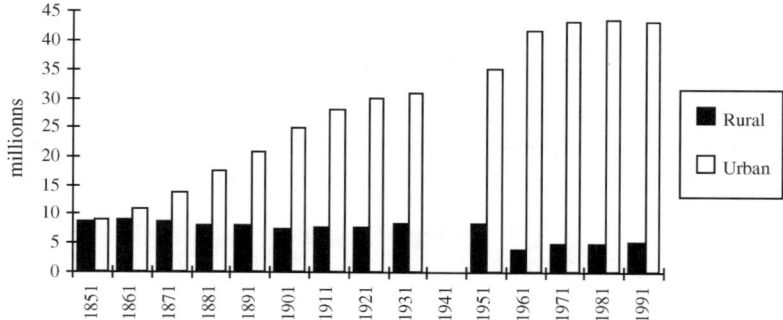

Figure 1.1: Urban and rural populations: England and Wales: 1851–1991. *Source:* Population Census, via Saville (1957), and OPCS (1981) and (1991).

areas, and, on the other are those urban dwellers with an interest in the countryside. The urban interest can be illustrated by the increasing demand for countryside recreation and in the more recent tendency for some urban households to relocate to rural areas.

The discussion so far has dealt with population as a whole. However, from the point of view of recreation demand, it is important to note the growth in the proportion of older people in the population. By 1901 more than half the population was less than 25, whereas by the end of the twentieth century, the proportions in the three age ranges — up to 24, 25–44, and 45 and over — were more nearly the same for both men and women. Indeed, the projection for 2026 shows the proportions in each range (up to 24, 25–44, 45–64 and 65+) approaching equality. The slightly larger number of women than men in the population comes about because women live somewhat longer than men and therefore have a higher proportion in the oldest age range.

4. Shifting Attitudes

Numbers do not tell the whole story. In particular, they tell us nothing about the changing attitudes to the natural world, which underpin the long British love affair with the countryside. These changes have been well documented by Thomas (1983), who notes that at the start of the early modern period[1] *"man's ascendancy over the natural world was the unquestioned object of human endeavour."* By 1800, however, the end of the period of Thomas' analysis, although it was still the objective recognised by most people, doubts and hesitations were being expressed *"about man's place in nature and his relationship to other species."* He considers four questions which were then under discussion in this context:

- Town or country?
- Cultivation or wilderness?
- Conquest or conservation?
- Meat or mercy?

Whilst it is undoubtedly the case that these questions all feature in contemporary debates about the countryside, it is still not clear which way subscribers to the "countryside ethic" would answer them. Love of the countryside is not the sole prerogative of the country dweller. Similarly, wilderness is by no means the only type of countryside favoured in Britain (which may be just as well, given that most ecologists would probably agree that there is now no real wilderness left in these islands). Conservation is generally valued but in many cases can only be achieved following some drastic alterations to the structure of property rights pertaining to land. Finally, while those who love the countryside are by no means all vegetarians, many are concerned with issues of animal welfare.

Thomas provides a thorough review of the way that attitudes to the countryside have evolved in this country over the centuries. In general, he stresses the shift towards a balance, preferring the second of each pair of alternatives. He found that, as urbanisation proceeded,

---

[1] Generally taken to be 1700.

enthusiasm for the countryside grew; as cultivation extended, wilderness was more highly valued; as wilderness was replaced by cultivation and development, its loss was increasingly lamented (often by those who had profited most from its destruction); and distaste for killing animals was expressed both by growing interest in vegetarianism and by attempting to conceal slaughter houses and butchery from the public gaze! However, we cannot assert a majority in favour of any of these positions without more evidence.

Another source of arguments about attitudes comes from the history of landscape. Ousby (1990) rebuts current commentators' received wisdom that tourism is a modern phenomenon and delves more rigorously into its past. He dismisses this view as "*a phantasm, compounded of modern self-dislike, intellectual snobbery and sentimentality about the past.*" He finds striking similarities between modern tourism and the tourism described in Chaucer's Canterbury Tales more than 600 years ago. Stopping short of claiming identity between the two periods, he nevertheless convincingly traces out a long sequence, starting from the crusades and pilgrimages of the middle-ages through to the Grand Tour of Europe which was a necessary step in every young gentleman's education. That was followed, in the eighteenth century, by increasing recognition of the visual and cultural pleasures on offer nearer home. A precondition for that to occur was the construction of roads and the introduction of the steel carriage spring. Spreading railways brought the countryside yet nearer to the towns and made for much easier access by urban populations. He also notes the important change in attitude, from one of regarding the natural world with awe, to recognising its romantic charm. Ousby develops his theme by analysing the evolution of tourism, through its treatment in the literature, with the country house and the crucial roles of information and changing attitudes. He skillfully links these factors in the emergence of the countryside and tourist phenomena.

A related theme is the landscape movement which led to the creation of many properties which are now the focus of many countryside visits. Mowl (2000) has documented the "*great age of the English Arcadia,*" from 1620 to 1820, when amateurs (Gentlemen) vied with professionals (Players) in designing the landed estates and their surrounds. These developments depended upon the availability of resources, which came from both industrial growth and improved agricultural efficiency, and on the interest of those developing their estates. The result has been to create artificial landscapes, which now add to the attractions of the countryside. Many of these properties are now in the hands of the organisations such as the National Trust and English Heritage.

An often cited, and early influential source of information on the countryside, is the poet William Wordsworth. The first edition of his Guide to the Lakes was published anonymously in 1810 and it has been in print ever since. The currently available paperback version (Wordsworth 1835) also contains his lengthy letter to the Editor of the *Morning Post* regarding the proposed railway link from Kendal to Windermere. In his guide he refers to the Lake District as of such importance that it should become a "*sort of national property*" which leads to the thought that he has discovered the concept of public goods. His concluding sentence to the main text is:

> In this wish the author will be joined by persons of pure taste throughout the whole island, who, by their visits (often repeated) to the Lakes in the North of England, testify that they deem the district a sort of national property, in

which every man has a right and interest who has an eye to perceive and a heart to enjoy (p. 92).

However, Wordsworth takes a restrictive view of the public, as his last few words indicate. Evidently he does not mean to include the whole public but only those who share his feelings about of the Lakes. Thus, in an appendix opposing the proposed Kendal and Windermere railway link he argues, for example, that *"the humbler ranks of society are not, and cannot be, in a state to gain material benefit from a more speedy access than they now have to this beautiful region."* Other passages in the text confirm this exclusive view of the countryside.

Of course, the countryside has been celebrated in all forms of communication. The BBC has the world's longest running radio serial in "The Archers — an *everyday story of country folk*" that has been a daily source of information and opinion on matters rural for half a century. More broadly, the rural novel has been an immensely popular literary form for more than a century and has doubtless done much to enhance awareness of countryside matters.

The first four decades of the last century have been surveyed by Cavaliero (1977) and many well-known novelists have contributed to the national enthusiasm for and interest in things rural. Further there are many other writers who bring countryside issues and affairs to the public in a more documentary format. An interesting case is film and television, which, because cameras work best with, or even require, good lighting conditions, may give a false impression of the amount of sunshine typically enjoyed by the countryside! No doubt experience will correct any misapprehensions quickly enough, but the point that much of the information available is by no means representative, is crucial.

A recent treatment of information on the countryside comes from Strong's (1996) review of the first century of the monthly journal *Country Life*. His assessment charts the evolution of ideas purveyed by that highly popular organ of mixed information and opinion. The evolving comparative roles of the different personalities contributing to the journal and the shifting editorial policies it has pursued, provide a fascinating and occasionally bizarre insight into the important impact of journalism in forming opinions and guiding tastes. The tenuous connection between analysis and text and the idiosyncratic editorial control revealed by Strong provide a significant warning about the quality of media information on the countryside.

5. From Town to Country

Taylor (1997) provides a detailed analysis of the countryside movement from the end of the eighteenth through to the middle of the twentieth centuries. He demonstrates in particular the great importance of means of transport from towns to the countryside, emphasising the role of trains and bicycles before access on foot was the main mode. Access on foot was only significant where countryside sites where close to centres of population and these became important where landowners tried to close traditional footpaths. Later, the focus of debate shifted towards questions of wider countryside access to larger spaces and the conflict with shooting became significant.

Trains preceded the bicycle as a means of access and were particularly significant where popular destinations, such as the Lake and Peak Districts were served. The availability of leisure time was also important and the gradual transition from the six-day week towards five and a half days was very important, as was the introduction of annual holidays, to say nothing of the gradual reduction of the working week, mainly during the twentieth century.

The first bicycles — the "penny farthings" — were not well suited to long distance excursions, but the advent of the "safety bicycle," in 1885, (with wheels of more even diameter) paved the way for cycle-based tourism. This use was further boosted by the invention of the pneumatic tyre, in 1888, making cycling both safer and tolerably comfortable.

Over the turn of the nineteenth century these technical innovations were accompanied by the establishment of many cyclist touring clubs. Many of these, including the so-called Clarion Cycling Clubs, were affiliated with the emerging socialist movement. However, none of this would have happened if there had not been enough leisure time available and Taylor (1997) describes the emergence of holidays in some detail. He refers to the early introduction of the "Wakes Week," which emerged in the cotton towns. Initially, in the 1870s, workers were allowed to take "summer holidays of three days beyond the weekend" at their own expense and it was another two decades before this became an official Wakes Week. This innovation led to the emergence of savings clubs, which enabled workers to take advantage of the leisure opportunity.

There were also vigorous campaigns to improve the quality of holiday experiences by encouraging workers to make full use of the countryside and fresh air and avoid the trashy trivialities of the commercial resorts, such as Blackpool, which were exploiting the new consumers vigorously. This lead to sometimes strident debates which involved various elements, including religion and socialism and their respective opponents.

These early development in recreation emphasise the importance of demand for the good and the technology available for its exploitation. These determinants of events are likely to remain important into the future. Availability of leisure time and the means of access to the countryside were then, and remain now, major determinants of demand for countryside recreation. Access possibilities now centre on the private car but there are other significant means of access including public transport and organised tours using chartered buses. If car use is to be more regulated and become more expensive then recreationists may turn to collective means of access. Such facilities are already available, for example the regular weekend outings organised by the Ramblers Association. These are cheap and accessible to urban dwellers and provide a popular alternative to the use of the private car. If motorists are to be obliged to bear more of the costs they currently impose on society, such means are likely to become more popular.

6. The Countryside in the Twentieth Century

Historians (e.g. Davies 1999; Hobbsbawm 1994) recognise the twentieth century as a turbulent period, dominated by two world wars, massive, economic recessions, the neo-liberal phase of the 1980s and 1990s and the subsequent partial recovery from it. Hobbsbawm (1994) divides what he calls the short twentieth century into three separate periods: 1914–1950; 1950–1975; and 1975–1990. The first and last of these he sees as savagely chaotic and the middle period as a golden age. The first period was dire, containing two world wars separated by a long bout of economic disruption and major recession. The period from 1950 to 1975 was one of considerable prosperity and some very positive progress: this included the formation of what is now the European Union.

Hobbsbawm saw the final period as one of chaos initiated under the neo-liberal regime of Margaret Thatcher. Many would contest his view, seeing positive benefits in the challenge she mounted to the established methods of managing the economy. Her government was certainly not afraid to innovate in public-sector management and notably in trying to improve its economic performance, typically by introducing private sector influence and expertise. Some aspects of this period are reviewed in later chapters but, at this stage, it is accepted that a considered verdict on the successes and failures of that period is only now becoming possible.

The twentieth century also saw the introduction of universal suffrage in the U.K., the raising of the school leaving age, the introduction of the welfare state, regular annual holidays, substantial extensions to the normal expectation of life and a massive increase in real incomes. In the prelude to the First World War, there was national concern as to whether there were enough fit males in the population to form an army. By the end of the century concern about the nation's health had switched to the problems of affluence. Poor nutrition due to inappropriate eating habits, the decline of sport in schools and the significant problems of substance abuse in the form of tobacco, alcohol and other drugs, had become disturbingly widespread by the 1990s.

Perhaps the most striking advances of the twentieth century were in communications. Transport increased in reliability, diversity and speed, as rail services were augmented by bicycles, buses, cars and air travel. These changes have transformed the accessibility of rural areas to the population at large. There have also been major improvements in the technology of sailing, with cheap and transportable boats, and in photography, which has become a familiar adjunct to countryside recreational experiences. Those who crave danger have been able to indulge their tastes with hang-gliding, paragliding and bungy-jumping, whilst those indifferent to the fabric of the countryside have been able to assail it with four-wheel drive cars and powerful motorbikes. Verbal communications, spoken written and visual have also expanded rapidly with the progression from telephone, and radio, through film and television, to email and the world-wide-web. This last group of advances has probably done more than any other factors to widen interest in the countryside. It has also provided a set of tools for the strategic management of participation in the countryside.

Thus, a major part of the positive legacy of the twentieth century has been the rapid emergence of the countryside as we now know it. This may contrast with the slow evolution of land use, but comes more sharply into focus when we recognise the crucial importance of the public demand for countryside. The growth of an important group of potential users of the countryside who are based in urban areas is mainly a twentieth century phenomenon, and one that has driven many relevant policy developments in the countryside over the last fifty years.

Another key feature of the twentieth century was the emergence of a land-use planning system after the Second World War. Various experiments in planning had been conducted between the wars but it was the 1947 Town and County Planning Act that first introduced a rigorous system of control of the conversion of land use through the development control process. Although significantly modified by subsequent legislation, the planning system persists, depending on the formation of plans at the local, county or district, level and a requirement that development will not be undertaken without permission (see Culingworth & Nadin 2002). A notable impact of the system is that, despite the construction of some millions of homes and many miles of road, the amount of land used for urban purposes only reached 3.6 million hectares (or 15% of total U.K. surface area) by the end of the twentieth century.

Similar legislation has also been applied to questions of conservation. In particular, the 1949 National Parks and Access to the Countryside Act established the National Parks Commission and the Nature Conservancy, the first with a remit for landscape conservation and the provision of recreational opportunities and the second with a focus on wildlife conservation. This Act might be seen as the formal initiation of countryside management as we now know it. It has been followed by numerous further policy advances that are reviewed in subsequent chapters.

During the period up to 1972 countryside management was perceived as an essentially domestic matter. However, on joining the Common Market, on January 1st 1973, the U.K. undertook to implement a number of policies which where to have a profound effect on the countryside. Initially, the most important of these was the Common Agricultural Policy (CAP), which sought to support the incomes of member state's farmers. However, the CAP has evolved in important ways and other European policies have also had an impact on the countryside. During the last decade there have been some attempts to limit the budgetary demands of the CAP and to reduce some of its adverse effects. These policy developments are reviewed later in this book.

7. The Demand for Countryside

We deal more extensively with the changing demand for and supply of countryside recreation in later chapters. Here a short outline of the themes will suffice. The urban population is now sufficiently numerous to justify recognition as the main source of rural recreationists. These are the "customers" for countryside management. They express demand for what it has to offer in various ways: demand which was generally seen as growing rapidly until recently. The main measurable sources of this growth are summarised in the data of Table 1.2.

Table 1.2: Indicators of growth in leisure demand: England, since 1891.

	1891	1951	1971	1991
Population (millions)	27.2	41.2	46.4	48.1
Average working week (hours)	56–60	44.8	40.4	40.0
Paid annual holiday (weeks)	Rare	1–2	2	4+
Licensed cars (millions)	Negligible	2.1	10.4	19.7
Foreign holiday-goers (percent)	Negligible	3	14	30

Source: House of Commons Environment Committee (1995).

Of course, such data do not give a complete explanation of the growth of recreation demand, but the main factors are there. The key factors include the almost doubling of population in the twentieth century, with most of the growth confined to urban areas; the increase in people of retirement age; some shortening of the average working week; the introduction of holidays with pay; and the phenomenal growth in the use of the car. The comparatively recent growth of foreign holiday-makers underlines the emergence of competition with other types of leisure activity, offering a partial explanation for the House of Commons Environment Committee's (1995) view that the number of holiday visitors to the countryside has not increased significantly in recent years. Careful interpretation of such data can offer useful indications of the present potential for growth in recreational pressure. Note, however, that changes in attitudes towards and tastes for open-air recreation are a significant contributor to this set of arguments, which are nevertheless difficult to measure. The technology underpinning recreation has also advanced in many ways during the last half century as improvements have been made in all types of equipment associated with outdoor recreation.

More fundamental questions arise relating to participation in countryside recreation and the observation that the demand for the countryside is not constant across all social groups. Thus certain social and ethnic groups are consistently under-represented in a range of countryside activities. Such a finding may reflect different tastes and preferences for leisure activities across groups, or more worryingly, the presence of barriers to participation in recreational activities that managers must work to remove. The existence of such barriers will not surprise those familiar with the works of a number of authors on social exclusion in the countryside (e.g. Pavis *et al.* 2001; Shucksmith 2000).

8. The Supply of Countryside

The supply of countryside goods and services arises, mainly but not entirely, as a by-product of primary land uses, particularly from agriculture and forestry but also from various sporting activities. The quality of the goods supplied depends on the local characteristics of farming and forest management as well as on the landform of the area, its location and infrastructure. Land under arable crops is subject to damage by recreational access and such areas are generally not open to the public. Grazed areas, especially semi-natural pastures managed without fences, can easily provide recreational access and can be used for a range of activities. These can be arranged to be consistent with the needs of livestock and may be constrained by use for other activities such as shooting.

Such constraints need not preclude recreation but it may be necessary to schedule recreational use to avoid conflicts with other uses. In the case of commercial forestry, access may well be unattractive or inconvenient during parts of the forest rotation. Perhaps recreational use will be limited to small parts of the forest, such as firebreaks and forest roads, that would generally be completely consistent with forest management. The analytical problem presented by these joint uses is that some, even a majority, of the goods in question are public goods, which means that their management may be problematic. Moreover they are often jointly supplied with private goods, a problem treated in more detail in Chapters 11 and 12.

9. What is Strategic Countryside Management?

To consider this question we can usefully separate countryside from the activity of strategic management. As described previously, the evolution of the countryside has generated an array of public goods which are in turn demanded by present and future populations. Strategic countryside management requires the consideration of all issues affecting the supply of and demand for these public goods, including how they are provided and how they are used. It is argued that our treatment differs from the majority of writing in this field of study, which concentrates either on questions of policy and their analysis, or on the more operational aspects of countryside management. The reason for presenting this book is that countryside managers increasingly find themselves dealing with strategic questions that are placed somewhere below the level of the formation of national policy but above the various operational and technical issues of grassroots management.

Most of the general literature on management, deals with business management at the level of the firm. Whilst this approach has been necessary to the development of the subject, it is nevertheless only of partial relevance to countryside management. This more public sphere of activity directs attention to the essentially public issues of accountability, of the legal aspects of policy, of finance and of a range of issues that are not of concern in private sector management.

Theories which seek to explain management systems and make them more rigorous are typically based on mixtures of political and social sciences. There is a long political-science tradition of analysing the public sector very critically, essentially from an economic viewpoint. It is this perspective that we will combine with some insights from the literature on organisational behaviour to form the basis of our treatment of this subject. This treatment borrows a number of approaches from the standard literature on strategic management and applies them in a public-sector context, with the emphasis on the particular strategic issues facing countryside managers.

The important elements of the countryside that managers have to consider are the availability of funds, the demands of countryside stakeholders, and the willingness of those "producing" countryside to continue to do so on a sustainable basis into the future.

Dillon (1980) proposed a useful definition of farm management as *"the process by which resources and situations are manipulated by the farm manager in trying with less than full information to achieve his goals."* This definition is broad but useful in emphasising the manipulation of situations as well as resources, and in drawing attention to the incompleteness of the information which managers typically face. Incomplete information is virtually always an ingredient of public sector management and requires managers to make judgements which can only be based on experience.

By drawing upon and extending the previous discussion, we arrive at a suggested definition of countryside management as:

> The manipulation of countryside resources and situations, often with incomplete information, to provide a sustainable supply of the countryside goods demanded by stakeholders.

This definition does not cover all aspects of countryside management and leaves scope for the judgement of the individual manager. There will also be a varying need for more conventional management skills from those responsible for the countryside.

Reflecting the title of this volume we use the word *strategic* to imply a particular level of managerial activity. Most agencies working in the countryside operate at several levels. They will carry out specific activities, often at a local level and small scale, as their main remit. But over longer periods they must pursue more substantial objectives and will be judged on the extent to which these have been achieved. Their effectiveness will be judged on the key question of whether or not their work maintains or enhances the level of public benefit generated by the countryside. *Strategic* countryside management is therefore defined as:

> The process of designing and implementing strategies, often with incomplete information, to ensure the sustainable and equitable use of resources in the countryside and to optimise the welfare produced from them over time for all stakeholders.

10. Using This Book

Countryside Management is the ultimate multi-disciplinary subject, and is evolving as we write. This means that no single text will cover all of the user's needs. Volumes of information of diverse quality are currently available from an array of sources and we refer to specific texts where appropriate. The disciplinary basis of countryside management includes all the underpinnings of any other form of management and also demands a thorough understanding of the countryside, how it is evolving and the pressures under which it has to work.

To keep up to date, managers must be aware of a variety of information sources. Many of these are official publications, often available free of charge, either on the web or through other media. One single journal, which covers many of the themes of countryside management is ECOS, published by the British Association of Nature Conservationists. For more fundamental treatments of issues, academic and professional journals are available. We refer to those in the text but we do not know at the time of writing what is being written everywhere, so constant attention to new source material is essential.

This chapter has illustrated the breadth of the subject and persuaded the reader that perusal of this book will be no more than the beginning of a substantial commitment of effort. The authors are well aware that we will be unable to give all subjects the depth of coverage that they deserve and the serious reader will find it essential to consult other sources. In particular we have not tried to summarise the town and country planning systems operating within the U.K., as this is well covered by many excellent texts (e.g. Cullingworth & Nadin 2002). Nor have we covered such specialist skills as human resource management or rangering. Moreover, those wishing to make more progress with the specific academic underpinnings of countryside management will have to consult the relevant specialist texts.

The remainder of the book can be loosely divided into five parts with each of the component chapters ending with a summary of the various strategic implications of the preceding material. The first deals in more detail with the context of countryside management, summarising the land use situation and the institutions governing it. It reviews the socio-political and the organisational contexts in which managers work and summarises the development of aims and objectives for management. The second part focuses on managing resources, including information management and financing the countryside including financial management, funding budgeting and assessing the impact of development. The third part discusses the supply of countryside goods, both public and private, the regulatory framework, the role of management agreements and the key theme of managing access. The fourth part deals with the management of demand, including the problem of uneven participation in countryside recreation, the notion of charging for countryside recreation and the role that marketing, education and interpretation play in visitor management. Finally, a single chapter considers the future of strategic countryside management.

References

Bedford Franklin, T. (1952). *A history of Scottish farming*. London: Nelson.
Callander, R. F. (1987). *A pattern of land ownership in Scotland*. Finzean: Haughend Publications.
Cavaliero, G. (1977). *The rural tradition in the English novel, 1900–1939*. London: Macmillan.
Central Statistical Office (2001). *Social trends 2001*. London: HMSO.
Cullingworth, J. B., & Nadin, V. (2002). *Town and country planning in the UK* (13th ed.). New York: Routledge.
Dahlman, C. (1980). *The open fields and beyond*. Cambridge: Cambridge University Press.
Davies, N. (1999). *The Isles: A history*. London: Macmillan.
Deane, P., & Cole, W. A. (1967). *British economic growth 1688–1959: Trends and structure* (2nd ed.). Cambridge: Cambridge University Press.
Dillon, J. (1980). The definition of farm management. *Journal of Agricultural Economics, 31*, 257–258.
Haldane, A. R. B. (1968). *The drove roads of Scotland*. Edinburgh: Edinburgh University Press.
Hobbsbawm, E. (1994). *The age of extremes: The short twentieth century 1914–1991*. London: Michael Joseph.
Hoskins, W. G. (1988). *The making of the English landscape* (with an introduction and commentary by C. Taylor, Revised Edition). London: Hodder & Stoughton.
House of Commons Environment Committee (1995). *The environmental impact of leisure activities, Volume I, Session 1994–1995*. London: HMSO.
James, N. D. G. (1981). *A history of English forestry*. Oxford: Basil Blackwell.
Mowl, T. (2000). *Gentlemen and players: Gardeners of the English landscape*. Stroud: Sutton Publishing.
Orr, W. (1982). *Deer forests landlords and crofters: The Western Highlands in Victorian times*. Edinburgh: John Donald.
Ousby, I. (1990). *The Englishman's England: Taste, travel and the rise of tourism*. Cambridge: University Press.
Pavis, S., Hubbard, G., & Platt, S. (2001). Young people in rural areas: Socially excluded or not? *Work, Employment and Society, 15*, 291–309.
Postan, M. M. (1972). *The Medieval economy and society*. Harmondsworth: Pelican.
Rackham, O. (1986). *The history of the countryside* (2nd ed.). London: J. M. Dent.

Roberts, L. N., & Hall, D. (2001). *Rural tourism and recreation: Principles to practice*. Wallingford: CABI.

Shucksmith, M. (2000). *Exclusive countryside? Social inclusion and regeneration in rural areas*. York: Joseph Rowntree Foundation.

Strong, R. (1996). *Country life 1897–1997: The English arcadia*. London: Country Life Books.

Taylor, H. (1997). *A claim on the countryside: A history of the British outdoor movement*. Stoke-on-Trent: Keele University Press.

Thomas, K. (1983). *Man and the natural world: Changing attitudes in England 1500–1800*. London: Penguin.

TNS Travel and Tourism (2004). *GB leisure day visits survey*. Edinburgh: TNS Travel and Tourism.

Wordsworth, W. (1835). *A guide through the district of the Lakes in the North of England, with a description of the scenery, &c. for the use of tourists and residents* (5th ed.). Kendal: Hudson & Nicholson.

Chapter 2

The Land Resource

1. Introduction

We saw in the previous chapter that the U.K. countryside has taken many years to evolve to its present state. Determinants of this evolution have changed over time and include the ownership of land, the incentives to which landowners and managers are exposed, and the extent of public interest in the countryside. Changes in the pattern of land ownership were particularly significant during the periods of enclosure and during the last century. The incentives confronting land managers were subject to change during much of the latter half of the twentieth century, whilst the demands of the urban population grew in line with cheap and convenient transport and with evolving perceptions of the countryside.

Economists examine questions of resource use and allocation in terms of supply and demand. This dichotomy will recur at several stages in this book and is useful because it separates two major groups of actors: those who own resources and produce useful things from them; and those who wish to consume the result. In this chapter we present an overview of the broad processes of land-use change, focusing on historical shifts in land use and on contemporary policy responses to such changes.

2. Land and Land Use

The distribution of land in the U.K. has changed over the past half century, particularly as land has been transferred from agriculture to other uses. The main data on land use for England and Wales are summarised in Table 2.1. The data for 1696 are included as a curiosity and are only loosely comparable with those for the more recent years. Broadly they underline the process of extending cultivation that has continued over a long period. The more recent data, covering most of the twentieth century, underline the generally slow pace of change during that period. Thus, in that period, agriculture "lost" 1.4 million hectares, from crops and grass, mainly to urban use, with some 0.3 million hectares transferring to forestry. But within agriculture more substantial transfers were recorded, particularly from permanent grass to cropping and rough grazings. The apparent transfer to rough grazing would also contain some statistical reclassification.

Expansion of the urban area in the U.K., largely at the expense of agricultural use, during the twentieth century, has been widely seen as undesirable. However, as Best (1981) points out, Britain is by no means the most densely settled country in the world. With

Table 2.1: The pattern of land use in England and Wales: 1696–1971.

	1696 (Millions of Hectares)	1901 (Millions of Hectares)	1971 (Millions of Hectares)
Crops	4.4	4.9	5.7
Permanent grass	4.0	6.2	4.0
Rough grazings	4.0	1.4	1.9
Forest and woodland	2.4	0.8	1.1
Urban land	0.6	0.7	1.6
Other land	–	1.0	0.7
Total land area	15.4	15.0	15.0

Source: Best (1981).

approximately 2.3 residents per hectare, it falls behind Belgium, Japan and The Netherlands, to name only three. Furthermore, there are wide disparities between various parts of the U.K. in terms of population density. For example if we compare the urban and the rural populations in terms of residents per hectare a wide range is found. The calculation for GB, in 1981, is presented in Table 2.2.

These rough estimates show that some 10% of the population inhabits 85% of the surface area, compared with 90% of the population which occupies some 15%. It is emphasised that these aggregate figures conceal a wide range of variation within both urban and rural areas. Thus in much of Wales, the North of England and the North of Scotland, rural population densities much lower than average will be found, whilst much higher densities will occur in many urban areas Moreover, it is an approximation to assign all urban land to urban areas, as has been done here. Also the basis of separating urban land from rural has almost certainly not been exactly the same as that used to separate the urban and rural populations. This distinction has important implications for the countryside, stressing that a substantial majority of the people interested in the countryside do not live there and can only visit it on a short-term basis from urban areas.

Table 2.2: Population density: Urban and rural Britain (1981).

	Land Area (Million Hectares)	Population (Millions)	Population Density (Residents per Hectare)
Rural	19.6	5.3	0.27
Urban	3.4	47.4	13.9
Total	23.0	52.8	2.29

Source: OPCS.

Table 2.3: Distribution of U.K. land by uses and country: 1999.

	Percent of Country					Area ('000 Hectares)	
	Agricultural Land			Forest and Woodland	Urban Land	Total Land	Inland Water
	Crops and Fallow	Grass and Rough Grazing	Other				
England	31	36	5	8	19	12,972	76
Wales	3	76	1	12	8	2,064	13
Scotland	8	67	2	16	11	7,710	169
Great Britain	21	50	4	11	15	22,745	256
Northern Ireland	4	76	1	6	13	1,348	67
United Kingdom	20	52	4	10	15	24,093	325

Source: Digest of Environmental Statistics 2001 (http://www.defra.gov.uk/environment/index.htm).

In Table 2.3 we update and extend the data from Table 2.1 to the rest of the U.K., bringing out variation between its constituent parts. In comparing the patterns of land use, it is immediately apparent that England has most of the cropped land of the U.K. whilst the other countries are more dependent on grass. Scotland and Wales also have a much greater share of their area under forest. Note that the data here show the per cent distribution within countries. The data must be expressed in hectares to show the U.K. shares of each country in a particular activity.

3. Primary Land Use

Two forces for change from agricultural land use during the past century have been particularly evident. First, there has been rapid expansion of the urban area as population growth has been concentrated in towns and cities. Despite rural birth rates generally being higher than urban rates, death rates have been more closely similar and the potential rural excess of population has been eroded away by rural to urban migration (see Figure 1.1). Although the direction of migration has reversed since the 1960s, it still leaves the great majority of the total population living in the towns and some 15% of the land under urban uses, including roads, railways and airports as well as housing.

Second, there has been considerable expansion of the area of land under trees under the influence of government policies to promote planting.[1] At first these policies were driven

---

[1] It should be noted that there is an implicit definition of "forest use" in such statements. However, the conventional definition of forest does not include hedgerow trees and an unknown number of small clumps of trees may also be excluded from such statements. These may make a considerable contribution to the landscape without being officially recognised as forestry.

by the perceived demand for timber, initially for strategic reasons but latterly follow more environmental and aesthetic motivations. In fact the Forestry Act of 1985 changed the objectives of the Forestry Commission by introducing a requirement to have regard for the environmental impact of its activities. A similar change of objectives was imposed on agriculture through the Agriculture Act of 1986. Forest policy during the twentieth century has promoted expansion of the area of the U.K. under plantation, from 5% at the beginning to 10% of land use at the end of that century. The picture emerging is therefore one of transfer of land from agriculture to both forestry and urban uses. However, a more detailed examination of primary land use is needed if conclusions are to be drawn as to the amount of "countryside" available.

4. Forestry

Some 15,000 years ago much of Britain was covered by ice or suffering from peri-glacial conditions. With the retreat of the ice, mixed-broadleaved woodland gradually established itself across the country, with some areas populated with the yew or Scots pine, our only native conifers. Grazing by mammals such as the auroch or bison, long extinct in the British Isles, may have created a dynamic and mixed landscape that was over subsequent centuries to be cleared by humans (Vera 2000).

Today, woodland typically classified as "ancient" dates back to the medieval period before 1600, with forests planted or naturally regenerated on open land between 1600 and 1900 classified as "recent" woodland (Peterken 1981). Typically ancient woodlands are valued for their higher biological diversity and are often the focus of the greatest conservation activity. Such woodlands have declined in the U.K. over the last century (Peterken 1981) and are now the subject of a variety of conservation initiatives such as those aimed at the Caledonian pine forests in Scotland.

After centuries of reducing forest cover, to provide timber and to make way for farming the land, the economy faced a drastic shortage of wood during the First World War, which led to the formation of the Forestry Commission (FC) in 1919. The Commission's first activity was to establish a planting programme designed to reduce U.K. dependence on imports. During its first 80 years, the area of forest land has more than doubled, now amounting to 8% of land cover in England, 12% in Wales, 16% in Scotland and 11% in Britain. The Forestry Commission owns more than one third of the forested area, the rest being in private ownership in both large and small estates (Table 2.4).

The ownership of the forest estate is also important because a significant share of it is publicly owned and public and private foresters are differently motivated and thus require different policies to support them. Whilst the state may be able to "take a view" about the desirability of particular forms of planting and adjust its activities directly, private foresters will have to be persuaded by different means. Following devolution, in 1998, state forests are now managed within their areas in England, Wales and Scotland by separate departments of Forest Enterprise. The Commission's other role, of encouraging new planting on private land and regulating its management, remains in the hands of its separate departments. The Forestry Commission has its main headquarters in Edinburgh and much of its business is conducted from there. The FC also has headquarters in Wales and England.

Table 2.4: Distribution of woodland by species, country and ownership: Great Britain, March 2003.

	Conifers (Thousand Hectares)	Broadleaves (Thousand Hectares)	Total (Thousand Hectares)
Ownership			
Forestry commission	699	87	786
Private woodland	887	1049	1936
Country			
England	372	739	1110
Scotland	162	122	285
Wales	1052	275	1327
Total	1586	1136	2722

Source: Forestry Commission (2003).

The majority of forest in Britain is in private ownership on farms and estates but the question of ownership requires qualification. Most of the private forest in Britain has been planted and managed under FC planting grants. Much of the rest consists of "dedicated forests" which carry with them important obligations in return for particular tax concessions granted in the past. For example, owners planting trees with grant support undertake not to fell them without permission and that permission will not be granted unless an owner accepts an obligation to replant within a stated period of felling. Others have received grants towards the cost of establishing their plantations which also require permission to fell and carry a replanting requirement. Thus, once land has been converted to forestry with state support, it is difficult to change its use again. Those who accept state support for afforestation are therefore foregoing important development options on their land. In the event of favourable changes in agricultural prices or the value of land for urban development they may be constrained from choosing those options by the conditions they accepted with their planting grants or tax concessions.

The first new forest plantations resulting from the policy of expanding forests were often of low aesthetic value and, as they became difficult to ignore in the landscape, those with an interest in the open countryside protested against this visual intrusion. Complaints about forest planting became vociferous during the 1970s and 1980s, as some of the plantations began to become dominant in the landscape. Aesthetic critiques, combined with increasing concerns about the perceived weak economic performance of forests, began to gain the attention of policy-makers and changes were introduced. Major policy changes have encouraged foresters to plant hardwood species and the proportion under hardwoods in Great Britain expanded from 21% of high forest in 1980 to 31% in 1999. The environmental pay-off from this will be relatively slow because of the long period of growth of deciduous trees.

Perhaps the main indicator of future environmental policies for forestry is to be found in the recent establishment of a series of urban forests in England. These will develop over the next half century and the expansion of low density tree planting is to be encouraged in their designated areas. This is to be achieved by persuading existing landowners to convert their land to forest, using grants were appropriate. As this move is environmentally driven it is not necessary to plant whole contiguous areas and the emphasis is on aesthetic configurations of planting. These recent innovations in land use policy arose at the initiative of the Countryside Commission in 1987 (Countryside Commission 1994).

Two distinct types of forest are being developed in this context. First, and largest, is the National Forest (NF) which covers an area of 50,000 hectares, centrally placed in England between Birmingham, Stafford, Nottingham and Leicester (Countryside Commission 1994). Second, on a smaller scale and at somewhat lower key, are the community forests, associated with major urban centres.

In 1995 the NF became a company limited by guarantee and it annual reports chart its progress (e.g. National Forest 2004). Within the NF boundary, 70% of the population of 187,00 lives in the four largest towns. At the start of this experiment 74% of the area was under agricultural occupation and only 6% was forested. One third of this forest was broadleaved, 9% was coniferous and the rest mixed (Countryside Commission 1994). The initial strategy sought to expand the forest area to up to a third of the total land area. It was recognised that this target might take several decades but by 2004 nearly 2,700 hectares had been established, more than doubling the original forest area. To achieve this, some five million trees had been planted.

In order to achieve their targets, the NF use an innovative Tender Scheme in which competitors may bid for a share of the sum set aside for the scheme each year. Landowners are invited to apply for funding, supplying details of the benefits they expect to follow from their planting and how much is needed for them to participate. These tenders are then scrutinised by the NF Company Board and the winners chosen can then enter into a 25-year contract.

Since 1989, as part of a joint initiative between the former Countryside Commission and the Forestry Commission, a number of Community Forests have been established in England. These forests are smaller than the NF and follow a specific policy of encouraging planting in particular areas. They differ from the generality of FC forests in being located in former industrial areas and having a greater emphasis on public access benefits.

The development of Community Forests began as a joint venture between the Forestry and Countryside Commissions and a range of local authorities (Countryside Commission 1989). The forests were planned to provide significant recreational opportunities for the populations of large urban areas, and by the end of 2002, 12 areas had been designated (see Table 2.5) (www.countryside.gov.uk). Each forest was intended to cover between 10,000 and 15,000 hectares and between 30 and 60% of the land will be planted with predominantly broad-leaved trees (Gilg 1996).

In their first 10 years Community Forests planted over 6,000 ha of new woodland, brought another 9,000 ha of existing woodland into management and opened up another 10,000 ha for recreation and access (Countryside Agency 2001). The programme has also created or improved over 5,000 km of public access routes and planted almost 800 km of hedgerows (Countryside Agency 2001).

Table 2.5: Community forests in England.

Community Forest	Area (Hectares)
Forest of Avon	57,300
Forest of Mercia (South Staffordshire)	2,100
Forest of Marston Vale (South of Bedford)	15,800
Great North Forest (Tyne and Wear, North Durham)	16,000
Great Western Community Forest (near Swindon)	39,000
Greenwood Community Forest (North Nottinghamshire)	41,400
Mersey Forest	92,500
Red Rose Forest (West Manchester)	76,000
South Yorkshire	39,499
The Tees Forest	25,500
Thames Chase Community Forest (East of London)	9,850
Watling Chase Community Forest (South Hertfordshire)	18,800

Source: www.cnp.org.uk.

The designation of a Community Forest has no statutory implication for planning and does not change any of the land use planning designations associated with the area (DETR 2001). A non-statutory Forest Plan exists for each forest, within which the local community forest teams set out their plans for the creation of the forest. The planned boundaries for the forests are then shown on structure plan key diagrams and in local plan proposal maps (DETR 2001).

While they provide considerable new opportunities to access the countryside, community forests additionally seek to enhance the environment at a number of levels. Thus, rather than creating large wooded areas, the community forest concept aims to create well-wooded landscapes that provide recreational, work and access opportunities. The creation of this kind of multi-purpose forestry, generating diverse benefits for local communities, reflects current trends in countryside planning and is supported by a range of grants, the most important of which are based on the FC's Woodland Grant Scheme (WGS). Landowners planting trees within Community Forests under the WGS attract a Community Forest Premium and if they incorporate facilities for public access can receive an additional supplement through the Community Woodland Contribution.

The Forestry Commission (2001) reported expenditure of £6 million of WGS funds in these areas over the previous six years. This has contributed to the planting of 2,700 hectares of new woodlands and management of "a substantial area of existing woodlands." A premium of £600 per hectare, for planting in the Community Forests, was paid until 2004. The initial contribution has been to establish forest planting on former urban land, much of it publicly owned. Further progress may depend upon the co-operation of more private landowners. Like most forest planting activities, expenditure is committed at the beginning of the process and benefits accrue over a very long period: indeed, efficiently managed forest constitutes a sustainable resource which need never cease to produce benefits.

A variety of community woodland initiatives have also been implemented in Scotland and Wales. Examples include the Central Forests Woodland project in Scotland which is designed to provide community as well as productive forest. In Wales the WGS has been used to encouraging public access to woods and has been used to support a number of community woodland developments.

5. Agriculture

Agriculture is the main land user in Britain, with 70% of the U.K. surface under its management. There are some 200,000 farms[2] although almost half of them are less than 20 hectares in size. A similar proportion are not run as full-time businesses. The remaining farms are full-time, in the sense that they would provide employment for at least one full time worker, and these farms provide the great majority of the output of agriculture. It is nevertheless recognised that the size of farm business does not necessarily tell us anything about its contribution to the environment.

Most farms are family businesses, although the amount of employment they offer to family or other workers continues to decline over time. Some farms are now managed by specialist contractors who provide the service of running the farm and pay the resulting profits to the farmer. The companies may also supply machinery services and other inputs which they buy efficiently in large quantities. Such arrangements are most common on mixed and cropping farms in the South of England. Some farm tasks are also undertaken by contractors who may bring advantages of expertise as well as supplying the services of specialised machines.

The current agricultural recession is credited with generating an increase in the exodus of workers from farming and the number of hired farm workers recorded is now less than the number of full and part-time farmers. Although there are currently anecdotal accounts of several thousand farmers "leaving the industry" such stories are not well documented because many farmers tend to reduce their commitment to farming without necessarily ceasing to be a farmer. The border between full-time, part-time and hobby farming is by no means consistently observed.

The number and nature of farm businesses in the U.K. may also depend on the long-term impacts of the Foot and Mouth Disease epidemic of 2001. Livestock enterprises in areas affected by the disease were faced with the prospect of having to restock at a time when the market offered little comfort to producers. Even farmers in areas unaffected by the disease were hit by export and movement restrictions. In some marginal upland areas the long-term impacts of foot and mouth disease may be to reduce or eliminate long-established patterns of grazing. This could lead to significant changes in landscape character, though positive ecological benefits may be found in some landscapes currently adversely affected by over-grazing.

---

[2] Strictly these are referred to as "holdings" which are the unit of enumeration in the Agricultural Census. However, one farmer may own or rent more than one holding so that there are probably more holdings than farmers. For convenience we will continue to refer to holdings as farms throughout this text.

The future of the farming and food sector in England was reviewed by Sir Donald Curry's Policy Commission on the Future of Farming and Food (Cabinet Office 2002), which made a variety of recommendations aimed at creating a profitable and sustainable industry that could compete in international markets and at the same time be a good steward to the environment. The Government response to this report "Facing the Future — The Strategy for Sustainable Food and Farming" (DEFRA 2002) was published in December 2002 and has the potential to achieve many of the objectives set out by the "Curry Report."

Another aspect of agricultural land use is a hangover from the enclosure process described in Chapter 1. Common grazing land still exists in England and Wales and is a considerable problem for those seeking to promote particular forms of environmental policy. Most remaining common land is in grassland areas and is particularly evident in the hills and uplands of England and Wales. These grassland areas are usually extensively grazed by sheep. Because of uncertainties as to property rights on such land and some lack of knowledge of the present owners of these rights, these areas have not been enclosed and continue in "common" use. This occurs where there are several "owners" of common rights and is also where problems of over-grazing are likely to arise. Committees of commoners manage some of them satisfactorily but others are less well run. There is a presumption on some commons that access is freely available, but the extent of this right is not well known. Various attempts to bring this under the regulation of the law have been slow to pay off (Aicheson & Gadesden 1992; Countryside Commission 1986). The total area of land held in common is not large (some half a million hectares, according to Aicheson & Gaddesden) but many common sites are strategically placed from the point of view of access.

It might be thought that common land provides an opportunity to enhance the delivery of public goods but the opportunity brings with a considerable challenge of trying to co-ordinate the behaviour of possibly large numbers of disparate individuals who may have no interest in public goods. Some interesting ideas have emerged regarding the management of the commons in England (see Capstick & Foulds 1991; Common Land Forum 1986) but the problem remains and becomes prominent whenever new policies are introduced to these areas. The 2000 Countryside and Rights of Way Act (see Chapter 15) has some further implications for reorganising the management of registered common land.

The importance of agriculture as an industry is sometimes inferred from its contribution to Gross Domestic Product (GDP), which had fallen to 0.9% by 2000. However, that is to ignore the significant value of the environmental public goods agriculture produces but which are generally not sold. In addition, agriculture accounts for a slightly larger share of total national employment compared to GDP, which implies that production per person in agriculture is below the national average. However, it would be a mistake to read too much into such data, as the margins of error in estimating the absolute size of the agricultural labour force are considerable.[3] Agriculture obviously accounts for a larger share of economic activity within the rural economy. Its share of the rural labour force is usually estimated to be in the region of 10%, though obviously varying from one area to another, but its contribution to *rural* output cannot be estimated accurately, in the absence of estimates of rural GDP.

---

[3] In particular it is not possible to weight the different types of worker to accurately convert the reported numbers to "full-time equivalent workers."

There are various well-established long-term trends observable in agricultural land use. The main change recognised during the twentieth century has probably been the restructuring of ownership and occupation as owner-occupation has taken over from renting. This process has been accompanied by a tendency for small farms to disappear, as they have been transferred to other land uses or amalgamated with larger farms, accompanied by the slower appearance of increasing numbers of larger farms. There has also been a sustained increase in the technical efficiency of food production.

Most of these changes in efficiency have been achieved by the introduction of more effective inputs, which has brought a notable price in terms of environmental impact. Thus, fertilisers and pesticides have been used in significant quantities and larger machinery has been introduced, encouraging the creation of bigger fields by removing traditional field boundaries. There was also a boom in investment in land drainage, which is now having its impact in downstream flooding following heavy rains. The process of intensification probably climaxed during the 1970s and 1980s and had begun to diminish as the century closed.

There is currently much apocalyptic language used in connection with farming. Thus the "plagues" of BSE and Foot and Mouth Disease are seen as disastrous and are taken as a basis for extremely gloomy predictions. Such views stand in stark contrast with the extremely high rate of technical innovation in agriculture, usually encouraged by short bursts of prosperity lasting only a few years, but allowing and promoting rapid development. This means that agricultural policy has to track such developments carefully if it is not to produce perverse outcomes. For this reason agricultural production and resource use is comparatively well documented and the DEFRA website is a useful source of information (www.defra.gov.uk).

The contrast between agriculture and forestry as users of land is worth noting. The major difference comes from the comparatively short production cycles in agriculture, which are much less than those which constrain forestry. Thus to produce a mature tree requires at least 40 years for softwoods and perhaps more than a century for hardwoods although the small amount of coppiced land is cropped much more frequently — every few years, depending on species. In contrast most crops grown on farms are annual, and some require only a few weeks to mature. Livestock enterprises may take longer to produce output, with more than two years from the conception of a calf to its slaughter for beef or joining a dairy herd. Pigs and sheep reproduce more rapidly and chickens for meat may be ready for slaughter within three months of hatching. Fruit trees require some years to reach full production but they are a minority crop in the U.K. The result of these short production periods is that farmers are much more concerned with comparatively short-term matters and are able to respond comparatively speedily to changes in markets, technology, policies and so on. Forestry is not insensitive to such forces but is nevertheless limited in its responses to changing conditions by its long production cycle. One obvious result of this is that farmers can quickly be persuaded to change their methods if there is a demand for it expressed by markets or policy makers. This has been seen in, for example, the rapid uptake of so-called agri-environmental policy during the past two decades, which has brought a large number of farmers into contracts with the government to produce public goods (see Chapter 12).

6. Urban Land-Use

According to Best (1981) the share of land under urban uses in the U.K. more than doubled between 1900 and 1971 (Table 2.1). However it still amounts to only 15% of the U.K. surface area, at the end of the last century (Table 2.3). This area cannot be distributed over different urban uses because the data are not available. Nevertheless we do know that a major user of land within the urban use share is in fact housing. Moreover, mainly due to the continued formation of new households, even within a static population, it is expected that a large number of new homes, perhaps four million, will be needed in the next two decades. This prospect is a "challenge" to existing planning designations — in particular Green Belt status — which constrain such developments. The current situation is that there is particular demand for new housing in the South East of England confronting a significant shortage of land which could be used for this purpose. Governments have tried to protect the situation by urging developers to use so-called "brown field sites" where possible. But developers are loath to do this because such sites are usually more expensive to develop than the "virgin" green field sites.

Resolution of this debate requires action by central Government and local planning agencies. Its importance for countryside managers is that expansion of urban populations in new areas will bring with it demands for access to local countryside. In that sense countryside managers will have to be aware of the activities of local planners in their area. They may also be called to give evidence and advice on some planning matters, especially those that affect the existing use of the countryside.

7. Land-Use Policy

Policies may be defined as sets of Governmental statements and activities designed to produce a particular result, which would otherwise not occur. They must have a purpose or set of objectives and a means of achievement as well as operating within the limits of cash availability and legality. Frequently purposes are enshrined in legislation and they may well have emerged from lengthy debates involving, committees of enquiry and more or less detailed research. It is also commonly the case that one particular agency or organisation will be charged with implementing the policy. In this overview we can cite only a few examples, which relate to the main land using activities described above.

U.K. forestry policy, going back to the establishment of the Forestry Commission in 1919, began with the comparatively simple objective of increasing the amount of timber produced in the Britain. The shortages of timber experienced in the Second World War led to the recognition of some further demand to grow trees in this country and gave a considerable boost to tree planting. By the 1960s people were beginning to use the countryside more for recreation and the unsightliness of early plantations became a substantial cause for complaint. The ensuing debate resulted in the FC acquiring the service of landscape architects for the first time. As noted above, early attempts at evaluating forest policy found it to be only marginally economic in terms of timber production. Even if some allowance was made for the value of saving imports it still seemed uneconomic as an activity. The

FC then raised the argument that the nation's forests provided a base for outdoor recreation and this also had value. The problem was to estimate this value. This line of argument was of crucial importance and the FC eventually succeeded in extending the issue of forestry's environmental contribution to its set of objectives in the 1985 Forestry Act. This officially broadened the basis of assessment of forestry policies allowing the recognition of benefits from recreation and, more recently, from carbon sequestration reducing the emission of greenhouse gases.

The problem with environmental benefits is that they are difficult to value in precise economic terms. However, methods are now available, although by no means beyond debate, which produce estimates of the relevant values. Assessments of the outcome of forestry policies, in terms of economic costs and benefits have now become much more complete (see for example Pearce 1991). There are more or less regular assessments of forestry as an economic activity and they produce informative reports. Generally, although the quality of these assessments has improved over the last three decades there remain some awkward analytical issues, which have not yet been satisfactorily resolved.

Agricultural policy differs from forestry in that faster responses to changes in incentive can usually be achieved. This makes it easier for the political system to produce identifiable results and reduces policy-makers' dependence on judgement. However, it also encourages undue concentration on short term outcomes at the expense of longer term results both positive and negative. The main problem with agricultural policy arises from the very large number of producers who are affected by change and whose responses to a new policy, even to a proposed policy, can destroy it. Further, the rapid entry of food into international trade can bring major disruptions to markets and substantial swings in prices and incomes, which can too easily add to policy costs.

Agricultural policy in the U.K. has had more than half a century of attention on a regular basis. Following the Second World War a system of annual reviews of agriculture was initiated in which the Government met the representatives of the farming interest and established what was the current state of the industry and how it had progressed in the preceding year. This review was followed by the determination of the farm-gate output prices, which were to be applied during the year then beginning. The system made allowance for certain cost increases which had occurred in the previous year and commodity prices were determined in relation to expected demands for home produced food. This policy was introduced immediately after a war in which Britain had had to operate a rigorous system of food rationing because of the submarine blockade which made importing food difficult.

Needless to say, that system became redundant once food supplies became adequate and rather than shortages, the problem for policy-makers was to avoid encouraging farmers to produce surpluses. Thus throughout the 1960s there were fierce debates with farmers' representatives about the appropriate internal prices to set for food. This phase of agricultural policy was in effect brought to an end when the U.K. joined the Common Market. Thenceforward prices were increasingly determined in Brussels and, as the Community enlarged, bore less and less relation to the specific needs of individual member states. Moreover the price level set through the CAP was generally much higher than had been experienced within the U.K. and showed considerable inflexibility downwards, with the result that the production of surplus food became an increasingly urgent European problem during the 1970s and 1980s. By the mid 1980s the CAP was absorbing some 70% of the

EC's annual expenditure, which seriously constrained the EC's capacity for introducing other types of policy as well as producing surpluses of food which could only be disposed of at great expense.

Various solutions to this problem were attempted (Harvey 1996) including the introduction of milk quotas in 1984. Other measures introduced included the development of agri-environmental policy whereby farmers where paid, through contracts, to modify their production methods in favour of environmental outcomes (see Chapter 14). These devices were accompanied, where possible, by reductions in farm gate prices. These changes were introduced under the pressure of the Uruguay Round of discussions under the General Agreement on Tariffs and Trade (GATT). A further round of discussions has now been completed and this may bring further reductions in price, if and when fully implemented.

In addition to the problems of setting agricultural price levels to achieve acceptable levels of income for farmers, there have been increasing numbers of policies designed to mitigate the undesirable side effects of agricultural policy. Policies have tried to respond to the increasing expressions of concern from environmental groups at the losses of environmental diversity and landscape amenity (Adams 1996) since the 1980s. As well as the introduction of agri-environment instruments, notable Government responses to this were the passing of the Wildlife and Countryside Act (1981). These changes signalled the recognition of the importance of environmental goods and the intent to check the rate of at which they were damaged.

Other modifications to agricultural policy have included significant changes in the structure of grants paid to farmers. These no longer lend such strong support to improvements in productivity and are increasingly aimed at enhancing the provision of public goods (Chapter 12). In addition to supporting environmental improvements, these measures also promote the adoption of various measures to promote animal welfare, the provision of safe and healthy food and the promotion of rural development. Rural development (see Mosely 2003) is a common element of other European rural policies and is now an increasingly important component of U.K. regional and agri-environment policy (see Chapter 14).

An important option for agricultural policy-makers which they are understandably reluctant to embrace has been the use of regulation as an alternative to price incentives. Inescapably there is an element of regulation attached to most policies. For example the use of intervention buying, whereby surpluses of commodities are bought up by the state and held until markets improve, require specification of acceptable quality, dates when policies will apply and conditions regarding payment, delivery and so on. Where contracts are made with farmers, there are conditions, which must be met, and in the case of default the extent of any penalty payable is spelt out in advance. However, there is a reluctance to use such methods more than is strictly necessary. Regulation was a major question for debate in the passing of the Wildlife and Countryside Act and many environmentalists argued strongly for compulsion rather than the system of negotiation and compensation which was eventually introduced. Critics dubbed that system "voluntarism", arguing that it was too weak and would prove extremely expensive because it encouraged farmers to seek compensation for not undertaking investments they had no intention of making anyway. In the event these policies have not proved so expensive as expected and rates of making agreements have been slower than expected. Compulsion is not much favoured by policy makers but it is, nevertheless, an option to be used if needed.

The third form of land use, development, has been regulated through a series of policies of increasing sophistication during the past century (Cullingworth & Nadin 2002). The introduction of a rigorous system of planning legislation came in the aftermath of the Second World War and is described in more detail in Chapter 13. One of the consequence of the planning system has been a process of land designation which has encompassed much of Britain's countryside. Some of the more common or familiar land designations are listed in Box 2.1.

Box 2.1: Examples of land designation used in the U.K.
Areas of Outstanding Natural Beauty (England, Wales and Northern Ireland)
Biosphere Reserves (international – via UNESCO's Man and the Biosphere Programme)
Environmentally Sensitive Areas (all U.K.)
Marine Nature Reserves (all U.K.)
National Nature Reserves (all U.K.)
National Parks (England and Wales)
National Scenic Areas (Scotland)
Ramsar Sites (international under the Ramsar Convention)
Sites of Special Scientific Interest (all U.K.)
Special Areas of Conservation (EU-based under the EC Habitats and Species directive)
Special Protection Areas (EU-based under the EC Birds directive)
World Heritage Sites (international)

This list is by no means exhaustive! It is also notable that the list is changing continuously as, for example, new areas are designated and as new forms of designation appear. Furthermore, some designations may easily overlap with each other, although some are, or should be, mutually exclusive.

An important designation not on the list above, is that of Green Belt, a planning device for indicating land, generally on the urban fringe, where there is a strong presumption against development. The designation of Green Belt is important as, being a means of preventing development, it is frequently subject to challenge and it does not always survive unchanged. This partly reflects the evolution of our attitudes towards land use as our demands for development land increase along with population. Green Belt land covers 1.5 million ha (12%) of England and over 156,000 ha in Scotland (Cullingworth & Nadin 2002). Advice to local authorities on Green Belt land is included in Planning Policy Guidance note 2 (PPG 2) published in 1995. PPG 2 sets out the purposes of Green Belt designation and the land (see Box 2.2) and covers a variety of other issues regarding the treatment of this land.

The application of a designation to a new area frequently changes the rights of property owners within the area and as a result is often strongly contested. The debate may be sufficient for the relevant government ministry to call for a public enquiry into the proposal. This does not necessarily happen for every development proposed but where it is a substantial issue an enquiry is more likely. Large enquiries may take years and involve large numbers of people. At the end of an enquiry the independent inspector produces a report and the appropriate minister then decides how to proceed. She may either find for or against the proposal or ask for further information — possibly even convening another enquiry.

> **Box 2.2: Purpose and use of Green Belt land.**
>
> **Purposes**
>
> - To check unrestricted sprawl of large built-up areas.
> - To prevent merging of neighbouring towns.
> - To safeguard countryside.
> - To preserve setting and character of historic towns.
> - To assist urban regeneration by encouraging recycling of derelict and other urban land.
>
> **Uses**
>
> - To provide opportunities for access to open countryside for urban populations.
> - To provide opportunities for outdoor sport and recreation for urban populations.
> - To retain attractive landscapes and enhance landscapes near where people live.
> - To improve damaged and derelict land around towns.
> - To retain land for agriculture, forestry and related uses.
>
> Adapted from: PPG 2, Green Belts and Cullingworth & Nadin (2002).

The delivery of rural policy came under increasing scrutiny at the beginning of the new millennium. This was motivated by a range of concerns, particularly the complexity of existing delivery mechanisms and a perceived need to change and simplify these mechanisms in response to the growing rural agenda. In England in 2002, Lord Haskins was invited to look at the arrangements for delivering the Government's rural policies in England. His report (Haskins 2003) recommended how rural delivery arrangements should evolve, and emphasise the need for devolution of responsibilities and for public services to be made more accountable and locally responsive. Significantly, the report supported the development of a more integrated approach to sustainable land management achieved by rationalising existing agencies with overlapping interests into a new agency responsible for land management.

8. Strategic Implications

The way in which land is used is critical in determining the nature and value of the countryside. The successful blending of agriculture and forestry is a major determinant of landscape quality. The location of urban uses within the countryside is unavoidable and must be sensitively undertaken if countryside options are to be fully available.

Developments such as the Countryside Agency's Countryside Character Programme (see Chapter 10) present a useful way forward in attempting to illuminate the process by which the physical characteristics of land interact with land use and other factors to establish distinctive regional patterns of landscape character. As well as categorising the landscape into different character areas, the approach also attempts to identify threats to landscape character and to set a policy agenda consistent with the objective of maintaining regionally distinctive landscape character. Such a policy agenda must take account of the wide range of land resource issues facing society at the beginning of the third Millennium. Many of these are addressed in subsequent chapters, and in particular Chapter 18 where we speculate about the nature of the challenges that will face the next generation of strategic countryside managers.

References

Adams, W. M. (1996). *Future nature: A vision for conservation*. London: Earthscan.
Aicheson, J., & Gadesden, G. (1992). Common land. In: W. Howarth, & P. Rogers (Eds), *Agriculture, conservation and land use: Law and policy issues for rural areas* (pp. 165–187). Cardiff: University of Wales Press.
Best, R. (1981). *Land use and living space*. London: Methuen.
Cabinet Office (2002). *Farming and food: A sustainable future*. Report of the Policy Commission on the Future of Farming and Food. London: HMSO.
Capstick, E. J., & Foulds, R. (1991). Lake District National Park Commons Project 1988–1990: A report to the Lake District special planning board and the Countryside Commission. Cumbria: Lake District National Park Authority.
Common Land Forum (1986). The report of the Common Land forum. CCP 215. Cheltenham: Countryside Commission.
Countryside Agency (2001). Seeing the wood for the trees. *Countryside Focus*, 16, 4–5.
Countryside Commission (1989). *Forests for the community*. CCP270. Cheltenham: Countryside Commission.
Countryside Commission (1994). *The national forest: The strategy: The forest vision*. CCP 468. Cheltenham: Countryside Commission.
Cullingworth, B., & Nadin, V. (2002). *Town and country planning in the U.K.* London: Routledge.
Department of the Environment, Food and Rural Affairs (2002). *Facing the future – The strategy for sustainable food and farming*. London: Department of Environment, Food and Rural Affairs.
Department of the Environment, Transport and the Regions (2001). The countryside – Environmental quality and economic and social development. Planning Policy Guidance 7 (PPG 7). London: HMSO.
Forestry Commission (2001). Annual report and accounts: Great Britain and England 1999–2000. London: HMSO.
Forestry Commission (2003). *Forestry facts and figures*. Edinburgh: Forestry Commission.
Gilg, A. W. (1996). *Countryside planning* (2nd ed.). London: Routledge.
Harvey, D. R. (1996). The role of markets in the rural economy. In: P. Allanson, & M. Whitby (Eds), *The rural economy and the British countryside* (pp. 19–39). London: Earthscan.
Haskins, C. (2003). Rural delivery review: A report on the delivery of government policies in rural England. London: Department of Environment, Food and Rural Affairs.
Mosely, M. J. (2003). *Rural development: Principles and practice*. London: SAGE.
National Forest (2004). Annual report: Financial year 2003–2004. The National Forest Company.
Pearce, D. (1991). Assessing the returns to the economy and society from investment in forestry. In: Forestry Commission (Eds), *Forestry expansion: A case study of technical, economic and ecological factors*. Edinburgh: Forestry Commission.
Peterken, G. F. (1981). *Woodland conservation and management*. London: Chapman & Hall.
Vera, F. W. M. (2000). *Grazing ecology and forest history*. Wallingford: CAB International.

Chapter 3

The Policy Machine

1. Introduction

In this chapter we reflect on the role played by government and other organisations in the countryside. The central state is the key agency here but it works with a variety of organisations at national, local, interstate and global scales. The relationship between these various elements determines the functioning of the "policy machine," as it is sometimes called: this chapter reviews the working of the machine as it affects the countryside.

We consider first the central state and its operation, including its dependence on established pressure groups and the delegation of its powers downwards towards local and regional government and upwards to multi-national organisations such as the European Union and many other higher level bodies. The work of the main administrative departments and their agencies which impact on the countryside are briefly reviewed. The main political science source for this chapter is Budge *et al.* (2000).

2. The Central State

Britain has no written constitution: a fact which is commonly overlooked by its population. This seemingly peculiar position is defended as allowing important flexibility in government and by reference to the slow pace of effective change in the processes of the state. Central government is the main policy-maker in this country. The main legislative body is the democratically elected lower House of Parliament (the Commons), which acts as a constraint on the Cabinet, which consists of chief ministers and is chaired by the Prime Minister. The Prime Minister is "appointed" by the monarch but is almost invariably the leader of the party with the most Parliamentary seats following a general election.

The Upper House of Parliament (the Lords), although undergoing a reform process at present, still has powers to modify legislation. The House of Lords consists of a number of hereditary peers and all those awarded life peerages. The traditional numerical dominance of hereditary peers in this House, having come to seem increasingly anachronistic, has been reduced in recent years, while at the same time increased numbers of life peers have entered the house including the so-called "people's peers," a nomenclature designed to highlight the fact that some members of the House are appointed on the basis of achievements that extend beyond the political sphere.

Meanwhile, the choice of Government is made democratically using a simple "first past the post" voting system with most candidates put up by the political parties. The main parties,

Labour, Liberal Democrat and Conservative, have been evolving for at least a century and support for each of them has varied widely over time, as have their respective political agendas. Liberals and Conservatives came originally from the so-called Whig and Tory parties respectively, whilst Labour had its roots in the workers' attempt to gain political power through the trade unions'. The Liberal Party has been small in size since early in the twentieth century and Labour formed its first major government in 1945 and was re-elected for a short term in 1950.

That Government pursued an ambitious agenda which set the direction of development for post-war Britain. Changes included the establishment of the National Health Service, reform of the educational system and the nationalisation of major industries. In the countryside it was responsible for the legislation which established the National Parks, the agricultural policy which applied for at least two decades, and the Town and Country Planning System, which remains in existence. Those Labour Governments were followed by thirteen years of Conservative rule before Labour formed the next two Governments, in the 1960s. They were succeeded by the Conservatives, for one term, after which Labour returned to power and was then replaced by a Conservative Government, under Margaret Thatcher, in 1979.

The last was a notably reforming administration, which was initially successful in transforming various ills which, until then, had appeared intractable. In particular they are remembered as the government, which reduced the power and influence of the trade unions and sought to remove several nationalised industries from public ownership through a process of "privatisation." However, as governments do, they "ran out of steam" after two terms of office and Prime Minister Margaret Thatcher was replaced by John Major in 1992 and the Conservative administration retained power until New Labour was elected in 1997. New Labour was re-elected with a large majority in 2001.

After 18 years out of office New Labour had an accumulated stock of policy changes in mind, and managed to implement some of these in its first term, which ended in 2001. These include reform of the House of Lords, an important measure of devolution of power to Scotland and Wales and the establishment of Regional Development Agencies (RDAs) in England. Initially the impact of these re-organisations will be slow to mature, but they are potentially highly significant agents in implementing a range of policy agendas across the countryside. Their role has recently been under scrutiny in a recent review of rural delivery mechanisms (Haskins 2003), which recommended that RDAs should deliver more to rural communities at a local level.

The essential role of the political parties is to organise the behaviour of politicians and voters so that they can carry out their key function of choosing teams of decision-makers from the competing politicians available. The democratic focus of this is the election, when the parties seek to attract voters with competing offers of what are thought to be attractive policies. Parties seek to present themselves as radically different from their opponents in the policies they offer and the means they use to implement them. However this should not detract from the widely recognised phenomenon of the substantial agreement, however tacit, between all parties over major aspects of government and public policy. In this sense, over many issues, it is often difficult to see what would be the difference of having one group in power rather than another.

3. Departments of State

There are many departments of state but we will concentrate here on those with relevance to countryside management and policy. The most senior Department of all is the Treasury, domain of the Chancellor of the Exchequer, and the body that regulates the economy and determines the financial flows to individual government departments. The main central departments are those of Health, Education and Employment, the Home and Foreign Offices, and the Department of Defence. Each of these departments is headed by a minister of Cabinet rank and they are assisted by junior ministers. They each produce annual reports, accounts and expenditure plans which show how they have spent their money and offer some explanations and justifications of policies pursued, including their intentions over the next few years.

The former Department of Environment, Transport and the Regions (DETR) and the Ministry of Agriculture Fisheries and Food (MAFF) were reorganised after the election of 2001, partly in recognition of the problems of the Foot and Mouth Disease epidemic of that year. Among other things that epidemic brought realisation of the economic interdependencies of rural areas, notably the close dependence of the major rural tourism sector on the (economically) much smaller farming sector. That provided the rationale for moving substantial numbers of civil service posts from the DETR to MAFF to form the new Department of Environment, Food and Rural Affairs (DEFRA). This now constitutes a dedicated "countryside ministry."

4. Central and Local Government

Central powers are delegated to a vast array of local agencies, some of which are critical to the operation of the countryside. The first of these, and the longest established, is the system of local government in the U.K. This operates through delegated powers which define its rights and obligations. The system is well-defined and critically important to the delivery of public services. The public management of land use and development also operates through local government in the Town and Country Planning System (see Chapter 13). This system operates by defining the local and central powers to control the pattern of development. Local authorities also have a range of other functions, of which education is the largest, that are continuously in flux as central government and other policies are amended. Operation of the local planning system is shared between counties and districts in England and Wales and between regions in Scotland, whilst in Northern Ireland it is managed by the Department of the Environment. Many other functions are delegated to the local level from central government and a majority of them operate at the county or district level. There are several other functions which operate on a similar basis (for example the police) and others, such as health and education, which may have some local management from local authorities but are also subject to direct budgetary control from the centre. Any type of devolution of power from one level of government to another is unlikely to confer complete freedom of operation to the lower level in the hierarchy.

A minor but important change in administrative style, introduced by the Major Government (1992–1997) in the interest of local co-ordination of central Government policies, has been the setting up of a system of regional Government Offices. These bring together the regional civil servants from the major central departments with a remit to ensure the co-ordinated local delivery of central policies. When they were first established, MAFF demurred over participating on the grounds that its policies were all centrally determined and it already had a functioning system of local offices arranged on a different geographical basis. DEFRA has now moved into line with other departments. As most central departments have some form of regional operation, it has become essential to tidy up the many different ways in which regions are defined. Progress has been made with this but the process is not yet complete.

Another shift in political structures has been the devolution of powers from central government that was introduced by the first Blair administration. This major change has yet to work through the governmental system fully. At present we have an elected Parliament in Scotland and an elected Assembly for Wales. The powers of these bodies differ, for example the Scottish Parliament has limited power to raise taxes for specified purposes giving it more local autonomy than the Welsh Assembly. Devolution is still very new and the possibilities inherent in this tendency are by no means exhausted. A further aspect of devolution also under way, but as yet the least developed, is the decentralisation of power within England to RDAs and Regional Assemblies. Their constitution and authority is now evolving and it remains to be seen what form their activities will take. The existence of elected or appointed bodies, responsible for certain government functions in various parts of the realm, has initiated a new era for central government, whose jurisdiction has now become quite diverse across the U.K.

Devolution has pervasive effects on administration in, for example, the forestry sector, where the Forestry Commission now has separate national offices for England and Wales, which report to Commission Headquarters in Edinburgh, where the Scottish headquarters is also located. The Commission is also now separated into two agencies — the Forest Authority, with an overall responsibility for administering forest policy and Forest Enterprise, which is responsible for the publicly owned forests of each part of the country. The Commission also has a general regulatory responsibility for the U.K. as a whole.

5. Non-Departmental Public Bodies

Each Government Department also has an array of non-departmental bodies[1] now known as Non-Departmental Public Bodies (NDPBs). There are many such bodies and they provide Departments with a means of extending their activities into new areas and introducing specialist expertise into their functions. Their numbers have been reduced from a peak of more than 2,000 in 1979 and they now number roughly 1000. The total annual expenditure

---

[1] NDPBs are often referred to under the nickname of quangos, an acronym for quasi-autonomous non-governmental organisation. NDPB is used here following official usage.

Table 3.1: Non-departmental public bodies attached to MAFF.

	Public Corporations	Executive NDPBs	Advisory NDPBs	Tribunal NDPBs	Total
Number	1	15	13	4	33
Employees	39	2,312	0	0	2,351
Members	4	58	502	302	866
Gross expenditure £m	6.1	171.7	0	0	177.8

Source: Cabinet Office (2001).

by Executive NDPBs amounts to some £23.9 billion, of which the Government funds £18.6 billion, and they employ 113,000 staff. In the same period the former MAFF had a set of NDPBs attached to it as shown in Table 3.1. Note that it accounted for a significant number of Advisory and Tribunal NDPBs with some hundreds of members.

In addition to the county- and district-based local-governmental systems, there are others which have specifically designed administrative structures. For example, since the 1995 Environment Act, National Parks have set up their own individual local authorities which are similar to county councils, although they differ in having their council appointed, rather than elected by the local population. This allows the Secretary of State for the Environment to ensure that the Parks are managed in the national as well as the local interest.

The Countryside Agency was formed in 1999, combining the former Countryside Commission and parts of the former Rural Development Commission. It is responsible for rural development and countryside management in England: nature conservation in England remains the responsibility of English Nature. This structure may change following the recommendations of Lord Haskins' Report on the delivery of rural policy across DEFRA and its agencies (Haskins 2003) and a possible consequence is the formation of a new, more integrated agency encompassing some of the functions of the Countryside Agency, English Nature, and the Rural Delivery Service, plus alignment of the Forestry Commission. This would require appropriate legislation to be enacted and any new agency is unlikely to be established before 2006.

Currently, DEFRA has budgetary responsibility for English Nature, the Countryside Agency and the Environment Agency, each of which provide advice to Government in policy areas that concern them. The responsibilities of the Environment Agency also take into account Wales, where the Countryside Council for Wales provides guidance on landscape, conservation and countryside recreation issues. In Scotland the Scottish Executive works with Scottish Natural Heritage and the Scottish Environmental Protection Agency (SEPA) to determine environmental and countryside policy for Scotland, while Northern Ireland has its own Department of the Environment and Department of Agriculture and Rural Affairs. The allocation of functions to different agencies within the various jurisdictions of the U.K. is detailed in Table 3.2. Note, however, that such a table can only be put together with some significant simplifications.

The main U.K. bodies dealing with environmental protection in the U.K. are the Environment Agency in England and Wales, SEPA and the Environment and Heritage

Table 3.2: Administration of rural issues by U.K. jurisdiction.

Jurisdiction/ Responsibility	England	Scotland	Wales	Northern Ireland	U.K.
Countryside	Countryside Agency	Scottish Natural Heritage	Countryside Council for Wales	Department of the Environment	DEFRA
Rural Development	Countryside Agency	Scottish Development Office	Welsh Development Office	Department of Agriculture and Rural Development	DEFRA (Department of Trade and Industry)
Conservation	English Nature	Scottish Natural Heritage	Countryside Council for Wales	Department of the Environment	Joint Nature Conservancy Council

Service (EHS) in Northern Ireland. The Environment Agency was created by the Environment Act 1995 and resulted in the amalgamation of the National Rivers Authority, the Inspectorate of Pollution and various local authority Waste Regulation Authorities. SEPA was created under the same Act from the old Scottish River Purification Boards and has somewhat more limited powers than its counterpart. The EHS is part of the Northern Ireland Department of the Environment and takes the lead in implementing environmental policy in the province. Its work includes pollution control, wildlife protection and the identification and protection of built heritage.

6. Non-Governmental Organisations

It is now well established that modern governments need pressure groups or non-governmental organisations (NGOs) in order to function properly. There are many hundreds of such groups, often run by unpaid but well-informed amateurs, which focus on an array of activities and represent the interests of their support group in the governmental process. A very well known rural pressure group is the National Farmers' Union (NFU) of England and Wales. This group was formed early in the last century and developed into the role of representing the farming interest in all agricultural policy matters. There are also separate unions for Scottish and Northern Irish farmers, whilst a Farmers' Union of Wales displays a Nationalist emphasis in the policies it proposes, to differentiate itself from the NFU. The NFU was particularly significant in agricultural policy debates during and after the Second World War when it was consulted annually about the economic state of the industry, when prices were determined each spring.

The NFU is a much studied NGO and it may be seen as having moved from a corporatist relationship with Government in the 1940s and 1950s to a more flexible and somewhat looser relationship more recently. Winter (1996) traces the roots of modern corporatism back to the Reform Act of 1867 which, by widening the franchise, created a need for party organisation and established the modern form of government. Corporatism emerged from this situation to meet the requirements of modern governments for reliable information from various parts of society on specialist matters. Corporatism is characterised by close working relationships between ministers, civil servants and pressure groups which gives the groups a central role in forming policy.

Such arrangements may be enshrined in formal relationships, as was the requirement under the 1947 Agriculture Act for the Government to consult annually with farmers' representatives to establish the state of the agricultural industry before it determined price levels for the coming season. In return for this valuable close consultation, the NFU undertook to discipline its members and provided a focus for policy discussions which was extremely useful to both Government and farming interests. The strength of this link was structurally weakened by U.K. entry to the then European Community in 1973, which shifted the locus of agricultural policy determination from London to Brussels and increased the number of participants in the debate. Other factors that have reduced the power of the NFU include the emergence of specialist pressure groups dealing with particular farm commodities (for example milk, pigs and poultry) and the emergence of competing groups, such as the Farmers' and Smallholders' Association and the Tenant Farmers' Association.

The U.K.'s entry into Europe greatly complicated the policy agenda and required a different model of policy formation. Winter (1996) argues that the appropriate model to describe present policy formation is the *policy network*. This recognises the different status of pressure groups and among which the NFU, in its early post-war mode, is seen as a "high-profile" insider. This model accords the farmers a place in policy formation but also recognises the many other groups with varying degrees of attachment to individual issues. The alternative to this model is the *policy community*, which describes a situation in which consensus exists amongst participants that more resources can usefully be applied to their policy field, in which they share deep common interest. Policy communities tend to be more cohesive and stable than networks (see Winter 1996 for a fuller review of the development of the political science models of lobbying).

A related pressure group, the Country Land and Business Association[2] (CLBA), represents the interests of some 50,000 agricultural landowners and rural businesses, many of which are farmers. There is substantial dual membership between the NFU and the CLBA and considerable overlap of interests. However, although this commonality of interest allows the NFU and the CLBA to "speak with one voice" on many issues it remains the case that the CLBA has a broader base of interest than the NFU. For example there is much more concern amongst rural landowners about such matters as hunting, game management, forestry and land use planning. The CLBA, though, is less concerned than the NFU with the detail of agricultural policy.

Beside these specialist agricultural interest groups, there are many environmental groups at work in the countryside as has been emphasised by Lowe & Goyder (1983). Although their book deals in detail with only five groups, they report a survey of the operation of 77 such groups, a majority of which have considerable rural interests and concerns.

---

[2] Up to 2001, the Country Landowners Association.

The book develops a convincing picture of the close interaction between pressure groups and their target government agencies. They distinguish between emphasis groups, which develop close links with particular parts of the government to the advantage of both parties, and promotional groups, which tend to challenge policies and procedures. They cite the interesting phenomenon of clientelism, that signifies the dependency which may develop between a Government department and its lobby, particularly with emphasis groups. Rather than mutual hostility between such actors, in practice each learns to use the other and an essentially symbiotic relationship may emerge. They give the example of the relationship between the former Nature Conservancy and the Wildlife Trust Partnerships in England. In the late 1970s the former, as an independent statutory body, managed to establish a mutually satisfactory relationship with its lobby. This allowed it to draw on voluntary labour and derive support from members of the former British Society for Nature Conservation (BSNC). In return it could make available expertise and administrative resources. Lowe & Goyder point out that the direction of pressure is not always from lobby to agency and that, in this case, the Conservancy was able to put pressure on the BSNC to reform it consistently with Conservancy needs. Although tensions may arise between such interacting bodies, they need not prevent either party from succeeding in its disparate activities as long as they share a core of agreement as to objectives. Lowe & Goyder also cite examples of Governmental agencies bringing lobby groups into existence to provide a platform from which to operate.

Although parts of Government may benefit from close links with their lobbies through clientelism, the costs to them of this collaborative style may be significant. They may be required to support Government activities with a possible loss of crucial independence and hence credibility with their membership. This delicate balancing act is one which can be observed daily as pressure NGOs join public debates, often in the media, arguing their case for a particular response from the public sector.

Rawcliffe (1998) has more recently examined the role of environmental groups and stresses their changing role and methods of operation. In attempting to explain how such groups work, he contrasts the U.K. with European experience of environmental groups where green political parties have been more in evidence. He sees the British political system as "*centralised, elitist and secretive*" policy-making which works through a system of:

> 'bureaucratic accommodation' through the progressive development of exclusive policy networks composed predominantly of 'policy communities' of government departments, government bodies and other established sectional groups and economic interests. These policy communities are relatively stable, reflecting the monopoly on the policy domains they represent.

By changing their operating policies, interest groups can generate significant shifts in membership and income. Thus, while membership of the Royal Society for the Protection of Birds roughly doubled in the decade following 1985, the smaller membership of Greenpeace increased by a factor of eight in the first half of that period and then lost half of that growth in the second half. Rawcliffe suggests that such differences in performance, which are crucial to the survival and effectiveness of groups, in part reflect the extent to which their policies match the *"wider public mood."*

7. Charities

Many environmental and countryside NGOs are, in fact, run as charities. The largest and best known of these is perhaps the National Trust, but there are many others. In the U.K. there is an important dividing line between charities and pressure groups in that charities are given particular favourable taxation treatment whilst pressure groups are not (see Chapter 7). So, in order to gain the benefits from charitable status, groups have to be careful to avoid becoming too "political" in their work. Issues connected with charitable status occasionally surface when a charity becomes too strident in criticising government policy. The advantages of charitable status are that they combine obtaining political support for a cause with securing membership. The disadvantages include the need to moderate their policy positions in order to retain charitable status.

One of the problems with charitable organisations is the extent to which they are an effective or efficient way of securing the services they deliver. In many cases the alternative of the state, or even commercial concerns, delivering services, is possible. Which should be chosen? One answer is that the state "could not" provide the many activities currently provided by charities. However, we must distinguish technical feasibility from desirability. It is probably the case that much of the work undertaken by charities could be delivered by other forms of organisation. But in many, even most, cases it is undoubtedly cheaper to arrange for charities to undertake such work. Without charities "the state" would have to be larger and this would have to be funded from tax revenue. A further strong argument is that the people working for charities derive pleasure from this service, an issue which is further explored by authors such as Parker (1992). Such arguments are powerful and provide a sensible reason for using charitable organisations where they are available. There are also some examples of effective co-operation between the state and charities, which produce valuable results — the National Trusts are a case in point (see Chapter 7). Hodge (1988) and Dwyer & Hodge (1996) explore the prospect of certain NGOs playing an increasingly important role in the provision of countryside goods (see Chapter 12).

8. The U.K. in Europe

Governing the U.K. does not stop at national frontiers. In fact any British government is constrained by a web of international commitments and obligations, both formal and informal, which have to be brought into the reckoning when action is being considered. Thus, not only are we members of the European Union (EU) and bound by its regulations and directives, we are also signatories of an array of international treaties and other arrangements, many of them going back over long periods.

The EU is a supra-national organisation, within which individual member states (including the U.K.) have devolved part of their national sovereignty in order to form a cohesive political unit (Alder & Wilkinson 1999). By 2004, when 10 additional states joined, the EU had enlarged to encompass 25 nations. At the heart of the EU is a group of nations bound together by treaty with the aim of promoting social, economic and environmental development through closer mutual co-operation and integration. Through its legislative powers the EU plays an important role in setting the environmental policy agenda across member states. The main EU institutions responsible for the development of legislation include the Council for the EU, the European Commission, the European Court of Justice and the European Parliament.

The Council is the main decision making body of the EU and consists of the ministers from each member state with competence in the matter under consideration. The Council of Ministers, as it is also known, meets regularly and initially different member nations took over the Presidency every six months and determining the policy agenda.

In June 2004 the heads of Government of the enlarged EU agreed on a new Constitution. This consolidates the various treaties and agreements upon which the EU is based and outlines the powers of the EU, where it can act and the powers of veto held by individual members. In practice the Constitution provides the EU with a greater role in the activities of its member states, though this varies across policy areas. In a number of countries, including the U.K., a referendum will be held over whether or not to accept the new Constitution.

The new Constitution requires the President to be elected by members of the Council (and for the election to be ratified by the European Parliament) and he or she will then hold office for two and a half years, rather than six months. This should provide greater coherence in terms of leadership and increase the influence of the President.

An important innovation of the Council, established under the new Constitution, is the principle of Qualified Majority Voting (QMV), which was originally introduced under the Single European Act of 1986. The use of QMV makes it more difficult for individual members to exercise a veto on EU proposals. Before the implementation of the EU Constitution the votes of members were weighted roughly according to economic size for decisions for which unanimity is not required. Under the Constitution, QMV will require the approval of at least 15 nations, comprising at least 65% of the population of the EU. Individual nations will retain powers of veto over defence, taxation and foreign policy. If outvoted, a member can take its case to the Council, though it may still be outvoted there. Where decisions require majority voting the European Parliament will have equal rights to the Council.

The European Parliament is a body of MEPs elected by their host countries to serve a five year term. As well as passing new laws, the Parliament scrutinises legislation through various committees, and controls the EU budget (see Alder & Wilkinson 1999 or other more recent texts for more details on EU legislative procedures). Once legislation is initiated it is considered by the European Parliament and if approved passed on to the Council for adoption. In practice, the European Parliament has increased in power over the years and legislation will not be passed without its approval. This growth in influence reflects the importance of the Parliament as the only EU body to be democratically elected. Any disputes over EU law may be settled formally in the European Court of Justice.

The European Commission is the body that proposes and executes EU law. It consists of a group of Commissioners appointed by member states for a set period. The Commission has a President, cabinet and various units of civil servants called Directorate Generals (DGs) which deal with different policy areas (e.g. DG VI deals with agriculture and DG

XI deals with environmental issues). The Enlargement Directorate has an important role in easing the entry of new members and assisting their cohesion to the EU. The main role of the Commission is to prepare proposals to be considered by the Council. Under the Constitution, from November 2004 the Commission will comprise of 25 members, one from each EU state. This number will be reduced after five years to produce a leaner body.

The U.K.'s relationship with the EU is perhaps the most important of its current international obligations. In the environmental field this is particularly so, which has obvious implications for countryside management. Having joined the EU[3] in 1973, the U.K., in common with other member states, was in a position to lobby for particular measures and to modify the proposals of other members in discussion at the Council of Ministers and other fora.

EU expenditure is funded by individual member states (Budge *et al.* 2000). The contributions include all agricultural import levies, customs duties, VAT and payments related to the size of member states' Gross Domestic Product. These amounts, and the share contributed, vary from year to year across member states.

Most EU policies are directed at regulation rather than payments and, in general, these funds are not used to make direct payments to individuals in the member states. Crucial exceptions to that generalisation are payments through the Common Agricultural Policy (CAP) and parts of the EU "Structural Funds." These are distributed in support an array of objectives, including the development of recently joined EU members to assist their "cohesion" to it, as well as funding certain agricultural payments.

Agricultural policy has always been a major element of EU expenditure. By 2003 it had been reduced to around 40% of expenditure although, at its peak, it had exceeded 70% of the total. The CAP is also the dominant rural policy which is determined in Europe. The U.K. has a special arrangement with the agricultural budget, which was negotiated by Margaret Thatcher at the Fontainebleau summit in 1983. Under this arrangement, the U.K. receives a rebate on its budgetary contribution each year, amounting to two thirds of the surplus of what it paid into the budget minus what it receives as agricultural payments. This arrangement, which is unique to the U.K., is often under attack from other member states and many would take the view that its persistence is surprising. We discuss the way in which the agricultural payments to the U.K. are varied in Chapter 8.

Following the publication of Agenda 2000 proposals on the reform of the CAP (CEC 1997), the EU Rural Development Regulation (RDR) 1257/1999 was introduced as the so-called "second pillar" of the CAP. The RDR broadens the emphasis of the CAP, moving it further away from a production focus and promoting the generation of environmental benefits and supporting the needs of rural communities. In 2005 the EU will publish a new version of the RDR and the revised Regulation will be implemented across member states in 2007.

Regulatory policies, although demanding a far smaller share of the EU budget than the CAP, have had a significant and widespread impact on many policy activities in the U.K.

---

[3] Or the European Community (EC) as it then was, having changed its name to EU in the Treaty of Maastricht, in 1991.

It is widely recognised that a significant proportion[4] of U.K. environmental policies have been implemented in response to EU policy and some of these are of direct relevance to the countryside.

The traffic has been both ways. For example, the U.K. was successful in persuading the Council of Ministers to add Article 19 to Directive 797/85, on Agricultural Structures. This provided for the designation of Environmentally Sensitive Areas in member states, leading to several other regulations (including the RDR) which provided for the financing and administration of what is now known as agri-environment policy (see Chapter 14). The U.K. relationship with the EU on environmental matters is detailed by Lowe & Ward (1998) who review the way in which the U.K. has managed to adapt EU regulations to its own circumstances. They argue that U.K. environmental policies can be seen to have been moulded by EU leadership in both style and substance and trace these effects through into the modification of administration and institutions.

9. Other Multi-National Arrangements

Other international environmental arrangements currently include the Kyoto Agreement of 1999 on measures to combat climate change, the Montreal Protocol on CFCs in 1987 and the Convention on International Trade and Endangered Species (CITES). Major trading agreements, such as the former General Agreement on Tariffs and Trade (GATT), under which constraints on trade were regulated by a series of agreements,[5] also constrain our activities and policies (Harvey 1997). GATT has now been replaced by the World Trade Organisation (WTO) and a further round of trade talks is underway. These are only examples from a very long list of formal arrangements which exist. Although frequently ineffective, these measures may become important in limiting the scope for adjusting existing policies or introducing new ones.

10. The Media

A significant element in managing the political process, and one which is often influential in determining its outcomes, is the modern communications industry (Curran & Seaton 1987). This is a major subject in its own right constituting a further important element in the political process. British consumers support a variety of regional and national newspapers, a majority of which are owned by conservative interests. A small number of these are large distribution "tabloid" papers that specialise in stories which catch the public imagination. They also take a somewhat simplified view of many political issues. Their great popularity, with daily sales running to millions, gives them significant influence with voters and it is notable that major tabloid newspapers have supported New Labour at the last two elections. The tabloids

---

[4] Lowe & Ward (1998) suggest that 80% of environmental legislation had its origins in Brussels.
[5] The last of these being the Uruguay Round, which reached a conclusion in 1994 and is currently being implemented.

contrast with "broadsheets," which are more demanding to read and are purchased by fewer people. The influence of newspapers has been greatly diluted by radio and television, which are also highly influential, though less obviously partisan, in affecting the behaviour of voters.

The work of the media is frequently controversial and its impact on events can be profound (Curran & Seaton 1988). They have played an important role in food and health scares in recent decades and their activities are not always helpful to policy makers. They can also play a very constructive role in purveying information quickly to large numbers of people. Public-sector managers can frequently make productive use of the media but may well find that their best-laid plans founder due to lack of attention to their presentation. Web sites now augment the battery of communications tools available to managers seeking to reach significant numbers of people.

Politicians react to the news media by making the fullest possible use of them to seek public support.[6] We thus have two separate parts of the political system — on the one hand democratically elected politicians, wishing to retain power and be re-elected — and on the other the media, driven by mainly commercial motives in seeking the support of their readers, listeners and viewers. Interaction between these two separate groups of interests often produces conflicting claims of distortion, dishonesty, incompetence and so on. What is not disputed is that the media have a significant impact on the working of the political system.

11. Strategic Implications

This chapter has presented a very brief synoptic account of the process of government in the U.K., concentrating on those activities which influence the countryside. Managers, and all others who work within laws, guidelines and policies promulgated by governments, have to have some understanding of this complex network of influence, power and authority. The formal parts of the process can be described but to understand the subtle ways in which the elements of the system work together, or fail to, requires experience. The key players in the process we have described include the electorate and their chosen politicians, paid public servants, voluntary workers, those employed by the media, and all kinds of participants in public decisions. The contrasting motivations which drive such a diverse set of people are an important determinant of their behaviour and an essential ingredient in the policy process.

It is emphasised that this chapter has not attempted to analyse all of the policies which flow from governmental activities. Many of these affect the management of the countryside and determine the scope of operation of countryside managers. There is a large literature devoted to analysing and criticising all types of countryside policies which is published in books and journals. Many of the relevant books are also cited at particular points in this text although we do not attempt a detailed critique of policy, aiming rather at helping countryside

---

[6] See, for example, Rawnsley (2001) for a detailed and entertaining analysis of the political background (the inside story, as he puts it) of the Blair Governments from 1997 to 2001.

managers to work *with* the policies which exist. We assume that strategic managers, for the most part, do not work by changing policies but by using them to the best advantage.

References

Alder, J., & Wilkinson, D. (1999). *Environmental law and ethics*. Basingstoke: Macmillan.
Budge, I., Crewe, I., McKay, D., & Newton, K. (2000). *The new British politics* (2nd ed.). Harlow: Longman.
Cabinet Office (2001). *Public bodies*. London: HMSO.
Commission of the European Communities (1997). Agenda 2000. Volume 1. For a stronger and wider union. Doc/97/6. Brussels, 15 July 1997.
Curran, J., & Seaton, J. (1988). *Power without responsibility; the press and broadcasting in Britain* (3rd ed.). London: Routledge.
Dwyer, J. C., & Hodge, I. D. (1996). *Countryside in trust: Land management by conservation, amenity and recreation organisations*. Chichester: Wiley.
Harvey, D. (1997). The GATT, the WTO and the CAP. In: C. Ritson, & D. R. Harvey (Eds), *The common agricultural policy* (pp. 377–405, 2nd ed.). Wallingford: CAB International.
Haskins, C. (2003). Rural delivery review: A report on the delivery of government policies in rural England. London: DEFRA.
Hodge, I. D. (1988). Property institutions and environmental improvement. *Journal of Agricultural Economics, 39*, 369–375.
Lowe, P., & Goyder, J. (1983). *Environmental groups in politics*. London: George Allen & Unwin.
Lowe, P., & Ward, S. (Eds) (1998). *British environmental policy and Europe*. London: Routledge.
Parker, S. (1992). Volunteering as serious leisure. *Journal of Applied Recreation Research, 17*, 1–11.
Rawcliffe, P. (1998). *Environmental pressure groups in transition*. Manchester: Manchester University Press.
Rawnsley, A. (2001). *Servants of the people; The inside story of new labour* (2nd ed.). London: Penguin.
Winter, M. (1996). *Rural politics: Policies for agriculture, forestry and the environment*. London: Routledge.

Chapter 4

Organisations and Management

1. Introduction

Countryside organisations work in a complex and dynamic environment, characterised by fundamental conflicts over resource use and the demands of an often perplexing institutional and regulatory framework. In this context the effectiveness of organisations can be improved if managers recognise the scope that they have to act in ways that complement their goals and reflect the needs of the external environment.

Increasing our understanding of how organisations deploy their resources and conduct themselves in a range of situations has been a major theme of the developing discipline of management studies. This has brought with it many books and articles aimed at increasing our understanding of how organisations and the people working within them function. While much of this work is focused on the private sector, many valuable insights are available for the public sector and for countryside management.

It is not the role of this text to give a comprehensive overview of this literature, but rather to highlight relevant material that can help us to answer some fundamental questions about organisations engaged in countryside management. These include:

(1) *What is the status of the organisation*? Is it in the voluntary sector, a government department or agency, a local authority, or does it operate in the private sector? The status of an organisation determines some of the parameters which define its structure and the amount of decision-making power that it holds. It may also determine the rules under which the organisation operates.
(2) *Who are their stakeholders*? Who is affected by the operation of the organisation? Who are its clients or customers? What other organisations does its work impact upon? Who are its competitors and collaborators?
(3) *What are the organisation's aims and objectives*? It is important to gain some idea of the organisation's strategic direction and the methods by which it intends to achieve these aims.
(4) *Under what constraints does it operate*? First there is the size of its budget and any constraints over the ways in which this has to be spent. Then the organisation may have to abide by certain rules and regulations or be monitored by some external party. There may also be legal constraints which will define the legitimate area of operation of the agency.
(5) *How does the organisation configure itself to deal with the external pressures that face it*? How do organisational culture and structure reflect the different aspects of its business

or the different needs of its workforce or stakeholders? Have culture and structure been designed to facilitate the strategic direction of the organisation or have they evolved as a response to the operational conditions that it works within?

(6) *What are the relationships between organisations and what impact do they have?* A number of public-sector organisations are under the budgetary or political control of other organisations, this may impact on the scope of their activities and their ability to act autonomously.

(7) *How can the literature on management inform the work of organisations working in the countryside?* Can existing models of business and public-sector management provide helpful insights to countryside organisations given the different conditions in which they operate?

Here we concentrate on the importance of culture and structure in achieving organisational goals. We also examine the nature of the relationships between the different types of public agency working in the U.K. countryside. Before this, we answer the final question and show how some well-established ideas from the management literature can be used to provide a framework for our exploration of the role of strategic management of countryside organisations (see Chapter 5).

1.1. The Role of Management in the Countryside

The development of management as an academic discipline has, in most cases, been aimed at improving the way in which managers do their jobs. This requires the design of programmes that will provide managers with an improved understanding of the tasks that they face, and at the same time help to develop the skills required to perform them more effectively. Early on in any such programme, students are asked to consider the role of management and to define the particular functions and tasks that managers have to perform within a particular organisation. This activity is equally appropriate for a student engaged in the study of countryside management.

It can be argued that perceptions of the basic functions of management have changed little over the last century. Take, for example, the work of Henri Fayol, a Frenchman writing in the early years of the twentieth century, who identified a robust typology of management functions that are summarised in Box 4.1.

Box 4.1: Fayol's Five Functions of Management.

Planning	Looking ahead, making provision for the future.
Organising	Providing the organisation with everything it needs to function.
Command	The direction of subordinates.
Co-ordination	Harmonising activities to achieve successful results.
Control	Ensuring that things happen as planned.

Source: Cole (1996).

Most of the management functions highlighted by Fayol are still regarded as important today, even if they are now applied in a rather different context in which rapid change, technological innovation, partnership and quality assurance play an increasingly dominant role. Fayol's work provides a rational framework for managing the activities of an organisation but, compared with more modern approaches, his categories neglect both the wider environment within which the organisation has to function and the needs of the workforce. The management of human resources and the relationship between the organisation and its external environment are now important elements in many management textbooks. To update the contents of Box 4.1 we could, therefore, replace "command" with "motivation" and extend the roles of planning and co-ordination to activities both within and outside of the organisation.

The next step in understanding what managers do, is to map the various management functions to the list of management tasks set out in Box 4.2. This is not an exhaustive summary and is designed to cover the main activities of countryside managers. Clearly, there are as many different managerial situations as there are organisations, and the relative importance of these tasks in any given context will be different.

Box 4.2: Management Tasks.

Strategic management
Setting objectives
Strategic planning
Monitoring and feedback

Resource Management
Human resources management
Financial management
Information management

Operational management
Operational planning
Inspection, maintenance and quality control
Fund raising
Purchasing
Monitoring and supervision

Demand management
Marketing and promotion
Education
Interpretation
Customer relations

First in the hierarchy is strategic management, where the planning and control functions are dominant. Strategic management is the central theme of the next chapter and its requirements inform the structure of this book. Second, comes the management of resources, an area encompassing elements of the functions of motivation, organisation and co-ordination. No plans or programmes can be implemented successfully if the required resources are not available, so resource management is the essential co-requisite of strategic management. The subject of human resource management is left to other more knowledgeable sources (e.g. Beardwell & Holden 2001), while information and financial management are covered in Chapters 7–9. Chapter 10 examines some assessment methods designed to provide additional information to decision makers working on projects or policies in the countryside.

Third comes operational management, the implementation of strategy within the organisation. This requires the organisation, control and co-ordination of resources to ensure that the organisation can undertake its core activities. This means ensuring the supply of goods and services to those who require them and securing the resources necessary for their provision. Chapters 11–15 address a variety of ways in which the supply of countryside goods is managed.

Supply is only meaningful where demand exists and the fourth, and final, task that we shall examine is the management of demand (see Chapter 16). This addresses the way in which organisations deal with the external environment when implementing strategy. No rational organisation should be content to allow itself to be completely at the mercy of the external environment, and most attempt to exert some control over their interface with the outside world. This interface encompasses activities such as marketing and promotion that can be used to modify the demand for the organisation's outputs, or to ensure a better fit between these outputs and the needs of consumers. It also includes approaches that discourage individuals from pursuing actions that conflict with the aims of the organisation. For countryside managers marketing, education and interpretation are the most relevant topics in this area, and these are discussed in Chapter 17.

2. Public-Sector Management

Many of the organisations dealing with countryside management are in the public sector, that is they are funded by public money and are, to a greater or lesser extent, under Government control. Public-sector management is often characterised by competition over funding and by the need to ensure that the services provided are appropriate and offer good value for money. Over recent decades it has become fashionable to criticise public sector management and compare it unfavourably with its counterparts in the supposedly more efficient private sector.

Some of this criticism has been justified, and in the past many aspects of public-sector management could be described as inefficient, unimaginative and slow to react to change. Since then, lessons have been learnt from the private sector and in many respects performance has improved as managers adopt new approaches and organisations redesign structures and hierarchies. Osborne & Gaebler (1992) give careful consideration to ways in which public-sector management can be modified to improve results. They identified a number of problems typical of ineffective public-sector management including:

- Excessive regulation and control of inputs and ignoring outputs.
- Over-concern for process at the expense of results.

- Excessively slow processes dominated by hierarchies and tied to place.
- An inability to recognise (what the sociologists call) the globalisation of living systems.

Rather than conform to this outdated and negative model, Osborne and Gaebler suggest that modern public-sector organisations should:

- Be responsive and deliver quality goods and services — giving better value for money.
- Empower citizens by pushing control out of bureaucracies and into communities.
- Be driven by goals or missions rather than by rules and regulations.
- Prevent problems rather than solving them after they have arisen.
- Earn money rather than simply spending it.
- Decentralise authority.
- Use market mechanisms rather than bureaucratic systems.
- Catalyse the public, private and voluntary sectors into action to solve the community's problems.

Many of these ideas reflect what is happening in the countryside today. Quality and value for money are important considerations in project appraisal, and securing public participation and community involvement are key issues for sustainable rural development. Similarly, the notion of strategic management and the need to drive organisations through a well-defined set of aims and objectives is well established in our public sector countryside organisations.

3. Organisational Culture

Culture is a phrase used to describe the ways in which a common set of attitudes, traditions, procedures and structures interact to generate a way of working specific to an individual organisation. Handy (1993) introduces the notion of organisational culture as *"sets of values and norms and beliefs — reflected in different structures and systems."* Schein (1992) expands on this idea and suggests that culture also embodies the ways in which groups of individuals begin to share the same sets of assumptions about how the world works and how best to tackle problems. The importance of organisational culture in modern management is widely recognised, and Rosen (1995) argues that culture largely determines strategy, and because of this is as important a factor in the success of an organisation as the goods or services that it produces.

The culture of an organisation may reflect a long tradition of public service, or a strong emphasis on quality; it may also embrace attitudes towards staff, to society, or to the environment. As Brown (1995) points out, separate parts of an organisation will often have different cultures. Within a university, for example, different cultures exist across groups of scientists, engineers and social scientists, and these cultures are to some extent informed by the way in which their disciplines teach them to view the world in particular ways. The visible manifestations of culture can be seen when the organisation interacts with its environment, and substantial clues can be found in mission and vision statements, rituals and dress codes, procedures and rules, logos, layout, customer interface and organisational structure (Handy 1993).

Professionals working in the countryside will often have to work with a wide variety of individuals and groups and can observe the different working cultures that exist across organisations and professions. One of the great challenges of such a multidisciplinary environment is to either create a common culture where these groups can work together productively, or to engineer conditions where cultural differences lead to creativity and innovation rather than conflict. Within an organisation, the creation or manipulation of culture can provide a powerful means of achieving change. For example, senior managers in an organisation undergoing management restructuring, merger or change of ownership may well decide to attempt to alter organisational culture as a means of underlining the changes that are occurring and moving away from the *status quo*. The art of deliberately planned cultural change is often put under the heading of organisational development (Rosen 1995), a growth area in postgraduate education and for continuing professional development.

The work of Handy (1993), Schein (1992) and others suggests a number of factors that influence organisational culture. These include:

- *History and ownership.* Are organisations private or public, or perhaps clubs, charities or membership organisations? Is there centralised or diffuse ownership? Is the organisation new or well-established?
- *Organisational goals and objectives.* Are these influenced by the desire to make profit or provide a service? Is the emphasis on quality or quantity? Are they influenced by wider societal goals?
- *Technology.* What is the nature of the work? Is it routine or changing? What level of investment is required and what resulting level of sophistication? How rapid is the rate of change of technology?
- *Size and diversity.* Is the group large or small? Are its activities homogenous or heterogeneous; specialised or diverse?
- *The external environment.* This encompasses the economy; markets and competitors; social and geographic factors; and the national culture.
- *People.* This includes the needs of the workforce, such as security or job satisfaction; their skills and talents and the availability of suitable individuals.
- *Scale.* At what level do individuals within the organisation work (e.g. the molecule, cell, organism, system) and to what extent do they see their activities as an object in themselves, or as part of a greater whole (e.g. does a stonemason think that he is cutting stones or helping to build a cathedral?)
- *Time.* At what time horizon do these individuals operate? The temporal perspectives of an archaeologist, a biologist and a financial planner might all be very different.

Handy (1993) provides a useful typology of the types of culture that can often be encountered within organisations operating under different conditions or at different stages of their life-cycles. These are illustrated in Box 4.3 and discussed in detail below.

The *power culture* is illustrated by Handy as a web, with a powerful central figure radiating lines of influence to subordinates who in turn link together to provide further structure and stability to the web. In common with spiders' webs, the power culture weakens after a certain size is achieved, and such a culture is generally only found in a small or new organisation where the charisma and personality of a leader, or group of leaders, motivates a modest workforce. Power cultures are all about personality, trust and effective communication and work well in times of rapid change when timely decisions must be made and then implemented quickly and effectively. They are not cultures of reflection and are heavily reliant on the quality of leadership available.

Box 4.3: Handy's Typology of Organisational Culture.
The Power Culture — The Web

- Small entrepreneurial enterprises with a highly centralised source of authority.
- Depends on trust and empathy for effectiveness, relies on personal communication, has little formal bureaucracy, puts faith in the individual.
- Innovative and react well in times of change.
- They judge by results, often regardless of the means.

The Role Culture — The Greek Temple

- Typifies what is often regarded as a bureaucracy — a culture of reason, logic and rationality.
- Depends for its success on the strength of its functional specialities co-ordinated by a narrow band of senior management.
- Relies on formal procedures and rules and it is the position rather than the person who fills it that is important.
- Work well in conditions of stability but are undermined by change.

The Task Culture — The Net

- Task or product oriented cultures, where the main emphasis is on getting the job done.
- A team culture often with common objectives, where the individual assumes the goals of the group.
- Influence is based on expertise as much as power or position and is more widely dispersed than in other cultures.
- Extremely adaptable and flexible and works best where speed of response is important.
- Hard to control, does not encourage depth of expertise and is inherently unstable.

The Person Culture — The Galaxy

- Individuals are the central focus and the organisation exists only to assist them.
- A communal culture where hierarchies can only exist by consent.
- Influence is shared and often based on expertise.
- Hard to achieve and therefore uncommon.

Source: Handy (1993).

Handy depicts his *task culture* as a net, where the strength of the organisation is a result of the individual strands or specialisations within it. The task culture is, as the name suggests, task or product orientated and relies on a set of very specific common goals. The task culture is one of co-operation, where individuals work together towards common aims rather than a more diverse set of goals. Here power and influence reside in those with expert knowledge and skills who can contribute most to the task at hand. This is not a culture of routine specialisation but of problem solving and innovation as new challenges continue to arise, and is exemplified in the recent expansion of *e-commerce* and the rise of the *dot.com* organisations seeking to exploit the new markets offered by the internet.

While task cultures tackle change and innovation well, they lack stability and can be volatile and vulnerable to the actions of individuals. If an individual in the task culture does not perform or leaves the organisation damaging gaps result. The frequency of such occurrences leads to a culture of "fire-fighting," where individuals must be able to perform a number of functions rather than concentrate on a particular area of expertise.

Role cultures are the most common cultural configuration, found in nearly all organisational sectors. The role culture is the almost inevitable result of growth, as the organisation expands, it requires new modes of working to accommodate its increase in size. Handy represents the role culture as a Greek temple where the upper pediment represents the core of senior managers, with a chief executive or managing director at the apex. Various pillars support the pediment and these represent the operating functions of the organisation, from middle management down to operational staff. Power and influence radiate from the apex through the pediment and down the pillars to the base or factory floor level.

The role culture is a reflection of the formalised bureaucracies that we shall examine later in this chapter. They are cultures of stability that rely on clearly-drawn hierarchies, highly-documented formal procedures, and well-understood lines of influence and communication. In the role culture, power comes from position rather than as a direct result of skills or personality. Nevertheless it is an effective culture for dealing with specialised, large or routine tasks involving many individuals and requiring reliable procedures and processes. Diversity can be dealt with through compartmentalisation and the different pillars of the temple can reflect different functional specialities of the organisation, each with a role culture that reflects the needs of that specialisation.

The efficiency that comes from increased specialisation means that role cultures perform well in times of stability. Diversification (see Chapter 5) allows the organisation to weather fluctuations in the external environment but may make it more vulnerable to any longer-term changes. The rigidity that underlies role cultures means that they are ill-equipped to withstand unforeseen change and replace unhelpful practices with ones more in keeping with the new organisational environment. Larger organisations may have to adopt a range of strategies to overcome the weaknesses that come with increased size.

Such strategies include directing a high level of resources into economic forecasting and market research: change is not such a problem for the role culture if it is expected and can be managed. Similarly, such organisations may attempt to lead a market and induce change to wrong-foot its competitors. Such innovations may be a result of a task culture being fostered in a particular arm of the organisation, e.g. research and innovation, to provide market drivers.

The *person culture* is drawn by Handy as a galaxy of individuals for whom the organisation is merely a convenient structure within which to pursue individual goals. In the person culture the organisation exists only to service the individuals who work within it. This unusual structure requires mutual co-operation and trusting relationships between participants and is rarely encountered. In the countryside such a culture may occasionally be encountered in craft co-operatives where groups of craft workers join together to share premises and to enjoy the benefits of the enhanced public interest that comes with the proximity of a variety of different outlets rather than a single craftsman.

Such cultures are rare because they are highly vulnerable to personality and require a high degree of trust and co-operation. Like students sharing a house, members of the person culture are only free to pursue their own interests if they are conscious of the needs of the collective. Therefore each member of the "galaxy" must ensure that his or her responsibilities are met or their failings will inevitably lead to the collapse of the group structure.

Miles & Snow (1988) adopt a different classification system (see Box 4.4), based on the behaviour of the organisation with particular emphasis on how it deals with the external environment. These descriptions can apply to organisations of different sizes and ages and relate to their planning systems and control structures. Indeed, they can be seen as providing a useful layer of additional detail over and above Handy's typology, so that an organisation with a role culture could further be described as having the characteristics of a defender, analyser or reactor.

Box 4.4: The Miles and Snow Classification of Organisational Culture.

Defenders — cautious, inward-looking organisations, reluctant to take risks. Characterised by little forward planning but rigid control systems. Perform well in the steady state.

Prospectors — more proactive and innovative and prepared to take risks. Relies on decentralised authority to enable it to react quickly to opportunities.

Analysers — rational organisations, with well-developed planning systems

Reactors — conservative organisations with loose control systems and little interest in forward planning. Concerned with maintaining the steady state and only react in crisis situations, often ineffectively.

Source: Miles & Snow (1988).

The different characteristics and objectives of organisations working within the countryside may suggest that one or other of these cultures would be appropriate for them or their component parts. Indeed, the diversity of modern organisations implies that different elements are likely to develop their own individual cultures in order to better reflect the nature of their activities. Schein (1992) argues that the complexity of modern organisations makes cultural models such as those proposed by Handy redundant. Instead he proposes models based on human behaviour which better depict the group learning process which underpins the development of organisational culture.

Many of the larger organisations and agencies will have little choice but to develop the more formal role culture, but may retain elements where the task culture provides a more effective means of achieving certain tasks. Some farms and rural micro-businesses may be modelled as power cultures, with a small staff working to the instructions of a central authority figure who has often founded, inherited or financed the venture. These may include organisations such as small haulage yards, fish and game farms, speciality food producers, outdoor pursuit centres, and catering or hospitality-based operations. Smaller organisations focussed on particular issues may adopt a task culture, especially if they require a high degree of specialism.

Typically, the type of culture that a group adopts depends upon the stage it has reached within its life-cycle and may also reflect external pressures that it has to face. In times of rapid change or upheaval, for example, organisations may adapt and take on characteristics of other cultures. This hybridisation of organisational culture is not uncommon and it is a logical method of dealing with change. Indeed, it is a common practice for organisations to adapt or alter certain facets of their culture to achieve certain ends.

Box (1994) reports on a process of conservation change that occurred within English Nature (EN) during the early 1990s following their creation out of the old Nature Conservancy Council. The strategy of the EN Management Board involved turning a bureaucratic, risk averse organisation into something more proactive and customer orientated. A fundamental part of this strategy involved changing organisational culture to help to facilitate acceptance of these new ideas. In particular it was felt important to create a "strong vision statement and powerful set of values" that could help to unify staff and motivate them in the future.

Box reports that the process of culture change began with the distribution of a culture questionnaire to EN staff. Analysis of responses identified a number of qualities lacking from the existing organisation, e.g. rapid decision making, risk taking, being outward-looking and proactive and having clear lines of delegation and authority. A gap analysis (see Chapter 5) was then used by the EN Board to suggest how far away from the desired situation the organisation currently was. A series of workshops and team meetings was then conducted to discuss the implications of achieving the characteristics desired by the Board. This raised the issue of cultural change and provided a baseline against which to measure improvement.

Initial improvements were achieved following further staff interviews, this time to identify restrictions or working practices that caused delays in operations. Remedies for these problems were implemented and provided an apt demonstration of how participation and self-help can lead to change and a reduction in bureaucracy. The new beginning for the organisation was further emphasised by a "Paper Clearance Day" in March 1993 when over 10 tonnes of paper was removed from desks and files and sent for recycling. Further culture changes were then encouraged at a local level in a bid to ensure that the ownership of such changes resided at grass roots rather than at a corporate level.

In his analysis of events at EN, Box makes the interesting point that scientists and other professionals distrust the cultural change process as it appears to be rather "*woolly and fuzzy*" to individuals who are used to dealing with hard facts rather than the manipulation of behaviour. Nevertheless, certain aspects of the culture shifts, e.g. feedback on team plans to assess how well they dealt with culture change, were felt to be quite effective and to help participants feel that the process was concrete rather than some abstract exercise that would not impact on the way that the organisation works.

This need for ownership and relevance seems particularly important in a countryside context, where staff may be suspicious of concepts that seem more appropriate in a commercial setting. Culture is as much a facet of countryside organisations as it is of those based in a more urban environment. Understanding and manipulation of culture are important tools in the management of these organisations and can help them to adapt and better respond to new pressures and opportunities. Handy (1993) suggests that different cultures suit different situations and recommends different strategies for organisations in crisis (power culture); dealing with innovation (task culture); and those concerned with managing the steady state or policy making (role cultures).

4. Organisational Structure

It is natural for organisational culture to be reflected both by the formal structures that exist within it and in the spatial relationships between its members. Thus, members of a task culture would be expected to be located closely together, possibly in open-plan offices with shared access to specialist equipment. By contrast in a role culture staff may be separated into groups that reflect different specialisms or areas of interest and these may be allocated different areas of physical space with different access characteristics with respect to common resources. The physical organisation of staff members may reflect cultural divisions or be broken down along the lines of the way in which the organisation has been structured by its senior management.

Mintzberg (1979) defines the structure of an organisation as: *"the sum total of the ways in which it divides its labour into distinct tasks and then achieves coordination between them."* This simple definition suggests that the structure observed within an organisation is imposed to help solve a set of problems surrounding the control, co-ordination and organisation of activities. Thus, organisational structure defines not only the hierarchies and lines of communication that exist within organisations but also the ways in which resources are allocated between different groups and functions.

Typically, organisational structure can be depicted in the form of a chart or diagram divided into layers that depict the levels of hierarchy (e.g. organisation charts or organagrams). Different groups or functions are shown in the diagrams as boxes, with senior management typically occupying the top layers or apex of the diagram. Subsequent layers depict the lower levels of management moving down towards the operational and support elements of the organisation. The arrangement of boxes across layers is used to depict the hierarchies that exist, while adjoining lines show how the various elements link together.

The structure of an organisation can be manipulated to achieve specified objectives, in particular it may be viewed as an important way of changing culture. The incidence of structural reconfiguration, especially in the public sector, especially following shifts in management or government policy, suggests that many managers feel that the physical remodelling of an organisation is an effective tool to promote change. This may be the case, but such restructuring often brings with it anxiety, uncertainty and reduced motivation, as well as impacting on productivity as time and resources are spent on relocation, retraining, redefinition and redundancy payments.

Clearly structural change is too disruptive to approach lightly, and should only be undertaken when circumstances demand. Structural change has been a fact of life for a variety of countryside agencies over recent years, often caused by a redefinition of roles and responsibilities coupled with the creation of a number of new organisations and the dispersal of others.

Cole (1996) identifies the key issues in determining organisational structure as the:

- Purpose or goals of the organisation.
- People within the organisation.
- Tasks undertaken.
- Technology utilised.
- Organisational culture.
- External environment.

In general, these issues map well onto the main drivers for structural change found in organisations in the countryside. Devolution of power to the regional level has seen responsibility for countryside issues moving to the regions, and this has meant that a variety of organisations such as the former GB Countryside Commission and Nature Conservancy Council giving way to new devolved organisations better equipped to meet modern challenges and more in tune with prevailing political attitudes.

As in the case of organisational culture, it is not difficult to begin to see some similarities between the configurations chosen by different organisations and on this basis to begin to categorise the ways in which organisations are constructed. Figure 4.1 provides an example of one such model as devised by Henry Mintzberg. This model looks at an organisation

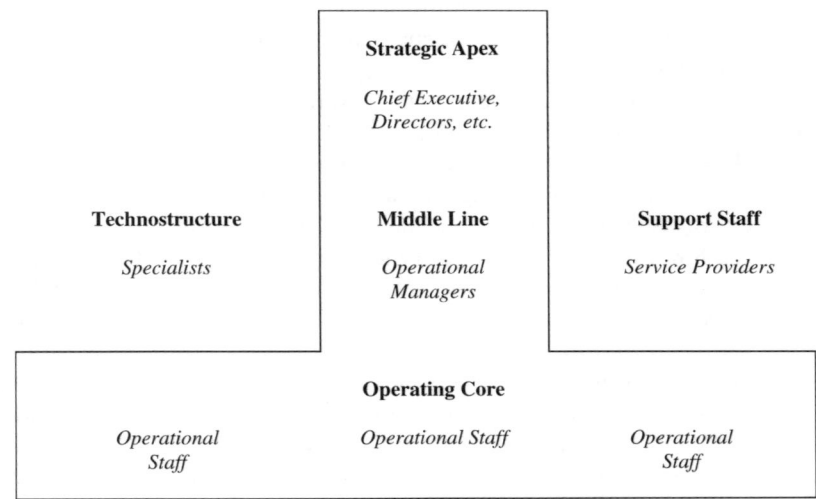

Figure 4.1: Mintzberg's model of organisational components. *Source:* Mintzberg (1983).

from the perspective of the roles played by employees and divides it into a set of functional components. Other models concentrate more on differences in outputs or geographical location, but like Handy's typology of organisational culture they each provide a useful framework for discussion and analysis at a classroom level.

The problem with such models is that although they tell part of the story, they tend to lack the complexity observed in the real world and are seldom directly comparable with what we might observe in practice. Mintzberg's model has the advantage that it does not attempt to imitate any particular organisational design, rather it presents a hierarchical structure typical of many organisations and demonstrates how different emphases within this structure can lead to different organisational configurations.

In the generic model shown in Figure 4.1, the strategic apex controls the main policy and decision making functions of the organisation. The middle line contains those business or operational managers responsible for implementing these decisions and managing the operating core who must, in turn, produce the good or service in question. Surrounding these main functions are a range of support staff and specialists providing services and expertise to the organisation. These can include clerical support, IT and maintenance functions, and technical expertise. For example, forest managers may wish to call upon the services of landscape architects, database managers, silviculturalists and other specialists to help implement a woodland management strategy, while local authority planners may wish to consult a field archaeologist or ecologist about a particular planning application.

Box 4.5 summarises the specific organisational configurations that Mintzberg discusses. Each configuration is defined on the basis of the dominant functions within the organisation and the key mechanisms for the co-ordination of these functions. Thus, Mintzberg's "machine bureaucracy" is dominated by the needs of specialists and relies on a well defined work process, while in a "professional bureaucracy" the standardisation of the skills of the core operating staff is critical.

It is relatively easy to see how certain countryside organisations fit into this pattern. Small organisations including a number of rural microbusinesses may fit into the mould of simple structures or adhocracies, while a variety of organisations concentrate on activities that revolve around specialist technical and scientific staff (e.g. the Institute of Terrestrial Ecology and various research institutes). Other agencies (e.g. the Countryside Agency or Scottish Natural Heritage) lie somewhere between the divisionalised form and professional bureaucracy in that while they rely on the skills of core staff there is still an element of specialisation and service provision to be achieved.

The way in which organisations configure their staff naturally leads to a variety of organisational designs that reflect their chosen structures. Cole (1996) identifies a number of common ways in which organisations design their structures.

Functional organisations group their staff by particular business functions, e.g. marketing, production, finance, etc. a configuration suggestive of the professional bureaucracy or Handy's role culture. This design is relatively efficient in that there are clearly defined roles and responsibilities within the organisation and greater scope for specialisation and economies of scale. As Cole points out, the drawback of such a structure is that staff tend to retain a rather narrow view of the scope of the organisation's interests, leaving room for rather parochial attitudes and interests to develop.

> **Box 4.5: Mitzberg's Organisational Configurations.**
>
> **• SIMPLE STRUCTURE**
> Basically unstructured
> Relies on direct supervision
> Strategic apex is key
>
> **• MACHINE BUREAUCRACY**
> Dominated by the needs of specialists
> Relies on standardisation of work process
> Technostructure is key
>
> **• PROFESSIONAL BUREAUCRACY**
> Dominated by skills of core staff
> Relies on standardisation of skills
> Operating core is key
>
> **• DIVISIONALISED FORM**
> Outputs/services are dominant
> Relies on standardisation of services
> Middle line is key
>
> **• ADHOCRACY**
> Shared dominance of core staff and support services
> Relies on mutual adjustment
> Support staff and operating core are key
>
> *Source:* Mintzberg (1983).

Output-based organisations group staff by what they produce, be it goods or services. These organisations might have a broader strategic apex than functional organisations in that the Chief Executive may be supported by a range of directors (e.g. finance, workforce planning, and marketing) beneath whom will be business managers in charge of the particular outputs (e.g. recreation, education, and customer services). Where appropriate these business managers will be supported by their finance, customer services and personnel managers. The concentration on output suggests a machine bureaucracy where specialists are dominant and there is an advantage in standardising work processes and purchasing specialist equipment. In smaller organisations a task culture may develop to support the highly flexible and innovative activities being undertaken. Again, there may be an opportunity for sectoral interests to develop at the expense of the remainder of the organisation.

The two examples reported above, begin to highlight a particular problem for corporate strategists, this is the question of how to distribute authority effectively throughout an organisation. The answer to this question depends very much on the nature of the authority in question. In some cases provided that key decisions regarding organisational vision and budget allocation are kept within the strategic apex there may be flexibility about what component units of the organisation do to implement strategy or allocate budgets to tasks.

Such devolution of authority may sometimes be termed decentralisation (the reverse of this process sometimes occurs as the top level of the organisational hierarchy claw back responsibilities from divisions). Decentralised structures are often devised in response to external pressures which suggest a greater need for specialisation or the need to structure the organisation around its activities. In such cases there is a need to delegate responsibility and authority and an obligation to ensure that an appropriate management structure is in place to take on this role. The advantages of decentralisation (Cole 1996) are that it:

- Spreads responsibility across a greater number of managers.
- Can permit greater responsiveness to local or specialised needs.
- Provides clarity for customers seeking a particular function or speciality.
- Allows different parts of the organisation to evolve independently free from the constraints of the broader organisation.
- Can lead to a higher profile for devolved elements of the organisation.
- Provides a potential marketing opportunity based on regional or functional distinctiveness.
- Empowers local staff and provides more opportunities for them to make a difference.

As we might guess, there are also numerous disadvantages to decentralised authority, (Cole 1996) including:

- The inability to recruit suitable senior managers to lead decentralised units.
- Problems with perceived equity and fairness in treatment across different parts of the organisation (i.e. the creation of functional ghettos).
- The need for highly effective communications mechanisms, particularly for the sharing of information.
- Cost inefficiencies due to duplication of certain roles.
- A lack of consistency in the way the organisation is presented to the outside world.
- In the long-run potential fundamental differences between the vision of the organisation and its components units.

Some of these disadvantages can be tackled by moving towards a more mixed structure that retains the most useful features of central administration and couples them with the greater flexibility of the more distinct decentralised units. Thus, in a more mixed structure some administration and support services can be shared by all units to avoid duplication, while a strong organisational culture can maintain consistency of vision and presentation by ensuring that devolved units are always aware of the organisational vision underlying their activities. Cole (1996) provides the following examples of such structures.

Divisionalised organisations are a hybrid of output-based and geographical structures where the organisation is divided up on the basis of both location and output. Again, key strategic and resource management responsibilities are retained by head office with some autonomy devolved down to regional or special project groups. The former Countryside Commission and its successor the Countryside Agency provide good examples of the divisionalised structure, combining a mix of regional offices and special project groups that concentrate on particular issues, e.g. Millennium Greens.

In each of the structural designs described above, decisions must be made over the level of control exerted by the strategic apex over the rest of the organisation. While control and co-ordination are necessary for the successful operation of any organisation, some level of local independence and autonomy may prove valuable. The ability to influence activities both within and between organisations is an important issue for Government agencies operating within the countryside. In the next section we examine some models of bureaucratic behaviour and introduce a classification of agencies that depends on how they spend and control their budgets.

Geographical organisations tend to conduct business on a national or international scale and structure their activities at a regional or national level. The strategic apex may be similar to that found in an output-based structure but supplemented by regional directors. The regional units will tend to share a common structure and will operate at a level of autonomy that depends on their ability to determine strategy and allocate budgets. Duplication of certain roles is made necessary by the scale of the organisation but there are generally clear lines of control reaching back to headquarters to ensure that overall direction is consistent. While many countryside organisations, e.g. English Nature, the National Trust, and DEFRA, have regional offices, the power vested in them is relatively small and focuses on the implementation of national strategies at a local level and with scope for local initiatives in marketing, land management, and project work. In some cases there is greater scope for innovation to tackle particular local issues and the Countryside Agency provides a number of good examples of important work led by regional offices.

It should now be clear how the structure and culture of organisations can reflect both the activities they undertake and their particular characteristics and outlook. In the case of the larger public-sector organisations working in the countryside, the role culture will predominate, coupled with structures that promote particular organisational goals. In the next section we look in more detail at how these larger organisations operate and in particular examine the important role played by their budgetary relationships with other organisations.

5. Bureaucracies and Public Choice

The word bureaucrat is often used as a term of abuse, which perhaps suggests that the people who use it fear or distrust a certain type of manager or administrator. Yet in today's society we cannot survive without bureaucracies and they have to be trusted and made to work. As much of countryside management is undertaken or heavily constrained by bureaucrats, we should examine the literature on the subject.

The sociologist Max Weber (1864–1920), who took a more optimistic view of bureaucrats, used the term bureaucracy to distinguish a particular organisational type that differed from other models in that authority within the organisation was not based on tradition, custom or loyalty but instead on the office or position of the person in authority as defined by the rules and procedures of the organisation (Cole 1996).

According to Cole, the main features of bureaucracies in Weber's philosophy are as follows:

- The continuous organisation of functions bound by rules.
- The existence of specified spheres of competence and authority.
- A hierarchical arrangement of jobs and authority.
- Appointments that are made on grounds of technical competence.
- Ownership of the organisation is kept separate from its operation.
- Official positions exist in their own right, regardless of the incumbent.
- All rules, decisions and actions are formulated and recorded.

The result of these features is that within bureaucracies authority is legitimate and not arbitrary. Weber considered this the most rational way of carrying out "imperative control over human beings" and especially important when organisations grew beyond a certain size or complexity. Later authors such as Handy (1993) recognised similar organisational cultures within modern management (the role culture) but their perceptions have been shaped by other writers such as Gouldner (1954), who argued that behaviour also plays an important role in bureaucracies. Gouldner's work suggests that successful bureaucracies take account of the beliefs and values of employees and that decisions and practices have to be regarded as legitimate if they are to be implemented successfully.

Many of our perceptions of bureaucracy are rather cynical and simplistic, but they survive because they can be found in the real world. We have all encountered officials too restricted by rules to be flexible, even in a good cause, similarly we have heard of people being promoted to the level of their own incompetence (the so-called "Peter Principle") and complained about "faceless bureaucrats" who place the needs of the organisation above those of the individual. Such convenient generalisations about bureaucracy should be avoided, not only do they miss out too much detail to offer a realistic view, but they also ignore the unobtrusive success of many large and absolutely essential bureaucracies. Nevertheless researchers have identified a number of disadvantages associated with the bureaucratic structure, these have been summarised by Cole (1996) as the following:

- Rules that become important for their own sake.
- Depersonalised relationships based on rights and duties rather than on the qualities of individuals, leading to rigid behaviour, potentially stifling creativity and imagination.
- Decision making that is pre-programmed and lacks originality.
- Rigid bureaucratic structures that may damage relationships with staff and clients.
- Poor responsiveness to change owing to standardisation and routine.
- Potential clashes between experts and general managers.

Some authors share Weber's optimism about bureaucracy. Dunleavy (1991) offers a more positive view which he contrasts with the work of Anthony Downs (1996) who presented a more pessimistic model of bureaucracy in the mid-1960s. Downs' central hypotheses were that:

- Bureaucrats try to attain their goals rationally. That is, they try to be efficient in allocating their time, and they are aware of the cost of their main input, which is information.

- The goals of the individual bureaucrat are complex, and would include the attainment of power, income and security, as well as those of loyalty, professional pride and a desire to serve the public interest. The important point is that every bureaucrat is assumed to be significantly motivated by his own self interest in addition to that of his employers.
- The organisation's social functions will strongly influence its internal structure and vice versa. This means that we should look at the environment within which an organisation works as well as inside it, if we are to understand its operation (Downs 1996).

The conditions under which bureaucrats work are characterised by Downs on the basis of three important factors: first, information is costly; second, decision-makers can only take in a certain amount of information and can usually only devote a small amount of time to making any individual decision; and third, there will always be some uncertainty about any decision, no matter how well informed the person taking it.

A central conclusion from much of the earlier literature on bureaucracy, including Downs, is that it will always grow. This gradual process of growth is sometimes described as "incrementalism" — as bureaucracies slowly increase budgets, size and influence. A consequence of this is the widely held belief that control of bureaucracy is a critical task facing society. A good example of this, are the frequent media demands that bureaucracy in the National Health Service (NHS) be reduced for the benefit of patient care. In times of public dissatisfaction with the NHS, management and administration are a softer target for criticism than those individuals, such as doctors and nurses, more directly involved with patient care. What is seldom mentioned is the inevitability of large bureaucracies growing to support services that not only employ large numbers of people but also utilise a large proportion of the public exchequer. In the absence of such necessary support networks, those concerned with patient care would be forced to spend much of their time on the less glamorous activities such as finance, human resource management, estate services and administration.

The pessimistic conclusion of Downs' work is that it will always be difficult to control bureaucratic growth because of the central interest of bureaucrats in securing expansion of their budgets as a means of expanding their empires. Such conclusions only serve to encourage those who would storm the bureaucratic Bastille and consign the bureaucrats to the tumbrels. Dunleavy, who comes from the Public Choice school of political science, has argued that Downs' view of bureaucracy is too simplistic. We will briefly examine Dunleavy's view of the world which usefully takes us beyond the budget-maximising position of Downs.

According to Dunleavy, public choice rests on four premises:

(1) People have sets of well formed preferences which they can perceive, rank and compare easily.
(2) Their preference orderings are transitive or logically consistent, so that if someone prefers socialism to liberalism, and liberalism to fascism, then they will also prefer socialism to fascism.
(3) People are maximisers who will always seek the greatest possible benefits and the smallest costs in their decisions. They will act rationally and pursue preferences efficiently. Rationality, note, does not mean we have to agree with the goals they are pursuing, only that they pursue them efficiently.

(4) People are basically egoistic, self regarding and instrumental in their behaviour, choosing how to act on the basis of consequences for their personal welfare.

These assumptions draw strongly on economic models combined with political science. Using them, Dunleavy attempts to replace the budget-maximising assumption with a model of behaviour which he calls "bureau-shaping." His reasons for asserting that rational bureaucrats will not maximise budgets are:

- Collective action problems (which arise to the extent that individuals do not all pursue the same collective goals) occur within agencies which are important in influencing behaviour.
- The enthusiasm of bureaucrats for maximising their budget varies across components of total budget and across different types of agency.
- Even where officials do budget-maximise they will not go beyond an internal optimal level.
- Senior officials are more likely to pursue non-pecuniary utilities than pecuniary ones. This would mean that collective strategies for re-shaping their bureaux, rather than pursuing growth alone, can best advance the interests of senior officials. The interest of senior officials in bureau-shaping or budget maximising varies with agency type.

Dunleavy suggests an alternative to the simple budget maximising model of a bureaucrat that starts from a hierarchy of agency budgets (see Box 4.6), and which can be applied to agencies in the countryside. This hierarchy is used by Dunleavy to define a typology of public sector agencies as described in Section 6.

Box 4.6: Dunleavy's Hierarchy of Agency Budgets.

Core Budget (CB) Covers expenditures directed at the agency's own internal operations. Includes the salaries, equipment and consumables used in the agency's basic functions.

Bureau Budget (BB) Includes all of CB together with any money that the agency pays out to the private sector (e.g. through contracts with private firms). This includes construction and major purchases of equipment that are purchased as a result of the agency's own decisions.

Programme Budget (PB) This includes the BB plus any other money that the agency passes on to other public sector bodies for them to spend. Inter-organisational transfers can only be included in the PB if the agency exerts hierarchical control over the ways in which the funding is spent.

Super-Programme Budget (SPB) This represents the PB plus spending by other bureaux from their resources over which the agency exercises policy responsibility or which it can limit or expand, or for which it can claim political credit.

Based on Dunleavy (1991).

6. The Role of the Agency

Dunleavy argues that we can distinguish different types of agency by the relative size of their budgets. He defines five types of agency as follows:

> *Delivery agencies* follow the models put forward by Weber. They have clear lines of authority and produce outputs or services directly using their own personnel to implement policy. They tend to be labour intensive and have relatively large budgets. PB is dominated by the CB plus minor additions to make up the BB, with little or no SPB increment. Countryside examples include the Farming and Rural Conservation Agency (FRCA).
>
> *Regulatory agencies* have the same budgetary relationships as Delivery Agencies. Their key tasks are to control individuals, enterprises or other bodies. They may use instruments such as licensing systems or performance standards to control activities and typically pass costs onto those who are being regulated. The agency may thus appear relatively cheap compared with Delivery agencies with similar scope. A U.K. example might be the Environment Agency.
>
> *Transfer agencies* are devoted to shifting money to their clients in the form of subsidies. DEFRA is an obvious example. Because the costs of paying out money are comparatively slight, CB would be expected to be only a small proportion of BB, with CB remaining relatively constant after the basic administrative structure is operating. Thereafter further money can be distributed without increasing the number of staff significantly. PB is mostly made up of BB, though in the case of the former MAFF a significant element of PB was used to pay for the work of the FRCA.
>
> *Contracts agencies* get work done by contractors. Their main effort is in research into project design and specification and the monitoring of implementation and a large proportion of their work is contracted to outside organisations. Their CB thus absorbs a small share of the BB, which constitutes the majority of the PB. An example of such an organisation is English Estates.
>
> *Control agencies* channel funding to other agencies as grants and transfers and supervise their activities. In this case both CB and BB are a minor part of PB which may increase substantially without them growing. Because control agencies may act in a supervisory role over other agencies their SPB may grow faster than their PB. The U.K. Treasury fulfils this type of role but with rather more complex power relationships than allowed for in the above description.

Based on this typology, Dunleavy puts forward an alternative hypothesis to budget maximisation, which is that bureaucrats seek to shape bureaux to their own ends. He begins by ascribing a series of positive and negative values to bureaucrats as shown in Table 4.1.

From these arguments he goes on to suggest that individuals' objectives can best be pursued by individual action until all opportunities for advancement are exploited. Thereafter there will be some interest in collective action. Dunleavy suggests this will be aimed by senior administrators by seeking to foster their work-related utilities. They will do this, not by budget maximisation, but by bureau shaping strategies designed to

Table 4.1: Positive and Negative Values Ascribed to Bureaucrats.

Positively Valued	**Negatively Valued**
Staff functions	*Staff functions*
• Opportunities for individual innovation.	• Routine.
• Broad scope of interest.	• Narrow scope of interest.
• High level of discretion.	• Low level of discretion.
• Low public scrutiny.	• High public scrutiny.
Collegial atmosphere	*Corporate atmosphere*
• Small work units.	• Large work units.
• Co-operation.	• Coercion and conflict.
• Predominance of elite personnel.	• Predominance of non-elite personnel.
Central location	*Peripheral location*
• Closer to centres of power.	• Remote from power centres.
• Metropolitan.	• Provincial.
• High status social contacts.	• Remote from high status social contacts.

Source: Dunleavy (1991).

bring their bureaux into "staff" as opposed to "line" functions. They will favour a "collegial atmosphere" and a central location: they will be more interested in power than in size of budget. Dunleavy suggests that they have five main ways to achieve this:

(1) *Major internal reorganisation*, concentrating expansion at the policy-making level and separating off routine functions.
(2) *Transformations of internal work practices* including a shift towards more sophisticated management and policy analysis systems. This means more high-level staff.
(3) *Redefinition of relationships with external partners* to reduce routine work and enhance policy control.
(4) *Competition with other bureaux* especially defending the scope of their activities and fighting others to take over new tasks which fit in with their ideal form of agency.
(5) *Load-shedding, hiving-off and contracting-out* provide the most radical opportunities for moving the agency in desired directions. Load-shedding is to subordinates, for example from central to local government, while hiving-off refers to the process of handing over certain activities to other agencies that have some autonomy over how they complete them. Contracting out involves moving activities to other departments within the agency or outside usually in return for a fee. In this model, although core budgets might fall as a consequence, contracted services are still in the agency's bureau budget.

So the alternative to bureau-shaping is a useful alternative to the older and simpler model of budget-maximising. In favour of bureau-shaping is that it captures more of the complexity of bureaucratic behaviour. This leaves us with the conclusion that bureaucratic survival is about power, rather than money.

7. Strategic Implications

Recent changes within the agencies that control many of the activities within the U.K. countryside suggest that survival has become an important goal of any organisation working in this area. As discussed in Chapter 3, the Haskins Report (2003) may lead to further organisational change in the agencies delivering rural policy in England.

The seemingly continual round of re-invention and re-definition as agencies seek to meet the challenges of the modern countryside may cause a certain amount of confusion and dismay both among the public and among managers. As illustrated in the previous chapter, the last 20 years have seen a plethora of new agencies born from the remnants of other older organisations which have been disbanded, split-up, devolved or merged. The importance of organisational culture and structure in the design and management of these agencies should not be underestimated. If organisational strategy is to be successful it must be supported by appropriate structures and by a culture that reflects corporate aims and objectives.

Dunleavy's typology of agencies provides one approach to examining organisations operating in the countryside. It provides limited insights, however, for the private sector and voluntary organisations that are important providers of countryside management. Even when applied in the U.K. it is hard to pigeonhole specific agencies under one heading as budgetary spending and interests are not always as clear as they are in Dunleavy's taxonomy. Nevertheless, Dunleavy's work provides a useful framework for analysing the relationships that exist between public sector organisations engaged in countryside management, as well as challenging the conventional bureaucratic model with a more positive framework that is consistent with the aspirations of many of those who work in the countryside.

References

Beardwell, I., & Holden, L. (2001). *Human resources management: A contemporary approach* (3rd ed.). Harlow: Financial Times, Prentice-Hall.
Box, J. (1994). Changing the conservation culture. *ECOS, 15*, 16–22.
Brown, A. (1995). *Organisational culture*. London: Pitman.
Cole, G. A. (1996). *Management theory and practice* (5th ed.). London: DP Publications.
Downs, A. (1996). *Inside bureaucracy*. Boston: Little & Brown.
Dunleavy, P. (1991). *Democracy, bureaucracy and public choice: Economic explanations in political science*. London: Harvester Wheatsheaf.
Gouldner, A. W. (1954). *Patterns of industrial bureaucracy*. Glencoe: Free Press.
Handy, C. B. (1993). *Understanding organisations* (3rd ed.). Harmondsworth: Penguin.
Haskins, C. (2003). *Rural delivery review: A report on the delivery of Government policies in rural England*. London: DEFRA.
Miles, R. E., & Snow, C. C. (1988). *Organisational strategy, structure and process*. New York: McGraw-Hill.

Mintzberg, H. (1983). *Structure in fives: Designing effective organisations*. New York: Prentice-Hall.
Osborne, D., & Gaebler, T. (1992). *Reinventing Government: How the entrepreneurial spirit is transforming the public sector; from Schoolhouse to Statehouse, City Hall to Pentagon*. Reading, MA: Addison-Wesley.
Rosen, R. (1995). *Strategic management: An introduction*. London: Pitman.
Schein, E. H. (1992). *Organisational culture and leadership* (2nd ed.). San Francisco: Jossey-Bass.

Chapter 5

Planning for the Future

1. Introduction

Any organisation, however simple, will have a set of objectives that it wishes to achieve within a given time-scale. The nature of these objectives will be determined by the underlying aims of the organisation, the resources available to support them and any constraints imposed by the environment within which it operates. All organisations must plan for the future and make decisions on how they can best achieve their objectives. Such strategic planning is a key task within an organisation, and those that operate within the countryside are no exception.

In this chapter we largely ignore the operational constraints facing managers and concentrate on how they can achieve a coherent, strategic approach to countryside management. We begin with an examination of the scope and goals of countryside management in the U.K. We illustrate this by examining the aims and objectives of a number of countryside organisations. We argue that the requirements of management at a national or regional level are sufficiently complex to demand the adoption of a strategic planning framework by countryside organisations. The process surrounding the crafting of such strategies is then described, along with a number of tools that can be used to help inform their design. Various approaches to strategy are then introduced and their suitability for countryside management is assessed. The chapter ends with two case studies and a broad definition of the objectives of strategic countryside management.

2. The Aims of Countryside Management

The aims of countryside management are many and varied and become more complex as the scope of the organisation widens and overlaps with other, broader national or regional priorities. To begin with a simple example, the chief aim of commercial farmers may be to produce sufficient food and fibre so that, once sold or consumed, they would achieve a basic standard of living for their family. Arising from this simple aim would be a series of objectives relating to the management of crops and livestock. In order to achieve these objectives, farmers have to plan how to allocate scarce resources — such as time, money, land and machinery — and, once these plans are implemented, they have to monitor their progress carefully and make any adjustments necessary to respond to external factors such as weather or the activities of pests and diseases.

In microcosm, these are the tasks facing any organisation in the countryside or beyond. All organisations must define the nature of their business and what they aim to achieve. These aspirations will evolve over time as organisations react to changes in the outside world, seek to exploit fresh opportunities, or respond to the changing needs of the groups that they serve. The latter is particularly relevant to public sector organisations who are increasingly under pressure to be more responsive to the needs of particular groups.

Where once the people were subjects of a sovereign, or citizens of a republic, they are now often classified as "stakeholders" whose needs must be considered by the organisations that work on their behalf. This attitude reflects the hierarchies of the private sector, where organisations are responsible to their shareholders or to investors, and has become widely adopted by public-sector organisations. Thus, health service organisations are told to become more patient-focused and educational establishments must respond to the needs of employers by imparting skills that are relevant to the workplace.

These changes in focus represent the beginning of a shift in attitude away from earlier paternalistic notions of public-sector management where the "powers that be" knew what was best for the public and set out to deliver it. There is certainly a good argument for public money to be spent in a way which maximises the welfare of society, and a greater emphasis on the needs of the groups that public-sector organisations interact with, may achieve a net improvement in social welfare.

For simplicity, we will consider the three broad categories of countryside organisation, private, public or voluntary, discussed in Chapter 4. This can be extended to include those organisations whose activities are only partly concerned with the countryside and which reach out into the town or beyond. Within each of these three categories the size and type of organisation will vary greatly, as will the aims and objectives that inform its activities. Even so, organisations within each category will often share certain broad aims.

The main aims of private-sector countryside management tend to be profit-led, and are generally focused on the production of goods and services that can be traded. Private sector organisations may also provide public goods that benefit the wider community but the provision of these goods is seldom an end in itself, unless encouraged by some form of Government support (e.g. through grants or subsidies).

By contrast, agency-led countryside management often concentrates on the production of public goods (see Chapter 12) and the elimination of public bads, and may have a mix of aims concerning the management of natural resources and the people who live in or visit the countryside. These aims must be achieved in an uncertain world subject to the constraints of government. Increasingly in the U.K., these constraints are set at a European or even international level, particularly where they concern public goods and bads, like biodiversity or pollution, that have trans-national implications. The voluntary sector can be described as having similar goals to the public sector, in some cases with the aim of maximising the welfare benefits to members subject to resource constraints. As we shall see in Chapter 12 the voluntary sector can make a significant contribution to the provision of public goods in the countryside.

Having addressed the broad aims of countryside organisations, we move on to assess the scope for strategic planning in the countryside. In some cases planning can be undertaken at a local or site level, e.g. through site management plans, local area strategies; or facility specific approaches. More significant is planning at the national or regional level. This can include various aspects of Government strategy outlined in White Papers, the corporate aims and objectives of the various countryside agencies, European strategies (e.g. the EC Birds Directive) and international strategies and agreements such as the Convention on International Trade and Endangered Species (CITES), the Kyoto Protocol and the Convention on Biological Diversity.

Whatever the goals of an organisation and whatever the level at which the organisation operates, some initial process must be undertaken to determine the goals that it wishes to pursue, and secondly the means through which it intends to achieve them. This process of setting aims and objectives is referred to in some management textbooks as corporate strategy.

3. Setting Aims and Objectives: The Role of Corporate Strategy

> [strategy is] the determination of the basic long-term goals and objectives of an enterprise, and the adoption of courses of action and the allocation of resources necessary for carrying out these goals.
>
> Alfred D. Chandler (1962)

Andrews (1987) draws a useful distinction between what he describes as corporate strategy, that is deciding on the nature of the environment in which the organisation will operate, and business strategy, which determines how it will operate within that environment. To some extent, organisations that operate in the countryside are limited in their choices, particularly where their functions are determined by government or statute. In some cases, flexibility exists and organisations can decide where to concentrate their efforts. For example, an organisation concerned with nature conservation must decide on how they will divide their efforts between political, educational and scientific activities.

Box 5.1: Aims and objectives of the Forestry Commission.
Mission

To protect and expand Britain's forests and woodlands and increase their value to society and the environment.

Objectives are to:

- Protect Britain's forests and woodlands.
- Expand Britain's forest area.
- Enhance the economic value of our forest resources.
- Conserve and improve the biodiversity, landscape and cultural heritage of our forests and woodlands.
- Develop opportunities for woodland recreation.
- Increase public understanding and community participation in forestry.

Source: www.forestry.gov.uk.

The starting point of the strategic management process is the decision on what aims will guide the organisation's future conduct and activities. These goals may be outlined as an organisational vision or set out in a mission statement, items that can often be found near the beginning of a corporate plan or annual report. The aims of an organisation broadly outline what it expects to accomplish over the long term and give rise to a set of more specific objectives which must be attained in order for these aims to be achieved. Box 5.1 provides an example from the Forestry Commission, note how the objectives support the mission statement and clarify the Commission's areas of interest.

Once these objectives have been defined, the organisation must go about the task of setting in motion the processes needed to achieve them. This task is often referred to as strategic planning and will be discussed in greater detail later in this chapter.

Private and voluntary sector agencies in the countryside also have well defined sets of aims and objectives under which they operate. Box 5.2 illustrates the aims and objectives of the John Muir Trust, an international organisation dedicated to the acquisition and sensitive management of key wild areas.

Box 5.2: Aims and objectives of the John Muir Trust.

Aims

To conserve and protect wild places with their indigenous animals, plants and soils for the benefit of present and future generations.

Objectives

- To conserve wild places and their landscapes, both for their own sake and for the sustenance and inspiration they give to humanity.
- To protect existing wild places so as to conserve their natural processes, and their indigenous animals, plants and soils.
- To renew wild places, where they have been damaged, by encouraging natural processes.
- To work with local communities and to encourage them to live in harmony with wild places.
- To promote an awareness and understanding of wild places for their own sake and for their value to the benefit of humanity.
- To stimulate public support.
- To protect wild places.
- To encourage voluntary participation in the conservation and renewal of wild places.

Source: Memorandum of Association of the John Muir Trust, www.jmt.org (2001).

The Trust believes that the best way of achieving the first three objectives is to own areas of wild land and oversee its management. Currently, the Trust owns and manages seven areas in the Highlands and Islands of Scotland, totalling 20,000 hectares (including Britain's highest mountain Ben Nevis, 1250 hectares of the Knoydart Peninsula and the Strathaird Estate on the Isle of Skye). Public participation is promoted through partnerships with local communities and through encouraging members to become involved in practical conservation projects such as tree planting, and repairs to paths and dry-stone walls.

As well as playing an important role in the strategic management process, an organisation's aims and objectives play a key role in the evaluation of performance at both a corporate and an individual level. This type of performance management is relatively common and was described by Drucker (1954) as "management by objectives." This approach to management emphasises setting standards and specifying results for all managers at an operational level, and assessing performance on this basis. Today, many regard management by objectives as too narrow an approach to meet the needs of modern organisations, but it is still commonly used in personal appraisal and review processes and may be the basis for assessing training needs (Box 5.3).

Box 5.3: The management by objectives process.

(i) Based on the strategic planning process define unit objectives.
(ii) Determine the major areas of responsibility for each individual manager and the results expected.
(iii) Define individual manager objectives and standards.
(iv) Determine key results and performance targets for assessment purposes.
(v) Review performance based on set targets, redefine individual targets as necessary, and identify appropriate training needs.

Based on Cole (1996).

A major task for many countryside managers is the design of local short-term management strategies. This may be achieved through designing appropriate management plans. This may be based on a broad set of fundamental aims for management which are supplemented by information from on-site surveys. This information can then be processed and analysed and a set of management objectives are drawn up. These objectives are translated into specific management prescriptions which can be translated into day-to-day site management activities. Leay et al. (1986) provide an early systematic description of the management planning process.

4. Managing the Wider Countryside

While all managers must learn to balance the sometimes conflicting needs of a variety of activities, particularly in the allocation and use of scarce resources, the broader countryside contains many examples where the needs of one interest group conflict directly with those of other groups. This was illustrated vividly during the 2001 Foot and Mouth crisis, where the needs of the livestock industry in combating the disease were frequently in direct conflict with the interests of tourism and related businesses. In many areas the restrictions imposed to contain the spread of the disease also prevented the public from using the countryside and led to substantial reductions in tourist visits and in the revenues of many local businesses.

80 Strategic Countryside Management

This was particularly strongly felt in areas such as Devon and Cumbria that rely heavily on tourism and which were also severely affected by the disease.

The Foot and Mouth outbreak represents a particularly extreme example of conflicting management aims, but such conflicts can always to observed in the countryside and can, in many cases, be attributed to the basic conflicts that exist between private and public land management. A number of public agencies, e.g. regional and national tourist authorities, may represent the interests of a number of private organisations, and this may bring them into conflict with agencies with a public-good remit. For example, could the English Tourist Board, English Nature and the National Park Authority all be expected to have similar management objectives for the Peak District?

In addition to the aims of public- and private-sector managers, the aims of the voluntary sector must also be considered. The voluntary sector tends to focus on particular issues or areas and in many cases does not become involved in the management of the wider countryside except when that management impinges on their own particular interests. There are exceptions to this, however, and some larger organisations, particularly the National Trust, have begun to take a much broader interest in the countryside and have engaged in a number of rural development projects. Indeed, the Trust's policy on rural sustainability, focused on providing a sustainable base for farming on the Trust's land with the aims of contributing towards the overall health of the rural economy (National Trust 2001).

Even organisations with broadly similar aims, e.g. conservation, may manage land very differently and have different management objectives. Thus English Nature and the RSPB may have different ideas about habitat management for particular species of bird. These differences can be attributed to differences in organisational culture and focus as well as to differences in resources and responsibilities.

Increasingly more than one agency has the power to influence management of the same piece of land, and this problem of multiple jurisdiction can be a major source of conflict and delay in countryside management (see Box 5.4 for examples).

Box 5.4: Examples of multiple jurisdiction in the countryside.

- The *Lake District National Park* where most of the land was designated by DEFRA as an Environmentally Sensitive Area and where some sites on this land are also designated as SSSIs by English Nature. Considerable areas of land in the National Park are also owned by the National Trust and some areas of grazing are managed in common.
- *Hadrian's Wall* different areas around the wall under the jurisdiction of private landowners, the National Trust, English Heritage, local authorities, Northumberland National Park, English Nature, and others.
- *The North Pennines AONB* is administered by nine local authorities, three County Councils (County Durham, Northumberland and Cumbria) and six district councils (Carlisle, Eden, Derwentside, Teesdale, Wear Valley and Tynedale). The area is included within both County Structure Plans and Local Plans.

It is difficult to combat the problems resulting from multiple jurisdiction with legislation. What is needed is constructive interaction between agencies at a local level, for example regular meetings and the determination of appropriate interagency protocols, preferably without tying up too much expensive management time.

In Chapter 1 we defined countryside management as the process of designing and implementing strategies, often with incomplete information, to provide a sustainable supply of the countryside goods demanded by stakeholders. This can encompass environmental enhancement, the provision of recreational opportunities and support to local businesses, economies and communities. The aims of any given organisation will determine their orientation towards these objectives, but increasingly the various countryside agencies are attempting to design programmes that deliver an integrated package of benefits to the rural economy which encompass economic, social and environmental objectives. Early examples of such integrated approaches include the Countryside Agency's Land Management Initiatives and DEFRA's Upland Experiment.

5. The Strategic Planning Process

At any stage in its existence an organisation must have a clear idea of:

- What it wants to achieve — its objectives.
- How it intends to accomplish these objectives.
- A time-scale within which the objectives must be achieved.
- How progress will be monitored and how policies and objectives will be revised.

These questions are usually answered by senior managers working at a strategic rather than an operational level, though there may be opportunities for workers from other areas of the organisation to take part through consultation. To ensure that this process works as smoothly as possible, the organisation requires a viable structure of leadership and a well-defined framework for decision making. Within this structure it should make appropriate use of physical and human resources and orchestrate the external environment into the overall plan (Cole 1996).

As summarised by Oldcorn (1996), the strategic planning process attempts to answer the above by asking managers to consider the following different, but related, set of questions.

5.1. Where are We Now?

For an organisation to move forward effectively, it must have a detailed knowledge of its current position, e.g. its strengths and weaknesses, the environment it works within, its competitors and collaborators. The importance of this information highlights the need for good quality, up-to-date, information upon which to base decisions and strategy.

5.2. Where do We Want to be?

Here the organisation must determine what it wishes to achieve in the short, medium and long term. This requires the development of a set of organisational goals and a formulation of the aims and objectives of the organisation as described earlier. Some authors, such as Thompson & Strickland (1990) see this step as merely an objectives-setting exercise, and separate from the development of the strategy, while others regard it as an integral part of the planning process.

The "distance" between where an organisation is now and where it would be if its aims and objectives were achieved can be termed the "planning gap" (Rosen 1995). The strategic planning process is about how managers attempt to close the planning gap.

5.3. Where Will We be if We do Nothing?

There may be good arguments for the organisation maintaining the *status quo* and not altering its strategic direction. Change is not always desirable and the upheaval caused by reorganisation or altering direction can significantly reduce performance. On the other hand, it may be tempting to do nothing as a way of avoiding necessary change. Such negative behaviour should be avoided. Successful organisations are responsive to change and are able to manage it successfully. An inability to deal with change can result in missed opportunities, reduction in competitiveness, failure to respond to the needs of stakeholders and eventually in the need for more drastic action. In the private sector this could mean a company going into receivership, while in the public sector wholesale reorganisation, merger with another organisation or even disbandment are options that could be considered.

In the countryside failure to respond to change is seldom an option. The countryside is a dynamic environment that responds to global and local forces. Rural businesses cannot ignore changes in technology and communications, farmers cannot ignore world markets, and our policy makers must adhere to European and international agreements on things such as pollution, sustainable development and biodiversity conservation.

Gap analysis (see for example Rosen 1995) is a technique used by managers to analyse the difference between where the organisation wants to be and where it would be if a "do nothing" approach was adopted (see Box 5.5). This is another way of identifying the

---

Box 5.5: Problems with a "do nothing" approach.

- Failure to adapt to changing environment.
- Failure to build on your strengths.
- Failure to eliminate your weaknesses.
- Failure to guard against threats.
- Failure to exploit new opportunities.
- A culture of complacency builds up.

Based on Oldcorn (1996).

planning gap. The technique is highly reliant on accurate forecasts of predicted performance and on any assumptions made about the behaviour of the external environment.

5.4. What Can We not do?

The activities of an organisation are usually limited by a variety of internal and external constraints. Internal constraints include ethics, organisational culture, political and religious beliefs, or personal preferences. Thus, some farmers may not adopt certain techniques on their land out of personal preference — e.g. they may stay out of milk to avoid having to work a seven-day week. More fundamental constraints include limited resources such as investment income, grant aid, time, skills and technology.

External constraints may include a range of laws, regulations, rules and codes of practice. Some of these, for example relating to pollution or food safety, may be legally binding, while others such as management agreements will have been undertaken on a voluntary basis.

5.5. How do We Fill the Planning Gap?

It is at this stage that managers must decide on the methods and approaches that they will use to fill the planning gap and determine how best they should be implemented. Thompson & Strickland (1990) recommend that following implementation, performance is strictly monitored, with the various activities evaluated and reviewed on a regular basis and adjusted as required. In general organisations tend to develop strategies along two lines:

(1) Those aimed at producing actions to meet objectives.
(2) Those aimed at ensuring that the resources are available to enable these actions to be undertaken.

These strategies are incorporated into:

- Business or corporate plans (longer term, between 1–5 years).
- Operating or tactical plans (shorter term, e.g. 6 months to 1 year).

There remains the question of how such strategies are arrived at and how managers can obtain the information required to help craft them. This is discussed in the next section.

6. Tools for Strategic Management

A number of approaches are available to managers to inform the strategic planning process. In this section we shall draw on the clearly designed and user-friendly strategic planning worksheets designed by Rosen (1995) to describe three techniques, SWOT analysis, PEST analysis and stakeholder analysis, which have particular relevance to managers dealing with the provision of public goods and services.

6.1. PEST Analysis

Politico-legal, economic, social, technological (PEST) analysis is designed to provide a framework within which a manager can gather relevant background information about the global macro environment within which the strategic planning process is taking place. Each of the four component factors is investigated in turn and any inter-relationships that could compound these effects are identified. Box 5.6 describes the PEST analysis process.

Box 5.6: PEST analysis.
The manager should identify and evaluate the following:

- External factors that may influence strategy.
- Future trends, developments, opportunities and threats that could be of strategic importance.

Note:

(1) The urgency and importance of each factor.
(2) When each event may occur and its probability.
(3) Any compounding inter-reactions.

Implications for each of the following should then be considered:

- The organisation.
- Its customers.
- The relevant sector.
- Intermediaries.
- Other stakeholders.

Based on Rosen (1995)

When undertaking PEST analysis the countryside manager must have a good grasp of relevant current and proposed legislation regarding land use and environmental protection. With the influence of the EU and the reform of the Common Agricultural Policy, the political environment within which the countryside manager operates is becoming increasingly complex. Among a variety of issues, managers may find themselves having to consider the implications of EU Directives on water quality or waste management and to review the impacts of changing patterns of agricultural support. They must also consider the latest strategies for sustainable rural development, biodiversity conservation, countryside access and the changing patterns of funding in the countryside. To add to the complexity of this analysis, the manager must consider not only the direct implications for her own organisation but any indirect implications caused arising from the impacts of these issues on customers, competitors and other stakeholders.

When complete, the results of this analysis may be fed into subsequent exercises such as SWOT analysis (see below) to help inform the design of appropriate strategies.

6.2. Stakeholder Analysis

Stakeholder analysis (see Box 5.7) is used by organisations to determine priorities and objectives, and according to Rosen (1995) is commonly applied in the public sector. The technique relies on a careful evaluation of the needs and priorities of stakeholders, that is individuals or other organisations who influence, or are influenced by, the decisions of the organisation.

Box 5.7: Stakeholder analysis.
The manager should identify and evaluate the following:

- The identity of all stakeholders.
- Their relative power.
- The importance of particular issues to each of them.
- Where and how stakeholders will exert their influence and power.

A *stakeholder map* should then be drawn to illustrate the following:

- Relationships between stakeholders (drawn as lines).
- Directions of influence (shown as arrow heads on the lines).
- Strength of influence (denoted by the thickness of the lines).

The manager must then predict how stakeholders will be affected by and respond to:

(a) Trends identified in PEST analysis.
(b) Continuation of existing strategies.

Then the manager must evaluate strategic significance of these findings for:

(a) Key stakeholders.
(b) The reactions of other stakeholders.

Repeat the above for possible new stakeholders who may be introduced by new strategies devised as a result of this analysis.

Based on Rosen (1995).

Public agencies or Government Departments tend to have the widest constituencies of stakeholders, while voluntary bodies tend to be influenced most by their members, collaborators and funding bodies. In the private sector, the decisions of the organisation will always concern its shareholders, staff and customers, but at the same time will impact on competitors and suppliers. The activities of any organisation will also be influenced by national and local government and by the activities of regulatory authorities and the decisions of the EU and various international bodies.

Again, the results of this analysis may then feed into subsequent exercises, particularly SWOT analysis where the needs of stakeholders will be used to inform potential strategies.

Box 5.8: SWOT analysis.
Managers must undertake the following tasks:

(1) Using findings from PEST and Stakeholder analysis and any other internal audits, identify all factors of strategic importance and list under strengths, weaknesses, opportunities and threats, noting the degree of urgency.
(2) Evaluate these findings according to their strategic significance.

Strengths

Identify under-exploited strengths and devise strategies that capitalise on them.

Weaknesses

Implement strategies to strengthen areas of weakness that undermine the success of current strategies or that may compromise future strategies.

Opportunities

Conduct an opportunity analysis (see Rosen 1995) to identify the most productive opportunities to exploit (i.e. those that best exploit internal strengths and external opportunities).

Threats

Identify any threats that compromise the organisation's mission and where appropriate devise strategies to overcome them.

In achieving the above managers must:

- Make qualitative judgements about current performance.
- Accurately predict future trends in the external environment.
- Develop a list of alternative strategies upon which to base a strategic direction, these must both fulfil objectives and ensure that sufficient resources are available to support required activities.

Based on Rosen (1995) and Cole (1996).

6.3. SWOT Analysis

SWOT analysis seeks to provides insights into potential new strategies by highlighting an organisation's *strengths* and *weaknesses* and identifying any relevant *opportunities* and *threats* that it will encounter in the future. It is frequently used by organisations seeking to re-evaluate their current position and devise new sets of aims and objectives that are better suited to new conditions.

The technique (see Box 5.8) is particularly effective as a means by which an organisation can begin to adapt to changes in its external environment. It explicitly evaluates external threats and opportunities and forces the organisation to evaluate how its current performance impacts upon its ability to deal with these stimuli. If an organisation's weaknesses are likely to prevent it from exploiting an important opportunity or dealing with a threat then these weaknesses must be eliminated. Similarly, any strengths that make an organisation well suited to meeting the challenges of the future must be fully exploited.

In the countryside one particularly important external environmental factor is funding. Funding opportunities can arise from a variety of sources, including Government grants, lottery funding, European structural or regional development funds or private investment (see Chapter 8). To achieve their objectives, the majority of countryside organisations must exploit these resources as fully as possible and must therefore not only be well informed about sources of potential funding but must be able to compete effectively for their share of the limited funds. Poor performance or perceived weaknesses may prove a serious a barrier to new funding, and organisations must emphasise their strengths and demonstrate how they will provide their benefactors with good value for money.

7. Strategies for Countryside Management

While the majority of authors who have considered questions of strategic management have concentrated on issues more relevant to the private sector, there are many lessons that can be applied to organisations dealing with the provision of public goods.

Ansoff (1966) developed a more formal approach to developing management strategies based on his product/market matrix. The vertical axis of the matrix denotes the organisation's external environment, i.e. its markets, while the horizontal axis relates to the products or activities that the organisation produces (see Figure 5.1). Within each cell of the resulting matrix Ansoff suggests the most appropriate type of strategy for the organisation to adopt.

Ansoff was particularly concerned about growth strategies in industry and where he lists market penetration and product development, these are replaced in Figure 5.1 with general improvement and expansion strategies. In many cases improvement and consolidation strategies are appropriate (see Box 5.9), particularly those that improve the quality and efficiency of existing core activities, e.g. English Nature may wish to reduce the costs associated with biodiversity conservation. Organisations dealing with the provision of countryside recreation may decide to increase revenues or justify funding by improving

88 Strategic Countryside Management

	Current Activities	New Activities
Current Markets	Strategies based on improvement or consolidation	Strategies based on expansion
New Markets	Strategies based on expansion	Strategies based on diversification

Figure 5.1: Ansoff's typology of strategies. *Source:* Adapted from Ansoff (1987).

market penetration and attracting more users to their facilities through imaginative use of the marketing mix (see Chapter 17).

Box 5.9: Improvement and consolidation strategies.
e.g. increasing the funding base, reducing costs, increasing membership numbers, contracting activities out to other providers

Advantages

- Quick to implement and comparatively inexpensive.
- Easy to measure outputs.
- Easy to control.

Disadvantages

- Organisations don't adapt to meet needs of a changing environment.
- Could generate adverse response from competitors.

Based on Oldcorn (1996) and Rosen (1995).

Cost-effectiveness may also be served by cutting internal costs by reducing infrastructure and contracting out certain activities to other providers. This strategy has been widely adopted in the public sector since the 1980s and has been used by local authorities and businesses to deal with activities such as refuse collection, catering, cleaning, and training.

Expansion strategies (Box 5.10) may be appropriate for commercial enterprises or voluntary groups with a limited scope that are seeking to attract new members and new funding by expanding their activity base. For example, a locally based heritage trust may expand its activities beyond its original area of concern or may extend its interest into other areas of heritage management.

Box 5.10: Expansion strategies.

(i) Expand into new activities, e.g. exploit identified opportunity by developing new goods or services using existing skills and resources.
(ii) Expand into new markets, e.g. expand geographical scope of activities, expand current activities into new markets, attract new users to existing goods and services.

Advantages of expanding into new activities

- Existing support systems and structures can be used.
- Can use existing knowledge base.

Disadvantages of expanding into new activities

- High start-up and development costs.

Advantages of expanding into new markets

- Relatively simple to implement.
- Uses existing skills, products and services.

Disadvantages of expanding into new markets

- Risky — what works in one area may not work in another.
- Needs new/expanded support structures.

Based on Oldcorn (1996) and Rosen (1995).

Diversification (see Box 5.11) is most often associated with commercial enterprises, for example farm businesses diversifying into bed and breakfast accommodation or into the provision of recreational activities such as angling, golf or horse riding. Similarly a country park or stately home may diversify by opening a shop or cafe. Sometimes organisations may diversify into what might be considered completely unrelated areas, though this is less common in organisations involved in countryside management. This probably reflects the often well-defined remits of such organisations which tend to prevent them straying too far from their original purposes.

The National Trust's recent efforts to become actively involved in rural development and its involvement in primary food production is an example of an organisation seeking to move sideways from its original core business into a wider, but related sector, that will arguably have benefits for the broader concerns of its members. Other voluntary organisations have sought to expand into commercial activities, for example in the early 1990s the Nottinghamshire Wildlife Trust diversified into commercial environmental consultancy.

Box 5.11: Diversification strategies.

Advantages

- May be the only option to move forward.
- As an insurance policy, i.e. spreading risk.
- Exploiting new opportunities identified by SWOT analysis.
- May be a better alternative than expansion.
- May create a positive synergy.

Disadvantages

- The organisation may lack required skills and knowledge.
- High start-up costs due to additional resource needs.
- Potentially high risk.
- May create a negative synergy.

Types of diversification

- Horizontal diversification — extension of current activities into similar areas.
- Same technology, different outputs.
- Conglomeration — diversifying into many different, unrelated activities.
- Vertical integration — moving into an area connected with your own.

Based on Rosen (1995).

Underlying these strategies is the need for organisations competing for resources or customers to attempt to maintain a sustainable competitive advantage. It is this that sets them apart from the competition and helps to maintain their position within the sector. Sustainable competitive advantage can be achieved through:

- Reducing costs — by doing things more efficiently you can be less expensive.
- Adding value — differentiation of your outputs from those of your competitors.
- Increased focus — excel in a geographic region or in a particular area of endeavour.

An organisation must be able to sustain its competitive advantage by becoming a "moving target" or creating barriers to others. Sometimes however, competition is not always fruitful and the activities of competitors may sometimes be beneficial. This is an example of the phenomenon of complementarity where one activity enhances the effects of another. This may be especially true in the countryside.

For organisations hoping to expand or diversify, co-operation may prove a fruitful strategy. This can come about through a variety of means. A merger means a take-over or the creation of a new organisation from existing organisation (e.g. the formation of the Countryside Agency in England from elements of the Countryside Commission and the Rural Development Commission). If an organisation lacks the skills and resources required for a particular project then it can work together with another organisation that has them in a joint venture (e.g. English Nature, Countryside Agency and English Heritage worked together on the Joint Character Map for England — see Chapter 10). In some cases a strategic alliance might be formed between organisations, that is a long term linkage where the objectives are similar to those of the joint venture, e.g. English Nature protocols.

8. Two Case Studies

8.1. Case 1: The Scottish Forestry Strategy (Scottish Executive 2000)

By 1900, many centuries of timber production and land clearance for agriculture had taken their toll on Scottish forests and only 5% of the country was forested. The introduction of the Forestry Commission in 1919 (see Chapter 2) began a sequence of events which was to lead to a substantial increase in the importance of forestry as a land use in Scotland, so that by 2000 16% of the country was covered. Scotland now has an internationally competitive wood processing industry and large areas are planted with high yielding species such as Sitka Spruce and Douglas Fir.

The 1995 Rural White Paper for Scotland identified a need for a continued "steady expansion of tree cover" but provided no long term target for this activity, stating only that "the quality of new woodland is at least as important as the physical area of expansion." This objective is consistent with recent developments in forestry policy which place more emphasis on the multi-purpose nature of forestry, rather than treating it merely as a source of timber. Thus, recreation, amenity, carbon sequestration and biodiversity conservation are all important goods associate with forestry, and used by the FC to help justify the grant in aid which it receives from Government.

Scottish devolution has enabled the development of distinct policies to deal with forestry and led to the production of a unique Scottish Forestry Strategy for the Scottish Executive, that extends to 2050 and beyond.

The strategy has a vision of Scotland as "*a land of fine trees*" and a resource that "both strengthens the economy and enriches the natural environment." It aims to "*promote confidence in the future of forestry*" while "*encouraging investment that will benefit current and future generations.*"

This vision leads to the following objectives for Scottish forestry which should:

- Promote sustainable economic growth.
- Enhance the environment, extend and enrich habitats and create attractive landscapes.

- Help to create a more inclusive society, offer employment opportunities and act as a "green lung" for towns and cities (Scottish Executive 2001).

The initial consultation paper for the strategy was published in March 1999 and 5,000 copies were distributed. A series of six regional seminars was organised during the summer of 1999 to discuss the strategy and over 250 written submissions were received concerning its content. A seminar was held in November 1999 to further discuss and refine the ideas in the consultation paper and a draft strategy was prepared early in 2000.

The strategy was developed by the FC which acts as the Scottish Executive's (SE) forestry department and has a statutory duty to promote the interests of forestry throughout Great Britain. The FC co-ordinated the design of the strategy through working with other SE Departments, relevant agencies, industry and local authorities.

The strategy had to take into account a variety of factors including international biodiversity obligations as interpreted by the U.K. Biodiversity Action Plan (see Case 2); European forestry policy (e.g. EU guidelines on sustainable forest management and biodiversity conservation); rural development policy (e.g. future implementation of EU Rural Development Regulation); and the resolutions of the Pan European Forestry Protection Meeting as interpreted in the "U.K. Forestry Standard" (1998).

The guiding principles of the strategy were:

(1) Sustainability, i.e. sustainable forest management and sustainable rural development.
(2) Integration, i.e. forestry should fit in with other activities, e.g. agriculture, deer management, fishing, conservation, recreation and tourism.
(3) The desirability of forests adding value to society.
(4) For forests to earn community support.
(5) That forestry should reflect the diversity and local distinctiveness of the land, forests and people of Scotland.

8.2. Developing the Strategy

The strategy required that the existing forest resource be developed to help realise the vision outlined above. This would be achieved by fulfilling the following objectives. Specifically, forestry in Scotland should:

(a) Contribute to the economy.

Current Position

- Adds about £600 million per year to the Scottish economy.
- 7,000 jobs directly provided by forestry and 3,000 in wood processing industry.
- Wood processing industry is investing up to £100 million per year on new equipment.

Strategic Direction

- To maximise the value to Scottish economy of wood resources becoming available for harvesting in next 20 years.
- To create a diverse forest resource of high quality that will contribute to the economic needs of Scotland throughout the twentyfirst century and beyond.

(b) Conserve and improve the environment.

Current Position

- Scottish forests may absorb up to 10% of Scottish carbon dioxide emissions.
- 15,000 ha of native woodland (2% of the land area) exist in Scotland and are a valuable resource for biodiversity.
- U.K. Biodiversity Action Plan priorities include the protection of ancient semi-natural woodlands and the creation new native woodlands especially ones linking existing woodlands.
- Forest management can increase biodiversity.
- Forests form a significant part of many landscapes.

Strategic Direction

- To ensure that forestry makes a positive contribution to the environment

(c) Enhance the quality of life for all communities.

Current Position

- Two million people visit woodlands in Scotland for recreation each year.
- £2 million per year is spent by FC on recreation facilities.
- A survey showed that 40% of residents had not recently visited a forest — the majority through lack of opportunity.

Strategic Direction

- To create more opportunities for people to enjoy trees, woods and forests.
- To help communities to use woods and forests to promote development.

Priorities for Action
Before these were set the following questions were answered:

- Why is it considered a priority?
- What are the potential benefits of addressing this priority?
- What needs to be done and what will it cost?

- Who needs to be involved?
- How will progress be judged?

Delivery

The strategy emphasises the importance of effective partnerships, i.e. with the Timber Growers' Association, local government, relevant agencies, e.g. Deer Commission, Scottish Natural Heritage, Scottish Environmental Protection Agency. The FC will manage the strategy and Scottish Enterprise will take account of the strategy in new policy development.

Scottish Enterprise published the Action Plan for forest industries in late 2000, with priorities for Action to be reviewed in the next five years.

8.3. Case 2: The U.K. Biodiversity Action Plan

The harmful effects that human activities have on the natural environment have long been recognised, but it is only recently that governments have been forced explicitly to acknowledge the extent of environmental degradation and to pledge their determination to curtail the activities which are destroying habitats, species, ecosystems and landscapes.

One indication that the environment has become an important international issue was the attendance of some 150 Heads of State or Government at the United Nations Conference on the Environment at Rio de Janeiro in June 1992. A central part of the "Earth Summit" was the signing of the Convention on Biological Diversity.

The term biodiversity attempts to describe the innate variability that exists among living organisms, particularly the biological and genetic diversity that is observed both within and between ecosystems (Johnson 1993). Weitzman (1992) attempts to describe this diversity in terms of the "degree of distance of dissimilarity or difference" between any pair of species.

Article 6a of the Convention requires contracting parties to:

> develop national strategies, plans or programmes for the conservation and sustainable use of biological diversity or adapt for this purpose existing strategies, plans or programmes...

The publication of the "Biodiversity — The U.K. Action Plan" early in 1994 represented an early response to this undertaking, and underlined the nation's commitment to the aims of the Convention. The document sets out the U.K.'s contribution to global biodiversity conservation over the next 20 years.

The U.K. Biodiversity Action Plan (BAP) identifies three different levels at which diversity can be assessed (HM Government 1994):

- *Genetic Diversity* is the sum of genetic information contained in the genes of plants, animals and micro-organisms on earth. Each species contains an immense amount of genetic information, with each individual being virtually genetically unique (Pearce 1993).
- *Species Diversity* is the number and variety of species on earth.

- *Ecosystem Diversity* refers to the variety of habitats, biotic communities and ecological processes that form distinct ecosystems.

Each of these must be considered when deriving the objectives of such a far-reaching strategy. Section 2 of the BAP describes the U.K.'s main areas of activity in terms of biodiversity conservation:

- Conservation within habitats.
- Conservation outside natural habitats, including the conservation of genetic material.
- Sustainable use of natural resources contributing to biodiversity and the impact of various activities, e.g. agriculture, forestry, tourism, transport, energy, recreation, etc.
- Partnership and education — environmental awareness and public participation with central and local government.
- U.K. support to Biodiversity Overseas — e.g. CITES, U.K. Aid Programme, etc.
- Information requirements and data sources.

Within this range of activities and supported by a variety of measures, the BAP required the U.K. to:

- Prepare action plans for threatened species in priority order.
- Ensure that identified species are increased by measurable amounts.
- Ensure that identified habitats or assemblages of plants or animals are measurably enhanced over the period of the plan.
- Develop a range of specific costed targets for key species and habitats for years 2000 and 2010.

The BAP therefore specified a comprehensive set of actions on habitats, species, public awareness and the global contribution of the U.K. to biodiversity conservation. Specific actions required by the U.K. in order to meet its BAP commitments included:

- Using existing incentive schemes to promote positive effects on targeted landscapes and habitats.
- Identifying prime biodiversity areas and agree a strategy to promote and enhance them.
- Continuing to protect ancient semi-natural woodlands and encourage forms of management that conserve their special characteristics.
- Continuing to encourage steady expansion of woodland and forest cover.
- Continuing to support measures for hedgerow management and restoration.
- Ensuring that summary management plans are prepared and where possible implemented for each biological SSSI by 2004.

Reports on the progress of the U.K. BAP were to be made every five years. As part of this reporting process an independent review of BAP progress way made by Consultants ENTEC U.K. Ltd. ENTEC decided to review the BAP on the basis of a set of criteria based on the activities necessary to achieve its objectives over the first five years (Knightbridge 2000). This review established how the BAP had been successful and went to identify a number of problem areas where progress had not been up to expectations.

High among the successes were the formation of effective partnerships required to implement the BAP and the agreement and adoption of a common agenda for the partners to follow. This has brought together not only national organisations but has also led to the formation of a range of local partnerships to support the development of local BAPs across the U.K. (Serjeant 2000). The formation of such partnerships is a clear pre-requisite to the success of a programme which has such wide-ranging concerns. Other important achievements were the completion and preparation of species action plans (SAPs) and habitat action plans (HAPs). As well as providing targets, these plans provide an important focus for action and research (Knightbridge 2000).

Knightbridge (2000) goes on to report a number of concerns identified in the ENTEC report. These highlight problems of scale, with the wealth of plans, initiatives and organisations drawn into the process. In common with many ambitious national strategies, the U.K. BAP is constrained by resources, and the ENTEC report recommended substantial increases in funding for HAP and SAP implementation, particularly in Northern Ireland and Wales.

Another concern identified in the report is communication. This is particularly important in strategies such as the U.K. BAP which require the co-operation and collaboration of a wide variety of organisations and individuals taken from a range of sectors. Unless very clear sets of objectives and targets are set for a process such as this, there is always scope for participants to have different perspectives about the nature of the process and the actions required to take it forward.

Another concern raised by some commentators, is the lack of any common vision for the countryside which the BAP was designed to influence. It is all very well to have firm targets for species and habitat conservation but how does this fit into the broader countryside of which they are a part? Does the BAP process, by dividing its efforts across a range of concerns, fail to place sufficient emphasis on some basic concerns, such as climate change? This failure to account for the "big picture" is not uncommon where complex strategies have to divided up into semi-autonomous components with overall control exercised at a distance by various committees and funding bodies.

Some authors (e.g. Green 2000; Marren 2000) have criticised the BAP process for being too concerned with attempting to preserve a particular snapshot of the countryside, with a checklist of species and habitats being conserved, while the "big picture" is largely ignored. Of course, what you see in the "big picture" depends on your perspective. For some, it may be the underlying global issues that threaten species, for others it the concern may mirror trends in land management, while others would prefer to set biodiversity conservation within a wider set of social and economic concerns.

The latter reflects the kind of holistic thinking that underpins some of the integrated approaches to rural land management mentioned in a previous section. These approaches are not restricted to consideration of environmental, economic or social issues but attempt to identify solutions that have positive impacts on each of these areas. Strategies for biodiversity conservation which look further than sets of targets and provide a range of other benefits may prove more sustainable in the long term than those which offer less advantages to society.

9. Strategic Implications

In Chapter 1 we provided a definition of strategic countryside management as:

> The process of designing and implementing strategies, often with incomplete information, to ensure the sustainable and equitable use of resources in the countryside and to optimise the welfare produced from them over time for stakeholders.

This led us to define a set of fundamental questions with which organisations working in the countryside are regularly faced. Their responses will depend on how well they understand the interactions between ecological, social, economic and political pressures that exist there. The tools described in this chapter provide a framework within which managers can improve their understanding of both their own organisation and the external environment within which it works. This better understanding of the context within which strategies have to be developed can be reflected in a set of organisational objectives such as those given below:

- To manage the supply of countryside goods for stakeholders.
- To ensure effective use of resources.
- To manage the demand for countryside goods to ensure that this does not conflict with other management objectives.
- To resolve conflict over land and resource use.
- To ensure sustainable land use.

The emphasis that any particular countryside management task will place on each of these objectives will of course differ depending on the particular circumstances surrounding their organisation. In each case it is important that managers approach their objectives with well defined criteria for success and associated milestones and completion targets. The use of a comprehensive strategic framework will assist in the planning of operations and provide a coherent mechanism for the achievement of the goals that organisations in the countryside set.

References

Andrews, K. R. (1987). *The concept of corporate strategy* (3rd ed.). Richard D. Irwin.
Ansoff, H. I. (1987). *Corporate strategy* (Revised ed.). Harmondsworth: Penguin.
Cole, G. A. (1996). *Management theory and practice* (5th ed.). London: DP Publications.
Drucker, P. (1954). *The practice of management*. London: Heinemann.
Green, M. (2000). Human nature. *Ecos, 21*(2), 47–52.
HM Government (1994). *Biodiversity: The U.K. action plan*. London: HMSO.
Johnson, S. P. (1993). *The earth summit: The United Nations Conference on Environment and Development* (UNCED). London: Graham & Trotman.
Knightbridge, R. (2000). The U.K. BAP – Five years on. *Ecos, 21*(2), 2–8.

Leay, M. J., Rowe, J., & Young, J. D. (1986). *Management plans: A guide to their use*. Cheltenham: Countryside Commission.
Marren, P. (2000). Did the Bittern read the BAP. *Ecos, 21*(2), 43–46.
National Trust (2001). Annual report to members 2000/2001. London: National Trust.
Oldcorn, R. (1996). *Management* (3rd ed.). London: Macmillan.
Pearce, D. (1993). *Blueprint 3: Measuring sustainable development*. London: Earthscan Publications.
Rosen, R. (1995). *Strategic management: An introduction*. London: Pitman.
Scottish Executive (2000). *Scottish forestry strategy*. Edinburgh: Scottish Executive and Forestry Commission.
Thompson, A., & Strickland, A. J. (1990). *Strategic management: Concepts and cases*. Richard D. Irwin.
Weitzman, M. L. (1992). On diversity. *Quarterly Journal of Economics, 107*, 363–405.

Chapter 6

Managing Information in the Countryside

1. Introduction

Information is a vital resource for the strategic countryside manager. The need for timely and accurate information is a key issue in the strategic management process and managers must determine how that information can be managed most effectively.

Of particular concern are the methods used for gathering information and the systems used to disseminate it. This chapter begins by outlining some of the information needs of countryside management and goes on to describe a number of different information gathering options from baseline field surveys to sophisticated methods of remote sensing. The move from conventional paper-based data storage to modern database management systems is discussed before a more detailed examination of the role of geographic information systems (GIS) in countryside management.

Following a brief description of GISs and their capabilities, several examples are used to explore the scope of GIS for countryside management, providing an introduction to the ways in which landscape ecologists, National Parks, local authorities and the Forestry Commission use GIS to provide a practical solution to their information handling needs. It will be shown that GIS is much more than a database but is a powerful tool for countryside managers involved in the strategic planning, conservation and environmental management tasks.

2. Information for Management

According to Handy (1991) information systems are *"the nerves of the organisation, without which none of the systems would function."* When considering issues regarding information systems, managers should ask themselves the following questions:

- Who is the information for?
- How will the information be used?
- How will the information be obtained?
- What sort of technology is involved?
- How can the information be managed effectively?

The diversity of land use issues in the countryside means that many specialist management functions exist in countryside organisations, each with their own particular information requirements. For example the information collected and used by a local authority archaeologist may be very different from that which is of interest to a rights-of-way specialist within the same organisation. These variations in information needs and sources mirror those found in the general population and themselves the subject of a number of studies (e.g. Valentine & Holloway 2001).

Many of these functions require access to a wide variety of information and they may "own" specialist data sets or utilise data that are held in common with other experts through some central facility. This information can then be used for a range of purposes. To illustrate the needs of the specialist, consider the data that might be useful to an ecologist working for a local wildlife trust. The ecologist's data sets might include:

- Grazing and hedgerow survey data.
- Water catchment data.
- Information on Trust reserves and local Sites of Special Scentific Interest (SSSIs).
- Data on the type and location of management agreements held by the Trust.
- Information on the location and numbers of various species in the Trust's area.
- Maps showing species distribution, wildlife corridors and other local habitat information.

General managers require data both for operational and for strategic purposes. Recall from Chapter 5 that one of the key tasks in the strategic planning process is to answer the question "where are we now?" Answering this question requires information on the organisation and its operation and on the role of the external environment. Tools such as SWOT and PEST analysis may be used by the manager to collate and analyse this information. Other tasks for which managers require good quality, up-to-date information include financial management and performance evaluation (see Chapters 7–9).

The activities of both specialists and general managers are dependent on the quality of their data and all should be aware of the problems that can make the data they use less reliable. Firstly, the quality of their data is closely linked with its means of collection. Managers should always take care to scrutinise the origins of the data sets that they use in order to ensure that they are what they are clamed to be. For example, it is important for a manager to know whether or not she is dealing with data generated by a complete census of information or data estimated from a sample. Sample surveys can be just as reliable, if not more so, than complete surveys. They are cheaper and quicker to implement and may be less prone to errors because more care can be taken over their conduct and on validating the resulting data. Even so, it is useful for any user to find out more about the nature of the sample that yielded their data; for example what areas did it cover, what proportion of the population was sampled? By answering these questions the manager will begin to get some idea of how representative the sample is of the population it has been drawn from and the likely degree of sampling error (i.e. the difference between the value estimated from the sample and the true population value).

When the manager is satisfied that the methodology underlying their data is satisfactory, she must still beware of the possibility that the methods used for data collection were inadequate. The best data gathering exercises include procedures for internal validation to ensure that those gathering data did their jobs well and that the data collected are reliable. Such procedures include random checks on the source of the data, or even statistical analysis to check for unexpected differences between different data collectors. Even if the data gathered in the field are reliable, there remains the danger of coding and transcription errors where mistakes are made in transferring field data records onto other media. Such errors can be kept to a minimum by the use of skilled transcription staff, or better still by ensuring that the data gathered in the field are downloaded into databases without additional transcription. This can be achieved through the use of computer-based data gathering techniques (e.g. CAPI — computer-aided personal interviews) where field researchers enter data directly onto laptop computers. Data are then regularly downloaded onto the main database via a modem.

One source of error in data that is easy to overlook, is the tendency in certain data sets for opinion or speculation to be presented as fact. Some data, even numbers, may be based on opinion or expert judgement (e.g. the valuations of stock or equipment used in accounts, see Chapter 7). Data generated through projections or forecasting techniques can be very useful for the strategic planning process but must always be treated with some caution. Forecasts by definition are speculation and even such "best guesses" are frequently proved wrong (if they were not we would all have become rich from gambling on the football pools or stock market!).

3. Gathering Data

There are a variety of primary and secondary data sources available to countryside managers. Secondary sources consist of data that have previously been collected and are available for the use of other managers. Primary data is original information which must be gathered by or on behalf of the manager. Secondary data tends to be accessed through databases and archives, while primary data must be gathered through a survey or some other method. Examples of primary data gathering include ecological surveys, visitor satisfaction questionnaires and footpath surveys (see Box 6.1).

Keirle (2002) provides a comprehensive introduction to gathering primary data about countryside recreation sites and associated visitors. In the case of the former, Keirle demonstrates the importance of both identifying the recreational potential of a site and also the associated constraints on land use (for example, through designations, such as SSSIs, or regulation, such as local by-laws) that may prevent certain activities. As well as information on the physical characteristics of the site (such as footpaths), Keirle recommends that comprehensive data is gathered on factors such as accessibility, interpretation and infrastructure. This type of information gathering could form part of a SWOT analysis for the site as described in Chapter 5.

Visitor surveys are an important part of site management planning, recreational demand analysis and the various appraisal and evaluation processes that are conducted to assess the impacts of projects and policies in the countryside. Keirle (2002) outlines the design and management of visitor surveys, emphasising the importance of understanding the potential information needs of the process which the visitor survey is intended to inform. Keirle describes the advantages and disadvantages of various devices used to measure visitor numbers. These include mechanical counters operated by pressure (for example from a vehicle passing over a pneumatic tube or pressure sensitive pad) and electronic counters (operated mechanically or by breaking a light beam). He goes on to outline the use of questionnaire surveys, including a discussion of sampling issues and the design of questions (for example, the use of open ended or closed ended questions to investigate visitor attitudes and preferences). Box 6.2 summarises the questionnaire survey design process. More novel, is his discussion of on-site observation-based surveys to determine visitor behaviour and distribution across a site.

Box 6.1: Footpath surveys

i. *Baseline Survey*. Describe the context within which footpath condition must be assessed. Assess each of the following variables:
   (1) Terrain and soil — e.g. natural, man-made, peaty, mineral based?
   (2) Slope — i.e. long slope, cross slope, angle.
   (3) Vegetation type along route of path.
   (4) Rainfall and drainage — i.e. to look at scope for erosion.
   (5) Temperature variation — i.e. how this may impact on growth rates.
   (6) Use Profile — e.g. how many visitors and at what times of year, proximity to settlements.
ii. *Ground Condition Survey*. Annually monitor the ground condition of whole length of the path using a process similar to the following:
   (1) Walk a set route recorded on a map.
   (2) Mark areas of erosion on map.
   (3) Note area and length of erosion.
   (4) Assess erosion on a damage scale relating to compaction, trenching and soil loss.
   (5) Photograph any severe damage.
   (6) Note any structures and record condition on a damage scale.
   (7) Implement fixed point photographic monitoring at section midpoints.
iii. *Boundary, crossing and waymark survey*. Along the route of the path record the following:
   • The type of boundary and its condition (e.g. stone wall in good order).
   • The crossing type and its condition (e.g. stone-step stile in need of some repair).
   • The landing type and its condition (e.g. compacted soil, some loss of subsoil).

Collecting primary data on countryside sites can be a time consuming and expensive occupation. Fortunately, a great deal of useful secondary data on land use is available to countryside managers. Some European countries keep an inventory of land uses which records both the ownership and utilisation of the land. While the U.K. does not have the equivalent of the Spanish *cadastre*, many secondary sources are available for finding information on land use. One such source is the Agricultural Census, a venerable system of information gathering, that is implemented on an annual basis through a questionnaire sent to virtually every farmer in the country.

> **Box 6.2: Designing a questionnaire survey of site visitors.**
>
> *Identifying the purpose of the questionnaire.* What information is the questionnaire required to deliver? How will it be used and by whom?
>
> *Identifying the population of relevance.* From whom do you require information? It is this population from whom you must take a sample.
>
> *Identifying the sampling frame.* What information do you have on the population of relevance that will aid sampling? A sampling frame could be a list of members or local residents on which a sample can be based or could reflect available information about the characteristics of an unknown but observable population of site visitors.
>
> *Determining sampling strategy.* How can you achieve a representative sample within the constraints of your budget? What type of sampling should be used — robust methods such as simple random sampling, stratified or cluster sampling, or a more pragmatic quota sample based on ensuring that your sample reflects known characteristics of the population of relevance?
>
> *Choice of sampling points and times.* At what points in the site (car parks, visitor centres, footpaths) and at what times of the year (high season or low season, week days or weekends) should the sample be conducted in order to ensure representativeness?
>
> *Choice of sample size.* How large should the sample be to provide reliable information? This may vary depending on whether qualitative or quantitative data is being gathered and on the levels of accuracy required. In general the more accuracy you require the larger your sample should be.
>
> *Design and ordering of questions.* The types question asked and the order in which they are asked. Choices range between more exploratory open-ended questions and discrete-choice closed-ended questions, sometimes based on scores or scales to provide qualitative information about attitudes and preferences.
>
> *Data entry and analysis issues.* Ensuring that the design of the questionnaire allows for easy data entry (to reduce errors) and that data is in the appropriate format for analysis.
>
> *Source:* Partly based on Keirle (2002).

The Agricultural Census has well-established limitations for modern users. Most of these stem from the fact that farmers are required by law to complete it and, as a result, they enjoy considerable protection of their privacy and this protection limits the use that can be made of the data. For example, the former MAFF used to make available summaries of the census at the parish level. There are approximately 13,000 parishes in England and Wales, with about 15 farmers per parish on average. However individual parishes may well have only one or two farmers. As the number of farms is declining over time, and at varying rates in each parish, it sometimes becomes possible to identify individual farmers. In order to protect the privacy of individual farmers, parishes with a small number of farmers are amalgamated with a neighbouring parish. This procedure introduces discontinuities into the data set which limit its usefulness in examining change at the parish level. Furthermore, although the census is compulsory, a number of farmers fail to complete their returns. The proportion of farmers doing this is not published and where non-responses occur the practice has been to utilise the last available return for that farm which may be several years old. The unknown impact of such non-response errors further limits the inferences that can be drawn from the census. Overall, the census has some disadvantages as a source of data for examining land use change. For that purpose, remote-sensed data becomes more attractive in that it is not subject to confidentiality problems.

An alternative source of information on land use change is to collect data over successive time periods about individual parcels of land. This can be done by remote sensing and is the method used by the Institute of Terrestrial Ecology's Countryside Survey. An early source of such information is the analysis of aerial photographs in Table 6.1. As an illustration, Table 6.1 shows the distribution of total land use in 1947 and 1980, respectively in the right hand column and the bottom row. These data show, for example that there was 4.7% of the surface area of Britain under broadleaved woodland in 1947 but only 3.6% in 1980.

The 1947 column and the 1980 row present the information that would be reported in an annual summary of land use. This provides some interesting observations. For example, the table shows that 2.8% of the surface area (i.e. approaching two thirds of the 1947 proportion) remained as broadleaved woodland from the beginning to the end of the period. The disappearance of 1.9% of area from broadleaved cover is accounted for in the other cells of the top row. The original 19 × 19 matrix that these estimates condense allows a more detailed interpretation but it is emphasised that this is sample data and is therefore subject to errors, which are inversely related to sample size.

The most dramatic change during that period was the expansion of the cropped area, mainly since 1970. The net change in cropped area from 1947 to 1980 was an increase of 5.2%. However, the turnover of land, as indicated by the sum of the off-diagonal cells

Table 6.1: Matrix of percentage land use change for Great Britain (1947–1980).

Percent Cover in: 1947/1980	(a)	(b)	(c)	(d)	(e)	(f)	(g)	(h)	Total (1947)
Broadleaved woodland	**2.8**	0.4	0.2	0.2	0.0	0.3	0.6	0.1	4.7
Coniferous woodland	0.0	**0.9**	0.1	0.1	0.0	0.0	0.0	0.0	1.1
Mixed woodland	0.0	0.1	**0.5**	0.3	0.0	0.0	0.0	0.0	1.0
Upland semi-natural	0.2	2.7	0.1	**21.6**	0.2	0.8	2.7	0.6	28.9
Lowland semi-natural	0.1	0.2	0.1	0.1	**0.3**	0.2	0.2	0.0	1.1
Crops	0.1	0.1	0.0	0.5	0.0	**18.6**	4.5	1.1	25.0
Improved Grass	0.2	0.2	0.1	1.4	0.0	9.9	**19.0**	1.7	32.5
Other and Urban	0.1	0.0	0.0	0.2	0.0	0.3	0.2	**4.9**	5.7
Total (1980)	3.6	4.7	1.1	24.4	0.5	30.2	27.2	8.5	**100.0**

Source: Derived from Adger *et al.* (1991).

in Table 6.1, shows a loss of 6.3 from the category offset by a massive 11.5% of the area which moved into this category (5.2 = 11.5 − 6.3). The main source of new crop land was improved grass, accounting for 9.9% of surface area, with a significant 1.4% moving to crops from semi-natural vegetation. This set of changes reflects the massive increase in the intensity of farming during the 1970s and 1980s.

The statistical richness of this presentation lies in the detailed information about the moves of land between use categories in the period: the change in land use. Thus, the sum of diagonal elements indicates that 70.6% of the area did not change use category, implying that 29.4% did change. Meanwhile comparison of the total column and row show the net changes in use category over the period to be, with rounding error, between 11.5 and 11.7%. Thus the matrix form of presentation yields much more information and identifies two to three times more change than the simple column and row totals more generally used. This amount of data is not easily available from censuses but can be obtained more readily from remote-sensed sources, such as the Countryside Survey.

The data in Table 6.1 shows what detailed descriptions of changing land use can be drawn from matrix presentations, but unfortunately such data is only collected from time to time and there is now no current matrix of land use change, apart from that based on the survey discussed above. We are therefore obliged to revert to more conventional presentations of data, using annual totals to tell a much less complete story.

Additional data on woodland cover can be obtained from the National Inventory of Woodlands and Trees which is now even more important given that some 60% of British forests are now privately owned. Other data sets exist, such as those owned by the Institute of Terrestrial Ecology, that provide useful information of the probable land cover in any given one kilometre Ordnance Survey map squares. These data sets rely on the extrapolation of existing survey data across much larger areas and cannot be regarded as totally accurate.

A range of spatially referenced census and survey data are now available to countryside managers. The Spatial Information Enquiry Service (SINES) provides details of around 600 geographically referenced data sets held by U.K. Government departments and agencies. The service is free of charge and enquirers can find out where and why data is held and contact details to obtain further information.

Perhaps one of the most important sources of information is the Population Census, which provides a "snapshot" of the distribution, size, structure and character of the people of Great Britain and Northern Ireland on a particular day every 10 years. The most recent census was conducted in June 2001. Census data can be accessed at a variety of scales, with Enumeration Districts (EDs) being the smallest unit. EDs cover at least 150 houses (500 in urban areas) and represent the area over which one census enumerator delivers and collects census forms. EDs aggregate into Wards and then into Local Government Districts. A spatial reference is attached to these units.

Map data is also very useful for countryside managers and all local authorities have detailed maps of the areas that they cover. In April 1993 a Service Level Agreement was negotiated between the Ordnance Survey (OS) and local authorities in England and Wales. This has made OS data stored in digital form, affordable to local authorities and has meant that Geographic Information Systems (see Section 5) can be used on a much wider scale.

Sources other than maps are available to provide information on what can be found on the surface of our planet. Since the early twentieth century the advantages of aerial photography in providing information about land use have been exploited with increasing frequency, especially in wartime. Some of the earliest sets of useful aerial photographs relating to the British countryside come from the German Luftwaffe in the Second World War. In the 1990s MAFF used this method to monitor progress in certain English ESAs. More recently the use of routinely captured satellite imagery has been found to provide data comparatively quickly and painlessly.

Remote sensing is a technique for obtaining data about the environment and the surface of the Earth from a distance. The technique employs devices such as cameras, lasers, radar and sonar and is often associated with the use of orbiting satellites. These data can be used directly or as backdrop to other data, to provide spatial context and to aid interpretation. Data from Global Positioning Satellites (GPS) can provide the user of a GPS tracking device with accurate information about their spatial location and could inform future visitor monitoring systems.

In the United States a system called Landsat has achieved considerable success in providing topographical and other data. Landsat is a system of remotely sensing satellites built by NASA, one of the most recent being Landsat 7 which was launched in 1999. Data are collected by measuring the reflectance of an area on the earth's surface to light. The scanned area varies in size from a few square metres to many hectares. In the U.K. the Environment Agency uses aircraft to produce Light Direction and Ranging (LiDAR), where a laser pulse is fired 5,000 times a second at the ground and after reflection can be used to measure height contours of land to an accuracy of 10–15 cm. The Environment Agency use this information for the purposes of flood plain and coastal zone mapping.

4. Managing Information

Traditionally the information used by managers in decision making has been stored on paper. This had the advantage of being relatively straightforward and cheap, and of providing a tangible record. Of course, this system was also time consuming, inflexible, space intensive, and could slow communications through difficulties in cross-referencing and communicating information to others. Such systems often relied on a knowledgeable administrator known as a collator who would use experience to make connections not readily available to others less familiar with the system. Information also tended to be stored in a variety of locations, some centrally and some close to its source, which made accessing information relatively costly.

Since the 1960s, organisations have increasingly begun to store information on magnetic media to be accessed via computers. The information technology revolution really took off with the advent of desktop microcomputers in the 1970s and 1980s. The advantages of computer based systems include their size, flexibility and speed, they also provide greater scope for data retrieval and the potential for making data more widely available. The advent of zip drives and digital data storage devices such as compact and digital versatile disks (CDs and DVDS) has increased the potential for data storage and retrieval still further. Initial problems with upgrading to electronic storage included the costs of software and hardware, plus the need for staff to acquire new skills. Over the years, personal computers have become as familiar a piece of office furniture as desks and chairs and the costs of equipment have fallen dramatically in real terms. This means that there is a greater potential than ever before for managers to utilise electronic storage and retrieval methods to enable them to get the most from their data sets.

The term information technology (IT) is now commonly used when referring to a variety of business and leisure related communications technologies. The U.K. Department of Trade and Industry definition of IT is:

> the acquisition, processing, storage and dissemination of vocal, pictorial, textual and numeric information by a microelectronics based combination of computing and telecommunications.

IT involves the inter-reaction of human operators with hardware (i.e. equipment used to store and transmit data, e.g. PCs, modems, and networks) and the software (i.e. computer programs) that are used to process information. Most of us are familiar with standard software packages used for word processing, and many of us will have encountered spreadsheet and database packages used for the storage and manipulation of data. With falling prices, digital imaging software is now readily available to many people. This can be used to produce images based on information stored digitally (e.g. photographs taken by digital cameras or files scanned from an external source). Similarly desktop publishing packages allow voluntary groups or small businesses to produce text of a professional standard for publications and newsletters.

Even more important have been the introduction of web browsers and easily available internet servers to allow greater access to information on the world wide web. As well as providing access to a wealth of information, the web provides unparalleled opportunities for groups to share information and ideas and to learn from the experiences of others. This provides particular opportunities for innovative applications of interpretation (see Chapter 17).

Information technology has been a particular benefit to remoter areas that have traditionally experienced problems with access to information. The information revolution has benefited private citizens, small business and even larger organisations such as the National Parks. Briggs & Tantram (1997) identify a number of areas where IT can provide positive solutions to countryside management problems within National Parks. These include how to:

- Ensure efficient handling of the information needed to manage the Park.
- Ensure that the information is high quality and therefore valued by colleagues.
- Ensure that a variety of specialists can access the data they need quickly and easily.
- Give specialists a feel for the "big picture" and show how their actions can affect others.
- Produce high quality maps as and when needed.

One particular IT innovation Geographical Information Systems has proved particularly useful in this context.

5. Geographical Information Systems

Geographical information systems (GISs) are computer-based systems designed for the collection, handling and display of spatially referenced datasets. They can store, manipulate and manage large and complex datasets with relative ease, though their most important feature are their use of spatial references to link specific items of data with their location on maps. GISs have three main components:

- A computer system: Hardware and software.
- A geographical database: Location, topology and attributes of geographical entities.
- An application: The need for the management and analysis of spatial data.

The software utilised tends to be some form of non-specific application software, packages range from simple map management systems (e.g. GGP) to desk-top mapping systems (e.g. MapInfo or ArcView) and full function GIS (e.g. ArcInfo). Various "turnkey systems" are also available to operators and these depend on a predetermined set of operations, prepackaged behind a graphical user interface. The complexity of the software and the required data analysis requires that the PC used for the analysis has a fast processor and sufficient RAM to run the software. High resolution colour graphics are also required, as are good quality input and output devices (e.g. scanners and colour printers).

GIS use data containing some form of spatial reference, for example a grid reference, an address or a pixel on a satellite image. Data collection and preparation is usually a very time consuming and expensive process. Originally the main source of data for GIS were paper maps. These could be entered into GIS using digitisers or scanners. Improved availability of digital data means that these approaches are becoming less common; however, the data preparation stage remains time consuming and expensive.

There are two main ways of storing spatial data within a GIS, either as a:

- *Vector:* An approach that uses points as the basic building blocks to model spatial data; or as a
- *Raster:* An approach that uses a grid matrix of cells to model spatial data.

Both approaches can be used to model most types of data, though the choice of approach can have implications in terms of the accuracy of the representation, amount of storage capacity required and the speed with which the data can be processed (Harmon & Anderson 2003).

Vectors can represent points, lines and areal features very accurately. Although much more efficient than raster data in terms of storage space, the method for storage and analysis for vector data is more intensive in terms of processing time. Vector data is input using digitising methods, where raster data may be scanned or remotely sensed.

Vector approaches are useful for applications involving irregular areas and boundary lines, such as local government or census areas, that require the system to register all features accurately to ground locations. Raster approaches are useful when applications involve the characterisation of extensive areas of land such as forests, and where detailed data is not required. It is also useful for making good use of satellite or terrain data or where slope and drainage analyses are to be conducted. The choice of models depends on the nature of the data used, the level of accuracy required, the amount of storage space available, and the form of analysis that you wish to undertake (Harmon & Anderson 2003).

GIS systems can also store data on geographical entities (e.g. roads, paths, rivers, hills, etc.) and their associated attributes. Attributes can be quantitative (e.g. the area of a reserve), or qualitative (e.g. the name of the reserve). For each entity there is a list of associated attributes, including the date and time at which the data was collected, this can be used to analyse changes over time.

Data within the GIS are stored within thematic layers, where each subject of interest or "theme" will have a particular layer. For example, on a local authority GIS there may be separate layers for roads, footpaths, rivers and woodland. When a map is produced the layers required are chosen and presented collectively. For large areas, such as the U.K., it is not usually possible to store all the map layers together. Instead it is conventional to break down the area into what are called "tiles," just as the OS break down Britain into a series of large-scale maps.

When conducting and interpreting GIS models, it is important that the quality of the data used is considered. Indicators of data quality provide an indication as to how good the data are and its suitability for the purpose used. General issues to be considered when assessing data quality are errors in data, accuracy, precision and bias.

Errors are flaws in the data, and occur if there is a difference between the real world and the GIS model. Accuracy is the extent to which an estimated data value approaches its true value. If a GIS database is accurate then it is a true representation of reality, however, it is clearly impossible for the data to be entered with total accuracy. Instead, data should be accurate within a certain tolerance which will depend on the application. Precision is the level of detail to which the data has been recorded. Precision does not, however, guarantee accuracy. If the data are not accurate then a high level of precision would not serve to improve the quality of the data. Bias is any systematic variation of the data from reality which leads to a consistent error throughout the whole data set for one coverage. This could be due to a technical or a human problem, for example a tendency for someone entering data from an aerial photograph to ignore all features below a certain size. Data quality can also be governed by the quality of the available map data.

6. The Features of GIS

Although there is some form of GIS in the vast majority of local authority planning departments, its use is dominated by cartographic (e.g. preparation of site maps and design briefs) and operational uses (e.g. checking planning constraints against an application), especially in the smaller district authorities. Other than the preparation of maps, there seems to have been comparatively been little use of GIS in strategic planning, for example comparative site selection and socio-economic analysis (Powe 2001). Even so the use of GIS in planning departments has increased and this trend is likely to continue into the future. One important possible use of GIS is to increase public participation in planning decisions as the public can be shown better representations of how planning decisions are likely to impact on local environments.

GIS relies on digital data storage. Data are stored independently of the map from which they are generated and can be used independently of the applications for which they were initially collected. This independence implies that application specific maps can be produced from the same data source and that data can be updated without having to redraw the whole map.

Other advantages include ease of access (maps are available on a network and do not have to be physically copied for everyone), the availability of querying facilities (the computer can search the data for you) and reducing space requirements (local authorities no longer require map libraries).

A range of different levels of access to GIS can be identified including:

- *Single users:* Individuals accessing their own data on their own machines.
- *Departmental:* Multiple users working for a single department (e.g. a National Park Authority) can access a departmental database and shared software.
- *Organisational:* Shared use across departments within an organisation based on a centrally maintained database.
- *Cross-organisational:* Data shared across organisations through a strategic partnership designed to facilitate co-operation and shared working and to provide access to a wider range of information. Such arrangements may be restricted to certain parts of participating organisations (e.g. local authority planning departments) and may require stricter protocols on maintenance and access.
- *Global:* Many people accessing many databases located all over the world, e.g. via the Internet.

Having a single means of storage provides a consistent central framework for all decision makers. Consistency is provided by new data feeding directly into the central database. This can cause difficulties, as some departments may not be prepared to release data for internal political reasons (see Gilfoyle & Wong 1998). There is currently progress towards local-authority wide spatial data standards in England and Wales: such a development would require standardised descriptions of sources, accuracy and format.

Spatial database queries can be made using GIS with the output in either a spatial or non-spatial form. Attribute-based queries can also be made using a GIS (e.g. all settlements where the population is less than 1000). Spatial data can be retrieved and attributes associated with the feature selected. Queries can be conducted to both gain information and to check the quality of the data.

Having created a spatial representation of the world it is possible to manipulate this data in order to calculate attributes of objects and create new spatial data. Given current technology the measurement of spatial feature attributes may be taken for granted, but prior to GIS these measurements had to be calculated manually. Once measured the data can be included as an attribute and used within further data manipulation. A number of GIS features are particularly relevant to countryside managers.

The creation of a buffer within a GIS application involves the creation of either a circular region around a point in space, or a corridor around a linear feature. The radius of the circle or the width of the corridor is defined by the manager. For example, the buffering of a SSSI or nature reserve might be useful to reflect notions of accessibility, or perhaps susceptibility to disturbance. Similarly, a linear buffer might be set around a proposed linear access route (e.g. a new footpath under Environmental Stewardship) to examine the extent of possible erosion due to walkers straying from the given route.

The overlay facility of GIS is used to compare different sets of data to find a set of feasible areas that satisfy given criteria. The manual predecessor of the overlay feature was sieve mapping (McHarg 1969), where a series of maps printed onto clear acetates were overlaid on a light table and areas of interest highlighted. This manual approach was used by some planning and nature conservation agencies as late as the 1990s.

In most cases overlaying is used to combine digital maps showing different features to give a composite map for the comparison of spatially referenced data, e.g. overlay a satellite map of land cover with a map of soils and river catchments to highlight potential pollution hotspots. Overlay allows for the statistical analysis of spatial association between features and permits the creation of a multitude of "new" maps demonstrating the association between different features. Overlay analysis may also help in policy design by permitting better targeting: for example by providing a better definition of the spatial areas to be covered by Groundwater Source Protection or Nitrate Vulnerable Zones, or by helping to determine which land designated as a Severely Disadvantage Area (SDA) for the purposes of agricultural subsidy payments is, in fact, moorland and therefore eligible for lower per hectare payments.

There are a number of problems with map overlay techniques. Overlays may be difficult to comprehend when a number of factors are involved, and most overlays do not allow for the case that the factors being examined may be of differing importance to the decision. Even so the technique provides a useful tool for countryside managers who need to understand how a variety of different factors impinge on a particular site.

GIS systems provide another useful tool for recreational planners through their ability to derive networks. A network is a series of linked lines that can be used by the GIS to calculate the distance or time for alternative routes between a set of points, e.g. between car parks and various visitor attractions. GIS can be used to solve the so-called "travelling salesperson problem" where a route has to be determined between a series of locations that minimises time, distance or cost. The GIS software assesses the alternative routes, taking account of constraints (e.g. river crossings, barriers, etc.) and displays the shortest route.

GIS can also be used to determine viewsheds. Here digital terrain models (DTMs) are used to identify how visible a particular feature, such as a new mobile phone mast or windfarm, is from a wide range of viewing points. Viewshed analysis has a wide range of applications and is particularly useful in assessing the landscape impacts of new developments in the countryside. As the view-shed analysis is based on a DTM, there is a need to account for features other than topography. For example, the height of the viewer, any intervening buildings and trees also need to be included in the model.

7. The use of GIS in Countryside Management

Since early 1990s GIS has been used increasingly in Countryside Management, for example all National Parks Authorities now use GIS routinely (see Box 6.3 for examples). GIS is used in a wide range of applications in the countryside and may provide scope for new problem solving methodologies as well as providing facilitates for the sharing of data across countryside management professionals.

> **Box 6.3: Use of GIS in National Parks.**
>
> *Brecon Beacons* — to manage data surveys of sheep grazing and visitor pressure as well as being used to generate draft local plans and for measuring and numbering field areas for local farmers.
>
> *Exmoor* — to analyse changes in land cover due to recreation, ploughing and grazing pressures over the past 50 years.
>
> *Lake District* — to predict the visual impact of new developments, e.g. intervisibility analysis for windfarms; to plot the altitude distribution of heather and bracken; and to plot the distribution of tourist accommodation to inform the local plan.
>
> *North York Moors* — to monitor countryside grant schemes.
>
> *Peak District* — for development control and land-use change inquiries.
>
> *Source:* Briggs & Tantram (1997).

GIS is useful in both the strategic and operational management context and is a powerful research tool. Briggs & Tantram (1997) identify a number of areas where GIS can aid the work of countryside managers by helping them to:

- Visualise conditions across wide areas more clearly and to better identify areas for management action.
- To combine and compare different data sets for the same spatial area (i.e. overlaying).
- Model potential environmental changes in order to investigate impacts.
- Monitor the effects of management, e.g. through change in land cover, changes in visit numbers, and changes in the distribution of facilities.

More specific applications of GIS in the countryside include:

- The storage and retrieval of spatial data.
- Production of site plans.
- Accessibility to services and employment centres.
- Visual impact assessment.
- Generation of management plans.
- Increasing and widening public participation in decision making.

This list is not exhaustive but provides some indication of the usefulness of GIS. In addition to its uses in managing data and producing maps, GIS can be used to analyse data and to model possible spatial changes. The latter allows possible future states of the landscape to be visualised in order to explore the implications of various policy options.

Pettit (1995) documents some early uses of GIS in the Brecon Beacons National Park, and in particular its use to inform the planning process. When a planning application is received the extent of the site is marked on a planning layer within the GIS and a check is run to identify any planning constraints. A table is then produced listing any constraints covering all or part of the site (e.g. tree preservation orders, archaeological sites, SSSIs, National Nature Reserves, and Wildlife Trust Reserves). This information can be passed on to the applicant and printed out in map form for future reference.

GIS is increasingly being used to apply the principles of landscape ecology to real landscapes. Landscape ecology considers entire landscapes as a set of interdependent habitats rather than just examining small areas of that landscape (Haines-Young et al. 1994). Aspinall & Humble (1997) demonstrate how GIS can be used to describe and interpret the components of landscape so that ecologists gain a better understanding of how ecology and geography inter-react. Their particular study shows how GIS can be used to investigate the structure, function and dynamic elements of landscape.

In this context, structure refers to the structural elements of landscape such as patches and corridors of habitat and their contexts (i.e. surrounding areas). This is described in terms of contiguity (i.e. the land adjacent to a patch of habitat) and connectivity (how different areas of habitat are connected). Function is the use of the structural elements of landscape by species, i.e. links species behaviour and landscape structure, while the dynamic elements of landscape refers to how their function changes over time, as does the way in which species use it (Aspinall & Humble 1997).

Aspinall & Humble (1997) report a study of Short-Eared Owls in the Orkney Islands which shows how detailed habitat knowledge can be combined with GIS to aid conservation and planning across a wide area. Short-Eared Owls depend on moorland for nesting and on grassland as the source of their main prey, the Orkney vole. At the time of the study, the Short-Eared Owl population faced major challenges in terms of habitat degradation, with moorlands becoming increasingly fragmented in Orkney, and grazing patterns have altered affecting distribution and abundance of voles. To construct conservation plans for the Short-Eared Owl it was necessary to understand:

- The scale of habitat fragmentation.
- Changes in the vole population.
- Any changes in the ratio of breeding to feeding areas.

This understanding was aided by the use of GIS to overlay land cover data, based on aerial photography, with data owl territories. Analysis of landscape areas allowed a ranking of habitat importance and it was found that successful breeding territories comprised dry heather moorland for nesting next to rough grassland for hunting. The dispersion of hunting habitat was also analysed (the owls require at least 50 voles per ha to stay in an area). Where fragmentation of hunting habitats was highest, vole density had declined and was close to this critical level.

The analysis identified the owl populations that were most likely to become isolated and also identified critical links in habitat corridors. Additionally the analysis suggested new ways of increasing connectivity between habitats and of increasing prey availability. This study provides a vivid illustration of the practical application of GIS in species and habitat management and for readers interested in this type of application, Johnson (1998) provides a more general overview of the use of GIS techniques in ecology.

The Forestry Commission has its own comprehensive GIS system called FORESTER. This has been in operation since 1999 and the FC claim that it is the world's most comprehensive forestry management database. The database can break the FC estate into the relevant forest districts and within them the forest sub-compartments (there are around 200,000 such sub-compartments on the FC estate). The GIS records basic information like the size of the sub-compartment, time of planting, type of tree and soil type and one of its uses is to produce stock maps for Forest Districts. A certain amount of information on non-mappable components is included in the database including data on species mix, thinning cycle and age classes and FORESTER can produce short reports on these components.

The GIS system has a variety of other uses and is especially important in the production of Forest Design Plans (FDPs). Each forest planning region has between eight and 72 FDPs and these are used as the building blocks for the strategic planning process within each Forest District. Each FDP unit has a life of five years, after which it may change (e.g. be combined with another unit). Individual FDPs are influenced by overall FC strategy and informed by a mixture of local knowledge from the forest manager and objective information from the database. For each FDP unit a score is entered by managers based on their assessment of the importance of the design plan unit for conservation, landscape and people. There is a high degree of subjectivity in the scores for landscape and people, though the score for conservation is based on a checklist which takes account of the presence of SSSIs and similar indicators.

FORESTER contains a DTM that records the height above sea level of discrete, non-overlapping spatial units (tiles) and can be used to produce a three-dimensional representation of the forest area. The system also uses a tool called *Spatial Analyst*, an extension of *ArcView* which can be used to provide an estimate of visible catchments, i.e. those area of forest visible from a particular point in space. Box 6.4 gives some other examples of useful data sets.

Box 6.4: Useful spatial data sets in the U.K.

LAND-LINE. Land-Line offers a comprehensive dataset depicting man-made and natural features ranging from buildings and roads to rivers and wetland and also includes administrative boundaries. The data is digitised at three different scales according to location (the most detailed being in urban areas).

ADDRESS-POINT^{TM}. Since 1996 ADDRESS-POINT^{TM} has provided a national grid co-ordinate and unique reference for each of 25 million postal address in Britain and has been created by matching the Post Office's Postcode Address File (PAF) with the Land-Line digital database.

PANORAMA. Land-Form PANORAMA is the 1:50,000 scale digital height dataset covering the whole of Great Britain and is available as either contours or digital terrain models (DTMs).

The Countryside Information System (CIS), developed by the Centre for Ecology and Hydrology, is a very useful source of spatial data about the countryside (see http://www.cis-web.org.uk/). The CIS package runs on Microsoft Windows and contains a variety of information, including data on landscape features, land cover and topography for each one kilometre square of Great Britain. Users are able to convert their own data into a format useable by CIS and it may also be possible to import data from CIS into a GIS application. The CIS Environmental Catalogue contains a list of all information available for the package, detailing the list of data collections and surveys where the CIS data originate. CIS is relatively straightforward to use and represents good value for money for countryside managers looking for a reliable source of spatial data.

8. Visualising Landscapes

Traditional maps assume the observer is positioned directly overhead and looking vertically down at the surface of the Earth. Maps are drawn as plane views and at a fixed spatial scale. Recent improvements in the capacity of GIS can now permit managers to visualise landscapes in three-dimensions (3-D), e.g. using the 3-D analyst module of ArcView. This facility is particularly useful in policy analysis.

Integrating GIS and Virtual Reality Modelling Language (VRML) helps to provide virtual images that can be used to investigate landscape change (O'Riordan *et al.* 2000). In order to achieve this analysts need to convert GIS databases to VRML with help of modelling tools such as *Pavan*. The resulting images can often be shown as a "fishnet" or "wire frame" diagram. This is an excellent means of displaying topographical data. Alternatively, a photograph could be draped over the digital terrain surface but this does not give a feeling of height to the view. It is also possible for trees, buildings and other features to be superimposed onto a surface. A common application is the combination of GIS location information and computer-aided design (CAD) packages that are used in, for example, building design. It is also possible to animate the view shown (see O'Riordan *et al.* 2000).

9. Strategic Implications

In order to make good decisions managers need access to accurate information at the right times. Recent developments in electronic data storage, communication and analysis mean that countryside managers have access to better information than ever before. The increased use of Geographic Information Systems has permitted that information to be used in increasingly novel ways, providing managers with not only baseline information but the opportunity to assess how their decisions might impact on the landscape. Ongoing developments in three-dimensional visualisation of landscapes will make this process even more informative and may be especially influential in facilitating public involvement in the decision making process, e.g. during planning inquiries or as apart of an environmental impact assessment process.

While GIS is an impressive tool it can never fully replace the local knowledge and experience of managers. Even today many decisions regarding site management are primarily based on the assessment of managers who over time have built up an understanding of site issues that cannot be replicated by a software package. At a site level it is appropriate for managers to use the GIS to replicate as much of their knowledge as possible and to use this and other information to provide them with new ways of visualising their data or presenting it in other revealing ways. This may simply mean more convenient and informative access to site information or it may aid the derivation of management plans. In some cases, as with the Short-Eared Owl described earlier, it may help ecologists to understand the complex interactions between species and the landscapes that they depend on.

Even more powerful is the ability of GIS to help planners and decision makers understand the consequences that different land management strategies may have on wider tracts of land. From a scenario-planning point of view GIS can provide a range of solutions to managers seeking a more holistic approach to management. Such holistic approaches reflect the growing movement away from treating individual areas as discrete packages of land but as part of the wider area to which it is a part. Biodiversity action planning and the Countryside Agency's Countryside Character Programme both provide examples of how decisions made in one area will have implications for wider priorities, implications which can be better understood by the use of GIS.

While GIS is an important tool in the countryside managers toolkit, we should not ignore the wider implications that the information revolution has had on the countryside. Issues of communications and information systems in rural areas are of considerable concern in the field of rural development. Improving communications in rural areas will have profound implications for the future economic and social wellbeing of local communities, and their ability to access such resources should be a consideration for strategists dealing with a variety of concerns from health and education to employment.

References

Adger, N., Brown, K., Sheil, R., & Whitby, M. (1991). Dynamics of land use change and the carbon balance. ESRC countryside change initiative. Working Paper 15, University of Newcastle upon Tyne.
Aspinall, R., & Humble, A. (1997, June). A wide ranging conservation. *Mapping Awareness*, 32–34.
Briggs, D., & Tantram, D. (1997). Using GIS for countryside management: The experience of National Parks. A Report on behalf of the Countryside Commission and the Association of National Park Authorities. Nene College, Northampton: Nene Centre for Research.
Gilfoyle, I., & Wong, C. (1998). Computer applications twenty years' experience County Council in Planning: Of Cheshire. *Planning Practice and Research*, *13*, 191–198.
Haines-Young, R., Green, D. R., & Cousins, S. H. (Eds) (1994). *Landscape ecology and geographic information systems*. London: Taylor and Francis.
Handy, C. B. (1991). *Understanding organisations* (3rd ed.). Harmondsworth: Penguin.
Harmon, J. E., & Anderson, S. J. (2003). *The design and implementation of geographic information systems*. Hoboken, NJ: Wiley.
Johnson, C. A. (1998). *Geographic information systems in ecology*. Oxford: Blackwell.
Keirle, I. (2002). *Countryside recreation site management: A marketing approach*. London: Routledge.
McHarg, I. L. (1969). *Design with nature*. Garden City, NY: Natural History Press.

O'Riordan, T., Lovett, A., Dolman, P., Cobb, R., & Sunnenberg, G. (2000). Designing and implementing whole landscapes. *ECOS, 21,* 57–68.

Pettit, A. (1995, November). Managing protected land: Brecon Beacons set the pace. *Mapping Awareness,* 28–31.

Powe, N. A. (2001). *Geographic information systems.* Unpublished manuscript, School of Architecture, Planning and Landscape, University of Newcastle upon Tyne.

Valentine, G., & Holloway, S. (2001). A window on the wider world? Rural children's use of Information and Communication Technologies. *Journal of Rural Studies, 17,* 383–394.

Chapter 7

Accounting for the Countryside

1. Introduction

As we have seen, the majority of the countryside is owned and managed by private organisations, public agencies and individuals. There is also a strong public interest in the countryside that is expressed through an array of policies and institutions, many of which receive public funds in return for providing the countryside services which are deemed to be demanded by the public. The funding of public-sector agencies is a critical resource issue, and an understanding of how these organisations are financed provides insights into their capacity to meet their objectives. Similarly, because many countryside goods are delivered by the private and voluntary sectors (sometimes supported by public money), countryside managers need to understand how such enterprises operate and must be able to judge their capacity to increase the supply of public goods. To achieve this we need to know how organisations in the countryside manage and allocate their finances.

The need to understand public accounts is an inescapable part of public accountability but the need to know about private finance is less common in public-sector management. It arises where strategies exist that encourage or subsidise private-sector actors to assist in the delivery of public policy objectives. This short chapter can provide no more than a brief introduction to this topic and begins by considering private accounts in the countryside, before turning to the financial management of public agencies.

Accounting systems are most widely used in the private sector and we consider this first before presenting examples of public-agency accounts. The main accounting tools are the balance sheet, the trading account and the flow of funds statement. These generate accounts of financial activities for reporting purposes and to justify choices that are made between various possible allocations of funds.

2. Farm and Private-Sector Financial Accounts

Private-sector organisations engaged in the supply of countryside goods include those concerned with agriculture and forestry, as well as recreational and tourist enterprises. Charitable or voluntary organisations in a sense fall somewhere between public and private agencies and they are treated at the end of the next section, with the public sector.

All such organisations have financial objectives and constraints. Private organisations are generally interested in making a profit in the long term, or at least in avoiding losses.

We could go further for private businesses and say that if they do not make a profit they risk losing the control and even ownership of the enterprise. Most such organisations also own assets of a capital nature that are not necessarily consumed within the individual accounting period. They will also spend money to service the various requirements of the business and receive payments for what they have sold or the services they have provided.

The problem for the accountant is how to combine these two different types of phenomena, the trading activity and the asset-owning activity, in an account which summarises the financial viability, or success, of the business. A further objective of accounting procedures is to shed light on the efficiency of the firm and indicate potential problems which require attention. How are these objectives met?

The accounting system reflects the financial flows in and out of the business and reports on the value of the firm. The latter is the *balance sheet* which records the value of assets at a fixed point in time. The *trading account* measures the value of flows into and out of the firm over the accounting period (virtually always, though not necessarily a year). There may also be a *financial-flow analysis* which gives an account of the availability of funds and the liquidity of the business during a specified period.

Box 7.1: Cold comfort farm, balance sheet, 3.4.2002.

Liabilities	£	Assets	£
Creditors	7,500	Cash in hand	250
Loans outstanding	10,000	Valuation (crops, livestock, cultivations and stores)	20,000
Tax Owed	2,500	Machinery	100,000
Bank Overdraft	5,000	Land and buildings	1,604,750
Mortgage	500,000		
Owner Equity (Net Worth)	1,200,000		
Totals	1,725,000		1,725,000

The balance sheet for a farm will record all the assets and liabilities of the business, (including unpaid bills and payments expected). Typically, it might be structured as shown in Box 7.1. Such a record shows what the business would fetch if it had to be sold on the day to which it relates. It is based on many valuations of items, some of which are estimates, often necessarily crude. For example, the valuation of livestock and growing crops requires detailed knowledge of markets, and of the costs of raising crops to the particular point at which the estimate is made. Valuation of stocks of inputs may also require estimation, in that they may have deteriorated in quality since purchase (e.g. hay) and may now be worth less than what was paid for them. The fact that this farm is owner-occupied is emphasised by the importance of land and buildings as assets. The value of some assets may change in important ways within accounting periods, requiring careful consideration for balance sheet purposes, because an increase in the value of assets may generate an increase in profit which is liable for tax (e.g. breeding livestock, milk quotas).

The trading account condenses the performance of one year into a single statement. The account is particularly useful for management purposes and starts with an opening valuation, at the beginning of the period and concludes with the final balance, at the end of the trading account period. These valuations feed into the balance sheets but the change in value is recorded here, being equivalent to income or expenditure. Box 7.2 presents the trading account for the farm where the difference between opening and closing valuations records the decline in capital valuations over the year.

Box 7.2: Cold comfort farm trading profit and loss account, 2001/2002.

Expenditure	£	Receipts	£
Opening value of assets	120,000	Sales of crops	0
Inputs: fuel, feed, fertiliser etc.	220,000	Livestock sales	120,000
Wages and salaries	20,000	HLCAs	140,000
Depreciation	20,000	Closing valuation	100,000
Interest on loans	40,000		
Profit (+) or Loss (−)	−60,000		
Totals	360,000		360,000

This farm is losing money: its valuation is falling because (realistically) the sale value of livestock is declining and the expected price, if the farm had to be put up for sale, is therefore falling too. In estimating such amounts, accountants face a serious dilemma as to how closely they should be based on current market prices. Most agricultural markets are subject to short-term fluctuations and there is no point in adjusting the valuations to follow them precisely. However, they should follow trends in the value of assets and they must therefore distinguish between short and long-term changes. Generally accountants tend to follow trading stock values but adjust breeding-livestock values more slowly. Such procedures may become problematic in times of volatile breeding-stock markets.

What advice could we offer the farmer on the basis of this trading account? Without extra information about the extent to which this is a "one-off" bad year, or merely one of a series, potential advice is limited. Clearly this has not been a good year for him, leaving him with a loss of £60,000 on his trading account. However, the change in the valuation over the year and the depreciation estimate does not require expenditure, so his cash flow situation will be £(20,000 + 20,000) = £40,000 better off. In *cash flow* terms, he therefore ends the year with a smaller loss of £20,000. Careful interpretation of accounts is necessary if performance is to be estimated with any precision.

The cash-flow statement is another means of summarising the economic status of a business over any time period — often less than one year. Setting out the expected cash flow for a short period provides a useful means of forecasting the credit requirements of a business, and can indicate whether particular purchases should be made now or in some future period. It may also show when a business is likely to be short of cash. The cash-flow statement generally differs from the trading account in including only actual payments made and sums received.

Having resolved the question of the viability of the business in the long term, the farmer may wish to consider introducing other enterprises onto the farm. This can be explored in a variety of ways ranging in sophistication from what is called partial budgeting, to mathematical models which require much effort to assemble the data needed to apply them. Here partial budgeting, which has a particular application in connection with calculation of compensation for management agreements is worth noting.

The partial budget focuses on the process of change and identifies the changes to the farm's accounts that will follow from a particular change of strategy. It seeks to determine only the net change in profitability from the change in enterprises. Consider the example in Box 7.3, which is taken from MAFF (1980) and which relates to a simple decision to change the acreage under potatoes by increasing the area under cereals. The partial budget considers only the direct changes to the accounts resulting from the change. This shows in the farmer will gain a net £1000 from the shift of resources, despite the fact that this represents a reduction in intensity of the farm.

Box 7.3: Partial budget.

Debit		Credit	
1. Extra costs incurred	4,500	3. Costs saved	9,500
2. Revenue foregone	12,000	4. Extra revenue	8,000
Change in revenue	16,500		17,500

A further simplification of partial budgeting was the introduction of gross margins (GMs) into farm management. These show the margin earned by any enterprise calculated as the difference between extra revenue and the addition to variable costs necessary for any expansion. Variable costs are those costs that have to be increased in order to expand the output of the enterprise. They would include feed and possibly "store" or breeding stock purchases for a livestock enterprise and seed, fuel, fertiliser and sprays for a crop. They would not usually include labour (except casual). This approach allows a partial budget to be calculated very quickly by comparing the GM of reducing one enterprise with the gain in GM from increasing another.

GMs are extremely helpful in that average GMs based on sample enquiries, such as the Farm Business Survey (MAFF 2000), can be and are made available by authors such as Nix (2000) and Chadwick (2001). These allow the quick estimation of the effect of expanding or contracting various parts of the farm business. It is, however, important to be aware of their limitations. They are sample averages and it may therefore be inappropriate to apply them to any specific farm. Variations in season, soil type and in the skills of the labour force (including the farmer) will make for a good deal of variability in the actual GMs achieved on individual farms and standard GMs must be applied with caution because they may be seriously inaccurate in particular contexts. Many of the handbooks present a range of values and leave the user to judge where a farm belongs in it and it is important to consider what are the particular characteristics of the farm in question before using such published information.

Partial budgets are an extremely useful device for making quick appraisals of the impact on a business of a change which is under consideration. In general, however, if a proposal passed the partial budget test it would usually be followed by a more detailed analysis before finance would be invested in a significant change to the business. It is emphasised that the example given above is a particularly simple one. For a more complex example, see Turner & Taylor (1998).

3. Public-Sector Accounts

The last section, outlining private-sector accounts, emphasised the way in which the financial performance of the individual firm or farm could be assessed in monetary terms. Performance is usually measured in terms of profit after due allowance for changes in the value of capital assets over the accounting period. Cash flow is another criterion that managers cannot ignore, although it is generally of more concern to private-sector managers than those in the public sector. In the private sector it is generally assumed that profit maximisation is the objective of the firm and profit thus becomes the obvious measure of effective performance. It is now widely recognised that other objectives also feature in private-sector decisions, but these would not necessarily change the optimum allocation of resources for a firm. Because the existence of several objectives greatly complicates the analysis, it is convenient to ignore it in the private sector and concentrate on profit maximisation.

By contrast, many public-sector produced outputs are not sold, and are difficult to value in monetary terms. So profit is rarely calculable and is generally not relevant to the agency, or its controlling department. Because there is usually no single measure of public-sector output and because many agencies have multiple objectives, analysis of their performance is rarely as clear-cut as in the private sector.

We begin by considering why accounts are necessary in the public sector. Many reasons could be adduced, but the first and main one is that the public sector uses financial resources voted to it by Parliament which itself is accountable to the electorate and which consequently requires reporting from public agencies on how they have spent the money they receive. Despite a requirement to record public expenditure by the agencies responsible for these activities, the accounts presented to Parliament are only the tip of the iceberg of the accounting process. Not only must public agencies report to Parliament on how they have spent the money, they also have to approach the Government to justify expected expenditure in future periods. This process is formalised at the departmental level in the annual Public Expenditure Survey (PES), a hectic annual round of discussions between the Treasury and "spending departments," usually with some public leaking of arguments and estimates. Forward estimation of expenditure requirements and particularly justification of increases in budgets over some notional base (which may of course be a reduction on last year's allocation) thus form a very important part of the public sector accounting process. Such analysis has to be *ex ante*, and therefore speculative, compared to the *ex post* presentation of conventional accounts. Thus, public agencies have to account for the money that they have spent, and in addition to that, have to make a case for any further allocations required to meet their objectives in forthcoming years. This broad process is termed financial control and it provides a second major reason for preparing accounts.

There are thus two main stages at which public sector accounts will be required, prepared and used. First there is the accountability mode and second there is a management/control/bargaining mode. They are dealt with here in that order.

Accountability requires public reporting, usually to Parliament, to demonstrate that past allocations of funds have been spent within the rules governing public expenditure. This will involve the production of a report summarising the financial year of the agency and reviewing its activities, its assets and its expenditure on research, development and grants, together with revenue received. Reports typically contain three important tables of accounts. They are:

- The income and expenditure account.
- The balance sheet.
- The cash-flow statement.

Table 7.1 presents the English Countryside Agency's first annual income and expenditure account for the year 1999/2000. The accounts are drawn up consistently with guidelines determined by the Treasury and their main purpose is to justify the money allocated by Parliament to the Agency.

The statement has been simplified, recording the relevant flows by broad headings. The Agency is a grant-in-aid body, drawing most of its income from the then Department of Environment Transport and the Regions (now part of DEFRA, see Chapter 3). As the accounts show, grant-in-aid is its main source of income. The small income from activities covers the things for which it may charge, such as the sale of publications. The income

Table 7.1: Countryside Agency: Income and expenditure account.

Item	Total 1999/2000 (£000)
Gross income	
Grant-in aid	48,664
Income from activities	1,023
Other grants received	3,192
Deferred government grant account	288
Total income	53,167
Expenditure	
Grants paid	27,382
Staff costs	10,368
Depreciation, administration and other costs	16,388
Total expenditure	54,138
Operating deficit	971

Source: Countryside Agency (2001).

from other grants received, refers to specific projects funded by other departments and the deferred grants are various adjustments to do with depreciation and property.

On the expenditure side, it is apparent that much of Agency's business requires it to operate as a Transfer Agency (see Chapter 4), with roughly half of its income defrayed as grants to other agents. These would include other public bodies as well as landowners, farmers and private organisations. Of this sum, roughly £14 million was devoted to what are called "Section 9 Grants." These are paid under Section 9 of the Local Government Act of 1974 to bodies undertaking activities which are "conducive to the attainment of any of the Agency's statutory purposes." These grants amount to nearly 30% of the Agency's grant-in-aid. The remainder of the report presents a balance sheet for the Agency's small stock of assets, at the end of March 2000, and a Cash Flow Statement for the year, which is simpler than the Income and Expenditure Account in Table 7.1.

Because the accounts report on public expenditure, they give only oblique clues as to the efficiency or effectiveness of the Agency's activities. Thus, they tell us only about money and the way in which it has been spent, they do not record anything about the outputs that are obtained from this expenditure (as spelt out by Osborne & Gaebler 1992), nor do they reveal much about the way in which administrative and other inputs are managed, or what they achieve. As a result we can merely examine these accounts and ask ourselves if they are reasonable. This comment would probably apply to the majority of public expenditure in the U.K., where further work and usually additional information is needed if conclusions are to be drawn on the efficiency of agency performance. The accounts reflect the public concern that there shall be honesty in the use of public funds but fail to recognise the possibly stronger case for considering the efficiency with which all an agency's resources are used. The main source for such an analysis is the companion volume to these summary accounts, which contains much more detail about Agency performance.

4. Scottish Natural Heritage

Established in 1991, SNH has a remit in Scotland equivalent to the combined responsibilities of English Nature and the former Countryside Commission for England. Its Annual Report typically presents its expenditure in two forms, reporting expenditure by heading and, separately, by programme. Each presentation is useful for different purposes. The two tables which follow are on a cash accounting basis, which presents more information than the conventional summary statements. The latter are presented in the report but are not summarised here.

Table 7.2 presents the annual spend in 1999/2000 comparing planned and actual expenditure in the first two columns and the previous year's actual expenditure in the third column. Comparison of the first two columns shows that planned and actual events were close whilst the previous year's results were not notably different from the latest year.

The presentation of expenditure by SNH programme, in Table 7.3 is of more managerial interest, whilst Table 7.2 is more useful for assessing SNH. Table 7.3 presents the same financial data arranged by outcome, rather than input. The item "Ring-fenced transfers" is significant as a reminder of SNH's relationship with other bodies, which it partly funds.

Table 7.2: SNH expenditure by head: 1999/2000.

	1999/2000 Planned £m	1999/2000 Actual £m	1998/1999 Actual £m
Salaries and superannuation	12.5	12.5	11.8
Administration	5.2	5.2	5.1
Capital	1.5	1.6	1.4
Maintenance of NNRs	0.8	1.1	0.9
Publicity, information, training.	1.0	1.0	0.9
Research and technical support	3.5	3.2	3.5
Grants	8.4	8.8	7.7
Natural heritage safeguard and management	3.8	3.4	3.6
Ring-fenced transfers (e.g. to JNCC)	2.5	2.4	2.3
Miscellaneous receipts	−0.2	–	–
Total expenditure	39.0	39.2	37.2

Source: SNH (2000).

JNCC is the Joint Nature Conservation Council a body which took on some of the co-ordinating roles of the former Nature Conservancy Council in 1990 (Adams 1996).

Arranging the data by activity headings, shows the importance of managing natural heritage sites, accounting for more than one third of SNH expenditure. Facilitating access and recreation was the next most important activity and the fact that it was less than one third of site management expenditure indicates the relative importance of these two activities. The comment on the limitations of the Countryside Agency accounts also applies to this presentation. In this case SNH published a very detailed companion volume to its accounts for 1999/2000 which would provide a useful starting point for a more rigorous analysis of its performance in that year (SNH 2000b).

5. Charities: The National Trusts

There are in fact two National Trusts operating within the U.K. The largest and oldest covers England, Wales and Northern Ireland and was established in 1895 and is referred to here as the National Trust (NT). There is also a National Trust for Scotland (NTS) which is similar to the other Trust but is more recent and covers Scotland only. The interesting aspect of the Trusts is that they are substantial public charities and they own considerable areas of land, which they manage for specific purposes. Both devote their funds and energy

Table 7.3: SNH expenditure 1999/2000.

	1999/2000 Planned £m	1999/2000 Actual £m	1998/1999 Actual £m
Maintaining and enhancing diversity	3.4	3.6	2.8
Managing special natural heritage sites	14.3	14.3	12.9
Implementing national parks	2.4	2.2	2.0
Promoting environmental education/public engagement	3.5	3.5	3.8
Improving land and freshwater management	3.5	3.2	4.1
Encouraging sustainable use of maritime areas	1.1	1.3	1.3
Facilitating access and recreation	5.3	5.4	4.7
Supporting sustainable development	3.4	3.6	3.5
Supporting Central Scotland Forest Initiative	0.8	0.8	0.8
Delivering special nature conservation functions	1.3	1.3	1.3
Total expenditure	39.0	39.2	37.2

Source: SNH (2000a).

to maintaining and conserving landscape and property which is of broad heritage interest. Their substantial memberships enjoy free access to their properties whilst non-members pay for access. There is also an arrangement between the Trusts that members of each have reciprocal visiting rights to the others' properties.

The Trusts are compared in Table 7.4, which shows that the NT is substantially larger than the NTS with more than 10 times as many members and three times the land area. However, note that the NTS has much more land per member than the NT. The annual visitor numbers will reflect the number of members of both Trusts as well as the comparative attractions of their properties. Also important will be the tourist cachment from which they draw. Thus the SNT has substantial numbers of overseas visitors, especially from the United States as well as attracting many visitors from the rest of the U.K. By contrast the NT has a much larger resident population to draw on and many more European and other visitors come to the South-East of England than to Scotland.

The National Trusts exist because of special legalisation which allows them to own property of a particular kind for the purpose of conservation. The Trusts may designate their properties as "inalienable" which means that it cannot be transferred to other uses

Table 7.4: Comparative details for the two National Trusts in 2003.

	National Trust for England, Wales and Northern Ireland	National Trust for Scotland
Number of members (thousands)	>3,000	256
Land area (thousand hectares)	251	76
Land area per member (hectares)	0.08	0.30
Annual visitor numbers (millions)	12.5	1.56

without stringent Parliamentary procedures. This unique arrangement gives the Trusts a great advantage in the ownership and management of property. The Trusts may also obtain property from estates whose owners are ready to relinquish them due to taxation and other problems. They may make arrangements which allow the original owners to continue residence as tenants of the Trusts.

The Income and Expenditure Account of the NT shows that about 40% of its income in 2002/2003 came either as membership subscriptions or as gifts (see Table 7.5): this compares with nearly half in 1999/2000. A further one fifth of its income is derived from its ownership of stocks and shares, admission fees and the rents payable on its properties. A significant proportion of the rents are agricultural and the NT pursues a policy of maintaining its rents at a low enough level to compensate its tenants for managing their farms within the conservation guidelines it sets. The NT also obtains government grants for various activities and owns a substantial chain of shops and other profit-making enterprises which

Table 7.5: National Trust: Income and expenditure, 2002/2003.

Income	£m	Expenditure	£m
Membership	75.6	Maintenance/running costs	97.1
Legacies	45.1	Capital projects	51.9
Investment income	22.1	Membership, publicity & recruitment	27.8
Grants & contributions	36.3		
Enterprises	68.7	Acquisitions	31.4
Appeals and gifts	16.0	Support costs	32.3
Sales of assets	3.3	Income generation	61.1
Admission fees & property income	36.5		
Total	303.6	Total	301.6
		General fund operating surplus	2.0

Source: The National Trust (2003).

Table 7.6: National Trust: Balance sheet: 28th February, 2003.

Funds	£m	Assets	£m
Tied funds		Fixed assets	22.3
Endowments	254.5	Investments	556.4
Other restricted	184.5	Current assets	
Designated Funds		Stock	7.3
Designated	137.4	Debtors	44.5
General	9.7	Bank and cash	5.4
		Current liabilities	−49.8
Total	586.1	Total	586.1

Source: The National Trust (2003).

by 2002/2003 contributed over 20% of total NT income. NT charges admission fees to non-members and this brings significant income too.

The expenditure side of the account is dominated by spending on property, either as maintenance or in the form of capital investment. These two activities together account for nearly half of NT expenditure. In 2002/2003 a further 9% was devoted to membership, publicity and recruitment costs, with 20% allocated to income generation. Notice that, in 2002/2003 there was a relatively small operating surplus, limiting the scope that the Trust has to invest in other activities.

The NT's capital situation is set out in its balance sheet in Table 7.6. Notice that the total assets owned by the Trust amount to only £586 million: less than twice its annual income. This is because the great majority of the NT's assets are held in inalienable property: since they cannot be sold they have no value. However, the Annual Report for 2002/2003 also recognised that the re-instatement value of its properties was £4.62 billion for insurance purposes, which would be a significant addition to its balance sheet in other circumstances.

Similar information is available for NTS and is reported in Table 7.7 and Table 7.8. The analysis for NT is not repeated here but the reader may easily compare the two pairs of tables to note the absolute differences between the two Trusts. Of more interest is how the two organisations might be compared through their accounts. Obviously some form of standardisation must be adopted to make comparison possible. There are three obvious contenders for this purpose. First the distribution of total income and expenditure and assets and liabilities could be compared as a proportion of the relevant totals. Second, the amounts might be standardised by the membership of the two or, third, they might be divided by area of land owned. The choice would reflect the focus of the analysis and how much information it is required to be retained.

In Table 7.9 the income of the two Trusts is compared on a per member basis. This is merely a matter of arithmetic, reducing the income columns of Table 7.7 and Table 7.8 to a comparable basis.

An analysis such as this, based on only one year's accounts, would clearly not be a sufficient basis for policy changes because any differences could reflect seasonal divergences

Table 7.7: National Trust for Scotland: Income and expenditure, 2002/2003.

Income	£m	Expenditure	£m
Membership	5.8	Routine maintenance/running costs	11.1
Legacies	2.5	Capital projects	5.2
Investment income	4.4	Membership, publicity, & recruitment	2.7
Grants & contributions	3.4	Acquisitions	0
Enterprises	8.5	Charity administration	4.1
Appeals and gifts	2.3	Income generation	7.1
Sales of assets	0.1		
Admission fees & property income	4.3		
Total	31.3	Total	30.2
		General fund operating surplus	1.1

Source: NTS (2003).

between the Trusts. However, if we ignore this, the Table does suggest some substantive differences that are worth noting. The total membership income per NT member is significantly smaller than per NTS member and the structure of the accounts reflects this and suggests possible explanations. Whilst the NT clearly had a greater volume of legacies in 2002/2003, NTS had a greater per capita income from investment and the grants paid in Scotland were evidently more generous too. A limiting complication is that of reciprocal membership rights between the two Trusts. In particular membership of either Trust confers reciprocal access rights to all the properties of both Trusts. This raises an interesting question as to whether one trust gains more from such an arrangement than the other.

Such comparisons need to be more broadly based than this example and should cover several years in order to provide a more accurate picture of the relationship between income

Table 7.8: National Trust for Scotland: Balance sheet: 28th February, 2003.

Funds	£m	Assets	£m
Tied funds		Fixed assets	10.2
Properties & reserves	6.8	Investments	90.9
Endowments	47.4	Current assets	
Other restricted	27.1	Stock	0.1
Designated funds		Debtors	3.3
Designated	17.9	Bank and cash	1.5
General	4.5	Current liabilities	−2.3
Total	103.7	Total	103.7

Source: NTS (2003).

Table 7.9: Comparative structure of income per member NT and NTS (2002/2003).

Item	Income Per Member NT (£)	Income Per Member NTS (£)
Membership	25.2	22.7
Legacies	15.0	9.7
Investment income	7.4	17.2
Grants & contributions	12.1	13.3
Enterprises	22.9	33.2
Appeals and gifts	5.3	8.9
Sales of assets	1.1	0.4
Admission fees & property income	12.2	16.8
Total	101.2	122.2

Sources: NT (2003) and NTS (2003).

and membership. Analysts would also have to consider the expenditure side of the two accounts and the evidence from the balance sheets too. It would probably also be worth testing other methods of standardising the accounts, as mentioned above.

6. Strategic Implications

This brief survey of financial accounting in the countryside has shown that there are many different ways of preparing accounts and diverse reasons for doing so. Accordingly, it is important to bear in mind the purposes for which they are prepared when trying to analyse a set of accounts. The chapter has presented accounts for private, public and charitable agencies in the countryside. They contain vital information which, often being highly summarised, requires careful interpretation. The very simplest manipulations of accounts can nevertheless facilitate comparisons, with other situations and other years, which may shed light on aspects of management strategy.

Accounts are usually aimed at showing that countryside funds are spent according to plans, commitments and proposals. They may also provide evidence in support of funding a desired management strategy. In particular they are an essential source of data for assessing managerial performance and for assessing the viability and financial requirements of possible future activities. Thus, while not a major strategic consideration, their importance is as a key part of the process of seeking funding for countryside projects and policies, as we shall see in the next two chapters.

Because public accounts are published for the express purpose of demonstrating that funds have not been misappropriated, they are not designed to present all of the information needed to assess the efficiency of public activities. They only provide the starting point for such an assessment and in many cases certain relevant information may not be available. For that reason the increasing practice of publishing substantial volumes of data alongside the published accounts is to be welcomed as an invitation to consider wider strategic questions more relevant than mere financial probity.

References

Adams, W. M. (1996). *Future nature: A vision for conservation*. London: Earthscan.
Chadwick, L. (Ed.) (2001). *Farm management handbook*. Edinburgh: Scottish Agricultural Colleges.
Countryside Agency (2001). *Annual Report and Accounts*. London: HMSO.
MAFF (1980). *An introduction to farm business management*. London: HMSO.
MAFF (2000). *Farm accounts*. London: HMSO.
National Trust (2003). *Annual Report and Accounts*, 2002/03. London: National Trust.
National Trust for Scotland (2003). *Your trust in Scotland: Annual review and accounts, 2002/03*. Edinburgh: National Trust for Scotland.
Nix, J. (2000). *Farm management pocketbook* (30th ed.). Ashford: Wye College.
SNH (Scottish Natural Heritage) (2000a). Annual report 1999/2000. Edinburgh: Scottish Natural Heritage.
SNH (Scottish Natural Heritage) (2000b). *Facts and figures 1999/2000*. Edinburgh: Scottish Natural Heritage.
Turner, J., & Taylor, M. (1998). *Applied farm management* (2nd ed.). Oxford: Blackwell Science.

Chapter 8

Financing the Countryside

1. Introduction

Where does the money come from to finance countryside management? Ultimately there are three sources: first, many projects and policies in the countryside are paid for out of the public exchequer; second, the public pays, funding the management either through some form of market mechanism, for example entrance charges, membership fees, or occasional sales of assets, and third, more directly, they may be funded through payments made out of a sense of altruism or self-interest.

As we saw with the example of the National Trusts in Chapter 7, each of these sources of funds can be important in the countryside. The payments routed through the public sector are generally transfers — usually subsidies or grants[1] — and are usually well documented at the national level through the conventional systems of accountability and reporting. By contrast, market-based payments are more easily overlooked and their value to recipients is much less clear. Some forms of direct payment, for example where citizens make particular bequests to a favoured cause, are documented officially. In other cases the extent of payments is unknown, for example where farmers are not fully compensated for the expenses incurred in making public goods available, perhaps, the costs of maintaining public footpaths over their land. Such contributions to the public good are difficult to account for and the value of such altruism is unknown.[2]

In the remainder of this chapter we review the main funding sources for countryside projects and enterprises and raise some questions about the effectiveness of the allocation system. In the next chapter we consider how the money paid to countryside agencies and actors is regulated.

---

[1] A grant represents a transfer of wealth between individual agents, whilst a subsidy reduces the cost of a good or service used in production or encourages the production of some good or service through an addition to its price or value. The distinction between these two is unclear, and they are used as if synonymous.

[2] A rare published example comes from the NAO (1997) report on Environmentally Sensitive Areas, which estimated the extent to which farmers were under-compensated through ESA contracts. As the NAO did not explain how this was estimated, readers are entitled to remain sceptical about the results.

2. Sources of Funds

Subsidies and grants are usually funded from Government revenues, which are collected in a number of ways. These include: direct and indirect taxation;[3] sales of services and assets; and fines. Taxation is the most important source of funds, and sales of assets, although second in importance, are comparatively minor, except during periods when privatisation of public assets is being pursued on a substantial scale, as it was during the 1980s and 1990s. The collection of public revenue from these sources is comparatively simple but the mechanisms of payment and the routes through which funds are channelled are often extremely complex. A particular example of this in the countryside is the finance of subsidies administered through the EU with funds collected from the member states.

Later in this chapter we discuss the rules which guide the distribution of public funds but there are some general concepts which are worth noting here. First, *hypothecation* of taxes is generally frowned upon in the U.K. public sector. Hypothecated taxes are those which are committed to a specific form of expenditure when they are collected. Thus it is sometimes suggested that a particular tax on inputs should be use to facilitate the use of those inputs. A common example is the motoring lobby complaining that road tax, paid by all motorists should be used to maintain and to even build new roads. The standard answer to this argument is that we do not hypothecate general taxes in this country. However, recent Governments have taken a somewhat more relaxed view of hypothecation and it has been introduced in one or two cases, for example the Landfill Tax, some of the revenue from which is used for environmental amelioration. Nevertheless, the general principle remains that taxes are not earmarked for any particular use, though tax increases may be justified by the need to provide additional revenue for particular public services such as health. A convincing argument for not hypothecating taxes is that tax revenue may vary independently of the need for particular forms of policy expenditure and it is not therefore wise to tie any line of expenditure too closely to a specific source of revenue.

Another principle, which becomes important in public expenditure from time to time, is that of additionality. This was widely quoted during the 1980s in the context of EU funded regional policies. When these funds were introduced, the EU insisted that its expenditure through the Regional Fund should be *additional* to what member states would have allocated if the European payment had not been made. Understandably the EU did not wish to see its policies being used as a substitute for public expenditure of internal origin in member states. Another area in which additionality is sought is in disbursing Lottery funds to projects within the U.K., as we discuss later. However, it was, and remains, virtually impossible be sure that the principle of additionality is rigorously observed.

3. Countryside Grants and Subsidies

Although grants and subsidies may be obtained through many different agencies, most pass through the Treasury at some stage, as tax revenue. The majority of funds are raised through

---

[3] Direct taxes are collected from the household sector and are related to the income of individuals. Indirect taxes are levied at various points in the economy — for example value added tax is collected on certain goods and services produced in the economy, and import duties collected on imports from other countries.

indirect taxes on various goods and services but a significant share is also levied directly on income. This is a reversal of the situation, which pertained in the late 1970s, when income tax accounted for nearly 40% of government revenue. Since then income tax has fallen, while indirect taxes and National Insurance have all increased considerably.

The routes by which public money reaches countryside agents are diverse. Some money comes indirectly from the Treasury, via bodies such as the Countryside Agency and local authorities, but some is routed via the EU, especially in the form of payments to support EU policy. Some EU policies have traditionally been funded fully from Europe, for example, Set-Aside and cash coming through the CAP commodity regimes. But other policies have been part funded, as with ESAs and Countryside Stewardship (see Chapter 14).

In all cases it must be remembered that all EU funds "belong" to EU member states in some sense. The EU is funded collectively by its members in proportions which are renegotiated from time to time. The main determinant of shares contributed is aggregate national income. The proportions do not necessarily correlate with the volume of funding obtained from the EU and some countries (including the U.K.) are net contributors to the budget whilst others are net gainers from it. Naturally such questions of budgetary status feature in the regular debates about sharing the cost of running the EU amongst members. As discussed in Chapter 3 the U.K. has a special and unique arrangement with the EU, negotiated in 1983, when the Council of Ministers was persuaded to adopt the Fontainebleau convention, whereby the U.K. receives a refund of two thirds of the excess of its contribution to the budget over its normal receipts from the budget, within each accounting year. There are obviously delays in determining the amount here because the precise sum has to be worked out after the event. It is nevertheless an important coup for the U.K. and one which is challenged at intervals. This "temporary" arrangement seems unlikely to persist indefinitely, although it has now been in existence for two decades.

The important aspect of subsidies to individual actors in the economy is that they are fully accountable. This means that the person receiving a subsidy may be asked to account for the money and those distributing it must also submit regular public accounts from time. Such public accounting is regarded as an essential part of the process of public expenditure. It serves to limit the extent of fraud and thus helps to keep down the level of taxation. But it is not just a matter of justice and there is obviously a limit to the amount of resources which should be devoted to preventing fraud.

This is a significant point which is too easily overlooked. The fact is that the public sector and indeed all parts of the economy will not devote major resources to preventing every kind of fraud. For example many employers give their employees the right to make free use of official telephones for social and domestic purposes. Several arguments could be used to defend such a practice: it saves employee's time, thus improving their productivity and perhaps contributes to morale in the workplace. So the economy would benefit from such a policy on the part of employers. Note that such a policy only makes sense when the telephone is comparatively cheap to use. Such an issue would be sufficiently trivial to be left out of the account in considering fraud. But there are many other similar questions which are less trivial and which require consideration. The use of official cars is one such example and there are many others, which are taken to be very important. Perhaps there is a sort of cost-benefit calculus at work here whereby employers will accept employees making use of facilities as a perquisite of the job as long as it does not cost very much and/or as long as productivity gains result.

The majority of public expenditure in the countryside is administered through various types of subsidy. Of these the largest in volume terms is the complex of payments made through the CAP. These amount in total to some billions of pounds per annum, the majority of which has traditionally been devoted to supporting farm incomes through what are known as commodity regimes, intervention buying and subsidising exports. There are other forms of subsidy directed to the countryside which would include the payments made through management contracts with landowners and farmers whereby they agree to undertake certain activities or accept particular constraints on existing activities. Although there are many thousands of such contracts in existence, and they may be seen as a subsidy to encourage the production and delivery of countryside public goods, the total amount of public expenditure spent through such channels is quite small.

Over recent decades, successive reforms of the CAP have led to an evolution in agricultural support policy, a process which will continue into the future as attitudes to agriculture and environment adjust over the enlarged EU. Significant changes to the conduct and focus of the CAP were included in the McSharry reforms of 1992 and the Agenda 2000 changes. More fundamental reforms were agreed by EU farm ministers in 2003 following the mid-term review of the CAP. These changes will move CAP payments further away from their traditional association with production levels, to a system of decoupled Single Farm Payments, as suggested by authors such as Falconer & Ward (2000). In addition, reductions in the overall level of support through the process of modulation,[4] have provided additional funds for rural development programmes.

Member states can opt to make full or partially decoupled payments, and provided that cross-compliance requirements are met there are no requirements to allocate land to particular uses. The U.K. will implement a fully decoupled system, incorporating existing levels of modulation through the Entry Level tier of the Environmental Stewardship Scheme (see Chapter 14). Single Farm Payments will provide agriculture support that is independent of production, though requiring the farmer to maintain eligible land in good agricultural and environmental condition.

The Single Farm Payment in England will be delivered at differential flat rates that apply to three separate categories of land. The first category, Severely Disadvantaged Areas (SDAs) corresponds to the former Less-Favoured Areas first introduced in 1975 under Directive 75/268/EEC on mountain and hill farming. The second category is all land outside of SDAs which, in recognition of its higher production potential, will be eligible for the highest per hectare payment. The final category is moorland within SDAs as defined by the so-called "Moorland line," first used in 1995 as one of the eligibility criteria for the Moorland Scheme, which provided grants to promote extensive livestock grazing. This land will attract the lowest flat rate payment as a reflection of its lower capacity for income generation.

Other forms of public subsidy to the countryside are distributed through local authorities in order to achieve countryside objectives. For example the cost of country parks is a general responsibility of local authorities and some of them, including the National Park Authorities, also operate their own systems of agri-environmental contracts. Whilst the expenditure of DEFRA is well documented and is clearly aimed at rural areas, many other sources of

---

[4] From 2005 direct payments to farmers will be reduced and funds transferred to rural development expenditure. The level of transfer will begin at 3% and be increased to 5% by 2007.

subsidy are not collectively documented. Nevertheless, if all public funds flowing into rural areas for all other purposes were all added together, they probably would exceed annual expenditure through the CAP.

4. Tax Concessions

Tax concessions, or breaks, are another mechanism for delivering public funds to agents and they are used in the countryside. Such concessions are frequently called for by people who recognise they are unlikely to receive a direct subsidy and are important in particular parts of the countryside. They are essentially special arrangements whereby favoured activities pay less than the full amount of tax. They used to be a major mechanism for funding forest planting until the early 1980s. Then they allowed people planting trees to not pay particular taxes, in effect granting them a subsidy. They are still used for the so-called Heritage Property (HP) arrangements under which property so designated does not attract taxation when its owner dies. In return owners have to provide access to the property. Such a mechanism has some clear disadvantages which are worth listing as follows.

First, because it is tied up with the tax system there may be a tendency not to reveal that these arrangements apply. Those entitled to access are unaware of the fact and are therefore unable to insist on access. Some HP owners are enlightened enough to acknowledge the fact that access is available as a right but many are not. Hence this subsidy is made available and the quid pro quo is not necessarily delivered.

Secondly, those who pay no tax, who are not necessarily the poorest — they also include those who can afford the best accountancy advice — will not be reached by such incentives.

Third, given that rates of taxation are adjusted regularly, the strength of incentive delivered through such a system will vary over time. In particular, since marginal rates of taxation have fallen steeply in this country over the last 20 years the incentives available through income tax breaks have been weakened.

Fourth, insofar as the tax which would have been collected is required for essential government activities, it will have to be collected somewhere else if individual taxpayers are allowed not to pay it. Some part of society will therefore have to pay for it. The Treasury usually opposes the use of tax concessions like this because they are uncertain how much they will cost. Those asking for tax breaks often support their case with the completely spurious argument that they "cost nothing." This is plainly not the case and there are also significant administrative costs attached to the arrangements.

Finally, much political effort has been expended in establishing a system of taxation, which is supposed to represent a social consensus about inter-personal justice. To set that aside in such a haphazard fashion is politically questionable.

So there are both political and economic arguments here. The strategic countryside manager will mainly be concerned with whether such arrangements produce the results desired in practice.

5. The National Lottery

The National Lottery was established by Parliament in the National Lottery Act 1993, as a means of raising money for worthwhile causes. It is overseen by the Department of Culture, Media and Sport, and since 1999 has been regulated by the National Lottery Commission, a task formerly carried out by the Office of the National Lottery (OFLOT). From every pound raised by the National Lottery, some 28 pence is donated to a variety of good causes, the definition of which is a result of public consensus, political expediency and determined lobbying. Up to 2000, six groups of good causes benefited from the Lottery, with money spent being divided up between the arts, sport, heritage, charities (17% each), the Millennium Fund (20%) and the New Opportunities Fund (13%). Since December 2000, when the Millennium Fund closed, a third of the Lottery budget has been allocated to the New Opportunities Fund which will merge with the Community Fund in 2005.

As we shall see, the Lottery has become an important source of funds for countryside management. Even so, critics argue that the Lottery suffers from a number of shortcomings as a source of funding for key activities in the public sector. First, not all Lottery revenue is available for funding projects. Not only are there substantial deductions made before the remaining 28% is distributed, but a share of the funds attracted to the Lottery would, alternatively, have been spent elsewhere in the economy. Thus it is recognised that other forms of gambling have lost revenue as a result of the Lottery (National Heritage Committee, Second Report 1996). Football pools are a well known example, but there have been other losers too, including charities. The Government has turned the knife in this wound by limiting the size of prizes to be paid by private lotteries to £25,000 and the total amount they might individually raise to £1m (Jenkins 1996).

Overall, the Lottery has proved to be a highly successful new source of funds though, as we shall see, a number of reservations have been expressed about the role that it plays in supporting good causes. A major advantage of the Lottery is its transparency in that the expenditure of Lottery funds is, (unlike our taxes) entirely hypothecated to particular programme segments (i.e. we know how Lottery revenue will be divided across expenditure streams before it is raised). One of the main concerns is that the Lottery should not to be allowed to substitute for, or reduce, public expenditure. Increasingly, Lottery funding, especially under the New Opportunities Fund could be seen to be encroaching into areas where the public might legitimately see as deserving of public funds rather than charitable donations which may not be secure over the longer term if Lottery income is reduced. Such reductions have resulted from less people playing the Lottery and in future may reflect internal competition for Lottery funds if, as has been suggested, special single issue games are introduced (for example to support a bid for the Olympic Games in 2012).

The concept of additionality relating to exchequer expenditure was mentioned above. In respect of the Lottery it is argued that any Lottery money used to fund public activities should only be additional to what would have been spent anyway. Such an objective is hard to achieve in practice and it seems unlikely that the concept can be applied rigorously in allocating funds.

Despite these concerns, the Lottery continues to make a considerable impact on funding for countryside management activities. The following sections briefly examine the activities of the three main Lottery funding bodies relevant to countryside management.

5.1. The Heritage Lottery Fund

The Trustees of the Heritage Lottery Fund (HLF) oversee the National Heritage Memorial Fund (NHMF) which was set up in 1980 to fund the U.K.'s outstanding national heritage (Gay 2000). The aims of HLF are to:

> secure, conserve and improve assets of importance to the national heritage, whether land, buildings or objects, and to enhance public access to and enjoyment of such assets.

Since the National Heritage Act (1997) eligible projects may include:

> things of any kind which are of scenic, historic, archaeological, aesthetic or scientific interest, including animals and plants which are of zoological or botanical interest...

The 1997 Act also broadened access to the HLF and now anyone can apply, if they can demonstrate a *"clear public benefit."* The HLF provides 75% funding for large projects, or 90% for small projects and has five main areas of concern, several of which are of particular interest to countryside managers:

- Land of scenic, historical or conservation value.
- Historic buildings and sites.
- Museums and collections.
- Archives and special libraries.
- Industrial, transport and maritime heritage.

Up to 2002, the HLF had allocated over £665 million in grants for projects in countryside, parks and gardens. This represented 22% of all grants and 19% of its total expenditure, and slightly exceeds the proportion of applications and funds applied for in this area over the same period (HLF 2001a).

Gay & Phillips (2001) see the HLF has been a "powerful force" in integrating different types of conservation and in securing public access to the result. They cite the example of the County Wildlife Trusts who, in return for the £25 million from HLF for the sustainable management of their reserves, have been encouraged to appropriately interpret and manage the ancient monuments on their land. Bishop *et al.* (2000b) highlight the potential for fruitful competition for funding generated by this kind of targeted funding.

Bishop *et al.* (1997) assessed the main impacts that the lottery has had on the countryside, arguing that the most important effects have been increased land acquisition by conservation groups. Much of this has been achieved through funding from the HLF, and Dalton (2000) highlights the purchase of the 33,000 ha the Mar Lodge in 1995/1996. Gay (2000) reports that HLF-funded land aquisition has safeguarded the future of over 50,000 ha of land. This includes many smaller areas of land, for example Mantle *et al.* (2000) report on how a £865,500 grant from the HLF helped the Wiltshire Wildlife Trust to buy Blakehill Farm in order to begin a major grassland restoration project. The Trusts' involvement in grassland restoration is a direct result of its ability to obtain funding from the HLF, who by 2000 had offered the Trust more than £3 million in grants for 16 projects.

Gay (2000) highlights the ability of the HLF to fund integrated projects that combine land purchase with measures to protect and enhance its ecological richness. Conservation and management are helped by HLF ability to support staff posts for up to five years when related to grant-aided capital expenditure. The Fund is also keen to support the creation of "buffer zones" around existing reserves and "corridors" between them. The HLF, in collaboration with the Countryside Agency, also funds the Local Heritage Initiative, designed to offer small grants to local community heritage schemes in England (Bishop *et al.* 2000a).

The HLF has also had major impacts on initiatives attempting to improve public participation and enjoyment in the countryside. Examples include a grant of £158,000 in 2001 awarded to the Council for National Parks and the Black Environment Network for the "Developing Links" project is aimed at broadening ethnic participation in National Parks. In the same year a grant of £89,500 was awarded to the North York Moors National Park to employ a full-time Links Officer to raise awareness of the opportunities that the Park offers to new audiences, particularly young and old people living in towns and cities (HLF 2001d). Also in 2001, the HLF awarded a grant approaching £100,000 to the Lake District National Park to begin a major programme of footpath repair and improvement as a means of promoting the tourist industry following the foot and mouth epidemic (HLF 2001). This kind of proactive funding to provide immediate support to a local economy badly hit by the disease illustrates the opportunities that bodies such as the HLF have to make an immediate difference to the countryside.

5.2. The Millennium Fund

The Millennium Commission (MC) was set up to assist "communities in marking the close of the second millennium and in celebrating the start of the third." This independent body used Lottery money to encourage projects which enjoy public support and which will be lasting monuments to the achievements and aspirations of the U.K. The first grants from the fund were awarded in September 1995 and overall it supplied some £2 billion of community based funding shared across capital projects, the Millennium Awards Scheme and the Millennium Festival and Experience, including the ill-fated Millennium Dome.

In addition to some 27 major capital projects across the U.K., a wide range of other projects from village halls and churches to woodlands were funded. Projects were funded in partnerships that include local authorities, government programmes, charitable organisation with private individuals and European grants. Box 8.1 provides some examples of projects funded by the MC.

The Millennium Awards ranged from £2,000 to £15,000 and were made to individuals through grant making organisations running a Millennium Award scheme in partnership with the Commission, e.g. £2 million was allocated across 5,000 conservation volunteers through the British Trust for Conservation Volunteers Natural Pioneers Millennium Award, £1.1 million was allocated in 270 awards from the Millennium Forest for Scotland Trust., and £1 million for Groundwork Millennium Awards for local environmental improvement projects.

Box 8.1: Some countryside projects funded by the Millennium Commission.

- Countryside Access for All (Northampton — £0.74m) — to turn a Country Park into a fully accessible amenity.
- The Millennium Forest for Scotland (£11.3m) — to restore and enhancing Scotland's native woodlands.
- The National Cycle Network (£43.5m).
- The National Wildflower Centre (Liverpool — £1.7m).
- The Trans-Pennine Trail (£5.33m) — to construct a multi-user trail from Southport to Hornsea.
- Woods on Your Doorstep (£10.6m — England & NI) two projects creating community woodlands (Millennium Commission 2000).

Source: www.millennium.gov.uk.

MC funds also supported the Millennium Green project, which was run in conjunction with the Countryside Agency (CA). A Millennium Green is an area of open space, to be enjoyed permanently by the local community, located in, or on the edge of a settlement *"within easy walking distance of people's homes."* The programme was managed by the CA under the direction of a National Project Team with a network of Millennium Greens Advisers based in regional offices throughout England. The MC funded half a £20m programme that helped some 250 communities in England to have their own Millennium Green by the end of the twentieth century. This was also supported by industrial sponsorship, notably from Bass Plc, who provided equivalent funding at 80 sites, including those in Box 8.2.

Box 8.2: Four Millennium greens.

(1) *Maryport Millennium Green, Cumbria* — a 1.2 ha site overlooking the sea and incorporating a circular path, mounded play area, seating, and traffic barriers.
(2) *The Old Station Millennium Green, Winscombe, Somerset* — a 1.94 ha site on old railway land, using the old station platform and including, seating, a play area, and interpretation highlighting the area's natural history.
(3) *Winston Millennium Green, County Durham* — a 2.5 ha site alongside the River Tees, with wonderful views and a 40 minute circular walk.
(4) *North Kilworth Millennium Green, Leicestershire* — a 1.35 ha site on former grazing land near the village hall, incorporating the remains of an old moated manor-house, and a ditched brook.

Source: Countryside Agency (2000).

The MC had a particularly important impact on tree planting, exemplified by the 15 months from Sept 1995 when the MC spent £29m on tree planting, virtually doubling the Forestry Authority's Woodland Grant Scheme in the same period. The Millennium Forest of Scotland received nearly £12m across 77 sites, while the Forest of Burnley project received £1.8m to plant 500 ha new woodland and preserve 200 existing woodlands. The Woodland Trust was awarded over £12 million to create community woodlands in England, Wales and Northern Ireland, and £4 million allocated to Black Country Urban Forest. The MC focus on tree planting was consistent with the strategic direction set by the 1995 Rural White Papers and with Forestry Commission strategy.

The Dales EnviroNet project (Bishop et al. 2000a) is a £9 million initiative (£4 million funded by the MC), involving a four-year programme of environmental and community improvements in the Yorkshire Dales NP administered by the Yorkshire Dales Millennium Trust Partnership. Match funding was received from a variety of organisations including the National Park Authority from NP Authority, the Forestry Authority, the Environment Agency, and the National Trust. Under this project local bodies put forward a wide range of proposals including planting and restoring native woodlands, restoring field barns and stone walls, creating nature conservation areas, repairing and improving footpaths and bridleways. The scheme encouraged co-operation and partnership strategies, though some of the component initiatives would have been eligible for other funding. This was applied particularly in areas outside the boundary of the Pennine Dales ESA, which also funded several similar conservation activities.

5.3. The New Opportunities Fund and Community Fund

The New Opportunities Fund (NOF) was proposed in the Lottery Act 1998. Its initial focus on health and education has since been extended to include the environment. Initial targets for NOF funding included a range of health, education and training initiatives, though environmental issues have become more prominent as the scheme has progressed. By 2003, the NOF was funding a range of major initiatives including a £125 million Green Spaces and Sustainable Communities Programme, from which grants provide children's play, sports facilities and playing fields, access to the countryside, and local environmental improvements.

A major scheme funded under this programme is Wildspace! a grant scheme administered by English Nature and devised to involve local communities in the management and enjoyment of local nature reserves. Organisations interested in managing and developing local nature resources, particularly in areas that lack access to natural open space, have until 2006 to apply for funding. Grants of up to £25,000 are available for project costs, with an additional £20,000 grant available for the employment of community liaison officers, and grants of up to £25,000 on offer for land purchase.

Also in England, the British Trust for Conservation Volunteers (BTCV) implemented the People Places grant programme in partnership with English Nature to support the creation and renovation of green spaces across England through one thousand grants, by 2006. Grants of up to £150,000 will be available from the Countryside Agency's Doorstep Greens programme. This is aimed at helping local communities in England to create or transform some 200 areas into community greens and open spaces.

Similar schemes are supported by the NOF in other areas of the U.K. The Creating Common Ground Consortium is a partnership of organisations in Northern Ireland, from which communities are able to apply for grants to improve their area through projects such as the creation of green public spaces and biodiversity management. The Scottish Land Fund, jointly administered with the Highlands and Islands Enterprise and Scottish Enterprise, was launched in 2001 to support sustainable development in rural Scotland. The £10 million scheme assists with land purchase and helps to fund development schemes on land where access and management agreements are in place. The £3 million Fresh Futures programme offers communities grants to projects which make the most of local green spaces. This is complemented by a £2 million suite of schemes aimed at promoting sustainable lifestyles. In Wales, the Enfys Partnership is a consortium of organisations running an open grant programme funded by a £7.5 million grant from the NOF. Applicants can apply for grants up to £100,000 to fund projects which among other things provide or improve green spaces and promote their understanding, use and enjoyment of green spaces. The scheme also supports community based projects that contribute to sustainable development.

From 2002, a range of disadvantaged communities in England, Wales and Scotland began to receive funds from the Communities Initiative, a "fair share" scheme jointly run between the new Community Fund and the NOF. This aimed to distribute some £169 million of Lottery funds to areas with high levels of disadvantage that have a poor record of winning Lottery funding (Countryside Agency 2002). A range of rural areas are included in this scheme, and the Community Fund is collaborating with the CA to allocate £10 million to rural England and this has been distributed across eight rural areas, mainly in the south and east of the country. The funding collaboration for this initiative reflects the proposed merger of the NOF with the Community Fund in 2005.

6. The Impact of the Lottery on the Countryside

The potential impacts that Lottery funding might have on the countryside were identified at the time of its inception (e.g. Newbould 1994). The amount allocated to the countryside cannot be accurately quantified, but Gay (2000) estimates that the countryside was allocated only 7% of the amount available for distribution during the first four years of funding. Even so, by 1998/1999 the Cabinet Office estimated that the Lottery was the second largest source of funding for rural areas. By the end of 1998 countryside conservation projects had received over £364 million (£15 per ha of land in the U.K.) and HLF funding alone had helped the voluntary sector purchase over 50,000 ha of land in over 200 sites (Bishop 2000). In an editorial for a special edition of *Ecos* focusing on the Lottery in the countryside, Bishop argues that it has become a force for "*joined-up conservation*" incorporating funding programmes that cover whole spectrum of natural and built environment. He goes on to suggest that the Lottery has played a number of key roles in the countryside, acting to:

- Shift the extent and direction of funding for countryside conservation.
- Create significant new funding agencies.
- Expand the scale of work of conservation bodies in the countryside.
- Support a wide range of diverse countryside projects.

Bishop *et al.* (2000b) expand this analysis into the key roles which Lottery funding has played in terms of countryside conservation policy, and highlights the following important contributions of Lottery funding:

- Improving the U.K. response to international conservation commitments, such as the Rio Convention on Biological Diversity.
- Facilitating the delivery of priorities across a wide range of public policy areas (e.g. social inclusion; sustainability).
- Encouraging the development of new policy opportunities by making more funds available (e.g. Millennium Greens, Millennium Forest for Scotland).
- Encouraging a more integrated approach to countryside conservation policy.

Bishop (1999) portrays the Lottery as "an enabler" providing funds for a variety of schemes and improving the capacity of the conservation sector to think and act in new ways. This is supported by a number of observations which demonstrate how the Lottery has enabled countryside organisations to expand the scale of their work in terms of biodiversity and landscape conservation and increasing public access opportunities (Bishop *et al.* 2000a, b). Another important contribution are the changes that the Lottery has brought about in the countryside agencies.

Bishop *et al.* (2000b) argue that since the advent of the Lottery, it has become a fundamental source of funding for organisations working in the countryside, with the traditional agencies used alongside other sources such as the European Union and the Landfill Tax to provide match funding. They further suggest that the countryside agencies now play other important roles in the Lottery funding process including providing advice (to Lottery Distributing Bodies, applicants, and Government) and becoming involved in new initiatives either as lead partners in an umbrella programme (e.g. Millennium Greens) or by providing support funds to help other organisations to prepare their bids.

Other concerns about the Lottery centre on the potential for the uneven distribution of funds across different social classes and geographical areas. The figures provided by the National Lottery Commission show that on average total Lottery spending is fairly evenly divided across classes with class C2 (unskilled manual) spending most and class E (e.g the unemployed, students, etc.) spending least (National Lottery Commission 2001). Information from sources such as the regular GB Leisure Day Visits Surveys small (e.g. TNS Travel and Tourism 2004), suggest that it is probably the middle classes who benefit most from the countryside in terms of per capita visits, and it may be the case that Lottery funding is acting as a form of regressive taxation and taking money out of the pockets of the less affluent to fund the pleasures of the middle classes.

Geographical inequities in Lottery funding are revealed by Bishop *et al.* (2000a), who report that, between November 1994 and December 1998, Wales had received the highest per capita and per hectare Lottery funding of the four home nations. Scotland received the second most per capita spending, while Northern Ireland received by far the lowest funding calculated on either basis (less than a third of that achieved by the Welsh per capita or per hectare).

Dalton (2000) reports concerns about the complexity of the application process which may disadvantage small organisations, who either lack experience with the process or who cannot afford the associated transaction costs. Recent moves to allocate more funds to small groups through a variety of means may address this problem. Indeed, the National Lottery web site suggests that over half of the awards made up to 2001 were for less than £25,000, many of which were for community based schemes. One important factor influencing this allocation was a change to the distribution rules for Lottery funds which allowed money to be used to pay for people running the projects.

According to Gay (2000), the land sector performs poorly, when compared to other sectors, in its ability to apply for and receive funding from the HLF. The fragmented nature of sector is advanced by Gay as one reason for the low levels of funding. She suggests that the national agencies have yet to define a clear role for themselves, whether as advocates for the sector, as applicants in their own right, or as providers of advice to other applicants. She compares countryside organisations with those dealing in archive and historical material which have been highly successful in making applications to the HLF, gaining nearly half of the available funding.

Gay also cites the high success rate of applications as evidence of lack of competition in the sector. This contrasts with the low diversity of applicants, with applications dominated by the Wide trusts. Gay points out that the National Trust and the World Wildlife Fund for Nature have made far less use of HLF finance than smaller organisations such as the wildlife trusts. This reflects the relatively low demand for Lottery funding in the countryside, with few organisations coming forward from this sector (Gay 2000).

Despite these concerns the Lottery has been shown to have some long-term implications for the countryside, including helping to increase the area of woodland and managed countryside; bringing more land into the ownership of voluntary organisations and significantly improving opportunities for public access and enjoyment. These gains can only be sustained if Lottery funding levels are maintained. Current trends suggest a gradual reduction in the popularity of our new national game, and this has in turn led to a reduction in the quantity of funds available for distribution. While this is a serious threat to the volume of funding, it must be borne in mind that the ability of the Lottery Distributing Bodies (LDBs) to distribute funding has always tended to lag behind the money available to them. Even so, LDBs, the regulator, and countryside agencies must remain vigilant if they are to ensure the continued survival of the goose that lays the golden eggs.

7. Charging Systems

These offer another source of revenue for countryside activities and are used by many organisations. The National Trusts are a case in point but many other organisations also make use of such options. The possibilities of charging are often limited by the non-exclucability of public goods, but there are often aspects of countryside facilities (e.g. car parking and the sale of maps, souvenirs etc.) for which charging is possible. There is often visceral opposition to charging for countryside goods on the grounds that such goods are public property. However this is simply not the case and to accept it is to ignore the possibly constructive use of charging as a means of discouraging congestion at particular sites and raising some revenue in the process (see Chapter 17). The evidence available on charging for countryside access is that it does not produce a vast revenue, however, covering a small share of costs of provision would be a useful addition to the revenue of a facility and good reasons would be needed for failing to use such an opportunity. Such reasons could include the possibility that charging may exacerbate or create problems of social exclusion within countryside recreation, though there is evidence to suggest that access charges are not the major deterrent in many cases (see Chapter 16).

8. Gifts/Donations/Covenants

Charities make use of such means of funding and they are considered, for example, in discussing the accounts of the National Trusts (see Chapter 7). Gifts and donations can make a useful contribution to funding particular projects. The main determinants of worthwhileness here will be the cost and convenience of the collection process in relation to the cash and any other benefits obtained. There may be a consideration that allowing people to contribute is important in itself, but the occasions when this will swing the balance of benefits to favour charging will be few.

Covenants of two kinds are relevant here. First, there are the covenants where taxpayers donate after-tax income to a charity under covenant and a proportion of the tax is paid to the charity in addition. This a particularly useful facility for large charities such as the National Trusts and the RSPB and it is also used by Wildlife Trusts. Whether the smallest charities are able to make effective use of such facilities is less clear. The second type of covenant involves landowners accepting a restrictive covenant on the use of their land. This provides a useful direct alternative to Government-farmer conservation contracts and has the advantage that it can be attached to the land so that it binds successive owners as well. In that sense, this mechanism offers a more secure stream of management or conservation benefits than those offered by shorter-term agreements (see Chapter 12).

9. Loans

Under certain circumstances it is permissible for public agencies to borrow money. Understandably this is carefully defined for each organisation to avoid the obvious problem of over-borrowing. Where, occasionally, public agencies get into financial trouble, central government may have to rescue them. As borrowing is an obvious and too easy way out of short-term trouble and into longer term catastrophe, it is not generally encouraged among public agencies unless the appropriate circumstances can be carefully defined. Although possible in principle, loans are not used for land use policy instruments of a conservation nature. However, there is an agricultural credit system farmers could use if they needed funding for a conservation activity on their land. If other more direct funding is available it would usually be seen as more appropriate than a loan at interest.

10. Sale of Assets

In certain circumstances this may be another obvious way of raising cash for public sector agencies and is equally very carefully limited by central government. For example, the policy of sale of council houses initiated in the 1980s provoked much indignation amongst local authorities who were not allowed to use the proceeds of the sales for building more houses. These sales generated £18bn over the 1980s and amounted to 43% of the take from privatisation. The really bitter pill for local authorities was in the direction as to the way in which the money could be spent. According to Jenkins (1996), part of the balance had to be used to reduce council debt and only part could be spent on housing. Unfortunately, the effect of sales was to shift the more desirable council properties into private ownership and leave the councils with the less desirable tenement blocks and estates. But at the same time the government had to introduce housing benefit, a costly subsidy paid for by central funds, available to tenants unable to pay rent. So we switched from a system of subsidising the cost of housing through (partly local) taxes to one of driving up rents and then giving a subsidy to the poor out of central funds to allow them to survive. For countryside managers, the message from this tale of woe would be to be careful about the sale of assets if you are running a local facility. Be sure you will be allowed to use the proceeds and that the subsequent situation will not be more costly to your agency.

Sale of assets might provide small amounts of finance for other activities. Where it does occur it is usually closely regulated to make sure that the proceeds are in fact used for an appropriate purpose. For example small amounts of Forestry Commission land may be sold into private ownership but the amounts sold and the revenue obtained are both small. Apart from the example of council house sales, there have been few major asset transfers in the countryside which would have provided significant funding for other activities.

11. Strategic Implications

There are many different sources of money for public sector activities. Several of those in the countryside rely on private contributions with or without the encouragement of the public sector. The publicly funded countryside is particularly important because it receives major sums of money and because the amounts are regulated and controlled.

This review has described a pattern of the availability of funds which is anarchic in its complexity. The problem of this rich mix is that it renders it virtually impossible to use funding as a systematic means of directing the development of the countryside. To make this system operate efficiently would require expenditure along lines stated at the beginning of the previous chapter. Yet that must be admitted to be impossible because of the lack of information, particularly regarding the value of benefits but also due to the wide range of possible sources and the agencies administering finance.

It is also significant that the allocation system we operate, based on annual allocations, makes it particularly difficult to aim for sustainable use of countryside resources through application of funds. The competition for public funds is so intense and the design of policies is frequently so crude that it would indeed be miraculous if the best possible allocation were to be achieved. In this situation accountability is one of the few financial controls available for regulating the public sector. It is therefore critical to make the most strenuous efforts to improve the quality of information which might guide public decisions at every level.

The strategic significance for managers must be to recognise where funds are available and to consider how funding will contribute most effectively to particular projects. That means having a good knowledge of the funding sources available and the way in which they are changing. It is vital to know which flows are coming on stream during a planning period and what constraints apply to their allocation. Managers must also have some means of assessing the comparative transaction cost to them of pursuing one source rather than another. As such information is collected, it becomes apparent where the best likelihood of success for each part of the programme lies. In the next chapter we consider the allocation side of the funding process from the point of view of the distributor of funds. How can funds best be assigned so as to serve the purposes of prevailing policies and their objectives?

References

Bishop, K. (2000). Gambling on 2020 vision. *ECOS, 20*(3/4), 1.
Bishop, K., Jones, M., & Phillips, A. (1997). Taking a gamble on the countryside. *ECOS, 18*(2), 77–87.
Bishop, K., Norton, A., & Phillips, A. (2000a). The impacts of the National Lottery on the countryside. *ECOS*, *20*(3/4), 11–19.
Bishop, K., Norton, A., & Phillips, A. (2000b). He who pays the piper – the impact of the National Lottery on countryside conservation policy. *ECOS, 20*(3/4), 20–28.
Countryside Agency (2000). Open space schemes prove a huge hit. *Countryside Focus, 8*, 4–5.
Countryside Agency (2002). Areas get their fair lottery share at last. *Countryside Focus, 20*, 3.
Dalton, A. (2000). Lottery funding in Scotland: Making a case for the countryside. *ECOS, 20*(3/4), 43–46.
Falconer, K. E., & Ward, N. (2000). Using modulation to green the CAP: The U.K. case. *Land Use Policy, 17*, 269–277.
Gay, H. (2000). Countryside conservation and the heritage lottery fund: An under-exploited opportunity. *ECOS, 20*(3/4), 52–60.
Gay, H., & Phillips, A. (2001). Natural and cultural heritage – exploring the relationships. *Ecos, 22*, 28–35.
Heritage Lottery Fund (2001a). *Lottery money targeted at areas hit by foot and mouth.* Press Release, 9.8.01.
Jenkins, S. (1996). *Accountable to none: The Tory nationalisation of Britain*. Harmondsworth: Penguin.
Mantle, G., Power, J., & Jones, A. (2000). The conservation of grasslands: HLF's effects in Wiltshire. *ECOS, 20*(3/4), 29–35.
National Audit Office (1997). *Protecting Environmentally Sensitive Areas*. London: HMSO
National Heritage Committee (1996). The National Lottery. Second Report, Volume I xxxv. London: HMSO.
National Lottery Commission (2001). *Facts and figures*. www.natlotcomm.gov.uk.
Newbould, P. (1994). Nature Conservation and the National Lottery. Countryside. *ECOS, 15*(3/4), 63–65.
TNS Travel and Tourism (2004). *GB leisure day visits survey*. Edinburgh: TNS Travel and Tourism.

Chapter 9

Allocating Funds

1. Introduction

Budgeting is a major tool in financial regulation and planning in the public sector. It is particularly useful to higher level control and transfer agencies in guiding the activities of subordinate agencies in the hierarchy. An effective working symbiosis between these two levels of organisation is an essential prerequisite for efficient operation throughout the public sector.

The importance of a budget is defined by two characteristics. First, the size of the budget will ultimately limit or constrain what the organisation can do. And second, the way in which the limits are set — the rules governing spending will also determine the extent to which a budget will limit what can be done. Obviously both levels of organisation share an interest in the outcome of the process.

It is a routine aspect of public life in developed countries that Governments set up agencies, allocate some funds to them and leave them a measure of freedom in allocating those funds amongst competing needs or objectives. Effective use of the budgeting system can make or mar agency performance and it is therefore very important to understand how these things are done. We therefore review some general aspects and principles of the process before turning to a case study of financing the National Parks.

2. Budget Setting

The main instrument for expressing the outcome of the financial allocation process is the budget, which is a forward statement of the amount allocated for a specific agency. Allocating public money amongst countryside agencies and controlling its use is achieved through an elaborate structure of forward budgets determined at various levels in the allocation process. As we saw in the previous chapter, most public agencies receive a majority of their finance from the Treasury, possibly through an intermediary department in Whitehall, whilst others have more complex arrangements, relying on a number of different sponsors and sources of finance. The accounts presented in Chapter 7 also confirmed this diversity of sources of finance. Many organisations use budgeting internally for regulating the flow of funds to its constituent parts. Budgeting is a therefore a vital process because it has widespread effects on the workings of the public sector.

Because of the significant size of certain expenditures they may be defrayed over several years and require even more years to deliver benefits. Such capital expenditures or investments are usually given special treatment in public expenditure. The essential characteristic of capital is that it produces a stream of benefits over a number of years — indeed some investments need never cease to produce benefits, whilst others have much shorter "lives." In either case, budgeting for capital expenditure would obviously require treatment different from the more typical annual round of short term expenditure. Capital budgeting encounters the problem of reconciling costs typically determined at the beginning of a project with benefits which may be delayed initially but which will usually continue into the future. These differences in flow over time are rendered comparable by reducing them to a value at a similar point in time, usually the present or the point at which the project is expected to start. Present values are obtained from future flows by a process known as discounting, which is essentially a kind of "compound interest in reverse." This ensures that events occurring in the near future are given more weight than events more distant in time.

Financial events occurring in a shorter time frame are presented in revenue budgets which provide a basis for a number of useful functions such as authorising and controlling income and expenditure, setting standards for evaluating performance, and co-ordinating the activities of multi-functional agencies. They may also have an important role in motivating managers and employees.

Table 9.1: Poverdale district council budget, 2001/2002.

	£ (000)
Expenses	
Employees	400
Running expenses	400
Premises costs	350
Transport costs	200
Debt charges	50
Revenue contributions to capital expenditure	150
Total	1,550
Income	
Government grants	700
Sales	55
Fees and charges	80
Rents	120
Interest	25
Miscellaneous income	45
Total	1,025
Balance to be met from council tax	525

Source: Adapted from Jones & Pendlebury (2000: 41).

Table 9.2: Loamshire Countryside and Parks Department: Annual budget, 2001/2002.

	£ (000)
Conservation programme	400
Access provision	350
Traffic management	90
Country Park purposes	100
Promotion	130
Interpretation	245
Planning	170
Research	150
Total	1,635

There are two sub-types of revenue budget, depending on the activity in hand. The first, line-item budgeting, focuses on the size and nature of income and expenditure. The second, programme budgeting, is driven by the purpose of the items in the programme. Such a budget would only assist with the some of the activities above. An example of a line item budget for a hypothetical small local district authority is given in Table 9.1.

Notice that this small local authority has insufficient income to meet its obligations and has to obtain further finance from Council Tax, which in fact is paid at another level in the system, namely at the county level.

For the more managerial purposes of controlling and planning of activities, a programme budgeting approach, focusing on the purpose of expenditure is required. A hypothetical example is given in Table 9.2 for the fictional County of Loamshire's Parks Department.

Such a budget would be much more interesting from the point of view of managing programmes and activities than a simple line item budget. In fact such budgets have been incorporated into an elaborate system of public sector management in the U.S., known as PPBS (Program Planning and Budgeting System) which has been widely applied and has also influenced events in the U.K. The case for making more of use of such a system would arise from a greater emphasis on efficient management rather than Government accountability.

3. Budget Setting in Practice

However, even if we do not make systematic use of methods such as PPBS, it is still possible to obtain some of the advantages they offer by more localised applications. The management orientation of Table 9.2 emphasises the functions of resource allocation, in contrast with Table 9.1 which is essentially about financial accountability. To consider how to allocate resources to get the best result from them, we must move into the delicate process of budget setting. For main Government Departments, this is dominated by an annual process in the U.K., which is carried out by the Public Expenditure Survey Committee (PESC) which meets and determines the expenditure plans for each main spending department over a five year period. These meetings, chaired by a senior minister, are frequently painful; each department is asked to accept cuts compared with what it would like to do and a negotiation procedure follows at the end of which the Government publishes a series of reports on Public Expenditure including a five year flow of funds for each Department. Leaks to the press and horror stories are used by participants in the process to try to engage public interest in the arguments, but this rarely succeeds perhaps indicating an intrinsic lack of political interest in public finance. The public expenditure reports are now highly technical documents, stuffed with information, which form the basis of the next year's activity and of the examination of out-turn at the end of the season. The longer run of years is more broadly indicative as the period over which the budget is spread increases. The final year of a five year series is unlikely to be accurate in the event, providing only an indication of what could happen.

The impact of the budgetary process is affected by the rules which apply to budget administration, especially in the flexibility they allow to budget holders. For example, if they are not allowed to carry over last year's unspent funds into this year's budget, budget-holders will do their best either to spend it before the year end, or divert it into another form of resource (e.g. physical stocks of some kind) which can be used in the next period. Such strategies can become extremely wasteful and should be avoided by the budget setting body where possible. In effect this means that the superior party must retain some flexibility in its allocation process so that, where unforeseen circumstances impose an extra load on a budget holder, relief can be given by amending the budget within the year.

An alternative way of allowing flexibility into budget use is to allocate a share of the budget to *contingencies*. So there might be a convention that all country park budgets in a county might be allowed to allocate 10% of their annual budget to contingencies. In such a case, the county treasurer will consider very carefully at the end of the year how contingencies have been spent and, if they are being used for expenditures which should have been foreseen, she may decide to amend the rules and remove the contingency allowance.

Another way of introducing more flexibility would be to allow a measure of *virement* between headings. This would mean, in the example in Table 9.2, that departments might be told they could transfer money between all headings up to a predetermined share. This capacity might be limited to particular headings, which were especially prone to fluctuation. Virement introduces a predetermined measure of flexibility into the process but the higher level authority has to be sure how far it may use it without risking an unacceptable loss of control.

Negotiation and determination of budgets is itself very demanding work. If managers are able to, they will bid for larger budgets than they can spend in the hope of reaching their preferred target level. Clearly those allocating the funds would not wish to be exploited in this way and must exert themselves to prevent it happening or accept that the budgets will not be fair to all participants. A politically skilled manager will secure a large budget for herself from this process. The Authority must then ensure that the funds are all spent within the year, or their next allocation may be threatened.

The difficulty of setting budgets generates a built-in tendency for officials to settle for the easiest method of determining budgets which, in most cases, would amount to issuing the same amount of resources as in the previous year. This may sound inappropriate, as indeed it often is, but careful studies have shown that this is what has happened over long periods of time. A thorough study by Danziger (1978) examined the expenditure budgets of four county boroughs of England and Wales, over the 86 years from 1888 to 1974, and found that the models which best described total expenditure over this long period are incremental. That is the best statistical predictor of next year's expenditure was found to be the level in the current year.

Another example closer to the contemporary countryside is that of the levels of finance in the National Parks of England and Wales. Until recently the Parks were supported by direct payments from the Treasury which were determined annually in discussions between each park and the relevant Government departments.

While some variation in funding between parks exists there is a notable similarity in the trends observed across parks. Budgets are generally highly incremental and the best predictor of one year's grant is that of the year before. It is difficult to believe that such an outcome is ideal. The size of parks is highly variable, as are, year to year, the pressures that each faces in trying to meet its objectives. Some parks have heavy visitor pressure at peak times, whereas others have comparatively few visitors. Similarly, some parks have serious conservation issues to resolve, while others are better endowed with landscape maintenance funds through the operations of other organisations such as DEFRA or the National Trust. Moreover these pressures change differentially over time and it would be reasonable to expect that their requirements for financial resources would not move so closely together.

These problems have concerned the relevant agencies for some time and have been considered by Government established committees in some detail. Recent moves have been introduced to tailor the funds allocated to the parks more closely to their annual expenditure needs and we discuss these in the case study below.

In principle the methods available for escaping incrementalism are well known. The obvious response of seeking to reproduce the PESC procedure, whereby each person seeking funds could be asked to stake their claim and fight their corner, with a PESC equivalent then judging the result, is taken to be unacceptable because it would be too time-consuming. Other options include the following approaches:

(1) One way would be to allocate shares to activities simply on the basis of last year's proportions — "*equal grief for all*." Anything else involves a departure from the past and arbitrariness becomes difficult to avoid. But starting the argument about shares from the previous years' budget is subject to objections of incrementalism which is inevitably wasteful.
(2) A partial escape from incrementalism would be to opt for a form of "*marginal incrementalism*" where only increases over last year's share are subjected to careful scrutiny. This could reduce the extent of incrementalism — at least it allows a gradual reallocation of resources over time. It runs into problems if demands for agency outputs change differentially and too fast for the incrementing process to keep up with.
(3) A more general form of this method is to "*top-slice*" part of the money by allocating it to essential/desirable new items and then share out the rest on the basis of the previous year's shares. Top-slicing is in effect a device for directing money towards particular objectives.

From the lead agency point of view there is a clear attraction of conducting multilateral negotiations in this way, in that it puts the onus back to the output points in the system and obliges budget holders to state their case. This would, incidentally, build up the authority of the lead agency. But to be really rigorous, a *"zero-based"* starting point should be applied whereby each spender has to start from the assumption that every penny has to be justified.

There are two main arguments against departing from established methods of allocation, which would probably apply also, to 1–3 above. First, that it is very time consuming to do so, tying up the talents of people who should be doing other (more creative) things. Second, that the best advocates, who may not necessarily be the best people to spend the money, will tend to obtain a disproportionate share of resources.

(4) Finally a system which has become popular in recent years, and which has much to offer as a means of avoiding the heavy bargaining costs of zero-based budgeting and non-incremental forms, is that of *"formula based budgeting."* Such a system would use a more or less mechanistic formula to allocate the available funds to sub-agencies. The crucial element is the formula. This has to encapsulate the demands placed on an agency and the particular resources already at its disposal. The obvious attraction of such systems is that they are less amenable to political log-rolling and that they could save an enormous amount of officials' time, which is currently tied up with budgetary negotiations. Budget formulae bring the desirable attributes of objectivity and transparency to what is normally seen as a very rough and ready business. Their weakness is in the arbitrariness they introduce. Budget formulae are now in use in many parts of the U.K. public sector.

Choice of budget allocation method used will have to bear in mind the possible benefits and costs of each one considered. The benefits include more precise control and placement of the available funds. The costs of each option will be the extent to which it wastes funds by misallocating them and the amount of staff time tied up in the process.

Formulae which seek to distribute the finance in a way which would maximise the output of all receiving agencies have a great deal to offer in certain contexts. They treat budget holders as a string of enterprises owned by the lead agency and direct resources to them in a way which will produce the greatest possible beneficial outcome. If this was a private firm seeking maximum profit, economic theory suggests that it would continue to spend money on the most productive activities (at the margin) still able to be expanded, until they ceased to be the most productive. Then other more productive activities would be expanded until the end of the budget was reached. Notice that this assumes a law of diminishing marginal returns will apply in each activity after some point has been reached. The optimum for each activity is then where the last unit of expenditure just equals the value of the marginal benefit it produces. In the more likely situation that the firm is short of funds for investment, the final optimum would arise where the ratio of each marginal product to the cost of producing it would be equal.

If it was felt that a simple formula, introduced without any regard for the continuity of the organisation, might be somewhat harsh in application, bringing serious discontinuities to established policies, then it would be possible to introduce it gradually. The lead agency could split the budget and allocate a top-slice on the basis of last year's shares and then distribute the rest on the basis of expected marginal results. The amount of top slice would, under these circumstances, reflect commitment to the previous year's outcomes, rather than the recognition of new possibilities. It would be expected that the share of top slice would eventually reduce to zero, once confidence in the budget formula had been established. Such trade-offs are in the nature of the budgetary process. This is a compromise which would work well if strictly adhered to, but it might be necessary for an agency, such as the Treasury, to ensure that the top slice was not too large or permanent and that the system did not tend to become a new sort of incrementalism in disguise. In essence the proposal is for the lead agency to operate a modified incremental rule, deciding how much (what share) is needed to fund inescapable commitments and then allocating what is left to its growth sectors.

Budgets are important at every level of government where superior agencies determine the funding at lower levels in the system. This may happen within individual organisations where the finance department, or a branch of it, determines the volume of funds available to other parts of the system or where one agency determines the funding of others.

At another extreme from the U.K. countryside and its agencies, the European Commission has to allocate funds to its member states annually. Countryside managers also need to be aware of how EU funds are redirected to its members. This has recently been subject to significant modification as a means of encouraging rural development policies (see Lowe *et al.* 2001, for a full account). In Chapter 3 we gave the background to these rather elaborate moves through which the Commission has offered member states an opportunity to move the policy emphasis away from farm commodities and modulate expenditure towards rural development and environmental amelioration. Under the rules of modulation the U.K. government have to match EU funds transferred from commodity support to rural development on a pound for pound basis. This allows the U.K. Government to increase substantially the funding available for rural development.

The operation is important because local public servants are increasingly finding themselves responsible for trying to raise funds directly from the EU. First, the member states contribute most of the funds in the EU's total budget, as explained in Chapter 7. These funds are then distributed by the different directorates of the EU, in support of its various policies. As agriculture has always secured a major share of these funds for the CAP, the EU devotes some policy energy to trying to regulate the CAP budget. When the policy debate shifted towards greater emphasis on rural development, at the end of the 1990s, it was important to the Commission that this should not become an excuse for re-expansion of the CAP budget, the share of which had just been reduced. Accordingly the concept of modulation was introduced whereby member states wishing to expand their rural development activities would be permitted to do so, partly by shifting funds from their agricultural sectors to the broader rural economy.

4. Budget Operation

We conclude, from this discussion, that budgeting provides a vital opportunity for controlling and guiding sub-agencies in useful and constructive ways. This opportunity must be grasped if the best use is to be made of the scarce funds available. Another important aspect of operating budgets is in the rules attached to their allocation, which regulate the behaviour of budget-holders. The following examples provide a brief account of some of the issues to be considered by budget holders.

156 *Strategic Countryside Management*

(1) The budget holder may, or may not, be required to return unspent funds at the end of the budget period. If he has to return any unspent surplus this puts pressure on him to dispose of all available funds within the stated period. It may also be possible for the agency to draw such funds and place them in a separate account for later spending. Such an aspect might be labelled the timing constraint.
(2) A budget may be broken down into more or less detailed spending categories. For example, so much for staff, so much for vehicles and so on. This categorisation may be relaxed to a degree by allowing a stated amount of virement between budget heads. For example it may be permitted to switch a declared share from one budget head to another, or another proportion of total budget may be moved without reference to the funding agency. *Virement* thus provides a constructive way of relaxing the budget constraint.
(3) Capital budgeting may pose a particular problem in that some capital items cannot be puchased/established within an accounting period. Building a road, a bridge or a harbour may take some years, yet the money may only be guaranteeable for the first year. Obviously a compromise between the budget holder and the funding agency will be needed here, and it will have to be specified. Commonly such problems are met on a "one-off" basis or at least separate budgeting arrangements are made for major capital items.
(4) Where inflation is rampant it can seriously undermine the budgeting process in that the money allocated may be reduced in value by the time it comes to be spent. If you are negotiating for a budget then a solution would be to get the money as soon as possible and invest it whilst waiting to spend it. You should be careful about where you invest it!

There are many other practical aspects to specifying budget constraints, which will be important in particular circumstances. The key conclusion is that a budget is not just a sum of money, but a flow of funds with particular rules, of varying flexibility, as to how it may be spent. We turn now to examine the way in which the National Parks receive their money and the ways in which the system is being improved.

5. A Case Study of the National Parks

The Edwards Report (1991) discussed the system of financing the National Parks in some detail. Since the establishment of National Park Authorities, under the 1995 Environment Act, and the formation of the Countryside Agency in 1999, a new budget setting system has been introduced which is formula driven.

The parties participating in this system include the Treasury, the Countryside Agency (CA), DEFRA and the National Park Authorities (NPAs). The Treasury's participation is not of great importance to the formula used — it is advised of the outcome by DEFRA once the results have been received. After some preliminary research, the Countryside Commission reported to the Government with recommendations (Countryside Commission 1998). A Commission working group, which included representatives of the National Parks, then agreed that although past funding bore a relationship to real needs, a greater share of funds should be allocated on an objective basis derived from management needs, using clear objective indicators. At this stage a set of indicators were introduced to reflect the real needs of the parks and the costs of managing land owned by Park Authorities. It was agreed to allocate a top slice of funds to NPAs, which did not have an Environmentally Sensitive Area (ESA) within them, to cover the cost of running their own agri-environmental schemes. The latter evens up the treatment between those with and those without that specific type of scheme.

The NPA's plans also contain an element of new bids for expenditure for the coming year. Annual Park budgets are now set in a series of steps involving the National Park Authorities (NPAs), the Countyside Agency and DEFRA. The steps are described in detail by Butterfield & Stevenson (2001), as follows:

(1) The CA sends advice on strategic priorities to the NPAs and DEFRA. These reflect the CA's view of the national priorities which should influence the plans of all parks. This advice is offered after consultations with National Park Officers.
(2) The NPAs then produce Best Value Performance Plans (BVPPs), which also contain an element of new bids for expenditure for the coming year, and submit them to DEFRA for consideration. DEFRA is statutorily required to obtain advice on these plans from the CA, which reviews the BVPPs and submits its advice.
(3) DEFRA then decides on the allocation and the result is published.

The formula proposed uses four boxes of indicators, as shown in Table 9.3 which are measured for each park and the results fed into the formula for determining each Park's annual grant.

Every one of these indicators is expressed in numerical terms and obviously the units used will partly determine the size and hence the influence of each indicator in the final sum determined. The number of indicators used here makes it likely that no single indicator will have a critical impact on the sum allocated through the final calculation. Nevertheless the formula is not fixed for all time — indeed it will be examined regularly by all who recognise its great importance to them. Given the publicly known shape of the formula it is easy for individual NPAs to argue their particular case, if they feel they are being inappropriately treated through the operation of the formula. An individual NPA can pursue its own interest by arguing for a modification of the formula, say by including new indicators or changing the weights used. However, in this essentially political process, it would be unwise for an individual NPA to push its own case to the detriment of others as this could provoke counter proposals. This does not constitute a criticism of the formula, merely a recognition of how it will work.

The main criticism which can reasonably be levelled at this procedure is that the indicators it rests on are mainly large aggregates, some of them not very certainly established, which do not change much from year to year. For example, estimates of the annual number of recreation day visits have already led to controversy but are unlikely to be re-estimated every year. Moreover simple counting of heads in a park gives only a crude indication of the demands of these visitors for NPA resources. Moreover the inclusion of park area in hectares in two of the baskets gives this variable substantial weight in the formula, but this is a very crude measure of park size. What is needed here is a measure of the proportion of park area which is attractive and available for recreation. Some of this is picked up by other variables such linear features, number of monuments and so on.

Table 9.3: Indicators proposed for allocating National Park grant.

Box Name	Indicators
1. Core Funding	• Park population. • Park area in hectares. • Number of authority members. • Number of planning applications processed.
2. Conservation of the natural and built environment	• Park area in hectares. • Area of land owned by NPA. • Length of linear features (walls etc.). • Number of Scheduled Ancient Monuments. • Number of listed buildings. • Number of conservation areas.
3. Recreation and visitor management	• Number of day visits per annum. • Length of public rights of way (PRoW) network. • Length of PRoW for which NPA has responsibility.
4. Special/local needs	• Traffic management schemes and sustainable transport projects. • Park run agri-environment schemes. • Cost of binding agreements for public access. • Match funding for projects attracting external grants.

Source: Robinson & Butterfield (1999).

However such measures are not only crude, but because they are totals, they do not recognise the costs incurred by an NPA *at the margin*. Thus the cost to an NPA of pulling in an extra visitor day to its attractions bears no necessary relation to the amount of money it would receive for doing so. Suppose an NPA did everything it could to attract, say one thousand more visitors in a year by opening access to some particular area within its boundary. If its previous year's visitor numbers stood at ten million, an extra thousand will only increase its total visitor numbers by 0.01%. The concern from the NPA point of view would be whether the expenditure it had made was in any way related to the amount of extra grant it received. Such a hypothetical example merely serves to emphasise that there may be little relationship between resources allocated and results achieved. To build such relationships into the formula may ultimately be impossible from existing information but it is an important touchstone in designing such formulae as new information is being provided all the time and methods of analysing it may finally allow the construction of a more appropriate formula. It is by no means unthinkable that it will eventually be possible to count visitors using remote sensing and that could completely revolutionise the data on visitor numbers adding precision to the formula.

To assess the benefits of better approaching the other NPA objective of conserving the countryside of the parks would be even more difficult to achieve than the objective of

Table 9.4: NPA and Broads Authority National Park grant 2001/2002.

National Park	Current Per cent of Total	Box 1–3 Indicators		Box 1–4 Indicators	
		2001/2002 Allocation Per cent Increase	2001/2002 Allocation Per cent of Total	2001/2002 Allocation Per cent Increase	2001/2002 Allocation Per cent of Total
Broads	8.4	−34	5.3	7.3	8.6
Dartmoor	10.9	12	11.7	7.6	11.2
Exmoor	9.1	−13	7.5	7.2	0.2
Lakes	15.9	40	21.2	9.7	16.7
Northumberland	6.7	3	6.6	7.5	6.8
North York Moors	12.3	26	14.7	8.3	12.7
Peak District	22.8	−14	18.8	3.7	22.6
Yorkshire Dales	11.8	26	14.2	8.1	12.2
Contingency	1.9				
Total	100	5	100	5	100

Source: Butterfield & Stevenson (2001).

promoting recreational use of the park. However approximately, progress on the latter can at least be assessed from visitor numbers. By contrast conservation is a very broad activity and progress in conservation is not easily measured across this broad agenda. Consequently it becomes more difficult to propose measures of success here. The simple presence of rare species or habitats would not suffice because such data cannot be aggregated together. Consequently those recommending final allocations will have to make judgements about the desirability of particular conservation activities and their outcomes one by one.

It is inevitable in an exercise such as this that some key variables will be omitted from consideration. For example there is an analogue of the treatment of parks, which do not have ESAs within them in the presence of the National Trust inside their boundaries. Parks certainly vary in the amount of NT property they contain and those with a large amount will benefit from the conservation activity of the Trust and its pulling power with visitors. An arrangement analogous to the treatment of ESAs would be to add to Box 4 in the formula an amount to compensate the parks for not having NT property and the contribution it would make to park purposes. Of course there are other variables omitted from the formula for which a case might be made. But there is a limit to the number of variables that can usefully be included without the process becoming unduly cumbersome.

This formula has now been applied to the determination of National Park Grant in England and the result is described by Butterfield & Stevenson (2001). The paper provides two examples of the way in which the formula could be applied, the first using only indicators in Boxes 1–3 and the second including Box 4 indicators but allowing them only 20% of the total weight of the determination. The results of these two calculations are presented and they are summarised here in Table 9.4.

Part of the reason for choosing the distribution in the final column of the Table was that the Government had evidently decided not to make any individual award less than the amount of the previous year's grant plus inflation. The inclusion of special needs specified in Box 4 makes a notable difference to the grant of several Parks and greatly reduces the variability of grants between the two years under consideration. Thus the Peak Park is lifted from a cut of 14% to an increase of 3.7% and the Lakes would have gained 40% which was reduced 9.7%, by the inclusion of Box 4 indicators in the formula. Thus the inclusion of this set of indicators did change the allocations quite markedly. It will be interesting to see how the use of this formula evolves over time. If it is working well, the pressure to adjust it each year will diminish as the fairness of the outcome becomes accepted.

6. Strategic Implications

This chapter has demonstrated the great importance of efficient and rational allocation of financial resources in the public sector and the considerable challenges of achieving such a result without either arbitrary determinations or the commitment of undue administrative resources to the process.

The process must start from an appropriate assembly of accounting and other information which describes the system of activities under consideration. From that we move on to consider ways in which the financial controllers of a system can appropriately deliver finance to lower levels in the organisation. The system of financial regulation and control emerges as one with at least two levels: a superior level from which funds are supplied and a lower level where they are directed to end uses. The working relationship between these two levels is critical to the success of the system. The higher level determines amounts and the constraints with which they are made available whilst the lower level has to make the best possible use of the resources available on an annual basis. The rules governing expenditure are a key part of the allocation process and can make a significant contribution to the efficiency with which lower level actors carry out their functions.

The inherent weakness in the system arises from the problem of negotiating annual amounts which will produce the best possible outcome. Over-exuberant administrators can easily demolish valuable motivations lower in the hierarchy. They can also waste time by being too zealous. The resources tied up with administering funds could usefully be applied to generating desired countryside benefits. The difficulties and frustrations of negotiating budgets push the system towards the inherent problem of incrementalism in budget setting. Allocating budgets without allowing them to become incremental is a critical need for those setting budgets. Efficiently carried out, the budgeting process can make a major contribution to the workings of the countryside.

We mentioned, in the introduction to Chapter 7, that the aim of allocating public funds in the countryside must be the achievement of the maximum possible volume of benefits for society from the funds available. The problem has been shown to be sufficiently complex to prevent that objective being achieved. Undoubtedly improvements in the system of allocating resources will be devised over time as better data come available for measuring outputs of the system. However, it must be recognised that until we are able to measure the value of the benefits produced and all of the costs incurred, it will not be possible to know that we have allocated resources efficiently in any rigorous sense. Meanwhile, we have to depend on the judgement of officials doing the best they can in a complex system with incomplete information.

References

Butterfield, J., & Stevenson, E. (2001). *National Park grant – 2001/2002*. Cheltenham: Countryside Agency.
Countryside Commission (1998). *Protecting our finest countryside*. CCP 532. Cheltenham: Countryside Commission.
Danziger, J. N. (1978). *Making budgets: Public resource allocation*. Beverley Hills, London: Sage Library of Social Research.
Jones, R., & Pendlebury, M. (2000). *Public sector accounting* (5th ed.). London: Prentice Hall.
Lowe, P., Buller, H., & Ward, N. (2001). Setting the next agenda? British and French approaches to the second pillar of the common agricultural policy. Working Paper 53. Centre for Rural Economy, Department of Agricultural Economics and Food Marketing, the University of Newcastle upon Tyne.
Robinson, T., & Butterfield, J. (1999). *New approach to allocating grant to National Park authorities*. AP 99/31. Cheltenham: Countryside Agency.

Chapter 10

Assessing the Impacts of Development

1. Introduction

As society places ever greater demands on the natural environment, it has become increasingly important for us to adopt systematic procedures that can be used to assess the magnitude and significance of the environmental impacts associated with new projects and policies in the countryside. This chapter discusses the scope and importance of such procedures for countryside management and examines three techniques that can be used in the appraisal of environmental quality and in the measurement of environmental impacts.

The importance of the techniques covered here is that they can help countryside managers to make more informed decisions about the consequences of planned activities in the countryside. Within the assessment process each approach offers different opportunities for incorporating the views of stakeholders and all can play a part in achieving the objective of sustainable research use. An alternative, economic appraisal technique cost-benefit analysis (CBA) is not described in this chapter. While this approach offers many advantages through its rigorous examination of the economic costs and benefits associated with the application of projects and policies, it is more specialised than the other assessment techniques described here and possibly less compatible with the objectives of sustainable resource use. A discussion of the method is left to more specialist texts (e.g. Hanley & Spash 1993).

Each of the three techniques that we examine in this chapter can play a role in sustainable decision making though, like CBA, none on its own is sufficient to ensure that we utilise the resources of the countryside in a sustainable way. What these approaches have in common is the potential to ensure that we maintain certain critical stocks of natural capital and reject developments that compromise the ability of current and future generations to enjoy their benefits. This notion of achieving an equitable use of resources, both within and across generations, is a necessary condition of sustainable development. The need to achieve an equitable distribution of resources is therefore more important than achieving an efficient distribution: while this may help to achieve sustainability objectives it cannot guarantee that the distribution of resources will be sustainable (Hanley *et al.* 1997).

The underlying similarity between each of the three approaches is that they attempt to provide additional information about the potential impacts of certain activities with respect to a particular reference situation. In the first technique, environmental impact assessment, practitioners seek to examine the impacts of proposed developments by comparing the state of the world that would exist if the policy or project was implemented, with another world state in which it is not implemented. This contrasts with the other two approaches, quality of life assessment; landscape character assessment, which concentrate on helping us to understand the existing state of the world and by so doing inform our future inter-actions with it.

Comparison with a reference situation is particularly important at the policy level, where the practitioner must make a judgement about the appropriate reference ("policy off") situation with which to compare the future ("policy on") situation. In some cases the appropriate reference situation may be the continuation of current policies, while in others this assumption may be unrealistic and the appropriate reference situation should be based on what would happen if some "best" alternative policy were adopted.

An important outcome from any appraisal process is the development of a set of management or policy aims which can be used to inform the development process or to further more general countryside management objectives. The techniques addressed in this chapter each offer different levels of assistance to the countryside manager in this area. Environmental impact assessment, for example, can help to shape the development process, while quality of life capital and landscape assessment can both lead to specific policy or management recommendations.

2. Environmental Impact Assessment

Environmental Impact Assessment (EIA) is a systematic, multi-disciplinary process used to gather information about the environmental impacts of a proposed development. The EIA process is used to inform decisions authorising the development and is designed to prevent or minimise any associated pollution and environmental damage. It also provides a vehicle for negotiation between the developer and the planning authority and permits public participation in development decisions. As such, it forms an important element of environmental protection process in the U.K. and other countries.

Following EIA, if a project is found to have a negative impact on the environment, then in extreme circumstances it may be abandoned. More often, the findings of the EIA form the basis of a constructive negotiation between the developer and the regulator, and may lead to new proposals, typically a change in design or implementation, so that the impacts of the development are reduced, or at least mitigated.

Clearly, EIA has an important function in helping to minimise the adverse environmental impacts of development and can also play a positive role in achieving sustainable development. In general, however, decisions on whether or not to proceed with a development are seldom based on the outcome of an EIA alone, but tend to take into account wider social, economic and political objectives (Lawrence 1994). This suggests that the exercise should be treated as an important aid to decision making and the development process rather than an end in itself. In order to fulfil this function, EIA must evolve to suit the changing set of values held by society relating to the environment and development. Sometimes this will mean that environmental issues take on a greater importance, while at other times economic and social impacts may be critical.

2.1. Background to EIA in the U.K.

The discovery of North Sea oil provided one of the major catalysts for the adoption of EIA in the U.K. The exploitation of this resource often required large developments in economically disadvantaged areas of high scenic beauty sometimes in relatively unspoilt areas. In 1974 the Scottish Development Department (SDD) noted that these and other large scale developments required "rigorous appraisal" and suggested that Local Planning Authorities (LPAs) implemented impact studies where needed. Subsequently, various EIAs were sponsored by SDD or LPAs or even by developers.

The Scottish Office and the Department and the Environment commissioned a manual to give LPAs make "a balanced appraisal of environmental, economic and social impacts of major industrial developments." This was issued to all LPAs in 1976 and updated in 1981. Despite this the main driver towards the use of EIA in the U.K. has been the European Union (EU). According to Glasson et al. (1995) the EU had three main reasons for establishing a uniform EIA system across all member states:

(1) a concern about the physical state of the environment and the prevention of further degradation (e.g. EC Action Programmes for the Environment from 1973 onwards);
(2) a desire that all members compete on a "level playing field" as far as development permission was concerned;
(3) the transnational nature of various environmental impacts, e.g. acid rain.

Drafting of an EU Directive on EIA began as early as 1975 and the first draft Directive was presented in 1980. Amendments were tabled in 1983 following extensive consultation process. Only in 1985 was the Directive 85/337/EEC finally adopted and implemented in July 1988. Individual member states were responsible for enacting their own regulation to implement the Directive and have considerable discretion over how this is done.

The Directive is very brief and extremely simple. It sets out a methodology for EA, in very few words and lists two categories of project to which it will apply. The first list, Annex I, makes EIA a requirement for a range of highly contentious projects such as oil refineries, thermal power stations storage for radioactive waste, iron and steel works, major chemical works, motorways and major airports, ports and waste disposal installations.

The second list, Annex II projects, leaves the decision on whether or not to carry out an EIA to the discretion of the member state. Typically, Annex II projects require EIA if they have significant environmental effects. The broad headings under which Annex II projects include agriculture, minerals extraction, various industrial developments (including the food processing) and various infrastructure or "other" projects. The projects listed under the agriculture heading include:

- restructuring of rural land holdings;
- the use of uncultivated or semi-natural lands for intensive agricultural purposes;
- water-management projects for agriculture;
- initial afforestation where this may lead to adverse ecological changes and land reclamation for the purposes of conversion to another type of land use; and
- the reclamation of land from the sea.

The introduction of Directive 85/337 as an important environmental constraint on land use in the U.K., was hailed as a major step forward by critics of the existing development control system. In the U.K., the Directive was given effect by the Town and Country Planning Act 1990, which made EIA a prerequisite of granting planning permission for specified projects. Most of the developments listed in Directive 85/337 are incorporated into the Town and Country Planning (Assessment of Environmental Effects) Regulations 1988 (SI 1988/1199 as amended) and the equivalent regulations for Scotland and Northern Ireland. In the U.K. the bodies responsible for deciding whether or not Annex II projects require EIA are the local authorities. A number of additional regulations have been put in place since 1990 to cover the requirement for EIA in various contexts where planning permission is not required (e.g. motorways, large-scale afforestation, and land drainage schemes).

Directive 97/11/EC amends the original Directive and suggests some changes to the specifications of projects under Annex I and Annex II. The U.K. implementation of the new Directive means that more projects require EIA than before and has led to some changes in procedures.

2.2. The EIA Process

The EIA process tends to divide the environment up into its physical (e.g. air, water, landscape, ecology, people) and socio-economic components (e.g. demography, employment, housing, services, culture). A development (i.e. a new project, policy, or programme) may impact on these components in a variety of ways depending upon the positive or negative nature of its effects, their temporal and geographical scope, and whether or not they can be readily reversed. The methodology of EIA can be clearly identified. This is spelt out in Article 5 and Annex III of the Directive, which requires the developer to supply the information listed in Annex III in an appropriate form in so much as:

- states consider it relevant to the consent procedure and to the specific project;
- the developer may reasonably be required to supply this information, given current knowledge and methods of assessment.

Article 5(2) summarises the information needed in the assessment, which is also spelt out in Annex III. Glasson *et al.* (1999) show that EIA process involves a number of steps and is ideally cyclical rather than linear in nature. They break the various steps of the EIA process down into the seven stages shown below.

2.2.1. Preliminary stages

2.2.1.1. Project screening This first element of the preliminary stages of EIA is used to determine whether or not the EIA is required. The EIA may be mandatory (i.e. an Annex I project) or discretionary (i.e. an Annex II project). Discretionary projects may require EIA on the basis of any or a combination of the following conditions: scale of the proposed development; sensitivity of the proposed location; or expectation of adverse impacts. There is no statutory requirement for the developer to apply for a ruling prior to seeking planning permission, about whether or not an EIA would be required. As Alder & Wilkinson (1999) point out, this reduces the opportunity for public consultation, as otherwise the first chance that the public has to comment is following the publication of the Environmental Impact Statement (EIS). This problem is partially addressed by Regulation 5 of the U.K. regulations which permits local authorities to decide whether or not an EIA is required prior to the planning application (Alder & Wilkinson 1999). Such decisions, were they required by law, could have a positive impact on the speed of the application process and improve the consultation process.

2.2.1.2. Scoping   Here the developer reviews the expected impacts of the project, direct and indirect, temporary, permanent, or cumulative, short or long term and any interactions between them. EIA is recommended where impacts may be significant or are currently unclear. Scoping is recommended but not statutory in U.K. It is often at this stage that the developer must contact various statutory and non-statutory consultees (e.g. English Heritage, the Countryside Agency) for their views.

2.2.1.3. Consideration of alternative approaches   If the project has significant impacts then various alternatives to the original proposal must be examined, e.g. size, location, design. These may provide effective means of reducing adverse impacts. This is required by Directive 85/337 but in the U.K. this requirement has been interpreted as discretionary and as a consequence many U.K. EIAs have failed to consider alternatives.

2.2.1.4. Description of the project   Schedule 3 of Town and Country Planning (Assessment of Environmental Effects) Regulations 1988 requires a detailed description of the project. This could include: the purpose or rationale of the project; the life-cycle of activities; location and physical presence of the development; description of processes involved; and details of the relevant planning policy context. The description will include any land-use designations as well as the levels of use of recreational facilities.

2.2.1.5. Identification of the environmental baseline   This stage identifies current environmental conditions and attempts to predict how will they change if the project does not go ahead. Department of the Environment (1990) suggests that the following topics should be addressed:

- population;
- flora, fauna and habitats;
- soil, geology, agricultural quality;
- water environment;
- air quality, climatic factors;
- heritage, architecture & archaeology;
- landscape & topography;
- recreational uses;
- other relevant features;
- policy framework and designation.

2.2.1.6. Identification of impacts This stage relates project characteristics to environmental baseline to determine likely environmental impacts. Various approaches to this stage exist, reflecting the diversity of potential impacts, e.g. overlays, checklists, etc. (see Glasson *et al.* 1999 for examples).

2.2.1.7. Impact prediction Here the magnitude of the predicted impacts is measured relative to the without-project position. This can be a complex undertaking and may require considerable expert knowledge.

2.2.2. Assessment stages

2.2.2.1. Impact evaluation Having predicted the nature of the impacts and their extent their significance must be assessed. Impact evaluation requires a distinction to be made between the size of an impact and its significance. The significance of impacts relates to their duration, magnitude, extent and permanence, i.e. long-lasting impacts affecting wide areas or large populations are generally more significant than impacts of short duration and limited geographical extent. Similarly, impacts that only affect a small area but for which there is a low probability of recovery, may be more significant than larger scale reversible impacts. To make these predictions more meaningful some measures of the likelihood of the impact (e.g. a 50% probability) should be included in the assessment. Such predictions may vary in accuracy as both objective and subjective approaches exist for impact prediction and will be used depending on the circumstances (e.g. in some cases accurate scientific data may exist to help predict for example habitat recovery following flooding, whereas in other cases forecasts may be guesswork based on limited anecdotal information). Other criteria for assessing significance might include some estimate of the value of the affected environment (this could be estimated using techniques based on either cost-benefit analysis or quality of life assessment).

2.2.2.2. Mitigation of impacts This is defined in Directive 85/337 as: "*measures envisaged in order to avoid, reduce and, if possible, remedy significant adverse effects.*" Mitigating measures are widely recognised as a second-best approach, particularly in the countryside where habitat creation and landscaping cannot replace lost or damaged natural features. Typical measures include: changes in site planning (e.g. mitigating effects on recreation by modifying boundaries of working sites; various technical solutions; aesthetic measures, such as landscaping; or ecological measures such as off-site habitat creation. The task of physically relocating sites (e.g. a grassland SSSI) may be considered in particular circumstances but is often impractical or too expensive.

2.2.3. Presentation stage The EIS can usefully be viewed as a report of the outcome of the developer's identification and assessment of the environmental impacts of the project. Glasson *et al.* (1999) make a number of recommendations about the contents of an EIS, which they say should be as brief at possible, yet at the same time cover the relevant issues as comprehensively as possible in non-technical language.

A review of EISs by Weston *et al.* (1997) showed that they were generally of a good standard, yet when the environmental information contained in them is examined, significant elements are often found to be missing. Even so, Weston *et al.* found the EIA process as a whole to provide sufficient information for the decision maker to make a reasoned judgement even if the EIS had shortcomings. However, when reviewing the usefulness of the EIA process, they recommend that we should not just look at the EIS, but at the totality of evidence collected by the process (often found in the various appendices).

2.2.4. Review stage EIAs may fail to meet statutory requirements or to provide sufficient information upon which to base the decision. The competent authority must review the submission and ask for more information if necessary. Non-mandatory review guidelines exist but until now have been used sparingly. In some countries independent review panels exist to examine quality of EIS.

2.2.5. Consultation This stage ensures that the public's views are taken into account in the EIA process. The consultation process helps the quality and effectiveness of the process and makes it more robust. In the U.K. this translates into various conditions about publicising the proposals and making the EIS available to the public. Consultation also occurs after the EIS is published. As amended by Directive 97/11/EC, the planning authority is requested to consult the relevant environmental and countryside agencies about the information included by the developed in the EIS.

2.2.6. Decision stage Typically, the EIS must be submitted with the planning application and then the local planning authority has a certain amount of time to make a decision (in England and Wales, 16 weeks). When the EIS is submitted it could reveal significant adverse impacts of development and could suggest the abandonment or modification of development proposal. Alternatively it may suggest ways of mitigating impacts. The planning authority must take into account the findings of the EIS, the views of statutory consultees (e.g. English Nature or English Heritage), and the public. The planning authority may then grant or reject planning permission or may ask for further mitigation measures.

In many cases, the consultation process which follows a planning application provides additional important information. Clearly, once an investment has been made in a full-scale EIA and the associated decision-making process, a certain momentum may have gathered that may prove difficult to ignore. This momentum may just tip the scales in favour of some form of development.

2.2.7. Post-decision stage The observed impacts of a project are perhaps the true yardstick by which EIA should be assessed. EIA establishes various conditions for the undertaking of the project and these must be kept in mind through the project's life cycle and monitored subsequently. Similarly, there is a need to ensure that the project's actual impacts are not more serious than those predicted by the EIA and that any mitigation measures perform as planned. Monitoring is not currently mandatory in the U.K.

2.2.7.1. Quality control in EIA In an ideal world EIA should be honest and unbiased. In reality it may prove to be too developer driven. This is understandable given that the developer is both paying for and hiring the practitioners who undertake the work. If the EIA process suffers from such "capture" then it could lead to decisions with unforeseen adverse environmental impacts. Potential for bias arising from this could be reduced if practitioners were selected by, reported to, or were monitored more closely by an independent authority.

Review of EISs gives some indication of the quality of the EIA, if only to suggest what additional information is required. Local authorities should now be increasingly experienced with EIA and the contents of EISs. In addition various independent bodies and institutions offer a review facility for Environmental Statements.

2.2.7.2. EIA in the countryside The Countryside Commission's role as a statutory consultee for major developments in England led them to become concerned with treatment of landscape and recreational issues in EIA. This concern inspired them to commission CCP 326 to provide guidance on these issues for assessors (Countryside Commission 1991).

Many of the recommendations of CCP326 were common to those contained in DoE (1989), but with an additional focus on landscape and recreational issues. The paper recommends early consultation with the planning authority and the Commission at the screening stage and recommends the use of countryside/landscape specialists in EIA process. It also stresses the importance of the consideration of alternatives and mitigation measures.

An understanding of the landscape is important in determining the potential impacts of development. Therefore the Commission recommends that the baseline information for the EIA should describe affected areas in terms of their landscape character. Similarly, consideration should be made of the subjective values associated with landscape and significance should be attached to any formal designation and cultural associations of the landscapes affected by development. Landscape character assessment can be used to classify landscapes and to provide an evaluation of their importance both locally and nationally. It can also be used to help assess the significance of the predicted landscape impacts.

If the development is likely to have significant impacts on recreation CCP 326 recommends that the EIS contains a description of available recreational resources and activities; including access to the countryside and estimates the levels of use of these facilities for recreation. The significance of these impacts must then be assessed within the local recreational context.

The scope of EIA in the countryside has been extended by EIA legislation in England and Wales to cover the use of uncultivated land or semi-natural areas for the purposes of intensive agriculture (DEFRA 2002). The land uses where this applies include meadows and grazing pastures, upland grassland, downland, heathland, scrub, moorland and wetlands. Activities that may require EIA range from cultivation, introduction of intensive grazing and vegetation clearance, to land reclamation, flood defence and drainage works (DEFRA 2002). Farmers will be obliged to inform DEFRA of plans to cultivate land and following a screening procedure DEFRA will determine whether or not there are likely to be significant environmental impacts and if there are the scope of the assessment. The main criteria that will be considered in the EIA will be designation, biodiversity, landscape character, archaeological or historical features, access and pollution (DEFRA 2002). Other legislation, the EA Forestry (England & Wales) Regulations (Statutory Instrument 2228, 1999) covers forestry and requires any project involving deforestation or afforestation to obtain consent from Forestry Commission.

2.2.7.3. Strategic environmental assessment EIA legislation in the U.K. currently includes no formal requirement for strategic environmental assessment (SEA). SEA is the application of the EIA process to significant policies, programmes and plans where consideration of environmental impacts early in the planning process may have significant benefits, particularly for sustainable development. Wood (1995) suggests that the implementation of SEA can increase the weight given to environmental issues in decision making and stimulate additional consultation and participation during policy formation He also suggests that carrying out SEA at a policy level, may help in the design of projects, generate generic mitigation measures, and encourage a more holistic approach to the treatment of the long-term and cumulative environmental impacts of policies and programmes. This could in turn reduce the number of EIAs required, as some projects will be designed to minimise environmental impacts.

SEA is provided for by NEPA in the United States and is also required by certain legislation in The Netherlands and New Zealand (Wood 1995). Its implementation is somewhat different from that of standard EIA because it must look at the long-term impacts of a wide-ranging policy or programme, rather than those associated with a geographically discrete project. Similarly, the organisations involved will not be developers and local authorities but Government departments and agencies. Wood (1995) identifies a number of other key differences between SEA and EIA which could impact on its usefulness. Foremost among these is the difficulty in predicting the long-term effects of policies and programmes, particularly where they may be linked with other factors. This is a generic problem and not specific to SEA and there seems to be much promise in using SEA as a formal framework for the review of the potential consequences of new policies and programmes in the countryside.

3. Quality of Life Assessment

Decisions relating to the management of the countryside will not only impact on the environment but on local communities and their social and economic wellbeing. Therefore it can be argued that an appropriate decision-support tool should explicitly consider each of these impacts in an integrated way in order to ensure that coherent decisions are made that will result in sustainable outcomes.

The Quality of Life Assessment (QLA) approach was devised as a joint initiative by English Nature, the Countryside Agency, English Heritage and the Environment Agency to "provide a consistent and integrated way of managing for quality of life" (Countryside Agency *et al.* 2001). To achieve this objective, the approach attempts to identify the consequences that plans, development proposals and management options will have on the wellbeing of society, and by so doing ensure that decisions will be better informed. It is designed as a tool that can be used to inform the planning process and to provide a systematic basis for management plans in environmentally important areas of countryside such as National Parks and AONBs.

Within the QLA framework, the outcomes of a particular decision are translated into changes in the stocks of environmental, economic and social capital. More importantly, the approach recognises the interdependence of these stocks, and that the economic and social benefits of a proposal may depend on environmental quality. This integration of the QLA approach was developed on behalf of the agencies by CAG and Land Use Consultants. Originally labelled Quality of Life Capital, the method envisaged as an approach to managing environmental capital, the remit of the project eventually broadened to consider social and economic capital and embraced the more general notion of human wellbeing or quality of life. The basic ideas that underpin QLA are not new, though the approach does provide a potentially useful framework for their consideration. Indeed, QLA provides an interesting contrast to the other techniques described in this chapter both in its relative simplicity and its focus on sustainability.

Quality of life has been used as an indicator of individual welfare for many years, particularly in health economics when comparing the benefits of alternative treatments for a chronic illness. Thus, in health appraisal, the effects that various projects or policies may have on health in terms of may be measured in terms such as "Quality Adjusted Life Years" (QALYs) or "Healthy Year Equivalents." Change in health status, for example, is first quantified using one of the different scales (health state is classified by potential disability and/or discomfort and in terms of the quality of life associated with these states), and then the effect is summed across the number of years associated with the change in health status to produce the QALY score associated with the change.

In contrast to the QALY approach, the QLA framework does not attempt to quantify the impact of a management option or potential development on quality of life. Similarly, no attempt is made to quantify the monetary costs and benefits associated with the change. In fact the approach has more in common with the scoping stage of EIA, in that it attempts to identify impacts and then make some judgement about their scale and significance.

The following section is based on the Overview Report on QLA (Countryside Agency *et al.* 2001) which describes the process as consisting of six steps:

>**Step A: Purpose.** Why is the study is being undertaken? It is important to understand the reasons for carrying out the QLA study and the type of decision-making process it is being used to inform. The Overview Report identifies a number of potential uses for QLA including: settlement planning; comparing alternative development sites; assessing development potential; identifying the benefits and services of landscape character areas; setting planning conditions and obligations; and involving the general public in the planning and environmental decision-making process.
>
>**Step B: Identifying what is there.** It is important to identify the sources of social, environmental and economic capital that the study will cover. These sources will provide a range of benefits and services to society that it may wish to protect or enhance. The scope of this investigation will depend on the purpose of the study. In some cases only local benefits and services will need to be investigated, while in others regional or national impacts may be of interest.
>
>**Step C: Benefits and Services.** Here, the approach identifies those benefits and services which could be affected by the proposed changes. Again, the purpose of the study will influence the range of impacts that the study

will concentrate on. The Overview report offers a checklist of potential benefits under the following headings: *health/survival* (e.g. environmental services like improving air or water quality); *biodiversity*; *appreciation of the environment* (i.e. aesthetic considerations); *sense of place* (e.g. aspects that impact on local character*); historical character; education; recreation*; and *value to the local economy* (e.g. employment and tourism benefits).

Step D: Evaluation: This stage of the process examines the benefits and services identified in Step C and asks the following questions:

- **Who do these services matter to, why and at what spatial level?** Some services such as open-access recreation may only be important to local users while others such as biodiversity will have national or international importance.
- **How important are they?** Some judgement must be made about the importance of maintaining these services – this will be related to the following questions:
- **Is the supply of these services sufficient?** Is enough of a particular service available to mean that it doesn't really matter if one source of it is lost? For example, in urban areas where open space is in short supply, a small patch of land for dog walking may be more valuable than an extra footpath in a National Park that is already well supplied with opportunities for walkers. In some cases, for example those relating to habitat loss, expert opinion should be sought to determine the implications of any supply changes.
- **What are the available substitutes for these services?** If a service is lost then are there ways in which that loss could be made up? This is similar to the notion of mitigation in an EIA in that it may be possible to replace a lost service with some equivalent (i.e. one piece of open land for another). Again, expert opinion may be required to determine what really constitutes a substitute for a particular lost benefit or service.

Step E: Policy and Management Implications. Based on the findings from Step D, this stage determines management and policy aims that will maintain or enhance the benefits identified in Step C. The nature of these aims will depend on the type of process the study is being used to inform. These aims should be drawn up by the practitioner in conjunction with the various stakeholders concerned with the site and where necessary in consultation with relevant specialists.

Step F: Monitoring. Performance indicators based on the benefits and services identified in Step C.

The Overview Report recommends that the outcomes from Steps C, D and E are recorded in the form of a "What Matters and Why Matrix." This is a table consisting of six columns. The first column lists the economic, social or environmental benefit or service that could be affected by whatever change is being proposed. The second column records who would be affected by the change, the reason why they would be affected and the scale of the impacts (e.g. local, regional, national, global). Column three attempts to classify the importance of the impact (e.g. high, medium or low), while the fourth column assesses the supply aspect of the benefit/service (i.e. is there sufficient, or is it over or under supplied?) The fifth column lists possible substitutes for the benefit or service and the final column lists the relevant policy or management aims.

The derivation of the "What Matters and Why Matrix" is the key element of the QLA process. By identifying the complete range of benefits and services that may be affected by a proposed development, strategic plan, or management option and then assessing their scale, importance and substitutability, the approach provides a convenient overview of potential impacts. By going on to provide management or policy aims to mitigate any potential loss or damage to these benefits and services the QLA approach provides valuable direction for decision makers and planners.

In terms of overall sustainability objectives, the approach provides a useful means of assessing the impacts of decision making at a relevant spatial scale. Identification of key benefits and services may be important in setting priorities for monitoring or action. The process also identifies where the loss of a service or benefit is irreversible, in which case the management prescription would be to refrain from the potentially damaging activity (as the only means of maintaining the current level of benefits).

Regarding its use in countryside management the QLA approach should provide managers with a useful framework upon which to base management plans, and in particular to identify ways in which site benefits can be enhanced. Gay & Phillips (2001) go somewhat further, and suggest that QLA, and similar approaches which take a multi-criteria approach, may provide the means for managers, policymakers and practitioners to share knowledge, pool skills and develop a broader vision across a wider range of interests. The technique also complements the landscape character approach by identifying the linkages between determinants of character and economic, environmental and social benefits with the result that a more coherent linkage might be made between these factors in the strategic planning process. This should result in more effective management of landscape character and a better integration between the broader countryside and designated areas.

The designers of QLA regard it as a useful tool for the scoping stage of EIA, and see it as a more useful approach to identifying priorities than those currently being used. They also regard it as a more robust alternative to CBA, as it provides a fundamentally different approach that does not attempt to enumerate benefits into a common currency.

Even so the technique suffers from a number of weaknesses. Assessments of the importance of benefits are generally subjective and even when informed by expert opinion could vary widely. Its concentration on the notion of substitutes is another potential weakness, especially given the tendency for practitioners to devise management or policy objectives that are based on substituting benefits and services across sites. One of the strengths of the QLA approach is said to be its aim to reject changes that would lead to the loss of complex benefits produced by the area as a whole, rather than any component. It could be argued that the very complexity of such benefits may mean that they are difficult to identify until they are lost, and that the QLA approach could easily fail to take adequate account of context. QLA also fails to deal systematically with inter-generational effects or with the question of non-use benefits.

4. Landscape Character Assessment

Landscape character assessment is a term that covers a broad range of techniques used to classify, describe and evaluate landscape and to make judgements based on an understanding of landscape character that will inform a range of different decisions. In the U.K. the term is probably most closely associated with a series of studies carried out on behalf of the former Countryside Commission in the 1980s and 1990s. At this time, the Commission were becoming increasingly concerned with the conflict between agriculture and the conservation of the broader countryside. These concerns motivated the development of a methodology that could be used to assess the character and quality of landscapes. This would lead to a better understanding of the factors that contribute to landscape character and quality and would help to identify potential threats to landscapes and thus inform policy development

The question was how to successfully incorporate issues of landscape quality into policy and management? The 1985 Public Enquiry into the designation of the North Pennines as an AONB brought this issue to national attention. The Inspector in charge of the enquiry was publicly critical of the Commission's approach to assessing landscape quality, concluding that it was both simplistic and subjective and incapable of making a convincing case that an area possessed outstanding natural beauty (Countryside Commission 1987). These proceedings provided considerable impetus to the development of a formal methodology for landscape character assessment (Swanwick 2002a), one of the first fruits of which was an assessment of the Mid-Wales landscape (Land-Use Consultants 1986).

The ramifications of the Inspector's comments can also be seen in Commission's first major statement on landscape assessment "Landscape Assessment: A Countryside Commission Approach" (Countryside Commission 1987). This document set an agenda for the Commission to adopt "*a comprehensive and practical approach to landscape assessment.*" The Commission's preferred approach to this task was a combination of objective assessment and subjective opinion, based on aesthetic taste and judgement, that would operate within a framework of consensus and common sense (Countryside Commission 1987).

Subsequent studies (e.g. Countryside Commission 1991a) investigated whether or not landscape assessment techniques could be adopted in a lowland context and aimed to develop a systematic approach to landscape assessment that would provide farmers with practical advice for conserving the rural landscape. This required both a detailed description and assessment of the landscape and an evaluation of the possible impacts of future landscape change.

Following the publication of landscape assessment principles by their sister organisation in Scotland (Countryside Commission for Scotland 1991), the Commission published "Landscape Assessment Guidance" (Countryside Commission 1993) their recommended approach to the art of landscape assessment. This document provided a systematic framework for landscape assessment including advice on the process and purpose of such exercises. The technique combines objective landscape description with subjective appraisal of aesthetic quality and as well as considering what makes a landscape characteristic or valuable, identifies those elements of landscape that reduce its value or which threaten its intrinsic character. Useful examples of field survey forms and landscape descriptions are provided in the guidance which provided the basis of a wide range of landscape assessments in England and Wales over the remainder of the 1990s, particularly those associated with the Countryside Character Programme.

4.1. The Countryside Character Programme

The steady erosion of local character has been a recurring trend in the second half of the twentieth century. This came about through a combination of factors, including the construction of new roads, the development of plantations of exotic tree species, removal of characteristic landscape features, the introduction of uniformity (e.g. through standardisation of the design of new houses) and has resulted in a slackening of the regional distinctiveness that characterised this country. Culturally, this represents our failure to recognise the importance of diversity in the English landscape.

The publication of Countryside Commission (1991b) heralded the introduction of the Countryside Character Programme. The objectives of this programme were to:

- identify, describe and analyse from a regional perspective the character of the English countryside;
- identify, again from a regional perspective, specific opportunities to conserve or enhance the character of the English landscape.

The approach was piloted in 1992 in the south-west peninsula (Countryside Commission 1995) and was extended across England following a consultation exercise into the aims of the Programme (Countryside Commission 1995). In 1998 the Countryside Commission published the first three volumes (Countryside Commission 1998a–c) in a series covering regional landscape character across England. For each character area in a given region these volumes outline:

- key characteristics;
- landscape character;
- physical influences;
- historical and cultural influences;
- buildings and settlement;
- land cover.

As well as illustrating the character areas using text, maps and photographs these documents also raise management and policy issues and identify pressures on landscape character and measures that could be adopted to address these problems. Raising these issues through the Countryside Character Programme was designed help to focus national policies that would have a major influence on the character of the countryside The implicit suggestion is that such policies should be applied flexibly to allow for regional variations that reflect local needs.

Since 1998 the Countryside Agency have produced the remaining seven volumes detailing the character of the entire 159 landscape character areas in England. The complete set represents a useful resource for countryside managers and planners, as well as a major reference source for students and the general public. To support this work, the Agency have also established a Countryside Character Network to provide a forum for discussion aid the dissemination of good practice in this area. The network now has more than 500 members gathered from a wide range of professions and countries.

Some commentators (e.g. Gay & Phillips 2001) give credit to the Countryside Character approach and similar initiatives developed in Scotland and Wales for helping to "raise awareness of the holistic nature of the countryside" and it is certainly true that a greater emphasis is now being placed on this issue by a range of organisations. One example of this is provided by English Nature whose Lifescapes initiative attempts to link biodiversity with other social, economic and environmental factors in an integrated way in order to predict future potential land use. The technique has also been used in the evaluation of policies with major landscape impacts such as DEFRA's Environmentally Sensitive Areas Scheme and by the Environment Agency to look at the landscape associated with river corridors and catchments (Swanwick 2002a).

More recently the Countryside Agency and Scottish Natural Heritage (2002) have published new guidance on landscape character assessment (Swanwick 2002b) which supersedes that given in Countryside Commission (1993) and Countryside Commission for Scotland (1991). This guidance builds on experience from a variety of major programmes of landscape assessment in the U.K. and reflects the evolution of the approach towards its current focus on landscape character and a commitment to the more active involvement of stakeholder groups (Swanwick 2002a, b). The guidance also reflects how landscape character assessment has been adapted in other contexts and incorporates links with methods for the assessment of historic landscapes as developed by English Heritage, Cadw and Historic Scotland (Swanwick 2002a, b) which are discussed in the following section.

The Landscape Institute and the Institute of Environmental Management (2002) is another publication providing a useful source of guidance for landscape and visual impact assessment, while Martin (2004) documents a range of examples of the application of landscape character assessment. Also of interest to practitioners, is a range of topic papers from the Countryside Agency and SNH providing guidance to practitioners on particular issues such as the use of geographical information systems and other computer-based methods.

4.2. Assessing Heritage Landscapes

Recently English Heritage, Cadw and Historic Scotland have each embarked on a series of initiatives designed to use landscape character assessment to improve understanding of historic landscapes in the British Isles. English Heritage's Historic Landscape Characterisation (HLC) programme considers the historic character of the English landscape. HLC is carried out at a county level and is closely associated with the Countryside Agency's Countryside Character Programme.

The HLC approach permits historic landscape character to be understood and managed appropriately and offers the potential to raise public awareness of the historic environment outside designated areas. In Wales HLC has been developed jointly by Cadw, CCW and the Welsh Archaeological Trusts and used to inform the management of the landscapes documented in their Register of Landscapes of Historic Interest (Cadw 1998). In Scotland the Historic Land-Use Assessment project was established in 1998 by Historic Scotland to create a detailed digital map of the character of the historic landscape of Scotland. Among the first tasks of this project were the assessment of the landscapes of the first two Scottish National Parks in the Cairngorms and Loch Lomond and the Trossachs.

5. Strategic Implications

The techniques discussed in this chapter each provide a useful tool to help decision makers evaluate the consequences of proposed developments and policy changes. None of them is designed to resist change but rather to ensure that change does not undermine aspects of the countryside that society values and will continue to value in the future. Landscape character assessment helps us to understand the nature and origins of landscape and how it may change in the future. It also helps to reveal what we value about local landscape character and in so doing provides a means of ensuring that our activities do not undermine these special qualities.

The quality of life assessment approach takes a broader view of the effects of development and uses a multi-criteria approach to assess how a proposed development might impact upon the benefits and services that a particular site provides to society. This may provide useful signals for the sustainable development of rural areas and in itself could form a useful precursor to more exhaustive and technical exercises such as Environmental Impact Assessment. The latter has an important role to play in ensuring that the impacts of development do not have a detrimental effect on the environment and local communities and works at various levels, both informing the design of development plans and helping planners to make decisions over whether or not to grant consents for developments to be undertaken. Strategic environmental assessment has the potential to provide important insights for sustainable development provided that it is informed by robust forecasts about the longer-term impacts of projects and policies in the countryside. As well as helping in policy design, this process may also improve the effectiveness of post-implementation monitoring and appraisal procedures by highlighting potential problem areas within a project that need to be examined on a regular basis.

What all of the techniques examined above have in common is their ability to be applied in a wide range of situations across the countryside and to provide important information to support the strategic management process. Each technique is flexible enough to permit adaptation to particular circumstances and they cover a wide range of concerns from the scientific to the social and aesthetic. One danger that they all face is the possibility of variable standards in application and the lack of any formal body to scrutinise their outcomes. Such variability will inevitably be reduced as the bodies responsible for using the resulting assessments become more experienced at evaluating the quality and scope of such studies. In the meantime they continue to provide decision-makers with a wealth of evidence which can provide considerable insights into how development can impact upon the countryside.

Strategically, it is important that these methods be applied proactively and used to identify opportunities to enhance the benefits that the countryside provides society, rather than merely as a means to protect the *status quo*. This requires a high degree of stakeholder involvement to ensure that the processes fully recognise the diversity of interests that developments can impact upon. Each of the assessment methods dealt with in this chapter is likely to be both better informed and more widely accepted if it fully engages with the appropriate stakeholder groups both during and after the assessment process.

References

Alder, J., & Wilkinson, D. (1999). *Environmental law and ethics*. Basingstoke: Macmillan.
Countryside Agency and Scottish Natural Heritage (2002). *Living landscapes: Landscape character assessment guidance*. Countryside Agency and Scottish Natural Heritage.
Countryside Commission (1991a). *Assessment and conservation of landscape character: The Warwickshire landscapes project approach*, CCP332. Cheltenham: Countryside Commission.
Countryside Commission (1991b). *Caring for the countryside: A policy agenda for England in the 1990s*, CCP 351. Cheltenham: Countryside Commission.
Countryside Commission (1993). *Landscape assessment guidance*, CCP423. Cheltenham: Countryside Commission.
Countryside Commission (1995). *The Countryside character programme*, CCP 472. Cheltenham: Countryside Commission.
Countryside Commission (1998a). *Countryside character. Volume 1: North East*, CCP 535. Cheltenham: Countryside Commission.
Countryside Commission (1998b). *Countryside character. Volume 2: North West*, CCP 536. Cheltenham: Countryside Commission.
Countryside Commission (1998c). *Countryside character. Volume 3: Yorkshire & the Humber*, CCP 537. Cheltenham: Countryside Commission.
Countryside Commission for Scotland (1991). *Landscape assessment: Principles and practice*. Battleby: Countryside Commission for Scotland.
Department of the Environment (1989). *Environmental assessment: A guide to procedures*. London: HMSO.
Department of the Environment, Food and Rural Affairs (2002). *Guidelines: EIA for use of uncultivated land or semi-natural areas for intensive agricultural purposes*. London: DEFRA.
Gay, H., & Phillips, A. (2001). Natural and cultural heritage – Exploring the relationships. *Ecos*, 22, 28–35.
Glasson, J., Therivel, R., & Chadwick, A. (1999). *Introduction to environmental impact assessment* (2nd ed.). London: UCL Press.
Hanley, N., Shogren, J. F., & White, B. (1997). *Environmental economics in theory and practice*. Basingstoke: Macmillan.
Hanley, N., & Spash, C. (1993). *Cost-benefit analysis and the environment*. Aldershot: Edward Elgar.
Land Use Consultants (1986). *Mid-Wales uplands landscape assessment*. Cheltenham: Unpublished Report to the Countryside Commission.
Landscape Institute and the Institute of Environmental Management (2002). *Guidelines for landscape and visual impact assessment*. London: E & F N Spon.

Lawrence, D. P. (1994). Designing and adapting the EIA planning process. *The Environmental Professional, 16*, 2–21.
Martin, J. (2004). Applications of landscape character assessment. In: K. Bishop, & A. Phillips (Eds), *Countryside planning: New approaches to management and conservation*. London: Earthscan.
Swanwick, C. (2002a). *Recent practice and the evolution of landscape character assessment*. Topic Paper 1, Landscape Character Assessment Guidance for England and Scotland. Countryside Agency, Cheltenham and Scottish Natural Heritage, Edinburgh.
Swanwick, C. (2002b). *Landscape character assessment: Guidance for England and Scotland*. Countryside Agency, Cheltenham and Scottish Natural Heritage, Edinburgh.
Weston, J., Glasson, J., Therivel, R., Wilson, E., & Frost, R. (1997). Environmental statements, environmental information, environmental assessment and the UK planning process. *Project Appraisal, 12*, 233–241.
Wood, C. (1995). *Environmental impact assessment: A comparative review*. Harlow: Longman.

Chapter 11

Country Sports and Other Private Goods

1. Introduction

Country sports provide one of the clearest illustrations of the ability of the countryside manager to deliver both private and public goods. They also provide a compelling example of the controversy which currently surrounds some traditional activities in the countryside. For the countryside manager the question arises as to whether new legal restrictions on country sports, such as hunting with hounds, fishing or game shooting, may reduce the public good benefits which they generate.

Long traditions of hunting and fishing in the countryside (see Rackham 1986) have been maintained by the owners of sporting and riparian rights. Typically, fishing and shooting are privately provided and are usually excludable. Such activities can therefore be priced and may be profitable to the provider. In the case of shooting, provision requires careful land management systems, that also produce other benefits, such as biologically diverse habitats, which may well bring pleasure to the non-shooting public. Rackham (1986) discusses some of the implications that sporting activities have had for the development of the British landscape.

The central issue in the provision of such private goods in the countryside is the way that the associated land and water is managed. This is particularly so in the case of all "sports of the chase," including hunting, shooting, fishing, deer stalking and falconry, where there is pursuit of a particular quarry. The hunting activity is extremely ancient, predating agriculture, and is surrounded by historic customs and laws, as well as being dependent on modern land use practices. As mentioned in Chapter 1, hunting used to be carried out in designated *forests* where the rights to participate were ascribed to the king and were tightly regulated. Fishing was also managed and fish were harvested for the table as required. Fisheries were often associated with castles, where moats could be stocked, and monasteries, where fish ponds might be used. Wild fish could be netted on rivers.

Initially the main purpose of hunting and fishing was to obtain food and the sporting aspect was subsidiary, although the reverse is now generally the case. Before firearms were available, dogs were used for hunting and James (1980) provides a long list of the types of dog used in various stages of the hunt. He also cites an important distinction between beasts of the chase and beasts of the warren. Wild populations important for food were carefully managed and medieval laws governed the extent to which forests could be used for grazing as well as rights to hunt in the forests.

Another designation of land was "the warren" which was an area where the owner had the right to hunt certain animals, whether for meat or to control their numbers. James lists hare, rabbit, fox, wildcat, wolf, badger and the squirrel as beasts of the warren, to which the roe deer was added in 1338. Fowls of the warren included pheasant, partridge and woodcock, and lark and plover could be added to the list.

The three motivations for hunting — to provide food, control pests or for sport, have varied in importance over time. Thus, whilst meat was important in medieval Britain animals once hunted for this purpose may now be treated as vermin (for example the rabbit). Originally, sport was limited to a comparatively small number of wealthy people, whereas now it is more accessible. During periods of rural poverty hunting rights have come under pressure from poachers, who risked heavy penalties if caught (Hopkins 1986). Deportation to the colonies was a common deterrent in the early nineteenth century. Illegal hunting is still discouraged but it is difficult to catch poachers and the deterrents available to the courts are comparatively minor. There also remains the notion that poaching is in some sense a socially acceptable crime.

This chapter briefly reviews the nature of private countryside goods before concentrating on summarising some of the key findings of two reports on the status of country sports in the U.K. These reports highlight some of the issues surrounding the contemporary debate over the future of hunting with dogs in the U.K. and illustrate the importance of participation in other country sports, notably angling.

2. The Nature of Private Goods in the Countryside

Private goods are those which are usually delivered through markets and the rate at which they will be made available is determined by their owners. They are called private, in contrast with the public goods we deal with in the next chapter, because it is possible to exclude people from them and because one person's consumption of the good precludes the consumption of that good by others. If one person catches a fish and eats it, no-one else can eat that fish. If a riparian owner wishes to have exclusive access to his fishing river he may exclude others from using it. Owners wishing to sell a good will be motivated by expected prices, both now and in the future, by the cost of making goods available, which is mainly the cost of production and delivery, and by the cost of potential liabilities to any other parties.

Two kinds of private countryside goods are of interest; first visitor attractions and second the various types of sport which may be pursued. Visitor attractions include the familiar, often historic, amenities of the countryside. Foremost among these are stately homes, and other sites with historic or wildlife associations, many of which are open to the public for the payment of an entry charge. There is also an array of private sites offering minor sporting activities, for example paint-balling, off-road driving or horse riding, for which people are prepared to pay. But the best known countryside sports are the so-called blood sports.

Attractions offered for private enjoyment share the common characteristic that it must be possible to exclude people from them if they have not paid an entry fee. Exclusion may be very expensive to ensure, especially on large unfenced sites, and in such cases private wardens or gamekeepers may help to secure it. Where exclusion is deemed infeasible or too expensive, the owner may fall back on treating the site as a public good, perhaps seeking some compensation from the public sector.

Where exclusion is possible at reasonable cost, the consideration of charging mechanisms must then be resolved. This issue is discussed in more detail Chapter 17. The National Trusts are probably the best known organisations that charge for access to countryside properties but there are many others, including charities and a wide range of public and private bodies. There are also some access points to the countryside equipped with voluntary contribution boxes. Such mechanisms may be an appropriate means of charging countryside users for access where the cost of collecting entry fees exceeds the likely revenue.

In the case of extensive areas of countryside it has also been possible to arrange access agreements with owners, through which they agree to forego their rights to prosecute people entering their land and, in return, receive compensation payments from relevant local authorities (see Chapter 14). For example, some shooting sites are extensive and are unfenced and on a subset of these, access is a right held by the public at large. In these cases, the existence of access rights qualifies the owner's right to exclude the public from his shooting area except on particular days when they must be informed that shooting is taking place. Such arrangements have been negotiated with landowners, for example in the Peak District National Park to ensure that access may continue but without danger to the public. In the Peak District there is provision for the negotiation of shooting management plans to regulate the relationship between shooting and access (Whitby & Falconer 1999). Such mechanisms are not necessarily straightforward where, as in this case, another section of the public wishes to prevent the sport from taking place. Then the owner may not wish to publicise his intention to organise a shoot because that might attract saboteurs. Sensitive management could achieve a compromise between these two positions. The 2000 Countryside and Rights of Way Act will open up further areas of open land in England and Wales for public access but owners will be able to exclude visitors on certain days of the year to allow sporting activities to continue (see Chapter 15).

3. Hunting with Dogs

Hunting with dogs and other "sports of the chase" may soon be a thing of the past in Great Britain. The original purpose of this activity was tied closely to the provision of food whereas today sport is the main motivation for participation. The removal of pests is an important rationale for hunting with dogs, especially in some upland areas, although where sporting methods are employed, involving large numbers of people and considerable expenditure, this activity seems to provide a secondary benefit. For example, Heydon & Reynolds (2000) demonstrate geographical variations in the rationale for fox hunting in England and Wales, suggesting that in some areas (e.g. the Lakeland fells in Cumbria) it is the most effective means of culling, while in others sport is the major motivating factor.

The debate about the future of blood sports in Great Britain has been under way for some decades and the first Blair government was committed to the elimination of hunting with dogs. In the event parliamentary time could not be found to honour that pledge but the commitment remains with the second Blair administration. In 2002, the Scottish Parliament banned hunting with dogs and it may only be a matter of time before controls or a total ban are imposed on other parts of the country. Previously, the National Trust had banned the hunting of red deer with hounds on its land in Exmoor following a report that suggested that the practice caused unnaturally high levels of stress (Bateson & Bradshaw 1997).

Those in favour of abolition see hunting with dogs as cruel and unacceptable, whilst some of those prepared to allow it to continue may take the line that it is a defensible traditional activity that the rest of society does not have the right to prevent. The latter libertarian position, whilst not a strong case, probably has wider support.

What are the strategic arguments for the defence of hunting? As discussed later, the economic arguments in favour of hunting have also been deployed and are generally weak. There is a measurable amount of employment maintained by hunting and this may be at risk if hunting is banned. However, arguments such as this are positing a counter-factual situation *without the event* in question, which is difficult to identify precisely. If hunting is to be banned what will happen to the horses and dogs currently maintained in order to participate in it and to the fallen stock that hunts currently dispose of for farmers? The answer to these critical questions depends on the extent to which some other forms of activity involving riding with hounds across the countryside replace hunting foxes and deer on horseback. If drag-hunting, involving the use of an artificially-scented trail for the dogs to follow, is taken up this could employ many of the horses and dogs currently used for hunting. In that event, the economic case for the defence of hunting is seriously weakened. It is difficult, however, to assess the likelihood of such an outcome and participants in the debate tend to substitute assumptions favourable to their own case (see Burns 2000).

Whilst it might be possible to attempt to predict the economic result of banning hunting with dogs it would doubtless be very expensive in terms of research resources and the result would probably not be beyond argument. In that sense this is a classical political problem where the uncertainties are such that they must be left for the political process to resolve. In that case, the role of the strategic manager is to assess the impact of any future legislation on the countryside she manages and design mechanisms which will re-instate whatever legitimate benefits are lost as a result of the policy change. This must be done within the existing legislative framework and initially without extra resources.

The report of the Burns Committee (Burns 2000) is a classic example of an attempt to feed decision-makers, in this case Members of Parliament, with the necessary information to make a decision. The decision in question here is whether to introduce a ban on hunting with dogs. The terms of reference of Burns were specifically: "To inquire into:

- the practical aspects of different types of hunting with dogs and its impact on the rural economy, agriculture and pest control, the social and cultural life of the countryside, the management and conservation of wildlife, and animal welfare in particular areas of England and Wales;
- the consequences for these issues of any ban on hunting with dogs; and
- how and when such a ban might be implemented."

The Report stresses that it does not try to answer the question of whether there should be a ban on hunting or to design a compromise solution, acceptable to the various parties involved. The resulting report is a unique compendium of information about hunting. For example, Table 11.1 summarises the information presented about the population of quarry

Table 11.1: Estimated population and annual kill of hunted species.

Species	Estimated Wild Population	Estimated Annual Kill	Kill as % of Population
Foxes	217,000	21,000–25,000	9.7–11.5
Red deer	12,500	160	0.1
Hares — hunted	630,250	1,650	0.3
Hares — coursed	–	250	–
Mink	18,000	400–1,400	2.2–7.8

Source: Burns (2000).

species and the annual kill through hunting. It is emphasised that these are estimates and vary in reliability.

In the final column of Table 11.1 the relationship between population size and annual kills by hunting is expressed as a percentage to give a comparative indicator of the impact of the hunting activity on the population. It can be seen from this that the annual proportion of foxes killed is much higher than for any other species but the possible margins of error, especially those of the total populations, would caution against placing too much weight on such calculations. The report discusses the impact of hunting on populations in some detail, concluding that a ban on hunting might actually reduce populations of some species because some habitats are at present managed with hunting in mind thereby maintaining populations at artificially high levels. The 2001 Foot and Mouth outbreak prevented hunting in many areas and Baker *et al.* (2002) found little evidence to suggest that a cessation in hunting had a significant impact on the fox population in either direction.

The comparative importance of these different sports in managing populations is only one aspect of their interest, however. For all of the activities, their importance is in the pleasure they bring to participants, and this need have little connection with numbers killed. Moreover, these numbers also reveal nothing about the comparative pain they bring to the quarry, nor the pleasure obtained from the hunt. It is also notable that most of these species are also hunted by other means — mainly with the rifle — and in most cases the main means of control is through methods other than hunting. Studies have shown that the hunt brings considerable stress to red deer and Burns discusses the extent to which the welfare of the different species is jeopardised by hunting.

Burns also examines the economic aspects of hunting, suggesting, for example, that direct employment generated by fox hunting is equivalent to some 6,000–8,000 full-time equivalent jobs. Of these 700 are directly employed by hunts. The key question is how many of these jobs would remain if hunting was banned? On this theme the report considers carefully to what extent the alternatives to hunting might provide a complete replacement for the activity. It suggests that the widely canvassed drag hunting alternative would not provide an effective replacement and that it is unlikely to be as widely popular as the present mode of hunting. Furthermore, the possible loss of jobs is small when compared with the numbers made unemployed as a consequence of the decline of many other traditional industries since 1945 (Ward 1999).

The question of replacement is one of the main arguments that has to be resolved if the impact of a ban is to be assessed. To do this the counter-factual situation *without hunting* has to be identified precisely and consequently it simply cannot be stated that hunting is necessarily desirable or undesirable. If that is recognised it tends to shift the weight of argument away from the economic impact of a ban and towards the libertarian arguments about the extent to which it is appropriate for society to constrain the freedom of citizens to pursue particular pleasures of their own choosing.

4. Game Management

A number of bird species are commonly hunted as game in the U.K. In lowland areas the pheasant and the English or Grey Partridge are the principal quarry species, while in some upland moorland areas the Red Grouse is a popular quarry. In wetland areas a variety of wildfowl fall prey to hunters, while mammals such as the hare and various species of deer are also hunted for the table.

Management of the countryside for game provides not only opportunities for sport but can have significant benefits for wildlife and landscape, particularly in lowland areas. These result from some of the land management practices adopted by estates that run shoots, or similar activities and include hedgerow maintenance, tree planting, coppicing, pond digging, building beetle banks, reducing the use of pesticides, woodland management and the creation of conservation headlands (Hill & Robertson 1988). The control of predators, such as crows and other corvids, by gamekeepers may also have positive benefits for some species of songbirds (Stoate 1994). Predation by foxes is also an issue, with the partridge particularly vulnerable due to its habit of nesting in hedge bottoms (Potts 1986).

The positive impacts of game management have been promoted by organisations, such as the Game Conservancy Trust (GCT) and the British Association for Shooting and Conservation, who make positive links between game management, less intensive farming methods and wildlife conservation (GCT 2001). Authors such as Ludolph *et al.* (1989) suggest that the wide rides cut through some woods to provide guns with good access to driven pheasants, have greater numbers and diversity of light-demanding species such as butterflies than the narrower rides used for forestry purposes. Other authors, such as Cox *et al.* (1996), point to the negative impacts of game management on nature conservation of some practices, including the siting of release pens in species-rich ancient woodland, the introduction of vigorous alien shrubs, and the creation of fast-growing game cover.

Of course the management of sporting estates varies as do the strategies for providing game. Some estates attempt to encourage wild birds by providing feed or improving woodland cover, whilst others adopt a more commercial approach breeding and releasing their own poults. Some practices carry risks, and excessive stocking or poor management can have adverse effects on wildlife. Problems such as these are tackled by codes of practice such as the Country Land and Business Association's Code of Good Shooting Practice (CLBA 2002) which attempts to set out means by which shoots can avoid environmental degradation. Other problems involve the conflicts that arise between game birds and natural predators. In the past the numbers of such predators have been kept down by shooting or the use of traps and poison. This has led to controversy in areas where endangered species such as the Red Kite have fallen victim to over-zealous game-keepers.

The positive impacts of particular game management strategies have been investigated at the GCT's demonstration farm on the Loddington Estate in Leicestershire. The estate, extending over more than 300 hectares is run as a business but farmed in a way that is compatible with game and the associated wildlife. The majority of the estate is arable land with significant proportions of permanent grass and woodland. Research by the GCT has established that numbers of certain birds such as the song thrush have increased dramatically since their experiments began in the early 1990s and point to reduced predation by crows and magpies as a significant factor in their resurgance.

Despite its many positive impacts on the countryside, game management is under increasing threat. Oliver Harwood, the CLBA's Head of Rural Economy, argues that shooting is facing a "death by a thousand cuts" as a range of issues make the activity ever more difficult to sustain economically. Problems facing shoots include: restrictions on game rearing resulting from animal welfare legislation; restrictions on marketing of game and use of lead shot through food safety and hygiene regulations; loss of the use of Emtryl, an anti-protozoal drug used to combat a range of serious infections in game bird populations; possible restrictions on the use of dogs; potential restrictions on shotgun ownership; and the effects of increased access to moorland and upland areas in England, Wales and Scotland following recent legislation on countryside access and land reform in these countries.

Better news for game management came from the subsidies available under the arable options introduced within the Countryside Stewardship scheme in England. These encourage practices that improve biodiversity (e.g. providing feed sources for birds and invertebrates, provision of conservation headlands and reduced use of chemicals) and help to restore conditions favoured by the Grey Partridge (Tapper & Aebischer 2001). Arable options within Countryside Stewardship also support the planting of small mixed blocks of cover crops within arable fields which if planted strategically can be advantageous to game species as well as providing cover and food for other species (DEFRA 2002). These options should persist in Environmental Stewardship which succeeds Countryside Stewardship from 2005. Other grants such as DEFRA's Farm Woodland Premium Scheme and the Forestry Commission's Woodland Grant Scheme already assist some shoots in providing funding for the creation and renovation of forests and woodland which may be vital in supporting commercial operations.

5. Participation in Country Sports

The current importance of hunting and countryside sporting activities has been documented by the Standing Conference on Countryside Sports for more than a decade in a series of reports (Cobham Resource Consultants 1997). The 1997 Cobham Survey is an interesting meta-study in that it provides a comprehensive collation of available research on country sports that allows conclusions to be drawn regarding the importance of these activities. The main challenge to those undertaking such studies is to be sure that included research is of an acceptable standard. Once this has been established the authors must then ensure that

Table 11.2: Number of providers and participation in countryside sports: GB.

Sport	Number of Providers	Number of Participants
Fishing		
Coarse	30,600[a]	1,640,000[c]
Sea	1,850–5,000	840,000
Game		820,000
Total fishing	32,500–36,000	3,300,000
Shooting and stalking		
Game, wildfowl and rough shooting	94,000	704,500
Deer stalking	3,650	14,500
Other	570	
Total shooting and stalking	98,220	719,000
Hunting		
Fox and Deer	230	183,000
Hare	125	32,500
Various	30[b]	13,500
Total hunting	385	229,000
Total, all sports	131,085–134,585	4,248,000

Source: Cobham Resource Associates (1997).
[a] Include both coarse and game fishing provision.
[b] Includes mink shoots and falconry clubs.
[c] For fishing the number of participants includes only single individuals.

the methods are sufficiently consistent across different studies to guarantee that results are comparable and, indeed, additive. We return to this question later, having summarised the main results of the 1997 study.

Table 11.2 presents a summary of the main findings of that study with regard to provision of and participation in countryside sports. The information here comes from a range of sources and the robustness of the sample estimates undoubtedly varies. The publication dates of the surveys reported range through the 1990s and the survey response rates from 23.5 to 100%. The latter arises where data are supplied annually by participating estates or where statutory returns are provided.

Perhaps the most notable finding from the report is the enormous participation in various types of fishing. This is obviously the most popular sport amongst participants and each of the three types reported commands substantial numbers of adherents. An important feature of the report is the efforts made to avoid double counting amongst those taking part in more than one type of fishing. This reduces the total participation, including multiple participants, by 1.34 million, to the reported 3.3 million. The grand total of participants in

Table 11.3: Direct expenditure on countryside sports in GB (£m, 1996 Prices).

Sport	Organisers	Participants	Total (£m)	% of Total
Angling	24	3,234	3,258	84.7
Shotgun shooting	115	255	370	9.6
Stalking	5	27	32	0.8
Hunting with hounds	17	159	176	4.6
Falconry	10	–	10	0.3
Total	171	3,675	3,846	100.0

Source: Cobham Resource Associates (1997).

all sports amounts to some 4.3 million annually. The study also estimates direct expenditure by both organisers and participants (see Table 11.3).

It is interesting that expenditure on angling dwarfs that for all other activities, accounting for 85% of the total. Note, too, that organisers' costs are generally small compared with expenditure by participants. Proportionately, the highest organisers' expenditure is on shooting, which would include mainly pheasant and grouse shoots. Falconry, still a minority sport, is as yet poorly documented. The total level of direct expenditure of all kinds is approximately £4 billion.

6. A Case Study of Competition Between Users

There is some evidence about the economics of particular sports that compete for the use of agricultural land and some of these are relevant to strategic management. For example grouse shooting has long been a traditional sport that has generated significant income for some landowners and pleasure for many others. The quarry here is the Red Grouse which is found in upland areas where heather moorland provides both food and cover for its young. Red grouse nest in the open and are therefore subject to predation by raptors and their habitat is commonly grazed by sheep. Many grouse moors are also prized areas for recreation and the interaction between these three land-uses (shooting, grazing and rambling) has fuelled substantial rows in the past.

These three activities have different requirements which must be reconciled in arranging land use. Those wishing to shoot grouse need a sustained population of adults that reproduces satisfactorily and successfully rears its chicks. The requirements of the shooters are thus a peaceful nesting period and low predator populations whilst the young are growing. This is well provided by a mixed age stand of heather, which generally requires periodic burning to keep it young. There have been cases of landowners, or their agents, killing raptors to reduce predation of grouse chicks. Moorland proprietors also try to minimise the use of their land by ramblers during the nesting season to avoid disturbance of the birds. Meanwhile those grazing sheep on this land, who are often the tenants of moorland owners, require as much grass as possible for their sheep and the ability to gain access to their flocks for supplementary feeding in winter. Left to themselves graziers would stock the land as heavily as possible and would not wish to maintain the heather. Under unregulated sheep grazing the heather would be likely to recede, as it has done in much of Britain during the past half century.

The problem of grazing management is exacerbated in some cases by the existence of common grazing rights which make it difficult to control grazing pressure. It has also been increased by the practice, for much of the last half century, of paying hill farmers a subsidy *per head* of breeding animals they keep on such land. Ramblers, wish to have access to the moors, with minimal restrictions and typically will have little sympathy for the shooting interest. These three competing interests pose a classic problem for countryside managers and has led to confrontations such as the "Battle of Kinder Scout" in 1932 (Stephenson 1989). This is an extremely intricate set of problems that has been under-researched as a result.

In a sample of 25 moors in Northern England and Scotland, Hooper & Whitby (1988) compared the income from sheep farming with that from grouse shooting and concluded that three types of moor were recognisable. First, eleven moors had let no shooting in the year of survey; a group of four moors had let shooting in that year but did not do so every year and a third group of ten ran its moors as a commercial shooting operation, letting shooting every year. They compared the net income from grouse with that from sheep, finding that, even for the latter group the net income from shooting was only a fraction of that from grazing sheep — although that need not mean that commercial shooting is unprofitable. The issue summarised here is complex and, because the various user groups have not been able to resolve the problem, heather moorland has been degraded. Another example which seems intractable is that of red deer in Scotland (Clutton-Brock & Albon 1989) where mild winters and the concentration of culling on males, which are prized for their antlers, have allowed populations to grow to such an extent that they are eroding agricultural and conservation resources. Many similar issues arise in the countryside. Where specific uses of available resources compete with others, such conflicts will continue to arise.

7. Strategic Implications

Many private countryside sporting activities have not been covered in this discussion. In particular, sports involving four wheel drive vehicles, mountain bikes, hang-gliders and small boats are now important and it is likely that participants in these sports will become more significant users of the countryside in the future. New activities will also swell the number of users of private goods in the countryside and their arrival will generate requirements for data where conflicts arise over access to resources.

Private goods are highly significant for countryside managers because they provide a very strong focus for many visitors to and users of the countryside for recreational purposes. For many, the associated activities also embody cultural associations that generate strong feelings that are both negative and positive. Because such goods are private at present this need not mean that they will always be private. The transformation possibilities between public and private goods are important to countryside managers because they determine who is responsible for their management. Furthermore, they also constrain the options for managing them, especially where ownership is an issue. Where conversion from public to fully private status is possible, management objectives could be achieved through regulation (e.g. through the planning system) or even via taxation. Where private to public conversion is contemplated this may involve an important change of ownership or property rights which would require political justification.

Having discussed the Burns Report and the Cobham Survey, we can compare and contrast their value for strategic management. Burns has the considerable advantage that it was paid for by the public sector and was addressed to comparatively specific questions, as detailed in its terms of reference. Consequently it is a much more focused document and it contains some information collected specifically for the inquiry. By contrast the Cobham Survey is a meta-study that draws together all available information on a particular rather broad theme. It thus faces the very considerable methodological challenge that it is presenting information from all sources available to its compilers. The cost of collecting such information would be very great and it is extremely useful as a starting point for anyone wishing to study this area. It cannot compete with Burns in terms of either accuracy or timeliness but, over time and with regular revisions being produced, it will probably become more generally useful.

The conclusions from these two reports are useful to countryside managers in different ways. Both present information about hunting, Burns in considerable detail and with some authority and the Survey offering a chance to assess the relative importance of the different sporting activities. Burns specifically focuses on one issue — the possible futures for hunting with dogs — whilst the Survey summarises a broader set of information and is less sharply directed to a specific issue. It is particularly useful in indicating the relative importance of different sports in terms of numbers of participants. From this comparison, angling emerges as the major sporting activity, even if we confine the view to inland fishing in rivers and lakes. Combining coarse and sport fishing gives a total of 2.5 million which is three times the number of people shooting and ten times those involved in hunting. This broad group covers a wide spectrum of activities from fishing in the local canal with cheap tackle to the most expensive sport fishing for salmon on Scottish rivers. The relative importance of fishing is highly significant because of its dependence on water quality.

However, an underlying reason for the production of the Cobham Survey is the perceived need to be able to promote and defend these sporting activities. What is happening to hunting today has already happened to shooting and fishing in some developed countries, and, indeed, has already happened here to a number of other sporting activities. When adherents of these sports need to defend their interest they will find the Cobham Survey and its successors a useful starting point for preparing their case. As Burns has shown, this is not just a question of the importance of these sports *per se* but depends also on their impact on all other values flowing from the land in terms of both primary products and conservation as well. Finally, decisions about the desirability of particular activities will be made by politicians and they need advice based on the best information available. In this particular case the Survey's authors are severely constrained by the methodology of the meta-study and are thus prevented from producing fully up-to-date and relevant information. When decision-makers recognise this gap in the available information they may feel a need to rectify it.

Meanwhile many issues of disputed rights and entitlements to use resources will raise issues for countryside managers. Some of these may be regulated through negotiation whilst others may require legislation. In yet other cases new technologies will facilitate more effective management as they become available. Such technologies may allow the "privatisation" of some public goods and in others they may offer other means of improving the way in which the countryside is used.

Acknowledgments

Thanks to Robert Earle for his assistance in researching this chapter.

References

Baker, P. J., Harris, S., & Webbon, C. C. (2002). The effect of a British hunting ban on fox numbers. *Nature, 419*, 34.
Bateson, P., & Bradshaw, E. (1997). *The behavioural and physiological effects of culling red deer.* Report for the National Trust, London.
Burns, Lord J. (2000). *Report to the committee of inquiry into hunting with dogs in England and Wales*. Secretary of State for the Home Department, London: HMSO.
Clutton-Brock, M., & Albon, S. D. (1989). *Red deer in the highlands* Oxford: BSP Professional Books.
Cobham Resource Consultants (1997). *Countryside sports: Their economic, social and conservation significance*. The Standing Conference on Countryside Sports, Reading.
Cox, G., Watkins, C., & Winter, M. (1996). *Game management in England: Implications for public access, the rural economy and the environment*. Cheltenham: Countryside and Community Press.
DEFRA (2002). *The countryside stewardship scheme; New arable options*. London: Department of Environment, Food and Rural Affairs.
Game Conservancy Trust (2001). *Conservation economics and game management*. Fordingbridge: Game Conservancy Trust.
Heydon, M. J., & Reynolds, J. C. (2000). Fox (Vulpes vulpes) management in three contrasting regions of Britain, in relation to agricultural and sporting interests. *Journal of Zoology, 251*, 237–252.
Hill, D., & Robertson, P. A. (1988). *The pheasant: Ecology, management and conservation*. London: BSP Professional.
Hooper, S., & Whitby, M. (1988). *Heather moorland management: An economic assessment*. Department of Agricultural Economics and Food Marketing, University of Newcastle upon Tyne.
Hopkins, H. (1986). *The long affray: The poaching wars 1760–1914*. London: Macmillan.
James (1980). *A history of English forestry*. Oxford: Basil Blackwell.
Ludolph, I. C., Robertson, P. A., & Woodburn, M. I. A. (1989). Changes in the ground flora and butterfly populations of woodlands managed to encourage pheasants. In: G. P. Buckley (Ed.), *Biological habitat reconstruction*. London: Belhaven Press.
Potts, G. R. (1986). *The partridge: Pesticides, predation and control*. London: Collins.
Rackham, O. (1986). *The history of the countryside* (2nd ed.). London: Dent.
Stephenson, T. (1989). *Forbidden land: The battle for access to mountain and moorland*. Manchester University Press.
Stoate, C. (1994). Does predation management benefit songbirds. *Game Conservancy Review, 25*, 55–56.

Tapper, S., & Aebischer, N. (2001). *Ecological evaluation of the arable stewardship pilot scheme, 1998–2000, Technical annex VI/3 grey partridge*. London: Ministry of Agriculture, Fisheries and Food.

Ward, N. (1999). Foxing the nation: The economic (in)significance of hunting with hounds in Britain. *Journal of Rural Studies, 15*, 389–403.

Whitby, M. C., & Falconer, K. E. (1999). Re-instatement, renewal or re-creation of access rights: The economics of a right to roam. Centre for Rural Economy, Working Paper 38, Centre for Rural Economy, University of Newcastle upon Tyne.

Chapter 12

Public Goods and Property Rights

1. Introduction

Historically many important countryside goods have been provided through traditional land management. Many of these goods have certain common characteristics that make them of particular interest to countryside management. Most important are the so-called public goods. While these provide society with a wide range of benefits, there is little incentive for private individuals to supply them, requiring Governments to intervene if they are to ensure that such goods continue to be available. Other freely available countryside goods are prone to problems of over-exploitation which leads to supply problems if demand is high.

In this chapter we examine the supply of public goods in the countryside and how this is influenced by the systems of property rights in place there. First, we introduce some key characteristics of countryside goods and show how these can be used to identify different categories of goods, each of which will raise particular concerns for managers. We then illustrate how the phenomenon of market failure has required Government intervention in order to ensure that society has access to the quality and quantity of public goods that it requires. This leads to a discussion of property rights and some of the different means available to countryside managers for increasing the supply of public goods by re-assigning these rights. This introduces a range of mechanisms underpinning government intervention, which are covered in more detail in Chapters 13 and 14. Finally, we examine the role of institutions, particularly non-government organisations, in the supply of public goods.

2. The Characteristics of Countryside Goods

A wide variety of goods are supplied in the countryside. Of those goods that interest countryside managers, many are produced as unintended by-products of other activities of particular land uses, such as agriculture or forestry. Such by-products are sometimes referred to as externalities (see Box 12.1) because their production is external to the market.

Externalities may either be depletable or non-depletable. Some goods, such as wildlife and common fisheries are examples of depletable externalities, where one person's use of the resource affects its availability and cost to other users. Non-depletable externalities are characterised by the situation that an increase in the consumption of the good by one person does not reduce its availability to others. The fact that an individual breathes clean country air can, as a reasonable approximation, be taken to leave the quality of air available to others unaffected. Similarly, in the absence of congestion, it costs virtually no more to admit 1001 visitors to a countryside attraction than 1000.

> **Box 12.1: Externalities.**
> **Positive externalities**
> Externalities which benefit society, for example landscape and recreational amenity may be positive externalities associated with agriculture.
>
> **Negative externalities**
> Externalities which cause a loss of well-being to society, such as the pollution of rivers and watercourses by chemicals may be negative externalities associated with agriculture.

Externalities are a major concern for countryside managers because their supply is not controlled by conventional markets, as is the case with normal goods. For example, if there is an unfulfilled demand for high-quality visitor attractions in the countryside, an entrepreneur may observe the gap in the market and arrange the supply of a new visitor attraction. The entrepreneur's motive for doing this lies in his ability to charge individuals a fee to visit the attraction and thus make a profit from the enterprise.

By contrast, where a good arises as the result on an externality, there may be little motivation for private individuals to increase the supply of that good. For example, most footpaths in the countryside originally developed as an externality associated with the need for local people to have access across agricultural land. If there is now a shortage of footpaths in a particular area, it is unlikely that an entrepreneur would arrange for new access routes to be developed. This is because casual countryside access through footpaths and bridleways generally does not attract a charge and with no possibility of profit there is little incentive for the entrepreneur to incur the cost of increasing the available supply. If the entrepreneur decided to open a new path and attempt to charge for access then it is likely that visitors would exercise their right to choose and use a substitute path. Furthermore, the entrepreneur would only have the opportunity to charge if they were able to restrict access to the path to certain points where payments could be collected. Many footpaths have multiple access points, making it difficult to exclude visitors.

The preceding discussion illustrates the notion that all goods, including countryside goods, can be described in terms of whether or not they display certain characteristics. A taxonomy of goods can be derived from three criteria related to these characteristics: the opportunity cost of their consumption; the property rights of the producer; and the property rights of the consumer (Winch 1971): this can be codified as (1,1,1) where all three attributes are present, and as (0,0,0) where they are all absent.

Private goods (1,1,1) are those that have opportunity costs of consumption (if one person consumes the good then it is not available for anyone else); producer rights exist which permit the owner to decide whether to sell the good and to whom; and consumer rights, which allow the consumer to decide whether or not to consume the good (see Chapter 11).

Non-congestion (0,1,1) characterises goods which have zero opportunity costs of consumption (consumption by one person in no way detracts from the good's availability to others), but which are subject to property rights: producers decide whether or not to sell, and consumers can decide whether or not to consume the good. Non-congested local authority country parks, museums, historic houses and gardens and a number of other non-depletable externalities are all examples of this type of good. Owners can institute a charge, but if some potential user would have derived utility from the good, at no cost to anyone (zero opportunity cost of consumption), but is prevented from doing so by a marginal price, the outcome is sub-optimal when judged against the criterion of Pareto optimality a test often used by economists.

The Pareto criterion defines as optimal, a situation where no one person can be made better off (according to her own judgement) without making someone else worse off. In theory, this state of the world occurs when free markets have resulted in the optimum allocation of resources to the production and consumption of goods and services. It thus depicts a pure level of efficiency in resource allocation but, importantly, excludes the problem of distributional equity between individuals. Although widely used as a key criterion in economic appraisals it nevertheless leaves the important issue of distribution to decision-makers to resolve by other means.

Open access or commons (1,0,1) is the case of a good where there is an opportunity cost of consumption, but exclusion cannot be practised by the producer, although consumer rights exist. Among the various forms of market failure affecting natural and environmental resources at an international level, the problems of open access and common property resources are dominant. Typical examples of this type of good are ocean fishing, radio frequencies, wildlife, and other depletable external benefits. In all of these cases, lack of ownership rights over the resource may lead to excessive exploitation and increased costs of consumption, for example to fishermen harvesting the resource. The open access problem can be solved by common agreement between all interested parties, and by governments assuming property rights over the resource or precisely assigning them to others.

Co-operative arrangements over commons generally seek to minimise over-exploitation. More generally the commons are managed by governments assigning property rights over the resource and regulating their use, as was done historically with the process of enclosure (see Chapter 1). More recently, the Wildlife and Countryside Act (1981) in England and Wales, was designed to help prevent the extinction of endangered species by making it a criminal offence to kill or destroy specified animals and plants and by protecting habitats, in which certain species are found, from commercial development.

Semi-public goods (0,0,1) are those with zero opportunity costs of consumption and no producer rights, but where consumer rights exist. Examples of this type of public good are radio and television reception: radio signals remain as strong no matter how many people receive them. In these cases there is zero opportunity cost of consumption and without a regulatory mechanism (such as the Television Licence) the producer cannot exclude consumers; however, a consumer can choose not to receive the signal. Provision of this type of good either provides positive or zero utility to the consumer. Consumer rights protect against the creation of a negative utility.

Pure public goods (0,0,0) are those with zero opportunity cost of consumption and where exclusion cannot be practised by producers or consumers. A large number of public goods fall into this category: national defence is the obvious example. Many environmental goods are also pure public goods: for example, air quality; flood protection; landscape; and nature conservation. The term "public good" does not reflect ownership, merely the particular characteristics of the good.

Garrod & Willis (1999) discuss the example of flood protection, which can be provided to residents and landowners on the flood plain by engineering works to the river bed, by raising levies or river banks, or by building a dam. The services are available to all at zero opportunity cost. Landowners cannot be forced to contribute to a private scheme of this type, and none can then be excluded from the flood control services except at great cost. Moreover, the benefits of such a scheme to any one individual are likely to be much smaller than the total project costs. Not only would a single individual contemplating such a project find it impossible to charge neighbouring residents, other individuals would have an incentive to become free-riders. This position is an example of the classic *prisoner's dilemma* situation where the optimal course of action for society is to institute flood control, but the gains to any individual are maximised by not participating in the scheme. Thus, without collective action this type of public good is unlikely to be produced.

Box 12.2: Key characteristics of countryside goods.
Ability to Choose
For some goods in the countryside it is not always possible to choose whether or not we consume them (except by not visiting an area); examples of these include landscapes, noise and pollution.
Rivalry in Consumption
There may be a level above which it becomes more difficult or even impossible to enjoy a countryside good. The notion of congestibility is similar to the concept of rivalry but on a sliding scale rather than in absolute terms.
Excludability
The right of the individuals who hold property rights over goods to exclude other potential users from them.

The taxonomy described above provides a useful framework for the consideration of a range countryside goods. Box 12.2 outlines the three key characteristics of countryside goods, while Figure 12.1 illustrates another common classification of countryside goods based on two of these characteristics, the ability to exclude individuals from the good and whether or not the good is rival in consumption.

3. Market Failure and the Supply of Public Goods

The classic public goods in the countryside include landscape, open-access recreation and nature conservation. As we shall show, it is likely that the provision of these goods will be politically determined. Some of these goods may, however, be provided by membership organisations, in which case they may become to some extent rival and excludable.

The failure of the market to supply public goods or to control public bads has resulted in a number of public strategies for their management. Public bads may be controlled by environmental regulation, taxes on pollutants or penalties to polluters. The supply of public goods may be enhanced by incentives for their supply and various other mechanisms.

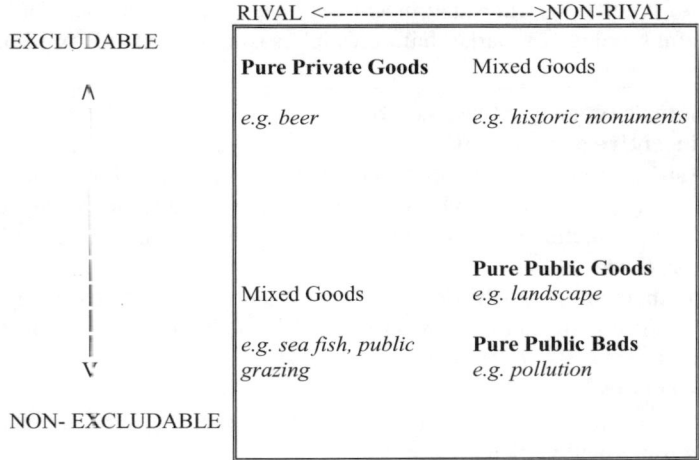

Figure 12.1: A classification of countryside goods.

Where the benefits of public goods are difficult to quantify, a cost-based approach to assessing priorities for environmental improvements is often appealing to regulators. This may be the case where budgetary constraints exist for specific environmental programmes. Governments thus tend to value environmental goods and services by estimating how much it costs to provide them, rather than by calculating the benefits of regulation to maintain or enhance them (see Garrod & Willis 1999).

The optimal provision of countryside goods occurs when the operation of competitive markets has led to an optimum allocation of resources to the production and consumption of countryside goods and services. In practice this almost never happens, the main reason for this being market failure.

Markets are places where goods are traded. While sharing many characteristics in common, markets differ through the extent to which they exhibit the following characteristics:

- freedom of information — how freely prices and other relevant information are available to all participants, and whether all producers and consumers are in contact; and
- restrictions that may prevent goods being freely traded.

The interaction between supply and demand produces *market clearing prices* that just exhaust the quantity of the good being offered for purchase.

Markets are said to fail if the conditions to achieve optimal economic welfare are not met. Government intervention in competitive markets, for example through subsidy, may lead to market failure. This can be illustrated in the loss of environmental quality associated with the intensive farming methods originally promoted by the Common Agricultural Policy in the EU. Conversely, governments may choose to intervene in markets that do not result in an optimal allocation of resources because of their economic structures. Examples of such corrective government intervention in the countryside include management agreements, and a variety of regulations, rules and incentives (see Chapters 13 and 14). Bator (1958) provides a useful typology of market failure which is summarised in Box 12.3.

> **Box 12.3: Bator's typology of market failure.**
> **Failure by incentive or by signal**
> Where price signals transmitted to producers or consumers fail to reflect social costs and benefits and where private costs and benefits do not fully include the external effects (i.e. externalities) of production or consumption decisions such as the pricing of fertilisers.
> **Failure by existence**
> Occurs where there are no established markets for the goods (or bads) being produced. Therefore there is no efficient pricing system which can be used to allocate such public goods and bads.
> **Failure by structure**
> Arises where there are not enough participants in the market to ensure efficient allocation of goods, e.g. rural land markets.
> **Failure by enforcement**
> Occurs where markets do not capture all aspects of the allocation process, as in the case where property rights are not fully defined by the legal/administrative system: for example the definition of the rights associated with common land; also where externalities of the consumption/production activity are not accounted for in the market mechanism, such as the pollution of rivers.
>
> *Source:* Bator (1958).

4. Property Rights in the Countryside

The concepts of public goods, rivalry and exclusivity direct our attention to the closely related phenomenon of property rights. Ownership of property is a key element in the economic organisation of any society. If land is to be efficiently allocated through market mechanisms, each of the multiple uses of land must have a corresponding property right that allows that use of the land to be allocated separately from all others.

The fundamental significance of property rights in determining the distribution of wealth in the economy is recognised by commentators on both sides of the political spectrum (though each side has their own ideas about the desirability of existing systems.). Commentators also emphasise the importance of "bundles of property rights," rather than the ownership of single assets and both sides accept that the prevailing system of property rights defines the legal and economic relationships between people and institutions. Based on this, what is the importance of property rights in the supply of public goods in the countryside?

The conceptual underpinnings of an answer lie in the economic theory of property rights, which amounts to a powerful descriptive model of land use, and indeed of the relationships between people in society. The theory has been modified and restated by many economists since it was first put forward in the last century.

Property rights are important because they are easily changed, and often inadvertently so, by governmental or private activities. The legal pattern of ownership of property rights is referred to here as the assignment of rights. Changes in the assignment of rights are important because they almost invariably involve transfers of wealth from one individual or group to another: in complete contrast with the *sale* of rights between willing agents. It is not surprising that the reassignment of property rights provokes argument. Important transfers of rights that took place in the last century include the nationalisation of development rights under the 1947 Town and Country Planning Act, whereby it was decreed that the rights to develop land were to be vested in the state. This was done without compensating the original holders of the rights. Other changes in rights which are important in the countryside arise with SSSI designation, where within a defined area of scientific interest those with user rights are constrained as to the activities that they may undertake (see Chapter 13). Box 12.4 illustrates some of the key consequences of changing the allocation of property rights.

Box 12.4: Key consequences of re-assigning property rights.

- Changes in the assignment of property rights almost inevitably lead to transfers of wealth from one individual or group to another, e.g. the Enclosure Acts.
- The assignment of property rights can be an important tool for Government in attempting to redistribute wealth or improve equity across society, e.g. nationalisation of major industries.
- Compensation may be required by those adversely affected by the re-assignment of property rights, e.g. compensation under the 1981 Wildlife and Countryside Act.

The theory of property rights seeks to explain the existence of rights and the relationship between their initial assignment and their final transfer to individuals who wish to use them. An important element in the theory concerns the costs associated with maintaining a given assignment, or with arranging a re-allocation of property rights. If the existing structure of rights encourages socially undesirable behaviour (pollution, for example) then a solution to the problem might be to redefine rights, separating the right to produce from the right to pollute and allocating the latter only to those producers who are prepared to pay for it (through buying a permit, for example). The feasibility of any such approach to re-allocating rights will depend on the magnitude of the costs associated with its implementation.

The importance of the assignment of property rights has been recognised by many commentators as a substantial, though largely political, problem. Distribution of rights is not only a matter of justice; it also affects the pattern of demand. This follows from the fact that changes in wealth, and hence income, will lead to changes in the pattern of consumption.

The role of governments in defining and assigning property rights is therefore critical to the efficient allocation of resources. Although theory indicates that this can be achieved irrespective of the initial assignment of property rights, this presupposes that there are no transaction costs involved with any re-assignment of rights and that the resulting distribution of wealth and income are acceptable. Since these conditions are unlikely to hold, it becomes apparent why many re-assignments of rights, for example through the planning system, are contentious.

It is important to emphasise that any given assignment of property rights is by no means static. Whilst the physical nature of much property and the ownership of it may be stable, the essential nature of property defined in terms of bundles of rights is perpetually changing. The two main factors responsible for this instability are changing demands and changing technology. Demands may alter as a result of shifting tastes and perceptions, as has been the case with the rise of environmentalism in the past three decades. Changes in demand may also result from demographic change.

Problems arise in the assignment of property rights when technological change introduces a new set of pressures in the economic system, the impacts of which must be borne by others. Those bearing the costs will seek remedy through the law and if necessary will demand new legislation or compensation. Legislation tends to generate new sets of property rights which switch asset values between individuals and groups. The social calculus applied here would require that the benefits to society as a whole, should exceed the sum of the benefits from the previous assignment of rights plus the costs of achieving the re-assignment. It would also require that the redistribution of wealth is fair and equitable. Depending on the effectiveness of such laws, and the costs of implementing them, society may be better off after adapting to new circumstances than it was before.

5. Multiple Land Use

From the above it could be concluded that a fully functional system of property rights must recognise the multiple nature of most demands on property. Under such a system land required for, say, grazing by sheep will be rented (or "owned") by farmers, whereas the collective right to enjoy the view of the same area of land remains the prerogative of the public. The landowner may own the exclusive right to shoot game on his estate, which he may rent to others on a daily or seasonal basis. Rights to pursue foxes on horseback may be acquired by the local hunt, and they may be obliged to pay for such rights at least to the extent of making good the damage that they inflict on other rights owners. Each of these multiple uses of land must have a corresponding property right which allows that use of land to be allocated separately from all others if the land is to be efficiently allocated through markets.

Other public demands on land are also recognised, including biodiversity conservation and recreational access. Also relevant is the concept of option demand, whereby groups and individuals may express enthusiasm for the continued existence of a countryside good in order to retain the option of experiencing it in the future. It is easy to discount such demands, but they are an extension of preferences for maintaining the existence of threatened species and habitats that an individual will never visit. If people have these so-called option and existence values (see Garrod & Willis 1999), and are willing to pay to maintain certain species and habitats, should they be prevented? Even if they are not prepared to pay, should their wishes be ignored?

A range of countryside goods are listed in Table 12.1. Ownership rights are indicated by whether or not others can be excluded from the good, whereas the other three categories

Table 12.1: Characteristics of countryside goods.

Good	Rival Excludable	Non-rival Excludable	Rival Non-excludable	Non-rival Non-excludable
Minerals	X			
Crops and livestock	X			
Fish and game	X			
Common grazing— stinted		X		
Common grazing — unstinted			X	
Linear rights of way			X	X
Heritage sites	X	X	X	X
Nature conservation				X
Landscape				X
Fresh air				X
Open access land				X

(user, occupier and public rights) become more evident as we move down the columns. Notice that the rival/excludable category of goods will require substantial transaction costs to sustain them in that condition. The non-rival/non-excludable goods also require substantial transaction costs if they are to be maintained. Such costs are usually less than would be required to move from one category to another, for example from non-excludable to excludable.

6. The Supply of Countryside Goods

In the U.K., agricultural intensification has led to a wide range of negative externalities in the countryside. As we have seen, Government intervention seeks to redress this with rules, regulations and financial incentives. A fully functional market system would ensure that the diverse rights in land match the demands of different groups if the land is to be efficiently used. Such a separation of rights would allow individual demands to be supplied more precisely. In practice, the delivery of many public goods in the countryside is achieved through an increasingly elaborate system of land use designations, which overlay the existing set of customary rights. These two systems are, in turn, being augmented by the activities of what are essentially private agencies set up to deliver countryside goods (Hodge 1988).

Bromley & Hodge (1990) suggest a radically different approach to these more traditional systems, where land managers are used to produce countryside and community attributes (CCAs) as well as conventional agricultural products. The desired level of CCAs would be set at a local or national level and enforced on farmers. This approach implies a shift in property rights away from farmers to society. Farmers would have to pay to avoid CCA conditions. In practice, property rights are held by both sides and a shift towards the alternative system would reduce externalities and the level of state subsidy.

7. Mechanisms for the Supply of Public Goods

The pressures on land use in the last 50 years have led to a reduction in many of the positive externalities of rural land management, such as hedgerows, hay meadows, wetlands, and woodlands. At the same time rising incomes and increasing demands for leisure and recreation in the countryside has placed a premium on these features. This has led to a rising social valuation of areas where traditional landscapes and landscape features have been maintained. While previous sections have demonstrated some of the complexities underlying the supply of public goods, this section attempts to summarise some of the mechanisms currently employed by Government to secure the supply of public goods in the countryside. This discussion is not exhaustive and a number of relevant regulatory mechanisms designed to prevent the loss of public goods, or mitigate against the effects of public bads, are discussed in Chapter 13.

Grant aid is typically used either for specific conservation purposes or to aid land purchase by voluntary-sector organisations. Conservation grants may be a fixed sum or a percentage of costs that contribute to the upkeep or conservation of items such as stone walls, woodlands, or hedgerows. A proportion of grant aid will be used for land purchase. Such investments offer the public good value for money because of the value that will be added by the purchasing body who will undertake site management and any tasks necessary to restore or improve the land.

Planning control has been used successfully in the U.K. since the late 1940s to prevent development from degrading the public goods benefits offered by certain areas of designated land. The role of planning regulation will be considered in more detail in Chapter 13 but its main contributions in the countryside include the designation and protection of green belt areas around large towns and cities and the planning restrictions that are in place in National Parks and other areas.

Covenants on land use As discussed in Chapter 8 these are legal arrangements between two people or agents, whereby one promises benefits to the other. In the particular case of land this may involve a landowner letting his land to a tenant on a tenancy agreement (lease) which restricts the agricultural practices the tenant may follow.

Covenants may be used by those wishing to promote conservation by buying land and then selling or letting it with restrictive covenants attached. Naturally the severity of the restrictions imposed will be reflected in the price or rent charged. The potential utility of such arrangements for conservation purposes would appear to be mainly limited by their legal complexity. These can be avoided by the agency responsible for the covenant making sure that its provisions are met, and carrying the associated costs of monitoring. Hodge *et al.* (1993) suggested that covenants might be used to provide longer term security to the conservation benefits secured through agri-environment schemes (see Chapter 14).

Management agreements will be discussed in detail in Chapter 14 but at this stage it is useful to point out that they can generally be classified as statutory or voluntary agreements. Various authorities, including the conservation agencies and the National Park Authorities, have statutory powers to enter into management agreements with individual land managers, for example management agreements in SSSIs. Some of these agencies can enter into discretionary agreements with land managers to conserve or enhance certain features such as stone walls, hedgerows or ponds, or to provide the public with additional rights of access.

This can be small scale (i.e. for features such as hedgerows) or large scale, with schemes covering landscapes or groups of landscape features across large geographic areas.

Public ownership of land has long been recognised as a means of securing public benefits associated with land ownership (see for example Orwin & Peel 1925) and is currently being promoted in some European countries, such as The Netherlands. The Ministry of Defence and the Forestry Commission in the U.K. already hold important areas of land on behalf of the public. The Forestry Commission is particularly active in promoting recreational and amenity use and has strategic commitments to biodiversity conservation. National Parks Authorities, Local Authorities, and the national nature conservation agencies all have legislative powers for compulsory purchase of land in order to protect landscape, amenity and wildlife values.

The public purchase of land can, therefore, be used to secure conservation benefits in the U.K. Land may be purchased directly by public agencies in pursuit of their recognised objectives. In practice, relatively small amounts of land are held in this way, for example in National Nature Reserves. The costs of public land ownership is the main barrier to this approach, though the capacity of the public sector to manage a growing portfolio of land is also in doubt.

More recently, as reported in Sections 8.5 and 8.6, the National Lottery has provided the resources for various charitable organisations to purchase land and manage it in ways consistent with their aims, which in many cases are consistent with Government policy on issues such as biodiversity conservation.

Cross compliance attempts to reduce the negative effects that agricultural intensification and price support mechanisms have on the supply of public goods. Cross compliance mechanisms link the right to price support to the recipient's ability to supply a public good — for example, set aside payments may be a condition for receiving cereal or oilseed rape subsidies, and livestock subsidies may depend on stocking rates. Cross-compliance measures underpin recent changes to agricultural support payments under the CAP, as payments are dependent upon keeping land under good agricultural and environmental condition.

8. Institutions and the Supply of Public Goods

Hodge (1988) emphasises the importance of stimulating the production of environmental benefits, rather than the more common objective of trying to prevent environmental damage. Protection of existing environmental benefits forms the basis of much regulation in the countryside (see Chapter 13), while more recently policy makers have attempted to change this emphasis towards one where environmental benefits are enhanced rather than merely maintained.

Such a change in focus by institutions dealing in the supply of public goods would lead to an environment which is of "*higher quality than is generally considered to be the responsibility of landowners*" (Hodge 1988). Hodge emphasises that it is not generally possible to reverse policies for controlling externalities to produce positive benefits; environmental improvement on agricultural land usually requires additional expenditure to that devoted to conventional agricultural production. In addition, organisations with different types of expertise may be required to facilitate this kind of change. Furthermore, a number of environmental valuation studies (e.g. Garrod *et al.* 2000) suggest that the general public tend to be willing to pay more to maintain current levels of environmental quality than to enhance them. This phenomenon can be explained by an examination of the underlying structure of property rights and the general tendency of individuals to have a greater preferences for maintaining current levels of benefits compared with increasing them to some hypothetical higher level.

Countryside benefits arise from variety and diversity in the landscape. This implies the existence of a wide range of benefit production methods from intensive and focused investment to absence of activity. Most countryside benefits have public good attributes and are not priced. Production of these benefits may require co-ordination of land-owners where scale economies in provision of habitat exist, Hodge (1988) describes this as non-separability of benefit functions between firms. Unless all actors work in unison the good will not be produced. Benefit functions may be discontinuous, producing thresholds at which sharp changes in availability occur.

Not all countryside benefits have all these characteristics but they are important enough to be recognised in designing policies and institutions. In designing such arrangements we should note that private agents in the economy are driven by the size of the profits which they generate. The private agent's ability to make a profit will depend on the assignment of property rights and the distribution of preferences. Where private costs and benefits are equated with social costs and benefits an "ideal" situation arises in that all benefits are captured and all costs paid.

To maximise this the economic agent will look for the best possible information. But, with location-specific public goods there is difficulty in finding the best allocation of resources. As there are few if any market signals for landowners to follow, they must understand the much more complex relationships between the familiar agricultural production elements of input and output and the less familiar habitat production relationships such as arable production and wetland.

Landowners need more information than for the strict control of pollution and beyond the production process. Such information signals must either be introduced from external sources, say by offering management agreements, or by creating new institutions to provide the necessary information. The objective of such a policy must be to minimise the sum of production and transaction costs.

9. Countryside Amenity and Recreation Trusts

Hodge (1988) introduced the term Countryside Amenity and Recreation Trusts (CARTS) to describe a range of organisation supplying public goods in the countryside. Examples include the National Trusts, the RSPB, the Woodland Trust and the Wildlife Trusts. CARTS have desirable incentive creating qualities. They can internalise many of the external benefits that they create by making them exclusively available to their members, whose fees for access and non-use benefits fund the organisation.

The constraints under which Trusts work are important. In the U.K. the law tends to separate political and charitable work. Thus, for example, charities are not allowed to become too heavily involved in political lobbying. Dwyer & Hodge (1996) introduce a typology of CARTs as shown in Box 12.5.

> **Box 12.5: A typology of CARTs.**
>
> *Primary Conservation CARTs* — nature conservation is their main role, i.e. buying and managing land for nature reserves, e.g. County Wildlife Trusts, Butterfly Conservation, Otter Trust, RSPB.
>
> *Primary Amenity and Recreation CARTs* — they acquire land mainly to provide public amenity and recreation sites, e.g. Buchan Countryside Group, Groundwork Trusts, Magog Trust.
>
> *Primary Heritage CARTs* — acquire land and landscapes because of its heritage value, e.g. National Trust, Landmark Trust, Oxford Preservation Trust.
>
> *Secondary CARTs* — non-commercial groups with aims other than CARTs but with similar management of open land, i.e. educational and recreational groups, e.g. Camphill Trust, Railway societies.
>
> *Source:* Dwyer & Hodge (1996).

Most CARTs wish to maximise benefits to members and perhaps also some non-anthropocentric benefits. CARTs have a number of features in common:

(1) their management of land may internalise the (previously) external benefits of land use. They may be able to make public goods excludable thus limiting congestion problems and ensuring revenue from their supply;
(2) they have an incentive to "produce" efficiently, minimising the sum of production and transaction costs;
(3) they can trade off the benefits of countryside goods and agricultural income, finding an optimal mixture, i.e. they have no requirement to maximise profits;
(4) long term ownership by CARTs drives them to take note of the long term consequences of land use;
(5) CARTS may acquire land and manage it optimally from the viewpoint of countryside and farming benefits;
(6) by running as a club they can share ownership, production costs and production benefits and can pool risks (Hodge 1988).

CARTs are likely to be more efficient the more homogeneous is their membership, the more closely management responds to the membership's demands and the more excludable are its benefits. (Hodge 1988). The ability of a CART to deliver public good benefits depends on its activities and, to a certain extent, on the level of altruism demonstrated by the people involved.

The National Trust in England and Wales (http://www.nationaltrust.org.uk/) is the largest example of a CART with over 2.5 million members (see Chapter 7). Table 12.2 reports the distribution of land use across the Trust.

Table 12.2: National Trust Sites (1994).

Land Use	% By Area
Hill farming	19
Lowland farming	23
Woodland	6
Parks and gardens	3
Commons	20
Coasts	17
Others	12

Source: Dwyer & Hodge (1996).

While a successful organisation the Trust is not without its problems. Many of these may be attributed to size and the consequent diversity of membership. At any given time the Trust has members who are for and against many issues of the day, for example development, road schemes, or hunting with hounds.

Boxes 12.6 and 12.7 highlight some key characteristics of two other major groups of CARTs the RSPB and the County Wildlife Trusts.

Box 12.6: Royal Society for the Protection of Birds (RSPB).

Largest conservation charity in Europe over 1 million members (150K under 18), and a large landowner with over 1,100 staff in 1996.

Registered charity. Gross income 1996 £37m, (cf. £30m 1994; £7 million in 1985).

In 1994 34% of income came from membership, 27% from legacies, 24% from grants and donations, 9% from enterprises — less dependent on grant aid than some CARTs.

Influential conservation and campaigning organisation with a clear single objective: the protection and conservation of bird species and their habitats.

Manages over 150 reserves across U.K. (across 250K acres), some with agricultural tenancies. 35+ reserves are used for teaching and field study. Claims 9,000 committed volunteers from almost 170 local groups.

Sources: Dwyer & Hodge (1996) and http://www.rspb.org.uk/

Dwyer & Hodge (1996) have carried out much interesting research on CARTs, including the County Wildlife Trusts who operate under the broad umbrella of the Royal Society for Nature Conservation (RSNC). On the basis of the data has collected from 47 Trusts, Dwyer & Hodge (1996) advance a typology of three separate groups, these are:

- *Type One*: the small group, having a membership of less than 3,000 and relatively modest incomes. There are usually fewer than five paid staff and usually include conservation, administration, membership and education officers. The latter may run a nature study and activity group.

> **Box 12.7: County wildlife trusts.**
>
> The county wildlife trusts, urban trusts and Royal Society for Nature Conservation have a combined membership of around 250,000 (from 115,000 in 1977).
>
> These groups are responsible for 55,000 ha, 0.26% of U.K. land area (30,000 ha in 1977). Their operating income in 1994 was in excess of £7 million rising from £0.5 million in 1977. Almost all County Wildlife trusts are registered charities.
>
> Wildlife trusts are involved in the ownership and management of over 2,000 nature reserves, though urban trusts may only have project-based control of management at some sites. They employ a growing number of professional staff, plus many volunteers.
>
> There are 46 U.K. Trusts, plus 50 urban wildlife groups all affiliated to the Wildlife Trusts Partnership.
>
> Most Trusts were founded between 1955 and 1970, with only a few new Trusts founded since the 1970s, e.g. Ulster, Sheffield, London, and Cleveland.
>
> *Sources:* Dwyer & Hodge (1996) and http://www.wildlifetrust.org.uk/

- *Type Two*: The developing and campaigning group. These trusts had grown sufficiently to develop strategies for conservation and environmental improvement. They may participate in the scrutiny of planning applications and provide environmental consultancies which earn them income. Many organise work programmes with mainly voluntary labour. Most of them have experience of combating environmentally damaging development, and most expanded over the 1990s. They tend to be well-known within their own county rather than having a broader field of operation. They run up to a hundred reserves from their moderate income and employ five to 12 staff.
- *Type Three*: The smallest group but nationally influential and with the largest incomes. They employ at least 15 staff and their field of operation extends well beyond the county to which they were originally attached. They may have helped to plan land management schemes which extend beyond their boundaries or successfully fought development proposals at public enquiries. They also produce research reports and lobby parliament. Some prefer to work through contacts within the establishment, whereas others work through the media. Due to their size and capacity to operate large projects, some have extracted environmental policy commitments from local industries and public agencies.

10. CARTs and the Supply of Public Goods

Hodge (1988) argues that the value of public goods and the costs incurred in their production, depends upon the assignment of property rights and the pattern of preferences. Ideally, economic agents engaged in the production of public goods should attempt to internalise all costs and benefits. Because benefits are the focus, Hodge suggests that information requirements may be more stringent than if costs were the focus (as in the case of pollution). Information is costly and it may be appropriate for it to be supplied by the agency for example in the form of management prescriptions or else to create new agencies modifying the structure of incentives and information. The objective of the new agency would be to minimise the sum of production and transaction costs associated with setting up the system.

Hodge (1988) argues for many more and smaller CARTs which would avoid the monopolistic position of agencies like NT and RSPB and promote specialisation in the benefits provided. He notes the following problems with CARTS:

(1) *Incentives and free-riding.* To the extent that they provide public goods, CARTs must cope with free riding. Insofar as they supply excludable goods they can use this to fund their activities. However, people may be prepared, from altruistic motives, to put up with some free-riding in a good cause. CARTs may create confidence in altruistic causes. Where CART operation is hindered by price distortions from other policies, then public support might be justified.
(2) *Spatial responsibilities.* These would vary with the type of benefit. For example, access might be of more local interest and conservation benefits more widely appreciated — even internationally. Defining appropriate spatial scales is important — if there are no scale economies to be reaped, then decentralisation to the lowest effective size unit has appeal. Some benefits will be identified more closely with widespread groups of people rather than according to spatial boundaries.
(3) *Inter-CART competition.* Where this existed it would allow individual's preferences to influence the provision of goods (at present often absent from countryside good provision). Competition could produce a varied range of options and a satisfying diversity of land use.

Access to funding does not guarantee control of land. Obtaining land depends on availability. NT has particular access because of its ability to hold land for the benefit of the nation under the National Trust Acts of 1907 and 1937 but there are few other such arrangements. Accumulation of land by CARTs takes time but it could be speeded up by giving them preferential access to land released by farmers taking early retirement.

Similarly, the high exclusion costs and diffuse benefits may make it difficult for CARTs to obtain land. Public ownership of land passed on to CARTs for management may be the answer to this problem. Substantial transfers of land to CARTs might engender a food shortage in the future if there was some major switch in demand. Such an outcome is, as Hodge concludes, unlikely but he argues that society needs to think more about public land management. CARTs have the attraction of offering land ownership with an incentive to provide public goods which would not be offered by private owners. But, non-excludable benefits and agricultural policy might warrant some form of public intervention.

Finally, Dwyer & Hodge (1996) make some predictions for the future role of CARTs which have important strategic implications for decision makers involved in managing the supply of public goods:

- CARTs cannot quickly replace private occupiers on the bulk of rural land;
- they will continue to work alongside the private sector;

- they will maintain their independence from government and agencies;
- they will continue to offer an alternative approach within a system that includes a range of land ownership formats;
- they will be more dynamic and entrepreneurial, seeking new ways to meet the demands of the collective interest within their resource constraints;
- they will continue to give weight to the needs of future generations;
- the interests of CARTs will continue to adapt in response to different patterns of public interest and conservation priorities.

11. Strategic Implications

One of the most important aims of countryside management is to increase or maintain the supply of public goods, while supporting the economic viability of those who manage the systems responsible for producing those positive externalities. In order to do this the following objectives must be achieved:

- implementation of an appropriate regulatory framework in order to protect and enhance public goods in the countryside, i.e. provision of disincentives for negative management;
- introduction of suitable incentives to promote the maintenance and improvement of public good provision in the countryside, i.e. the provision of incentives for positive management;
- achieving the support of groups and individuals engaged in maintaining or improving public good provision by ensuring that advice, assistance and resources are made available to them.

In this chapter and the two that follow, we describe a range of mechanisms that managers can use when attempting to achieve the first two objectives. Some of these mechanisms will also go part of the way towards achieving the third objective, though it will be important for managers to understand the dynamics and objectives of organisations such as the CARTS discussed in previous sections.

While Government intervention to protect and enhance the supply of public goods in the countryside is clearly of critical importance, the role of CARTs as niche providers of particular public goods will become increasingly important. The specialist interests of CARTs and their independence from prevailing Government and agency policies mean that they provide valuable diversity in the arena of public goods supply. If as Dwyer & Hodge (1996) suggest, CARTs become increasingly entrepreneurial, while retaining the ability to change their focus in response to the preferences of their constituents, then they may continue to lead the way in public goods provision.

References

Bator, F. M. (1958). The anatomy of market failure. *Quarterly Journal of Economics*, 72, 351–379.
Bromley, D., & Hodge, I. (1990). Private property rights and presumptive policy entitlements: Reconsidering the premises of rural policy. *European Review of Agricultural Economics*, 17, 197–214.

Dwyer, J. C., & Hodge, I. D. (1996). *Countryside in trust: Land management by conservation, amenity and recreation organisations*. Chichester: Wiley.

Garrod, G. D., & Willis, K. G. (1999). *Economic valuation of the environment: Methods and case studies*. Cheltenham: Edward Elgar.

Garrod, G. D., Powe, N. A., & Willis, K. G. (2000). Economic evaluation of River Hardham artificial recharge. Report to Southern Water. Centre for Research in Environmental Appraisal and Management, University of Newcastle upon Tyne.

Hodge, I. D. (1988). Property institutions and environmental improvement. *Journal of Agricultural Economics*, *39*, 369–375.

Hodge, I. D., Castle, R., & Dwyer, J. (1993). Covenants for conservation: Widening the options for control of land. *ECOS*, *13*(3), 41–45.

Orwin, C. S., & Peel, W. R. (1925). *The tenure of agricultural land*. Cambridge: Cambridge University Press.

Winch, D. M. (1971). *Analytical welfare economics*. Harmondsworth: Penguin.

Chapter 13

Protecting the Countryside

1. Introduction

Organisations in the countryside operate within a complex legislative framework, any changes to which may have important implications for countryside management. Legislation tends to impact on countryside management in one of two ways. One approach to legislation is to provide mechanisms for regulating activities in the countryside in order to achieve particular objectives. This is often done by altering the systems of property rights that exist within the countryside and which determine whether or not particular individuals or groups have the right to undertake certain activities in a given area.

Some regulations are therefore designed to remove or restrict the rights that people have to damage the countryside, while others assign improved rights to particular groups. Mechanisms designed to alter the structure of property rights tend to operate on a "command and control" basis and are based on sets of rules designed to ensure that the desired outcome is achieved. Those regulations relevant to countryside management tend to operate through the planning system, or through a variety of measures designed to prevent environmental damage and protect landscape, flora and fauna.

Rather than attempting to alter the structure of property rights, a second approach to legislation attempts to provide a framework within which individuals and organisations are provided with incentives for countryside management. These tend to be aimed at land management and agriculture and includes grants or subsidies that promote desirable management practices. The role of incentive-based mechanisms in the countryside is discussed in Chapter 14, which focuses on the use of management agreements. In this chapter we concentrate on the how legislative measures are used to protect the environment. Chapter 15 then discusses how both regulatory and incentive-based mechanisms have been used to increase public rights of access to the countryside.

This chapter begins by reviewing the role of the European Union and U.K. Government in constructing the legislative and regulatory frameworks that impact on the countryside. We then review a range of approaches applied to environmental protection by various authorities in the U.K. and examine the role of the planning system in controlling development and managing the countryside. The chapter goes on to discuss some important land designations and examines the impact that these have on various countryside management objectives. This is followed by a short section summarising some of the measures available to protect historic features in the countryside.

2. The Role of Government and the European Union

Although all U.K. laws are made by the Queen in Parliament, the bulk of environmental and countryside legislation is created under powers delegated by Acts of Parliament, or in the case of European law through delegated legislation (Alder & Wilkinson 1999). Many Bills also contain wide enabling powers, allowing potentially unpopular or controversial provisions to be brought in at a later date as statutory instruments. Parliamentary Select Committees, such as the House of Commons Environment Committee, review and debate existing and proposed legislation and have proved influential in a number of areas concerning the countryside. Most Acts of Parliament are instituted by Government, though in some cases new legislation is generated by Private Members Bills.

Much of the legislation that impacts on Britain's countryside reflects the requirements of our membership of the European Union (EU) or is influenced by European law and policy. In turn many of the drivers of EU environmental policy reflect international law and commitments. The structure and operation of the EU is described in Chapter 3.

EU environmental policy is embodied in a number of the treaties and programmes that have emanated from the EU. These have included five Action Programmes for the Environment from 1973 to 2000 covering issues from pollution prevention to environmental impact assessment and sustainable development (the latter under the Fifth Action Programme "Towards Sustainability" which was launched in 1993). Member states are bound to incorporate EU law into their own statutes and in some cases EU instruments can be enforced directly under domestic law. Indeed, even domestic laws passed before comparable European laws must be interpreted in line with the latter's requirements (Alder & Wilkinson 1999). Most EU measures concerning the environment are in the form of Directives which provide objectives which member states must then implement in their own way. This allows member states considerable scope to ensure that, wherever possible, the implementation of EU policy is moderated by national interests.

3. Strategies for Environmental Protection

A wide range of environmental protection measures impact on the countryside. In recent years many of these have been put in place in response to European Directives and implemented by the relevant Government Departments and agencies. Many of these Directives are informed by the needs of sustainable development, or by the precautionary or polluter pays principles, both of which are discussed below.

Because of uncertainty regarding the impacts of pollutants on the environment, it is sensible for regulators to ensure that caution is exercised when setting emission standards. Therefore the emphasis in any pollution strategy may be placed on reducing pollution at source, rather than relying on pollution treatment mechanisms. Environmental economists describe the logic underlying this approach as the "preventative principle." A more strongly framed version of this notion is embodied in the "precautionary principle," which argues that in the presence of uncertainty it is better to take precautions to protect human welfare, even if there is no firm linkage between harm and the proposed activity and despite the costs of such an approach (Hanley et al. 1997).

The precautionary principle is closely allied to the notion of sustainable development and reflects the realisation that we may not know enough about the potential effects of pollutants on the environment to be confident about permitting emissions. Its objectives have led to it being incorporated into a number of international law and policy instruments including EU law through Article 174 of the 1992 Maastricht Treaty and several subsequent Directives (Alder & Wilkinson 1999). It also informs the use of environmental impact assessment (see Chapter 10).

While such principles provide a cautious route through the maze of new technology that society is faced with, excessive caution could result in valuable opportunities being lost and the overall welfare of society being reduced. For most purposes a compromise must be made between the potential benefits associated with the adoption of a new technology and its possible environmental impacts. The preventative principle is less extreme and more amenable to economic arguments about the costs and benefits of associated activities.

The waste management regime introduced by the Environmental Protection Act (EPA) 1990 is based on the preventative principle (Alder & Wilkinson 1999). The same Act embodies the notion of integrated pollution control (IPC) a notion consistent with EU policy on co-ordinated approaches to environmental problems. IPC attempts to implement a holistic approach to pollution control on land, air and water, taking account of the processes that lead to pollution and recognising the inter-relationships between pollution across all three. IPC involves the regulation of emissions and setting of standards for control. IPC is informed by consideration of sustainable development and its objectives must be cost-effective (Alder & Wilkinson 1999). The BATNEEC criterion (best available technique not entailing excessive cost) underpins the IPC approach to ensure that the twin goals of environmental protection and economic efficiency are achieved.

Production of a good has various costs to society, for example, it may use natural resources and may cause pollution. These costs are generally not reflected in its market price. Adopted by OECD nations in 1972, the polluter pays principle (PPP) seeks to rectify this example of market failure. PPP stresses that the price of a good or service should fully reflect the total cost of production, including the costs of all resources used (Turner *et al.* 1994), i.e. polluters must internalise the costs of the use or degradation of environmental resources. To prevent trade distortion, the PPP should be applied internationally, otherwise market distortions will appear. providing a cost advantage to firms in those countries that do not adhere to the principle, and providing an incentive to consumers to purchase goods from sources where costs are kept low by a failure to manage pollution.

The standard interpretation of PPP requires the polluter to pay for the control of effluent down to an acceptable level, and not to pay for the damage caused by that pollution. This can be extended to make polluters pay for the damage they cause. According to Turner *et al.* (1994) the principle is widely applied but not generally as a way of setting specific environmental quality targets — rather, it is used as a source of revenue which may be given back to the polluter, e.g. as grants towards treatment plants. The PPP was incorporated into the First EC Action Programme on the Environment in 1973 and embodied in the Single European Act of 1986. Many aspects of U.K. law allow for the costs of pollution prevention to be borne by the polluter, or charges to be levied on those found to be polluting. The Water Resources Act 1991 and the Environment Act 1995 both contain provision for polluters to be made liable for the pollution damage (Alder & Wilkinson 1999). The PPP is not always, applied, however, and agricultural policy provides a number of examples where farmers are compensated for giving up the rights to damage the environment through their activities.

While the notion of polluters paying for the damage that they cause to the environment is satisfying, some problems exist with adopting this idea in practice. It is not always easy to identify polluters, nor to link environmental damage with particular agents. Indeed, in some cases it may be difficult to determine whether or not an externality associated with some process is a pollutant or not. The costs involved in monitoring pollution may be high, and when internalised within the polluting industry can lead to problems of competitiveness, particularly if the activities of the polluter are judged to be in the national interest (Turner *et al.* 1994). Even where polluters are identified, the damage due to pollution may be hard to define or attribute and the resulting costs may be difficult to estimate. Additional problems may also arise from the uneven distribution of pollution caused by regulatory mechanisms such as pollution permits or discharge consents. Economics provides a number of techniques (e.g. contingent valuation, see Garrod & Willis 1999) for measuring the costs of environmental damage, which though controversial, are applied by the Environment Agency in appraising projects.

4. Regulating Pollution on Land and Water

Pollution can affect the countryside in a number of ways. Later in this section we consider some of the legislation surrounding the management of water quality in the U.K. First we briefly consider some of the legislation associated with land-based pollution, particularly where it may impact on ecosystems or human health. Two important areas concern the control of pesticides and the identification and remediation of contaminated land.

Pesticides make an important contribution to human wellbeing. They enable crops to be produced more efficiently, reduce the contamination of food by toxic fungi, and control insects that spread human diseases. Pesticides also have the potential to harm humans and other species and they can have certain undesirable side-effects (DEFRA 2001). It is therefore important to control the use of pesticides, and the U.K. has a well-evolved system of pesticide regulation involving various government agencies and departments, the independent Advisory Committee on Pesticides and a range of committees and agencies within the European Union. DEFRA (2001) summarises some of the more important legislation relating to pesticide use in the U.K., these are supplemented by various statutory and voluntary codes of practice, notably the Voluntary Initiative on Pesticides which was developed by various industry groups in England as a means of avoiding the imposition of greater statutory controls on pesticide use.

The Environmental Protection Act (1990), as amended by the 1995 Environment Act, provides a regulatory regime for the identification and treatment of contaminated land. This is land where pollution could cause significant harm to human health or other interests. In England and Wales local authorities have the responsibility of identifying contaminated land following its own investigation or information from the Environment Agency or another concerned party. Following identification, the Environment Agency and other appropriate individuals must be notified and a consultation process about remediation will commence.

In April 2000 the Contaminated Land (England) Regulations 2000 (S. I.2000/227) came into force, providing an improved system for identification and remediation in cases where contamination leads to unacceptable risks to human health or the wider environment. Similar measures for dealing with contaminated land have been introduced in Scotland and Wales by the Scottish Executive and the National Assembly for Wales. The new regime provides explicit definitions of contaminated land based on the risks associated with the contamination and places specific duties on local authorities with regard to remediation. Liabilities for polluters are to be calculated in line with the PPP.

There are a number of important policy areas surrounding the management of water resources that have direct impacts on countryside management, including EU water quality Directives and pricing polices set by the industry regulator. Water companies have statutory duties to safeguard Special Protection Areas, National Nature Reserves, Sites of Special Scientific Interest, and other designated nature conservation sites. In addition, the Environment Act 1995 placed a duty on water companies to promote the efficient use of water by their customers, and to further the conservation and enhancement of flora, fauna and geological or landscape features of special interest.

The impacts of activities, such as agriculture, on drinking water are also important and 68 areas in England and Wales have been designated as Nitrate Vulnerable Zones (NVZs) under the EC Nitrate Directive (91/676/EEC). In England, 32 Nitrate Sensitive Areas were designated within these zones, predominantly in the centre and east of the country. Within Nitrate Sensitive Areas, farmers were eligible for payments to compensate them for changing their farming practices to reduce the use of nitrates which could contaminate drinking water supplies. The scheme was closed to new entrants in 1998 but payments continued to be made until 2003. Since 1998 various statutory measures have been implemented within NVZs to ensure that ground and surface waters are protected from excessive nitrogen from chemical fertilisers and manure.

Other EU Directives help to improve water quality and may impact on habitat management by altering consents for such activities as discharges and abstractions on designated conservation sites. The EU Urban Waste Water Treatment Directive and the EU Bathing Waters Directive each require greatly improved levels of treatment for sewage discharges. This will reduce local pollution, but will not address other causes of water quality such as run-off from surrounding farm-land of nutrients and chemicals. The EU Water Framework Directive (2000/60/EC) provides better protection for the aquatic environment by improving the regulation of certain toxic substances that have a negative impact on certain key habitats.

While regulations exist to protect the countryside, the responsible agencies have a choice about the manner in which they enforce them. Lowe *et al.* (1997) provide an example of the sensitive use of regulation in their study of farm waste management. Prior to the 1980s waste management on farms was covered by a system of voluntary regulation based on codes of practice. From the mid 1980s concern about farm-level pollution increased as more pollution incidents occurred and productivity became less important. At the same time a number of contributory factors (e.g. the possible privatisation of water authorities and a deterioration in river quality) led to an increase in the pressure for increased regulation of farm-based pollution. By 1987 the House of Commons Environment Committee was calling for a "far more interventionist and regulatory approach to farm pollution."

The National Rivers Authority (later to be subsumed into the Environment Agency) was subsequently granted enhanced powers to deal with farm waste. Pollution inspectors were given new authority to deal with farm waste pollution and to prosecute offenders where appropriate. However, Lowe & Ward (1997) point out that following this increase in regulatory power only 10% of farm pollution incidents resulted in prosecution. They go on to suggest that pollution inspectors only prosecuted as a result of serious incidents or in pursuit of "rogue farmers" who were persistent deliberate offenders. They argue that this approach to regulation secures better co-operation from farmers as it is more consistent their own notions of justice and fairness.

5. Development Planning

The Town and Country Planning system embodies a number of fundamental measures to regulate the rate and location of development. After some initial experiments in the inter-war period, the first major planning instrument was the 1947 Town and Country Planning Act. Under this Act the post-war Labour Government effectively "nationalised" the right to develop land, giving county councils unprecedented powers to control development. This radical change constituted a major shift in the assignment of property rights in land, by requiring landowners wishing to develop their land to ask permission to do so. The main exemptions to development control under the Act were agriculture and forestry. Other powers included in the Act were the designation of "green belt" and "green wedges" in and around towns to act as recreational resources and buffers against development and the establishment of Tree Preservation Orders to control the felling of trees on amenity grounds (Gilg 1996).

Critical to such a system, is the means of knowing where the planned development will occur. Such information was to be published by local authorities in a development plan which indicated how land use was to evolve in its area. The plan set out broad proposals for land use in its area and landowners could then see where they were likely to be allowed to develop. The related activity, in effect implementing the plan, was the so-called development control process. Would-be developers were required to seek permission to develop and their proposals would be scrutinised by a development control committee and permission would be granted or denied (Cullingworth & Nadin 2002).

In the case of major developments, or following appeals against the decisions of the local authority, a public inquiry may be called where the planning inspector will hear evidence for and against the development. The verdict is then confirmed or rejected by the Secretary of State, with a right to appeal to the High Court against the decision. One such appeal which recently proved unsuccessful, concerned the decision of the planning inspector to uphold Teesdale District Council's rejection of an application by National Wind Power to build a wind farm consisting of 25 turbines, each 54 metres tall, near Barnard Castle, County Durham. The development would have been on the borders of the North Pennines Area of Outstanding Natural Beauty and the Yorkshire Dales National Park and the public inquiry found that it would have a "discordant visual impact" on surrounding landscapes (Countryside Agency 2000a).

Until recently, development strategies have been encompassed within either Structure Plans, Local Plans or Unitary Development Plans (combined Structure and Local Plans for metropolitan areas). Structure plans were introduced by the 1968 Town and Country Planning Act, and are drawn up by county councils to set the overall planning policy framework within which district councils develop Local Plans. The latter were established by the 1971 Act, and contain detailed policies and proposals set within the context of the structure plan. The 2004 Town Planning and Compulsory Purchase Act will abolish Structure Plans and replace Local Plans and Unitary Development Plans with Local Development Frameworks (LDFs). In addition, the Minerals and Waste Plans produced by county councils will be replaced by new Minerals and Waste Development Frameworks.

LDFs will be prepared individually by the relevant district, unitary and National Park authorities and will comprise a series of Local Development Documents (LDDs), some of which will act as development plans and others as supplementary planning guidance. Regulation will inform local authorities which LDDs they are obliged to produce. The framework for production of these documents will be set out in a Local Development Scheme.

One important aspect of LDFs, is that they should contain a "Statement of Community Involvement," which will set out how the local community will be involved in both the continuing review of the Framework and in consultation over planning applications. Community involvement is an important issue, as LDFs are obliged to take account of local priorities and strategies. Under the 2000 Local Government Act local authorities have a duty to develop Community Strategies in conjunction with other public, private and community sector organisations. These should promote the economic, social and environmental well-being of their areas and contribute to the achievement of sustainable development. LDFs must be informed by these Strategies and should provide a mechanism to help them to achieve some of their objectives.

6. Planning Guidance

The numerous planning acts since the war have often been worded in a rather vague way that deliberately leaves room for interpretation in the line with contemporary Government policy or to suit particular circumstances (Gilg 1996). Since 1988 such interpretation has been provided by Planning Policy Guidance notes (PPGs) for statutory planning, which have covered a range of development issues as shown in Box 13.1 PPGs have been supported by a series of Regional Planning Guidance Notes which provide a more local perspective on planning issues. As well as helping with the interpretation of legislation, PPGs and Regional Planning Guidance Notes inform development plans. Other guidance is provided by the Royal Town Planning Institute and statutory bodies such as the Countryside Agency (e.g. Countryside Agency 2000b).

The 2004 Planning and Compulsory Purchase Act introduced Regional Spatial Strategies (RSS) to replace Regional Planning Guidance. These should be consistent with national policy and will outline specific regional or sub-regional policies, whilst addressing the location of major development proposals. The change in name reflects how the planning system is gradually moving away from a focus on land use to a more spatial-based approach more in line with regional development.

> **Box 13.1: Current national planning policy guidance notes.**
>
> **PPG 1**: General Policy and Principles
> **PPG 2**: Green Belts
> **PPG 3**: Housing
> **PPG 4**: Industrial and Commercial Development and Small Firms
> **PPG 5**: Simplified Planning Zones
> **PPG 6**: Town Centres and Retail Development
> **PPG 7**: The Countryside: environmental quality & economic & social development
> **PPG 8**: Telecommunications
> **PPG 9**: Nature Conservation
> **PPG 10**: Planning and Waste Management
> **PPG 11**: Regional Planning
> **PPG 12**: Development Plans
> **PPG 13**: Transport
> **PPG 14**: Development on Unstable Land
> **PPG 15**: Planning and the Historic Environment
> **PPG 16**: Archaeology and Planning
> **PPG 17**: Sport and Recreation
> **PPG 18**: Enforcing Planning Control
> **PPG 19**: Outdoor Advertisement Control
> **PPG 20**: Coastal Planning
> **PPG 21**: Tourism
> **PPG 22**: Renewable Energy
> **PPG 23**: Planning and Pollution Control
> **PPG 24**: Planning and Noise
> **PPG 25**: Development and Flood Risk

Other reforms to the planning system are under consideration, including a review of all PPGs. PPG 7 on the countryside will be one of the first to be reviewed. Revised PPGs should be shorter and clearer and in the future it will be easier to separate guidance on policies that must be followed, from advice that can be interpreted in a more flexible way.

7. The Planning System and Countryside Management

The protection of the countryside has always been one of the main motivations for the existence system of development control in the U.K. Following their foundation in 1926, the organisation now known as the Campaign to Protect Rural England (CPRE) was among the first bodies to campaign against urban sprawl. Their efforts soon bore fruit with the 1932 Town and Country Planning Act and the 1935 Restriction on Ribbon Development Act. The former was the first piece of legislation to accept the need for universal rural planning. As we shall see in the next section, the CPRE's efforts to achieve the establishment of National Parks were also to prove successful.

Regulation through the planning system provides important safeguards for a number of land uses in the countryside. For example, policies in statutory development plans are important to the long-term protection of landscape and biodiversity in that they set out the framework for land-use change. Since the enactment of the Planning and Compensation Act 1991, they provide a key reference in determining development applications. Powers under the Town and Country Planning Act 1990, as amended by the Planning and Compensation Act 1991, are regulatory; although planning also has a role in co-ordinating efforts amongst organisations promoting environmental improvements and searching for funding sources (Cullingworth & Nadin 2002).

In general, planning authorities now place more emphasis on protecting landscape and wildlife, both in formulating development plans and in reaching decisions on development applications, through the use of procedures such as environmental impact assessment (see Chapter 10). These plans are also informed by other priorities such as the maintenance of landscape character (see Chapter 10) and biodiversity action planning (see Chapter 5). In addition, as local authorities increasingly pursue Local Agenda 21 policies, this too results in greater action to protect and conserve wildlife species and habitats especially at local levels. In these cases planning policy will support particular countryside management objectives, a tendency which will continue if sustainability continues to be the driving force in future planning policy.

Section 106 agreements under the Town and Country Planning Act 1990, permit local authorities to enter into planning agreements with any person having rights to land, to secure "planning gain." Planning gain accrues when, in connection with obtaining planning permission, the developer offers or is obliged to incur some expenditure, surrender some right or concede some other benefit which could not be embodied a valid planning condition. Section 106 agreements have been used in a number of cases to negotiate developer's contributions to the delivery of country parks, nature reserves, footpaths and woodland planting (Countryside Agency 2000c). One such example of planning gain, was reported at Coulby Newham near Middlesborough where, alongside a major new housing scheme, developers have been involved in tree planting, hedge-laying, the creation of new footpaths and cycleways, and have helped to pay for a new nature reserve (Countryside Agency 2000c).

Local Agenda 21 policies may have regional impacts and help to contribute towards some management objectives. Occasionally, local planning authorities have, in partnership with other organisations, secured funding for wildlife projects, often where this contributes to wider community benefits. For example, as part of its project to restore the coastline, Durham County Council set aside £1.3 million to acquire or seek the donation of land for the creation and management of semi-natural habitats in conjunction with the National Trust (see Leonard 1998).

The granting of new development rights may conflict with some aspects of countryside management. These conflicts will vary geographically, as development pressures are stronger in some regions than in others. Removal of the constraints on the use of prime agricultural land for the commercial and housing developments could, for example, have serious long-term effects on habitat and recreational management.

A more strategic consideration of countryside management issues in the planning system would offer the potential to help deliver particular objectives and the new Regional Spatial Strategies may introduce measures that have positive impacts on countryside management. Similar progress may be made following reviews of Planning Policy Guidance.

Future reviews of planning policy may lead to a greater emphasis on "positive planning." An illustration of this, is the recent work of the Countryside Agency on concept statements with local planning authorities in England (Countryside Agency 2003). These documents aim to support sustainable development by identifying appropriate locations and building designs for proposed developments. This should make planned developments more acceptable to local communities and thus reduce the time taken by planning authorities to make decisions. Unlike traditional development briefs, concept statements concentrate on creating "a better place to live" rather than merely seeking to overcome the normal constraints on development (Countryside Agency 2003). By providing a brief and clear statement of the type of place a new development should create, and how this will contribute towards the vision of the local authority, a concept statement should provide better information to local communities and facilitate a more informed level of debate about proposals. The emphasis on environmental quality within concept statements is consistent with both the Landscape Character and Quality of Life Assessment approaches documented in Chapter 10. Moves towards more positive planning legislation will represent a significant advance away from policies of the last half-century which have retained the duality between planning on the one hand and its implementation through development control on the other.

The process of planning involves designation of land for particular use categories. Designation is a quite general system of regulating land use and it is used in an array of contexts in the U.K. Thus there are many policies regarding land use which begin by designating the land to which they apply. Some of the key land use designations are covered in the following sections. Others, such as sites of local conservation interest or sites of nature conservation importance, which occur at a more local level and are the responsibility of the local authority, are not discussed here.

8. The Creation of National Parks

In 1872 the United States became the first country to designate National Parks, with Yellowstone being the first site to be so honoured. The National Park concept grew from these beginnings and in 1916 the U.S. set up their own National Park Service. A number of other countries followed the example of the United States but it was not until the late 1920s that any substantial campaign was launched for National Parks in the U.K.

Among the leading lights of this movement were the CPRE and other organisations whose membership had an interest in outdoor recreation (Evans 1992). This campaign led to the formation of the Addison Committee in 1929 with the objective of investigating the feasibility of establishing National Parks in the U.K. as a vehicle for promoting recreation and nature conservation. This small victory focused the conservation movement and resulted in considerable activity and lobbying. The eventual publication of the Addison Report in 1932 was favourable to the notion of National Parks but offered little practical guidance towards their creation and, indeed, somewhat confused the issue by making a distinction between the need for "National Reserves" for conservation purposes and "Regional Reserves" near towns for access and recreation (Curry 1994).

In 1936 the Standing Committee on National Parks was formed. This comprised of a consortium of the CPRE, the Friends of the Lake District, the newly formed Ramblers

Association and a number of other sympathetic organisations. One of the main achievements of the Standing Committee was the publication of "The Case for the National Parks" a short, but widely circulated, pamphlet setting out their definition of a National Park and proposing separate National Parks Commissions for England and Wales, and Scotland (Evans 1992). Pressure from this group was probably at least partly responsible for the much derided 1939 Access to the Mountains Act, a weak piece of legislation that made no significant impacts on improving access to the countryside (Evans 1992; Gilg 1996).

The formal designation of National Parks and Areas of Outstanding Natural Beauty (AONB) in Great Britain moved closer following the report of the Scott Committee of 1941, which reviewed rural land use issues, including the provision of amenity land. In 1942, at the heart of the Second World War, the Government decided that following the conflict it would establish the first British National Parks. John Dower, a leading member of the Standing Committee on National Parks, was asked to set up a study into the feasibility of this plan. Dower was a veteran of this debate and had previously circulated a list of 20 potential National Parks for Great Britain covering some one third of the total land area and worked on policy strategies for National Park designation (Evans 1992). In May 1945 Dower published the report "National Parks in England and Wales" (Dower 1945).

Unlike Addison, Dower did not consider that there was a need for separate types of National Park to deal with conservation and recreation, rather he considered that the needs of recreation would provide ample justification for the conservation of the relevant areas (Curry 1994). Dower suggested three categories of nationally important landscape. The first two categories included those landscapes that should at some stage be designated as National Parks, while the third category listed a further 34 areas that, while not suitable for designation as National Parks, were nevertheless important areas of natural beauty that had an important role to play in terms of public amenity.

The Dower Report became the blueprint for National Parks within the U.K. Box 13.2 summarises the main elements of Dower's vision for National Parks. The report recommended some 22 potential parks, a personal selection made *"in close accord with the consensus of informed opinion."* The question remained of how of to embody Dower's

---

Box 13.2: Dower's vision for National Parks.

A National Park may be defined in application to Great Britain as an extensive area of beautiful and relatively wild country in which, for the Nation's benefit, and by appropriate national decision and action:

(a) the characteristic landscape beauty is strictly preserved;
(b) access and facilities for public open-air enjoyment are amply provided;
(c) wildlife and buildings and places of architectural and historic interest are suitably protected, while
(d) established farming use is effectively maintained.

Source: Dower (1945).

ideas in legislation at a time when a number of vested interests vigorously opposed to the designation of National Parks in their areas.

The Hobhouse Committee, established in 1945, continued the work begun by Dower and made the final decisions on recommending areas for designation. In 1947 the Committee made its recommendations on National Parks, which largely followed those of Dower (Hobhouse 1947a). Overall, the report suggested that the bulk of the designated area should be uplands, with some lowland areas such as the South Downs and Norfolk Broads also designated. In all, 12 areas were suggested as potential National Parks, with a further 52 designated conservation areas (Evans 1992). Areas of high landscape and conservation value in Scotland were felt to be under insufficient pressure to require their designation as National Parks, though many were eventually designated as National Scenic Areas under which some additional development control powers became available (Gilg 1996). This lower-level designation (similar to an AONB designation in England and Wales) was in spite of several reports on behalf of the Scottish Council for National Parks which suggested five priority and three reserve National Parks (see Evans 1992 for details).

Following the work of Dower and the Hobhouse Committee, the National Parks and Access to the Countryside Act became law in March 1949. The passage of the Act was probably eased by the fact that Lewis Silkin the Minister of Town and Country Planning and Hugh Dalton, the Chancellor of the Exchequer had both been active in the Ramblers' Association (Curry 1994). The Act provided the legal framework for the creation of National Parks in England and Wales as areas of:

> beautiful and relatively wild country in which landscape beauty is strictly preserved; access and facilities for open-air enjoyment are amply provided; wildlife and places of historic interest are suitably protected and established farming use is effectively maintained.

Paragraph 35 of the 1949 Act sets out that the "*essential requirements of a National Park are that it should have great natural beauty, a high value for open-air recreation and substantial continuous extant.*" The term "natural beauty" is not explained but some clue is provided by the interpretation section of the Act, where in paragraph 114.2 there is a reference to the "*preservation of flora and fauna and geological and physiographical features.*" This emphasises the importance of the underlying physical features of landscape as well as the wildlife interest to be found there. No formal definition of natural beauty was provided until the 1968 Countryside Act.

The 1949 Act also provided the basis for the establishment of the National Parks Commission in England and Wales, an overarching body to provide advice and guidance for the individual Parks. The 1968 Countryside Act led to this body being replaced by the Countryside Commission, an organisation with a far wider range of responsibilities over the countryside. Previously the Countryside (Scotland) Act of 1967 had paved the way for the establishment of a similar organisation in Scotland.

The designation of the 10 new National Parks (see Table 13.1) did not occur until the 1950s when, as Gilg (1996) and Evans (1992) point out, a range of issues regarding the objectives, management and resourcing of the new Parks came to light. Conflicts arose at a management level where, following Dower's vision, the local National Parks Committees

Table 13.1: National Parks in England and Wales 2003/2004.

National Park	Year Established	Annual Visit Days (Millions)	Population (1991)	Area (Hectares)
Brecon Beacons	1957	7	32,000	135,144
Dartmoor	1951	4	29,100	95,570
Exmoor	1954	1.4	10,645	69,280
Lake District	1951	22	229,198	229,198
Norfolk & Suffolk Broads	1989	5.4	5,500	30,292
North York Moors	1952	8	25,500	143,603
Northumberland	1956	1.5	2,200	104,947
Peak District	1951	19	38,100	143,833
Pembrokeshire Coast	1952	4.7	22,842	62,000
Snowdonia	1951	10.5	26,251	214,159
Yorkshire Dales	1954	9	17,980	176,869

Source: Council for National Parks, www.cnp.org.uk.

were told to manage the Parks to both preserve natural beauty and encourage open-air recreation. Where conflicts over land-use objectives arose, Parks had few resources in terms of staff or infrastructure to resolve them (Gilg 1996).

The years between the 1950s and 1970s were hard ones for the fledgling National Parks, with a number of battles being fought and lost with the development lobby. Evans (1992) lists a number of damaging large scale developments in National Parks during this time including the military installation at Fylingdales in the North York Moors, the Meldon Grange Reservoir in Dartmoor, power stations at Trawsfynydd and Dinorwic in Snowdonia, limestone quarrries in the Peak District, and the A30 Okehampton bypass in Dartmoor. These developments suggested the planning system was not powerful enough to protect even National parks. Mechanisms such as Landscape Area Special Development Orders (LASDO) which had been introduced into the Lake District, Peak District and Snowdonia as early as 1950 had some positive impacts. These regulations meant that local authorities had to be notified about any new buildings in the Park, after which they had 14 days to call for a full planning application if the development was likely to prove unsatisfactory (Evans 1992).

The results of the National Parks Policy Review Committee were published in 1974 in the Sandford Report (Sandford 1974). This recommended that LASDO provisions be extended across all National Parks. Despite extensive lobbying, these proposals did not come into effect until 1986, when they were applied to new roads and buildings as well as to forestry and farming (Evans 1992). The Sandford Report noted that in some cases the conflicts between conservation and recreation in National Parks had become irreconcilable (Gilg 1996). After some delay, the Government endorsed this view and agreed that, where conflicts could not be resolved, conservation needs should take precedence — the so-called "Sandford Principle" (Department of the Environment 1976). This policy was consolidated by PPG 17 (Department of the Environment 1991) which stipulates that in National Parks, AONBs and Heritage Coasts, conservation should always take priority over recreation.

The Local Government Acts of 1972 and 1974 led to a number of important changes to the ways in which National Parks were run. From 1974, all National Parks had to have a core of permanent staff overseen by a National Park Office. This group would be responsible for the production of a five-year management plan. This was achieved by a doubling of National Park budgets.

9. National Scenic Areas

For over 30 years from 1957 no new National Parks were created in Great Britain. In 1980, after a number of false starts, the Countryside Commission for Scotland established a pilot programme in Glen Lyon and Loch Rannoch that was the forerunner of the eventual 40 National Scenic Areas (NSAs). Land in these areas was to be designated on the basis of their "unsurpassed attractiveness which must be conserved as part of our national heritage" (Countryside Commission for Scotland 1978). These areas are now established under the Natural Heritage (Scotland) Act 1991 and cover some 1,001,800 hectares, Although the designation has no statutory basis (SNH 1999), NSAs are recognised by the International Union for the Conservation of Nature as Category V (protected landscape) areas. Following their 1999 review of NSAs, several initiatives have been implemented by SNH to establish coherent management strategies for NSAs, and this process is likely to continue.

10. Developing National Parks

In England and Wales there were no significant developments in National Park designation until 1988 when, after a period of great controversy, the Norfolk and Suffolk Broads Act gave the area equivalent status to a National Park. The area is under the administration of the Broads Authority which in addition to its duties in conserving and enhancing the natural beauty of the area and promoting public enjoyment must also protect the interests of navigation (Gilg 1996).

In 1994 it was decided that the New Forest would also benefit from the same planning policies as those used in National Parks, though it would not be able to use the title (Gilg 1996). Given the pressures faced by the area (it receives an estimated 22 million visits per year) such largely cosmetic designations as the New Forest Heritage Area were unlikely to prove adequate and, as we shall see, the case for the areas designation as a National Park was soon to be revisited.

The Edwards Report of 1991 reviewed National Parks and made a number of recommendations including the formation of independent, free-standing National Park Authorities (similar to the Broads Authority) to replace the existing county council committees. These were established in the 1995 Environment Act which, in addition, redefined the conservation and recreational roles of National Parks as recommended in the Edwards Report. The Act defines their statutory purposes as:

- to conserve and enhance the natural beauty, wildlife and cultural heritage of the National Park;

- to promote opportunities for the understanding and enjoyment of the special qualities of the Parks by the public.

In keeping with the Sandford Principle, the first of these objectives takes priority in cases of conflict. Currently the Government allocates 75% of the National Park budget direct to individual National Park Authorities and contributes a further 25% via constituent Local Authorities. This amounted to £35.5 million in 2003/04.

Following the Environmental Protection Act 1990 and the Natural Heritage (Scotland) Act 1991, the designation of National Parks in Wales and National Scenic Areas in Scotland has became the responsibility of their respective national agencies (Countryside Council for Wales and Scottish Natural Heritage), subject to confirmation by the Secretary of State. Since 1999, the National Assembly for Wales has been responsible for National Parks and AONBs in Wales, advised by the Countryside Council for Wales. Similar post-devolution arrangements exist in Scotland for National Scenic Areas and any new National Parks. After 1990 National Park designation in England remained the responsibility of the Countryside Commission; however, in April 1999 this task was passed on to its successor the Countryside Agency.

The National Parks (Scotland) Act 2000 was passed in July 2000. The Act provides the powers for National Parks to be established by means of a designation order. Scotland's first National Park, The Loch Lomond and The Trossachs National Park, was established in July 2002, while the Cairngorms National Park was designated in March 2003. The National Parks designation subsumes some of the former National Scenic Areas and is intended to offer greater levels of protection and opportunities for management. As in the case of other National Parks in the U.K., these areas are now managed by fully functional National Park Authorities.

In addition, the case for the designation of the South Downs and the New Forest as National Parks has been reviewed recently. This case for the South Downs is supported by the England Rural Development Programme which includes a regional objective for the south east of England for "enhanced, restored and recreated open downland" with the objective of recreating that landscape *"particularly within the South Downs"* (MAFF 2000). Following a lengthy process of consultation and review, boundaries for the proposed National Parks were drawn up. A Designation Order for the New Forest National Park was made in February 2002, with a similar order for the South Downs published in December of the same year.

Public enquiries into the designation of the New Forest and South Downs were undertaken in 2002/2003 and 2003/2004 respectively, though at the time of writing only the New Forest had had its status as England's first new National Park in nearly 50 years confirmed. A National Park Authority for the New Forest should be established in 2006.

The designation of new National Parks in England and Scotland will provide new challenges. What advantages will designation have for the Scottish sites that tightening existing legislation could not achieve? Is this an exercise more in marketing than protection and a chance to place Scottish sites on a more equal footing with their equivalents in England and Wales and internationally? In the case of the South Downs, having a new National Park so close to an expanding urban area will certainly lead to conflicts but could provide considerable economic benefits by capitalising on one of the area's greatest, and most fragile, assets.

11. Areas of Outstanding Natural Beauty

In addition to the areas that were eventually designated as National Parks, a number of other areas were designated as possessing outstanding natural beauty. Section 87 of the 1949 Act gave power to the newly constituted National Parks Commission to declare AONBs, while Section 5 gives the criteria for selection. The main difference between the two designations was that AONBs had no specific responsibility to create opportunities for recreation, though such activities are permissible provided that they did not conflict with the conservation of natural beauty and the needs of agriculture and forestry.

Unlike National Parks, AONBs were originally managed by local councils, or more recently by joint advisory committees composed of local authorities and representatives of other interested groups such as land owners or local communities. There are currently 37 AONBs in England and four in Wales (though the Wye Valley AONB straddles both countries), covering approximately 15% of the land area (Clarke 2000). Another nine AONBs are designated in Northern Ireland.

The publication of a Countryside Commission report on AONB management (Countryside Commission 1998), voiced many of the concerns expressed in England over the years about the problems of effective management in AONBs. These concerns included the lack of any statutory management structure and any sound basis for forming partnerships with local landowners or other interest groups. Particular concerns centred around the problems experienced in AONBs under multiple jurisdiction (e.g. the North Pennines AONB is covered by parts of six district and three county councils). A further shortcoming was the lack of any obligation for local authorities to provide management plans, potentially losing a valuable opportunity to enhance the social, economic and environmental benefits provided by these important areas.

In response to this report and other concerns, the 2000 Countryside and Rights of Way Act updated the provisions of the 1949 Act and conferred the same protective status to AONBs as that enjoyed by National Parks. To achieve this, the Act obliges all public bodies, statutory undertakers and Ministers to have regard to the purpose of AONBs in conserving and enhancing natural beauty. As Clarke (2000) points out, such an improvement in status is consistent with the International Union of Nature Conservation classification of protected areas, in which AONBs, NSAs and National Parks are all designated under Category V "protected landscapes and seascapes." These areas are expected to have distinctive character and "*significant aesthetic, ecological and/or cultural value*" and often have high biodiversity values.

The 2000 Act also obliged the relevant local authorities in England and Wales to produce management plans for AONBs. These management plans were based on extensive local consultation and used guidance provided by the relevant national agencies (e.g. Countryside Agency 2000b, 2001a). In some cases management plans were prepared by Conservation Boards. Such Boards were established with the aims of conserving and enhancing the natural beauty of the AONB, while at the same time promoting the public understanding and enjoyment of the area. The Boards are also responsible for working in partnership with other local organisations such as the local Regional Development Agencies to ensure the social and economic well-being of the areas (see Countryside Agency 2001b). Conservation Boards already exist in some AONBs, notably the Sussex Downs. A three year funding package to support these new management responsibilities was launched in 2001, with the new Statutory Management Plans (SMPs) coming into force from April 2004.

12. Sites of Special Scientific Interest

Sites of Special Scientific Interest (SSSIs) are the flagship of Government efforts to protect and conserve natural heritage in the U.K. They safeguard the quality and diversity of a range of habitats and species, encompassing the entire range of natural and semi-natural ecosystems, as well as protecting important geological and physiographical features (Evans 1992). A key element of SSSI strategy is to protect these areas from encroachment from agriculture (e.g. over-grazing or cultivation), from development and from general neglect. Other important objectives of SSSIs are to provide habitats for vulnerable species and to provide a protected reservoir of genetic diversity.

SSSIs had been a minor element in the report of the Huxley Committee in 1947 (Huxley 1947, Cmd. 7122) and were introduced by Section 23 of the 1949 Act to cover areas that have particular biological or geological interest. Originally, SSSIs were designated by the Nature Conservancy, which from 1965 became part of the National Environmental Research Council (NERC). In 1973 following concerns over NERC's management of conservation sites, the Nature Conservancy Council (NCC) was formed under an Act of the same name (Evans 1992). Since 1991 the notification of SSSIs has been the responsibility of the NCC's successors.

Notification of a new SSSI takes place at a local level following careful consideration of site information against published criteria. At this stage exploratory discussions take place with owners and occupiers (EN 2002). Following initial notification, all owners and occupiers of the land, the local authority and a range of other public bodies must be informed about its new status. In England, objectors have four months to make representation against the notification.

The responsibilities of owners and occupiers of SSSIs in England are outlined in EN (2002) and include the need to provide written notice before beginning any of the operations listed in the notification as likely to damage the site. These could include such mundane activities as cultivation, grazing, mowing, fertilising and pesticide use (Evans 1992). Once a site has been officially notified, the local authority is obliged to inform EN about any planning application regarding land within the SSSI, and must have regard for the status of the site when making their decision.

Public bodies own some 20% of land designated as SSSIs in England (EN 2002). As well as their requirement to inform EN of their intention to perform any operations that may damage the site, the 2000 Countryside and Rights of Way Act places a general duty on these bodies to take all reasonable steps to *"further the conservation and enhancement of the features"* for which the site has been notified (EN 2002).

In their early years, notification of a site as an SSSI did not offer a guarantee of protection. Unlike National Nature Reserves (see Section 13), SSSIs could not be purchased, leased or held under management agreements: Evans (1992) catalogues a number of examples demonstrating how notification failed to protect certain sites. This situation was improved by a range of new legislation introduced subsequent to the 1949 Act.

SSSIs are now established by notification of the conservation agencies under Section 28(1) of the 1981 Wildlife and Countryside Act (as amended). This Act offered a substantial improvement to the protection offered to SSSIs. The provisions of the Act were designed to prevent owners from damaging sites until the NCC or its successors had a chance to enter negotiations for a management agreement (Section 28(5)). These agreements could be made under either the 1949 or 1968 Acts (Alder & Wilkinson 1999). For example, Section 15 of the 1968 Countryside Act permitted voluntary management agreements to be offered to land-owners to compensate them for income lost under SSSI designation (see Chapter 14).

Under the 1981 Act, the agency may consent to an activity proposed by the landowner on a SSSI or, if it did not, was allowed three months to negotiate a management agreement. If an agreement is not made within this time, then the activity can be carried out. In extreme cases, where no agreement can be reached, the agency can evoke the power of compulsory purchase under the 1949 Act. Although these powers were extended by both the 1968 and 1981 Acts this remedy seems only to have been used sparingly.

In exceptional circumstances where the special features for which the land has been designated are not being properly conserved, statutory agencies have the power to issue a management notice on a SSSI. If the owner or occupier does not remedy the situation within a given time (subject to appeal to the Secretary of State), then the agency has the power to enter the land and carry out the work itself. Schedule 11 of the 2000 Countryside and Rights of Way Act provides English Nature or CCW with the power to issue stop notices in specific circumstances. These have a similar effect to the withdrawal of consent under the 1981 Act and are also subject to the owner or occupier's right of appeal.

The 1981 Act did not address the problem of damage occurring to sites in the three months leading up to designation. The Wildlife and Countryside (Amendment) Act (1986) closed this loophole, and increased from three to four months the time allowed for the NCC and land occupier to negotiate a management agreement.

In 1992, protection for SSSIs through the planning system was increased, after the Government indicated that the Secretary of State would call in and determine any planning applications that would impact on sites of national or international conservation importance. At the same time advice was issued for the use of environmental impact assessment (see Chapter 10) to assess developments on SSSIs. Local authorities were also obliged to consult the relevant conservation agencies over development proposals likely to affect SSSIs.

The 2000 Countryside and Rights of Way Act considerably tightened up the protection offered to SSSIs and other conservation sites in England and Wales. English Nature is confident that the Act will bring vastly improved protection to SSSIs, consistent with the Government's target is to bring 95% England's SSSIs into "favourable" condition by 2010 (www.english-nature.org.uk). The provisions of the Act include:

- extending powers of compulsory purchase and increased penalties for damaging SSSIs by owners, occupiers or others;
- giving further protection to SSSIs through allowing EN and CCW to impose permanent restrictions on land to prevent damage;
- giving conservation agencies the power to secure management of SSSIs.

The 2000 Act also introduced a new offence of intentional or reckless destruction or damage to the special features of the site, or disturbance of fauna. If convicted, those who damage SSSIs may face fines of up to £20,000 on summary conviction or more following conviction on indictment. In addition, courts can force owners to restore land to its former condition or face fines of up to £5,000.

Austin (2001) suggests that the 2000 Countryside and Rights of Way Act has shown that wildlife law in Scotland is outdated and sometimes ineffective. He cites damage to SSSIs, particularly as a result of slow deterioration through causes such as overgrazing, neglect and pollution and quotes evidence to suggest that "key habitat" on more than half of Scottish SSSIs is in "unfavourable condition." The Scottish Executive has sought to address some of these problems with the objective of improving levels of protection so that they match those now achieved in England and Wales (Scottish Executive 2001).

Some authors, such as Pennington (1996), argue that non-government organisations (NGOs) such as EN and SNH, encourage regulation as a means of increasing their own budgets and workforce. This echoes the arguments of Downs (1966) who argued that that: the central interest of bureaucrats was in securing the expansion of their budgets (see Chapter 4). Pennington argues that the designation of SSSIs does not necessarily have a positive impact on conservation, indeed, he suggests that successful conservation is not in the interests of the conservation agencies: "*As the theory of bureaucracy predicts, the more damage to environmental sites, the greater the demand for new sites and the extra budgets to 'protect' them.*"

In 1993 equivalent prices, EN's budget had tripled between 1980/81 and 1990/91, increasing from £18.8 million to £56.7 million: at the same time staff numbers increased from 530 to 858. In addition 1,200 new SSSIs were designated between 1981 and 1995. Pennington argued that the nature conservation agencies would rather increase designation than spend money preventing damage on existing stock of SSSIs because the former activity requires a higher level of staff and budget. In 2000, EN estimated that their staff carried out some 6,277 visits to assess the condition of SSSIs.

Between April 1997 and March 1998, 87% of all damage to SSSIs in England was the result of overgrazing of upland heath, grassland or moorland (EN 1998). This damage is reversible and reducing sheep numbers will enable the vegetation to recover in most cases, others will need remedial habitat management. By the end of 2002, figures suggested that 40% of the assessed area of SSSIs in England was in unfavourable or declining condition, with a further 13% in unfavourable but recovering condition (DEFRA 2003). This figure rose to 70% for some specific upland habitats (EN 2000). The most significant problems with the condition of assessed SSSIs in England (see Table 13.2) were found on calcareous grassland, upland acid grassland, upland dwarf shrub heath, bog, and river and stream SSSIs (DEFRA 2003).

Development activities account for some 13% of all cases of reported damage and 8% of the total damaged area (EN 2000). A significant cause of damage is the exercise of existing planning permissions for mineral extraction which are difficult to revoke under current legislation. An important issue for managers dealing with SSSIs on wetland sites include problems of water quality and quantity (EN 1998).

By 2003 there were over 4,100 SSSIs in England covering over 1 million hectares (some 7.5% of the land area) and involving some 26,000 owners and occupiers

Table 13.2: Habitat condition in assessed sites of special scientific interest.

Broad Habitat Type	Favourable or Recovering (Ha)	Favourable or Recovering (%)	Unfavourable (Ha)
Broadleaved, Mixed and Yew Woodland — Upland	9,862.44	70.91	4,045.95
Broadleaved, Mixed and Yew Woodland — Lowland	43,985.67	73.88	15,552.57
Coniferous Woodland	21,407.37	91.79	1,914.82
Boundary and Linear Features	448.8	64.43	247.81
Arable/Horticulture	13,465.61	97.78	305.52
Improved Grassland	787.72	83.68	153.64
Neutral Grassland — Upland	3,879.80	60.39	2,544.62
Neutral Grassland — Lowland	29,956.50	67.96	14,125.26
Calcareous Grassland — Upland	4,431.01	32.51	9,199.89
Calcareous Grassland — Lowland	20,502.82	54.00	17,462.41
Acid Grassland — Lowland	4,491.99	58.56	3,178.67
Acid Grassland — Upland	7,992.40	37.01	13,601.88
Dwarf Shrub Heath — Upland	42,947.84	29.41	103,104.96
Dwarf Shrub Heath — Lowland	26,447.36	69.01	11,879.21
Fen, Marsh and Swamp	13,280.47	66.87	6,579.33
Bogs	53,578.70	32.68	110,360.85
Standing Water and Canals	13,146.96	69.04	5,896.51
Rivers and Streams	2,589.14	40.48	3,807.25
Montane Habitats	12.13	1.40	852.16
Inland Rock	4,276.02	50.93	4,120.32
Built-up Area and Gardens	10.46	12.20	75.29
Supralittoral Rock	5,215.09	87.49	745.59
Supralittoral Sediment	8,983.82	64.66	4,909.86
Littoral Rock and Sediment	120,883.77	79.44	31,279.04
Littoral Sediment — Saltmarsh	21,163.03	74.46	7,257.75
Inshore Sublittoral Sediment	1,256.75	78.87	336.76
Earth Science	20,417.73	94.24	1,247.06
Other	16,212.87	92.61	1,293.82
Total	511,634.27	57.64	376,078.80

Source: DEFRA (2003).

(www.english-nature.org.uk). They range in size from the very small (about 130 are less than half a hectare) to thousands of hectares, the largest being The Wash, an area of intertidal mudflats, which covers 66,050 ha. There are some 1450 SSSIs in Scotland covering over 950,000 ha, which represents over 11.5% of Scotland's land area.

Recent targets for SSSIs state that by 2010, 95% of all sites should be in favourable or recovering condition. This equates to nearly a million hectares of land. By April 2002 only 56.5% of that area had achieved this target (DEFRA 2003). This objective will be supported by the publication of a Code of Guidance under Section 33 of the 1981 Wildlife and Countryside Act that will explain the revised SSSI legislative framework.

13. National Nature Reserves

The 1949 National Parks and Access to the Countryside Act confirmed the official status of the Nature Conservancy (NC), which had been set up in November 1948 (Evans 1992). One of the duties of the NC under the 1949 Act was to notify local planning authorities about the designation of SSSIs and National Nature Reserves (NNRs). Today, NNRs represent some on the best SSSIs and in England some 35 NNRs are treated as "spotlight" reserves where English Nature make special efforts top improve public access and information provision (DEFRA 2003).

Under the 1949 Act, NNRs could be purchased or leased from owners or managed subject to a binding legal agreement. The first NNR in Britain was Bienn Eighe in North West Scotland. The separation of NNRs from the National Park system runs counter to Dower's original vision and was more in keeping with the proposals of the Addison Committee. Despite the concerns voiced by commentators of the time, NNR designation has proved successful, and the number of NNRs designated by the NC's successors far exceeds that originally anticipated.

NNRs provide examples of the best areas of natural habitat in the country and are now declared by the relevant national agencies under the 1949 Act. They are owned or leased by those agencies, or alternatively established under formal agreements under which the owners and occupiers agree to manage the land for the benefit of wildlife and their habitats. NNRs may also be established under the 1981 Wildlife and Countryside Act to include land managed as a nature reserve by an approved body, such as a County Wildlife Trust (e.g. the Sussex Wildlife Trust manage the Pevensey Levels NNR).

NNRs cover a wide range of vegetation and habitat, much of it scarce or threatened. Coverage of NNRs ranges from coastal salt-marshes, estuaries, dunes and cliffs to chalk downs, lowland heaths, meadows, bogs, and native woodlands. This coverage means that NNRs are filled with rare and interesting species which can be actively protected and studied by scientists. Significant opportunities for access also exist on NNRs, and English Nature's web site highlights over 30 where recreational access is encouraged.

By 2004 there were over 200 NNRs in England, covering in excess of 80,000 hectares. The Reserves can be found throughout the country, from Holy Island in the North to The Lizard Peninsula in Cornwall. This compares with 128 NNRs covering 43,270 hectares, in 1991 and the 73 NNRs across Britain originally recommended in 1947 by the Wildlife Conservation Special Committee of the Hobhouse Committee which accounted for only 28,350 ha (Evans 1992). Over 60 NNRs are designated in Wales ranging from only five hectares to over 2,000.

In 2000 SNH undertook a review of the aims of its management of its 72 NNRs (covering over 116,000 ha) to take account of changing priorities in nature conservation. Following this review they found that only 31 sites were close enough to the key attributes and purposes that had been set out for NNRs. A further 26 had doubtful status and 14 were so deficient that they faced having the designation removed (SNH 2000).

14. European and International Sites

The U.K. also contains a number of conservation sites that are protected under international or European designations. International designations include Ramsar sites and Biosphere Reserves, while European sites are defined as Special Areas of Conservation, candidate Special Areas of Conservation and Special Protection Areas. PPG9 (Nature Conservation) (DETR 1994) provides details of the protection afforded to these areas. PPG9 was revised in 2003 providing new guidance on nature conservation issues.

Biosphere Reserves are areas of ecosystems located either on land or water, that have international recognition under UNESCO's Man and the Biosphere Programme which was launched in 1971. Biosphere Reserves are nominated by national governments and are expected to meet three complementary aims covering conservation; sustainable economic and human development; and the support of education, research and training related to issues of conservation and sustainable development. The U.K. withdrew from UNESCO in 1985 and by the end of 2000 had failed to revise either the criteria for designation of Biosphere Reserves or the management objectives for the 13 existing reserves across the U.K. Such revisions have already taken place at a UNESCO level.

In 1976 the U.K. Government ratified the Convention on Wetlands of International Importance especially as Waterfowl Habitat (the Ramsar convention). Under this Convention the Government is committed to designate "Wetlands of International Importance" (Ramsar sites) and to ensure that the use of these wetlands does not compromise their ecological value In 2001, English Nature reported that there were 78 such sites in England alone covering some 365,726 ha. A total of 35 Ramsar sites had also been designated in Scotland, covering an additional 70,000 ha. Strategies for the management of these sites is regularly debated at an international level, with for example, the Sixth Ramsar Conference held in Brisbane in 1996 setting Ramsar strategy for the period 1996–2002. In Britain this led to a review of all Ramsar sites under the guidance of the Joint Nature Conservancy Council.

Under the 1979 EC Directive on the Conservation of Wild Birds (79/409/EEC) the Government is obliged to designate Special Protection Areas (SPAs) to conserve the habitat of a range of rare or vulnerable birds (both native and migratory). Some SPAs and Ramsar sites qualify for joint status. To comply with the Directive the Government must ensure that these designated sites do not experience significant pollution disturbance, or deterioration. In practice this means that these sites (and Ramsar sites) are also protected by SSSI designation. Around 65% of the area of SSSIs are SPAs (DEFRA 2003). English Nature and their partner organisations across the U.K. are involved in the identification of these sites, their notification as SSSIs and are responsible for carrying out consultations on the proposed designations with the various interested parties.

The Habitats and Species Directive (92/43/EEC), which builds upon the 1979 Berne Convention and the commitments of the 1992 Rio Earth Summit, requires member states to submit a list of sites which will make a significant contribution to the favourable conservation status of habitats and species which are considered of European nature conservation importance. Member states had until 2004 to designate these sites as Special Areas of Conservation (SACs).

Establishment of these sites should contribute towards the Directive's aims of ensuring the long-term survival, variety and population stability of the species. Regulations 16 and 89 of the Conservation (Natural Habitats &c) Regulations 1994 (SI 1994/2716) provide the power to make management agreements at European sites. Both SACs and SPAs will contribute to a EU network of protected areas known as "Natura 2000" sites. At present over 80% of the area of SSSIs has been earmarked for designation as SACs (DEFRA 2003).

15. Protecting Countryside Heritage

A large number of protected sites and designated areas in the countryside have been established to offer protection to historic sites, buildings or monuments. Architecture and heritage are recognised as an important element of landscape character and the protection of archaeological interest is also incorporated into agri-environment measures such as DEFRA's Environmental Stewardship Scheme (see Chapter 14).

The most important heritage designation from an international perspective, is that of World Heritage Site (WHS). This designation was introduced by UNESCO in the 1960s as a means of highlighting those sites that had outstanding natural, cultural or environmental importance and which were worthy of exceptional international efforts in order to ensure their preservation. A World Heritage Convention was drawn up by UNECSO in 1972 and ratified by the U.K. in 1984. Candidate sites are proposed by their host countries and considered by the World Heritage Committee, which decides whether or not they designation. By 2003 there were more than 20 WHSs in the U.K. including Hadrian's Wall, Stonehenge and Avebury, the St Kilda archipelago and the Giants Causeway in County Antrim, Northern Ireland.

WHS designation brings great prestige and is a potentially valuable marketing tool, but it does not afford sites any additional statutory protection. PPG15 "Planning and the Historic Environment" ensures that local authorities take account of this status in the development planning process and at some sites this is supported by the existence of a WHS management plan. These plans are not binding, but provide a framework within which the management and development of the site can be co-ordinated with the special qualities of the site and the interest of other groups (Cullingworth & Nadin 2002).

The Avebury WHS Management Plan (English Heritage 1999) which relates to management of the unique area around Avebury in Wiltshire provides a good example of this approach. The area encompasses some 5000 years worth of evidence of the impacts of history on landscape and the management of the 22.5 square km site is a particular challenge. A third of the site is owned and managed by the National Trust with the remainder mostly in private hands, much of it used for agriculture. The area is also part of the North Wessex Downs AONB, testifying to its important landscape value. The management plan seeks to ensure that the character of the area is protected and to introduce positive management that will benefit both the heritage and economic interests of the area (English Heritage 1998).

Completion of the plan was aided by a comprehensive database of the economic and cultural assets of the area held by English Heritage on a GIS.

English Heritage is the principal Government agency responsible for the management of historic sites in England and the provision of advice to Government and local authorities about historic and archaeological issues. Welsh Historic Monuments (Cadw), Historic Scotland and the Environment and Heritage Service (EHS) in Northern Ireland fulfil similar roles in the remainder of the U.K. Part of English Heritage's job is to ensure that the country's heritage contributes directly to the social and economic health of the nation and, since their merger with the Royal Commission on the Historical Monuments of England in 1999, they have been the national body for architectural and archaeological survey and record.

English Heritage have been instrumental in assessing and mapping the historic elements of the landscape at a county and national level. This work has informed both the Monuments Protection Programme and the Countryside Character Programme. This co-operation with other agencies reflects the notion that archaeology in the landscape can best be understood and protected as part of an integrated approach to landscape conservation.

A schedule of ancient monuments has been kept since 1882 in order to ensure that the nationally important historical sites and buildings are given special protection under law from development and damage. The Ancient Monuments and Archaeological Areas Act 1979 provides the legislative framework for the protection of historic monuments and incorporates a system of consent for works to be carried out on Scheduled Ancient Monuments (SAMs). Owners of SAMs are encouraged to adopt sympathetic land uses and advice on this and financial support may be provided by a local monuments warden. The relevant national agencies compile the Schedule which is then approved by the responsible Government body. The scheduling process may be assisted by other agencies such as the regional Welsh Archaeological Trusts or the Ancient Monuments Board of Scotland.

Archaeological sites in England and Wales that are not scheduled, are given some protection under PPG 16 "Archaeology and Planning" (Department of the Environment 1990). This ensures that developers carry out proper archaeological investigations during development and means that if a site is likely to be damaged or destroyed as a result of development that it will be fully recorded. If damage to sites is likely to result from natural causes such as erosion or flooding, then the relevant agency may fund investigation and recording work.

Local Authorities have the ability to designate conservation areas at sites where the historical or architectural character are worthy of protection. So far over 8,000 conservation areas have been designated in England. This designation permits planners to restrict activities such as demolition, alterations and tree removal. English Heritage and the other regional agencies are also involved in providing advice to Government over the listing of buildings of particular historical or architectural importance.

The listing process is enabled through the Planning (Listed Buildings and Conservation Areas) Acts of 1990 and 1997 (Scotland), and provides protection against inappropriate development. There are many listed buildings across the U.K. (the Historic Scotland web site estimated that in 2003 there were some 43,000 listed buildings in Scotland alone) and any changes to them require listed building consent. Listings categorise buildings as having various levels of importance and this impacts on the level of protection afforded to them. In

Scotland for example listed buildings are Category A, B or C depending on whether they are of national, regional or local importance.

English Heritage is currently engaged in an exercise to provide a comprehensive photographic data-base of all Grade I and II listed buildings in England. This will include addresses and information about their significance. Understandably, this has caused some concern among the occupiers of these, mostly privately-owned, buildings. While unlikely to provide a threat to the buildings themselves, this example provides an illustration of the delicate balance managers must tread between the protection of our national heritage, be it built or natural, the desire of public agencies to ensure that the public is fully informed about their activities, and the rights of the private individuals and institutions who own or occupy the sites in question.

16. Strategic Implications

This chapter reports some of the wide variety of regulatory mechanisms that have been used in the U.K. to protect the countryside. The planning system provides the means for protecting important areas of landscape, as well as land used for amenity and the built environment. In addition, a range of mechanisms exist to protect man and the environment from the harmful impacts of pollution from chemicals and waste products.

The sheer volume of regulation, coupled with its tendency to change and adapt over time, provides a considerable challenge to the countryside manager who must understand the ramifications that various pieces of legislation may have for the land that she manages. In such an environment, it is easy to feel that the individual is relatively powerless and that opportunities for strategic behaviour are limited.

To some extent this is true, as we must all abide by the law of the land. What this does not take account of, however, is our ability to influence the development of new legislation and regulation in ways that may benefit our objectives as countryside managers. New legislation does not appear overnight and there are many opportunities to shape the development of that legislation before it enters the statute book.

In the case of European Directives and our obligations under international agreements, several years may pass between their establishment and their implementation in the U.K. In these cases individual countries may have the ability to frame these laws in ways which best suit their own interests. The precise nature of these interests will be determined, at least in part, by the activities and lobbying of various groups and individuals. In some cases countryside agencies and interest groups may be included in the consultation process and presented with an opportunity to directly influence policy direction. Even when this is not the case many countryside and environmental organisations have become powerful lobbying groups with the ear of a variety of senior politicians and their aides. The activities of both Government and non-government organisations, such as the Countryside Agency and CPRE, in the area of rural planning provide examples of the ability of countryside organisations to help develop or interpret regulation in ways that are consistent with their objectives.

Where influence can be brought to bear, what should the strategic priorities of countryside managers be? Some of the problems highlighted by Pennington, and the recent review of NNRs in Scotland by SNH, suggest that regulation and designation alone are not sufficient to protect our countryside. Designation must be continually reviewed to take account of changing management objectives and must be supported by a legal framework within which consequences of damaging sites act as a genuine deterrent. The changes to the penalties for SSSI damage put in place in England and Wales by the 2000 Countryside and Rights of Way Act represent a step in the right direction. Furthermore, the lessons that we have learnt from the management of National Parks and AONBs have demonstrated that designation must be accompanied by an effective management structure and this must in turn be adequately funded. Only then can we begin to ensure the appropriate design and implementation of management strategies.

The arguments of Pennington suggest that where resources are constrained, the quality of management may be of greater importance than the size of the area designated. If designation exceeds the ability of existing funds to manage it, then in an ideal world those funds should be increased. We do not live in an ideal world, however, and in some cases it may be preferable to ensure that funding is targeted at those sites considered to be of most importance. This reflects some current practice, where resources, for example for monitoring, are directed at those sites assessed to be at greatest risk. The extension of such risk-assessment methodologies into the management of protected sites may provide the greatest benefits for the available budget, as efforts will be directed at the protection of those sites most vulnerable to damage or degradation. At the same time, some managers may judge it important to move further in the direction of positive management rather than merely protection. Some developments in this direction are illustrated in the next chapter in the context of incentives for countryside management.

Another important management objective can be to ensure an equitable distribution of benefits across different groups in society and across different geographic areas. Managers should also be aware of the question of inter-generational equity and the possibility that, in the future, society may place different values on certain aspects of the countryside compared with today. In view of this, there may be merit in designing regulations that help to ensure that certain critical levels of natural or human capital exist in order to provide the option for future generations to gain these benefits. These type of considerations underpin the philosophy of sustainable development and are consistent with our definition of strategic countryside management (see Chapter 1).

Managers may wish to consider the desirability of regulation that is based on a more broadly defined set of objectives than is sometimes the case. While protection must still be a priority, legislation should also take account of the environmental, economic and social well-being of the countryside and those who live in and visit it. Following this precept, we can help to protect the countryside by putting in place some of the foundations required for a sustainable future.

References

Alder, J., & Wilkinson, D. (1999). *Environmental law and ethics*. Basingstoke: Macmillan.
Cadw (1998). *Register of landscapes of outstanding historical interest in Wales*. Cardiff: Cadw; Welsh Historic Monuments.
Clarke, R. (2000). AONBs: Invited to the Ball? *Ecos*, *21*(3/4), 60–62.

Countryside Agency (2000a). Farm plan has wind taken out of its sails. *Countryside Focus*, 5, 8.
Countryside Agency (2000b). *Planning tomorrow's countryside*, CA60. Cheltenham: Countryside Agency.
Countryside Agency (2000c). Developers getting the green message. *Countryside Focus*, 12, 6.
Countryside Agency (2001a). *AONB management plans: A guide*, CA23. Cheltenham: Countryside Agency.
Countryside Agency (2001b). *AONBs: A guide for partnership members*, CA24. Cheltenham: Countryside Agency.
Countryside Agency (2003). *Concept statements and local development documents — Practical guidance for local planning authorities*. Cheltenham: Countryside Agency.
Countryside Commission (1998). *Protecting our finest countryside: Advice to Government*, CCP532. Cheltenham: Countryside Commission.
Countryside Commission for Scotland (1978). *Scotland's scenic heritage*. Battleby: Countryside Commission for Scotland.
Cullingworth, B., & Nadin, V. (2002). *Town and Country Planning in the UK* (13th ed.). London: Routledge.
Curry, N. (1994). *Countryside recreation, access and land use planning*. London: E & FN Spon.
Department of the Environment (1976). *Report of the national park policy review committee*. Circular 4/76. London: HMSO.
Department of the Environment (1990). *Archaeology and planning*. Planning Policy Guidance Note 16 (PPG 16). London: HMSO.
Department of the Environment (1991). *Sport and recreation*. Planning Policy Guidance Note 17 (PPG 17). London: HMSO.
Department for Environment, Food and Rural Affairs (2001). *A guide to pesticide regulation in the U.K. and the role of the advisory committee on pesticides*. Pesticides Forum Papers PF101. London: Department for Environment, Food and Rural Affairs.
Department for Environment, Food and Rural Affairs (2003). *Sites of special scientific interest PSA target delivery plan*. London: Department for Environment, Food and Rural Affairs.
Department of the Environment, Transport and the Regions (1994). *Nature conservation*. Planning Policy Guidance Note 9 (PPG 9). London: HMSO.
Dower, J. (1945). *National parks in England and Wales*. London: HMSO.
English Heritage (1998). *The Avebury WHS management plan*. London: English Heritage.
English Nature (1998). *Annual report and accounts 1997–1998*. Peterborough: English Nature.
English Nature (2000). *Annual report and accounts 1999–2000*. Peterborough: English Nature.
English Nature (2002). *Sites of special scientific interest: Working today for nature tomorrow*. Peterborough: English Nature.
Gilg, A. W. (1996). *Countryside planning* (2nd ed.). London: Routledge.
Hobhouse, A. (1947a). *Report of the national park committee (England and Wales)* Cmd 7121. London: HMSO.
Leonard, R. (1998). *Turning the tide: The programme for the restoration of the Durham coastline*. Paper to a Seminar on Local Agenda 21 for the Northern Branch of the Royal Town Planning Institute, Newcastle, 24/6/1998.
Lowe, P., & Ward, N. (1997). The moral authority of regulation: The case of agricultural pollution. In: E. Romstad, J. Simonsen, & A. Vatn (Eds), *Controlling mineral emissions in European agriculture*. Wallingford: CAB International.
Lowe, P., Ward, N., Seymour, S., & Clark, J. (1997). Farm pollution as an environmental crime. *Science and Culture*, 25, 588–612.
Ministry of Agriculture Fisheries and Food (2000). *Rural development plan for England*. London: HMSO.

Pennington, M. (1996). *Conservation and the countryside by Quango or Market?* London: Institute of Economic Affairs.
Sandford, Lord (Chairman) (1974). *Report of the national park policy review committee*. Circular 4/76. London: HMSO.
Scottish Executive (2001). *The nature of Scotland: A policy statement*. Edinburgh: Scottish Executive.
Scottish Natural Heritage (1999). *National scenic areas: Scottish natural heritage's advice to Government*. Battleby: Scottish Natural Heritage.

Chapter 14

Incentives for Countryside Management

1. Introduction

Management agreements are voluntary arrangements between a land manager and a countryside organisation, where in return for a payment, the former agrees to manage the land in accordance with the prescriptions of the latter. In the U.K. a number of organisations, including English Nature, Scottish Natural Heritage, the Countryside Council for Wales and local planning authorities have statutory powers to enter into such agreements with landowners and tenants.

Schemes based on management agreements may need to ensure an appropriate level of participation across potential agreement holders in order to ensure that underlying management objectives are achieved. The success of management agreements depends on the appropriateness of their prescriptions, whether or not they offer land managers sufficient incentives to adopt the practices required of them and on the costs of administering the schemes that underpin them.

This chapter begins by examining a range of criteria that may inform the design of management agreements and goes on to review a number of management agreements currently in operation within the U.K. and their effectiveness as mechanisms for the provision of public goods (see Chapter 12). In particular this chapter will focus on management agreements implemented through agri-environment schemes in the U.K. and their role in securing an increased supply of public goods.

2. The Design of Management Agreements

Various criteria can be used to evaluate policy instruments and these provide a useful framework within which to discuss the design of effective management agreements.

- *Information costs* — how much baseline information is required to establish and administer a scheme based on management agreements? Gathering and processing information is costly, time consuming and prone to error. Information costs may be particularly high when designating areas within which agreements are available. Costs can be kept down by the use of secondary data or by designating on the basis of information that is relatively easy (and cheap) to obtain.
- *Administration costs* — what are the non-financial costs of implementing a particular type of management agreement? These include the costs of publicising and negotiating

agreements, plus the costs of any monitoring. Management agreements offer incentives for a high degree of self-regulation, where possible reducing the need for excessive monitoring. Any element of design that can reduce the need for costly monitoring may prove beneficial, though this should not be achieved at the expense of effectiveness (e.g. reduced monitoring on SSSIs may lead to an increase in the proportion that are damaged annually). Similarly, costs can be reduced by keeping schemes simple and transparent, thus reducing the amount of time and effort required to explain and negotiate the scheme. Negotiation costs can also be reduced if participation is non-competitive, though this may prove less efficient in terms of delivering maximum benefits at least cost than a so-called "challenge scheme" that only accepts applicants who can show that they will offer the highest levels of public benefits.

- *Equity* — management agreements must offer fair incentives to all participants, with increasing rewards for levels of participation that incur additional opportunity costs. Similarly, agreements must not be seen to favour one target group more than another as perceived inequity can lead to dissatisfaction and reduce uptake levels. Management agreements are often voluntary and securing the goodwill and enthusiasm of participants can reduce administrative costs and can be an important factor in their success.
- *Reliability under uncertainty* — management agreements should be robust in their ability to deliver policy objectives under a range of external circumstances. Thus, they should be able to retain participation under changing circumstances. This means that incentive levels must be reviewed frequently to match changing opportunity costs and that penalties for withdrawal must represent a sufficient disincentive for managers thinking of ending their agreements early.
- *Adaptability* — similarly, management agreements should be flexible and be capable of adaptation to suit changing circumstances. Thus, payments should be linked to opportunity costs as closely as possible and there should be an ability to change management prescriptions to take account of new management priorities. Shorter agreement lengths or renegotiation clauses may be devices that allow periodic changes to be made to schemes.
- *Dynamic incentives* — well-designed management agreements offer increasing incentives to land managers who supply the greatest volume of public goods. Thus management agreements should offer incentives for farmers to increase environmental quality rather than merely maintain current levels. The tiered approach offered by the Environmentally Sensitive Areas Scheme is a good example of a dynamic incentive. As we shall see in the next point, however, the desirability of differentiated payment levels may be reduced by the resulting increases in administration costs.
- *Economic efficiency* — do management agreements achieve policy objectives at lowest cost, or would, for example, better regulation, achieve the same for lower total expenditure? Similarly, could the same expenditure be used to achieve more? This is an argument that has often been used to criticise Government expenditure on certain high profile agri-environment schemes. Efficiency may be improved by adopting certain design criteria, for example when attempting to reduce the negative impacts of agricultural production it may be useful to ensure that agreements cover whole farms rather than only part of a holding which might allow farmers to increase inputs into areas not under agreement (the so-called "halo effect"). Commonly, the efficient delivery of scheme

outputs may conflict with the need to reduce administration costs. Schemes may be designed to offer more differentiated payments that target desired outputs more precisely than undifferentiated mechanisms. The costs of ensuring that participants comply with such differentiated schemes will be higher than those incurred by an undifferentiated payment mechanism and in the past this has led to a concentration on schemes that are easier and less costly to administer even if they are less likely to achieve the desired outputs (Moxey & White 1998).

While these criteria provide some guidance over the design of management agreements it may prove more difficult to evaluate the effectiveness of different management agreements following their implementation. One simple way to compare instruments is to calculate how many hectares of land they protect. This approach is examined further in Section 11.

3. Participation in Management Agreements

While the criteria set out above are important in helping to guide the design and delivery of schemes based on management agreements, it is important to consider the needs of the population at which these mechanisms are aimed. U.K. agri-environment schemes are voluntary and if they are to successfully deliver their objectives they must ensure adequate levels of participation (Wilson 1996). Participation in such schemes depends on the inclinations and circumstances of individual farmers (Green 2002). A variety of studies over the years (e.g. Brotherton 1991; Ilbery & Bowler 1993; Morris & Potter 1995; Morris et al. 2000; Ohlmer et al. 1997; Wilson 1996) have examined farmers' motives for participating in schemes based on management agreements.

Whitby (2000) suggests that the voluntary nature of these agreements creates certain problems in terms of their continuity, however, he reports little evidence of farmers failing to renew contracts on the basis of their first decade of existence. Green (2002) argues that while some schemes, such as Countryside Stewardship, have been over-subscribed, others that are more demanding (e.g. the upper tier agreements in some ESAs) have not been so well supported. As well as the demands of the schemes this observation also reflects the smaller areas of eligible land under the respective schemes.

Morris & Potter (1995) examined motives for farmers' participation in ESA schemes. They found wide variations in levels of commitment and sympathy with the wider aims of the scheme and categorised farmers into two groups: active and passive adopters. Enrolment in the scheme is not the only sign of its success, tangible evidence that the attitudes of those within the scheme have been altered in a desirable way is. Morris and Potter concluded that some participants will enter the scheme opportunistically for financial benefits and the net effect of their participation may be low, e.g. if the incentives are seen as a payment for "resting" land.

Lobley & Potter (1998) emphasised the importance of the scheme fitting into the established farming system allowing farmers to adapt their practices rather than adopt radically different methods of working. Battershill & Gilg (1996) provided some evidence to support this view in their study of participants in agri-environment schemes in South

West England. They concluded that that traditional farming systems should form a much larger and more focused part of agro-environment policy.

Wilson (1996) suggests that payment levels are the prime factor in determining participation, and Lobley & Potter (1998) also conclude that the possibility of financial benefit may be the deciding factor in the decision over whether or not to participate. Hanley *et al.* (1999) suggest that a conflict between the financial incentives offered by management agreements and the financial benefits of other aspects of the CAP, such as headage payments, may also reduce uptake rates. In such cases larger farms may have more to lose from joining such schemes.

As well as financial motives, farmers' attitudes towards schemes and their objectives may also prove important for scheme adoption. Lobley & Potter (1998) highlight resistance among certain farmers to agreements that seem contrary to established agricultural practice or which compromise the farmer's independence. Wilson (1996) noted that age, length of tenure and education influenced attitudes to management agreements, while Morris & Potter (1995) proposed a "participation spectrum" which enabled them to classify farmers by their attitudes in a continuum between active adopters and resistant non-adopters.

Beedell & Rehman (2000) make some useful observation about the roles of environmental and farming groups in promoting agri-environent agreements. They used a social-psychology model, the Theory of Planned Behaviour, to investigate the conservation-related behaviour, of a sample of Bedfordshire farmers. Farmers who were members of the local Farming and Wildlife Advisory Group (FWAG) were found to be more influenced by conservation-related matters and less by farm management concerns than other farmers. In addition such farmers appeared to be more influenced by farming and conservation groups, grants and conservation advice. This suggests that careful choice of organisations involved in promoting agri-environment schemes might be an important element in increasing uptake.

Wilson & Hart (2001) compared the attitudes of a sample of U.K. farmers to agri-environment schemes, with those of farmers in other European nations. They found marked differences between attitudes in northern European countries to those in Mediterranean countries. The study did, however, identify a range of common factors influencing participation, including financial considerations, "goodness of fit" of schemes, farm size, tenure, and farm type. They suggest that financial motives do not necessarily mean that farmers will not have equally important environmental concerns. They go on to argue that current agri-environmental policy may fail to adequately address the structural and socio-economic characteristics of farming populations, and suggest that understanding participation should only be a first step towards assessing the effectiveness of agri-environment instruments. They suggest a need for research to investigate the impacts that scheme participation has on farmers' incomes, environmental attitudes, and on the environmental quality of the associated land.

4. Management Agreements for Conservation

The use of management agreements between statutory bodies and land managers was initiated in the 1949 National Parks and Access to the Countryside Act (Section 16). This Act permitted local authorities to negotiate and finance management agreements with land owners and farmers in National Parks and AONBs. Management agreements have been used for a variety of purposes in National Parks. One use for these arrangements has been to forestall agricultural development, for example to aid the conservation of managed heather moorland in the Exmoor National Park. The scope for public financial support for such agreements was extended to open country outside the designated areas under the Countryside Act of 1968.

Many early management agreements concentrated on achieving increased recreational access (see Section 5) but gradually this mechanism became more commonly used to provide an incentive for more environmentally friendly land management. Payments to promote conservation are commonly based on the need to compensate farmers for the profits foregone by not undertaking particular damaging activities, though Green (2002) notes how payments have gradually evolved to encompass incentives for positive management practices. The main objective of compensation payments over the years has been to prevent damage to SSSIs. Payments are generally made through management agreements between the relevant statutory authority and the land manager. The present system involves compensating farmers for their net loss of profit when they are prevented from carrying out operations that are likely to damage the scientific value of a site.

The significant cost elements in this system are those of compensation, negotiation and monitoring. There may also be indirect cost savings to the Exchequer, following adjustments to farm output and reductions in production subsides. Economic costs would include all losses in resource productivity measured at their social cost and would be offset by the benefits to society of improved conservation.

Monitoring of SSSIs concentrates on site integrity and quality. The former aims to determine whether or not the site is intact, if all its habitats are in condition, and to assess potential threats to the site. Assessment of site quality requires more detailed investigation and may involve collecting data to measure ecological and physical changes to the site. In England, one third of sites are checked for integrity each year, and 5% for quality. The cost of these procedures is not published but will form a significant part of the overall costs of SSSIs.

While management agreements could help to prevent damage to SSSIs, they may not ensure their appropriate management. Monitoring revealed worrying variations in quality across SSSIs and indicated that a number were particularly vulnerable as a result of inadequate management. In an attempt to combat these shortcomings English Nature (EN) introduced the Wildlife Enhancement Scheme (WES) in 1991 as a means of improving the management of SSSIs. Through WES EN sought to "*develop an effective partnership with managers of land in SSSI.*" The schemes provided incentives for the positive management of SSSI land with the aim of generating a more proactive response to the delivery of conservation goods. Enhancement Schemes have operated in a number of SSSIs: e.g. Culm Grasslands in Devon and Cornwall; Craven Limestone Grasslands of the Yorkshire Dales; Dorset Heathland; and the Magnesian Limestone Grasslands of Tyne and Wear.

Despite the introduction of the WES, site monitoring statistics throughout the 1990s suggested that a more wide-ranging approach to introducing positive incentives for management across all SSSIs was required. Progress towards this objective was made in 2001, when new guidelines on management agreement payments for SSSIs were published. These were motivated in part by the fact that the EU had classified SSSI management agreements as a form of state aid. This classification meant that the Government was required to comply with the rules associated with this kind of aid, and in particular were obliged to calculate payments in the same manner as those made through DEFRA's agri-environment schemes. Thus, payments are now calculated on the basis of income forgone, any additional costs resulting from any site management activities and the need to provide an incentive for land managers to enter into the agreement.

5. Management Agreements and Recreation

Management agreements have been used to provide recreational access in the U.K. for over 50 years. Such agreements were first adopted in National Parks, where costs have traditionally been high. This was often due to the use of wardens to regulate access, while other expenditure could include legal costs, maintenance and administration. The high level of costs when compared with the associated benefits of additional access may explain why such agreements remain relatively uncommon. More recently many access agreements have been negotiated under agri-environment schemes many of which now include an access element. This topic will be revisited in the next chapter.

6. Management Agreements and Heritage

Organisations involved in heritage management often work closely with other countryside organisations. For example, English Heritage inform English Nature about newly scheduled ancient monuments, while the latter informs English Heritage about newly designated SSSIs, NNRS or Marine Nature Reserves. This ensures that both heritage and conservation concerns are incorporated into site management. DEFRA recognises the importance of maintaining links between landscape and heritage in their Countryside Stewardship Scheme (see Section 8).

On entering the Stewardship scheme archaeological sites are protected from activities such as cultivation and a range of grants is made available for the restoration of traditional buildings; old orchards; historic parks; hedges, walls and banks; and water meadows (Middleton 1998). Many other archaeological features may be present on Stewardship land including hill forts, industrial remains, old field systems (e.g. ridge and furrow), burial mounds and other earthworks and these may be protected or enhanced by the Stewardship agreement In some cases farmers participating in this scheme may seek specialist advice from the County Archaeology Department or, in the case of Scheduled Ancient Monuments, from English Heritage (Middleton 1998).

7. Agri-environment Schemes

Whitby & Lowe (1994) outline the development of environmental policy in relation to agriculture. They identify the origins of concern for the rural environment as going back to the late nineteenth century when the major concerns were the expansion of urban and industrial development. More serious environmental concerns began to surface following the rapid post-war transformation of U.K. agriculture which brought with it a decline in certain species of farmland birds, the loss of hedgerows and significant areas of heathland, moorland and wetland (Whitby & Lowe 1994).

Whitby & Lowe (1994) identify the 1970s as the turning point in changing perceptions of the consequences of countryside change in the U.K. A series of influential reports in this and the following decade identified the major threats that intensive agriculture posed to landscapes, habitats and species. This threat was exacerbated by a system of agricultural support encouraging production at the expense of environmental quality. The U.K.'s increasing involvement in the CAP did nothing to ameliorate the growing concerns of the environmental lobby. In 1981 the Wildlife and Countryside Act provided additional powers to regulate agricultural practices to protect areas designated as being of particular biological importance. Such measures did little to protect the broader countryside and a variety of important landscapes, features and habitats within it.

By the mid-1980s, a variety of factors conspired to make Government ministers more receptive to the notion of reforming policies on agricultural support to tackle problems of overproduction, increasing costs and environmental degradation (Whitby & Lowe 1994). The flagship of the U.K. Ministry of Agriculture, Fisheries and Food's (MAFF) commitment to agri-environmental policy was the Environmentally Sensitive Areas (ESAs) Scheme which is designed to protect areas of national environmental significance whose management depends on traditional farming practices. This arose from Article 19 of Council Regulation 797/85 on "Improving the Efficiency of Agricultural Structures" (EC 1985), under which member states were encouraged to introduce special national schemes in environmentally sensitive areas with the aim of promoting farming practices favourable to the environment.

In the U.K., MAFF envisaged ESAs as discrete and coherent areas, whose national environmental significance was threatened by agricultural change but could be conserved by the retention or extension of certain farming practices. Effectively, ESAs are areas of landscape, conservation or archaeological interest where farmers are offered financial incentives to comply with a set of management practices designed to secure conservation objectives. On this basis, Article 19 was implemented in the U.K. through Section 18 of the 1986 Agriculture Act. Different ESAs encourage and discourage different sets of management practices — depending on the needs of the area.

Following a period of consultation, the first round of ESAs was designated in 1987, followed by a second round in 1988. This encompassed 10 areas in England, five in Scotland, two in Wales and two in Northern Ireland. These original ESAs were designated for five years and all were redesignated in 1992 and 1993, several of them with much increased areas and virtually all with changes in their management prescriptions. Two further stages of designation followed, with the amount of eligible land roughly twice that of the first two stages. Agreements are open to all applicants within the designated area and are available for 10 years with an option to withdraw after five years.

The rate of uptake of ESA agreements and the area they protected grew steeply during the year following designation. Typically, by the end of the second year after designation more than 90% of the final area of agreements had been negotiated. Agreements have been taken up enthusiastically by farmers, which may be partly explained by the comparatively slight constraint they impose on the practices of many participants.

A wide range of landscapes were designated under the ESA scheme, but what they all had in common is a dependence on the continuation of agricultural practices which tend to be extensive and largely livestock based. These practices and the landscapes which they have helped to create were threatened either by a decline in markets and global prices or by agricultural improvement and intensification. The variation in average size of ESAs reflects a range of factors such as the extent to which new rounds of designation have concentrated on extensive grazing areas.

The initial rounds of ESA agreements offered annual payments to farmers in return for them following a set of management prescriptions that varied depending on the physical and farming characteristics of the ESA. The scheme offers different tiers of participation each requiring increasing levels of environmental benefit and offering differential payment levels. ESA schemes may also provide additional recreational and educational access.

Many ESAs coincide with other designated areas such as National Parks, Areas of Outstanding Natural Beauty, SSSI, Special Protection Areas and Special Areas of Conservation. The current set of 22 English ESAs comprises:

> *Stage I:* West Penwith; Pennine Dales; South Downs; Somerset Levels and Moors; the Broads.
> *Stage II:* Clun; Test Valley; North Peak; Breckland; Suffolk River Valleys.
> *Stage III:* Exmoor; South Wessex Downs; Avon Valley; North Kent Marshes; South West Peak; the Lake District.
> *Stage IV:* Upper Thames Tributaries; Dartmoor; Blackdown Hills; Essex Coast; Cotswold Hills; Shropshire Hills.

The adoption of Agri-Environment Regulation 2078/92 provided for "accompanying measures" to CAP reform to help farmers adjust to a new era of lower prices and to protect or conserve the agricultural environment. The objectives of schemes arising as a result of Regulation 2078/92 were to include a reduction in the use of chemicals on agricultural land, lower stocking rates, more extensive land use, effective management of 20 year set-aside, and the promotion of access for the recreational use of land. MAFF responded to this by designating more ESAs, more Nitrate Sensitive Areas (a designation now replaced by Nitrate Vulnerable Zones), a moorland scheme, habitat schemes, set-aside management schemes, and by adding access to ESA objectives. Like the ESA Scheme, all of these operated on a voluntary basis. Currently ESAs cover approximately 10% of agricultural land (i.e. 1.15m ha) in England.

In 1991 in a move to broaden the scope of agri-environment policy away from particular areas to incorporate particular habitats and landscape features, the pilot version of the Countryside Stewardship Scheme (CSS) was introduced by the Countryside Commission. The objective of the scheme was to provide incentives for land managers to undertake specific measures to conserve, enhance or re-create important landscapes and to provide access to them for the general public. In 1994, CSS was merged with the Hedgerow Incentive Scheme (HIS), a series of measures designed to improve the management of hedgerows.

A thorough programme of monitoring and evaluation was undertaken following the introduction of the pilot CSS in order to evaluate its effectiveness. Following a policy review in 1995, which judged the pilot phase of the scheme to be a success, administration and funding for CSS were handed to MAFF. The transfer also saw the addition of new options targeting traditional stone walls and banks, and unimproved areas of old hay meadows.

The CSS was open to farmers and land managers who agreed to enter land into 10 year agreements with a view to changing the management of that land in ways that would produce conservation and recreational amenity benefits. In return for entry, land managers would receive annual payments, with capital grants available for a range of one-off activities such as tree planting. The scheme had a fixed budget and as a result entry was at the discretion of its administrators and dependent upon the ability of applicants to deliver the objectives of the scheme. This approach challenges applicants to deliver the greatest possible volume of benefits and is arguably the greatest strength of the CSS in terms of its ability to offer value for money. The initial budget was £13 million for the first three years but this was increased to £25 million by the second year of the scheme to allow for its expansion across a range of landscape types.

The initial focus of the scheme was on the management of five landscape types: lowland heath, coasts, upland, watersides and chalk and limestone grassland. This was soon extended to include historic landscapes, old meadows and pastures. In the third year of the scheme urban fringe and a field margin element were added. The incorporation of HIS into the scheme added whole farm hedgerow restoration to the scheme.

The number of Stewardship agreements has increased from around 6,000 in 1996 to over 13,000 by 2004 and the three most common types of stewardship agreement are on chalk limestone grassland, waterside and upland habitats. The flexibility of the system is illustrated by its expansion into new habitats and features and by the element of negotiation that is required over new agreements.

A recent extension to the scheme has been the introduction of new arable stewardship options. These aim to increase biodiversity on farmland and should benefit species associated with arable land. The various arable stewardship options promote management practices that create suitable habitats for farmland species or which improve the food sources for available to them. Specific measures include leaving cereal stubble unploughed over winter and the provision of conservation headlands, areas adjacent to arable crops that are not treated from pesticides. The scheme was piloted in the West Midlands and East Anglia and introduced across England in 2002.

In Wales, significant changes to agri-environmental policy took place in 1999 with the introduction of Tir Gofal. This is a whole-farm scheme that applies to all agricultural land in Wales. The scheme encourages production methods designed to protect the environment and maintain the countryside in a range of target landscapes.

The scheme is administered by the Countryside Council for Wales (CCW) and is "designed to maintain and enhance the agricultural landscape and its wildlife; and to provide new recreational opportunities" (CCW 2001). It replaces former schemes such as ESA. Tir Cymen, Habitat, Moorland and the Countryside Access Scheme. Farmers are asked to enter into ten year agreements with a five year break clause and there is a minimum eligible holding size of three hectares. There are four principal elements of Tir Gofal as shown in Box 14.1.

Applications for Tir Gofal are selected, as with CSS, according to the degree of environmental benefit that they are likely to generate. The selection procedure takes account of existing environmental features on the farm, and of the benefits that could come from using voluntary options to restore or create habitats or features. A process such as this tends to provide incentives for land managers to maximise the level of environmental benefits generated by participation. This in turn ensures better value for money and allows project officers to target a wider range of management objectives. These objectives will be made explicit through a whole-farm management plan which will be drawn up by the farmer (or his agent) in conjunction with the project officer. The plan will then form part of the formal management agreement between CCW and the applicant.

> **Box 14.1: The principal elements of Tir Gofal.**
>
> - land management — whole farms must enter and holdings must comply with various management prescriptions for key habitats. There may be options for the restoration or creation of certain habitats or features;
> - creating new permissive access — an optional element of the scheme which in common with other U.K. agri-environment schemes seeks to create new linear routes, area-based access, or educational access;
> - capital works — payments for additional work to protect and manage habitats and features and to support new access provision;
> - training for farmers — including courses on managing specific habitats, such as wetlands and woodlands and practical skills, e.g. drystone walling and hedge laying.
>
> *Source*: CCW 2001.

The next two sections describe some more recent developments in agri-environment policies within both the EU and the U.K. that have led to the introduction of a range of new schemes.

8. Developing Agri-environment Measures

The reforms in terms of land management offered by measures such as ESAs and CSS are limited as they are restricted to certain geographical areas, landscape types or landscape features. These measures have been criticised for tending to deal with symptoms (e.g. hedgerow loss) or react to EU directives rather than deal with the underlying causes. However, these schemes have introduced various concepts that are important to a more sustainable approach to land management. These include making payments for traditional farming techniques which benefit the landscape and a move towards encouraging proactive management rather than merely preventing environmental damage.

The House of Commons Agriculture Committee's Second Report of Session 1996/97 "ESAs and Other Schemes Under Environmental Regulation" considered U.K. responses to Regulation 2078/92. It recommended integration of all schemes into "a single national framework" to aid efficiency of monitoring and administration and make life easier for the farmers. The committee saw "no strong case for the designation of further ESAs" and called for MAFF to encourage farmers onto higher tiers and to draw up conservation plans. It also recommended the introduction of an appeals procedure for farmers on ESA boundaries seeking to be allowed in.

The recommendations of this committee were somewhat overshadowed by developments in Europe. In 1997 the European Commission published Agenda 2000 (CEC 1997), a comprehensive statement of how European policies should develop in order to accommodate the challenges facing a more integrated and enlarged Union. This document encompassed agricultural and structural support, and would have important consequences for the budgetary resources devoted to these areas of spending. Proposals included extending agri-environment payments, with plans to reorganise the rural development measures in the CAP and structural policy.

The 1997 publication offered little detail as to how these particular proposals were to be implemented. Things became clearer following the introduction of the new EU Rural Development Regulation (RDR) 1257/1999 as the so-called "second pillar" of the CAP. The RDR has had significant consequences for those organisations in member nations with responsibilities for tackling environmental, economic and social issues in rural areas. As well as offering support for rural communities, the RDR seeks to meet society's demands for a high quality rural environment.

The major instruments for the implementation of the RDR in Britain are the Rural Development Plans for England, Scotland and Wales. Each of these seven-year plans shares common priorities and objectives but approaches them in different ways that reflect their particular national viewpoint. Among the priorities relevant for countryside managers are:

- maintaining and enhancing biodiversity and landscape quality in the countryside while at the same time increasing protection from pollution and over-exploitation by agriculture;
- keeping the majority of land farmed or forested, especially in remote areas; and
- increasing competitiveness in rural areas by promoting diversity, adding value and increasing investment.

The first two priorities are likely to have large potential benefits for biodiversity conservation and in particular the objectives of the U.K. Biodiversity Action Plan (see Chapter 5), while the third will aid the broader rural community as well as countryside organisations.

The Rural Development Plans (RDPs) represent a significant commitment by the Government to promote sustainable production systems and improve the countryside. The spending plans outlined in each of the RDPs reveal that the largest proportions of their respective budgets will be devoted to agri-environment instruments, forestry and to the support of less favoured areas (LFAs).

There are four RDPs in the U.K., one each for England, Scotland Wales and Northern Ireland. Priorities and funding for these programmes are shown in Table 14.1 The RDPs were developed in 2000, shortly after devolution in Scotland, Wales and Northern Ireland in 1999 had established new institutions and responsibilities affecting rural development. Funding for RDPs was enhanced by the decision in December 1999 to apply modulation to secure additional funding for RDR measures. Without modulation the U.K.'s historically low levels of spending on the RDR's preceding measures, had resulted in an allocation of

Table 14.1: Priorities in the U.K. Rural development programmes.

Programme (Total Budget in Million Euro)[a]	Total Public Expenditure on AESs (Million Euro)[a]	Priorities
England (2,254.00)	746.0	Priority A: Creating a productive and sustainable rural economy Priority B: Conserving and enhancing the rural environment
Northern Ireland (401.60)	120.5	Priority 1: Agri-environmental measures Priority 2: Less Favoured Areas Priority 3: Forestry
Scotland (1,077.90)	131.5	Priority 1: To assist the viability and sustainability of Scottish farming (LFA and forestry) Priority 2: To encourage farming practices which contribute to the economic, social and environmental sustainability of rural areas (agri-environment)
Wales (698.80)		Priority 1: To create stronger agriculture and forestry sectors Priority 2: To improve the economic competitiveness of rural communities and areas Priority 3: To maintain and protect the environment and rural heritage

Sources: Ward 2002; DG Agriculture 2003.
[a] Including appropriations from the use of modulation.

only 3.5% of total EU funds, despite the U.K. having 12% of the EU's agricultural land (Ward 2002).

Across the U.K. for the 2000–2006 period, the RDR will represent approximately 10% of annual CAP expenditure (although this proportion will vary from year to year on a generally rising trend) (Ward 2002). All schemes under the RDR in the U.K. will be fully match funded from domestic sources, via DEFRA for the England RDP (ERDP) and via the Scottish Executive, the National Assembly for Wales and the Northern Ireland Executive (Ward 2002).

The ERDP aims to redirect spending on agricultural support from production support to schemes that boost the broader rural economy and advance environmentally beneficial farming practices. Measures put forward under the plan will be financed by a combination of EU funding for the RDR, proceeds from modulating farmers' payments under CAP direct production subsidies, and new Government match-funding of the receipts from modulation and existing budgets.

More recently, proposals have been put forward in several influential reports (e.g. DEFRA 2002) to introduce a more inclusive level of management agreement through entry-level agri-environment schemes that reward environmentally-friendly management and go beyond the requirements of existing regulation or market-based assurance schemes. The aim of such schemes is to increase the availability of management agreements to all farmers and provide benefits across the wider countryside. The scope of these schemes and the relatively low restrictions that would be placed on participants have led them to be described as "broad and shallow" schemes. "broad and shallow" schemes. According to DEFRA (2002) the aims of the proposed entry-level scheme in England include:

- rewarding farmers for positive countryside management;
- reversing the decline of farmland birds, and other wildlife and plants;
- retaining features that contribute to local distinctiveness;
- protecting natural resources from damage; and
- safeguarding archaeological sites and monuments.

9. Agri-environment Measures Under the Rural Development Regulation

The allocation of spending on agri-environment measures within RDPs is greatest in England, accounting for 60% of spending, compared with 40% in Wales, 25% in Northern Ireland and around 20% in Scotland. The use of modulation has enabled the scale of the agri-environment component of the programme to be doubled. Each of the four countries will utilise a range of agri-environment measures as documented below.

9.1. England

Originally ERDP measures comprised three schemes, all of which were voluntary: CSS, ESAs and the Organic Farming Scheme which provides five years of support to farmers converting to organic production. From 2005 ESA and CSS will be replaced by the Environmental Stewardship scheme. This new agri-environment scheme comprises two levels:

- Entry-Level Stewardship (ELS).
- Higher-Level Stewardship (HLS).

ELS will be open to all farmers and will encompass the whole farm including any woodland. The main aim of the scheme is to encourage a large number of farmers over a wide area to deliver simple but effective environmental management. Applicants must prepare a simple environmental farm record and will choose from a range of environmental management options to include in their applications. These options will help achieve targets in at least one of the following areas: biodiversity; protection of historic features; maintenance of landscape character; and reduction of diffuse pollution. Targets for ELS will differ according to the needs and characteristics of the different English regions.

Specific options for ELS management include:

- Hedgerow management.
- Maintaining stone walls.
- Woodland rides.
- Buffer strips.
- Low input grassland.
- Upland grazing management.

Farmers choose from the available options (each allocated a certain number of points) and much achieve a set points target to qualify for funding, i.e. 30 points per hectare or 15 points for extensively grazed uplands. Pilot payments were set at £30 per hectare or £15 for extensively grazed uplands.

HLS is based on existing the ESA and CS schemes and seeks to build on their success while extending the area that they cover. Like the ESA Scheme, HLS will use a tiered approach offering 10 year agreements with a five year break clause, and existing agreement holders will switch to the new scheme from 2005. Unlike the ELS, entry to HLS will be discretionary and applications will require farmers to undertake an environmental audit.

HLS will focus on particular target areas and features. and to achieve its objectives will support some capital works. The five main objectives of HLS may be summarised as:

- wildlife conservation;
- protection of historic environment;
- maintaining and enhancing landscape character;
- promoting public access;
- natural resource protection.

The HLS will have "a clearer focus on measurable environmental outcomes" than current schemes, with less emphasis on prescription than CSS or ESA. To support this the application process will focus on outcomes rather than processes.

HLS will be discretionary and highly targeted and its focus will be on high priority areas and features. In some areas this will require a whole-farm approach to be adopted while in others the scheme will be targeted only at key features. As with ELS, HLS will rely on clear national and regional targeting guidelines. Regional targets will be set first at the Joint Character Framework level then on county basis.

There will be four tiers to the scheme, three aimed at maintenance, restoration and re-creation of high quality environmental features, with a fourth "Support Tier" used to offer additional access to ELS options and additional HLS options to farmers offering high quality management but outside target areas/features.

9.2. Scotland

In Scotland, agri-environment programmes account for under a quarter of the total allocated budget, but modulation has allowed the scale of the agri-environment programme to be expanded. The two schemes, both voluntary, offered are:

The Rural Stewardship Scheme (RSS) is a whole farm scheme which was introduced in 2001 and applies to all of Scotland's agricultural land. The scheme promotes production methods designed to protect the environment and maintain the countryside in a range of target landscapes. The Scheme combines and rationalises two former schemes the Environmentally Sensitive Areas Scheme and the Countryside Premium Scheme. Agreements are for 5 years with the aim being to encourage participants to remain in the scheme for a further five years. The Organic Aid Scheme was first established in 1994, and provides five years of support to farmers converting to organic production.

9.3. Wales

In Wales, agri-environment programmes account for 40% of the total allocated budget, again expanded through the use of modulation. Like Scotland, there are two voluntary schemes Tir Gofal (see Section 7) and the Organic Aid Scheme, established in 1994 to provide five years of support to farmers converting to organic production.

9.4. Northern Ireland

In Northern Ireland, agri-environment programmes account for just over 25% of the total allocated budget for the accompanying measures programme. The use of modulation has enabled the scale of the agri-environment programme to be expanded by about a quarter. There are three voluntary schemes:

- The *Environmentally Sensitive Areas (ESAs)* scheme (see Section 7). Approximately 20% of the Northern Ireland land area is designated as ESA.
- The *Countryside Management Scheme (CMS)*. This was launched in 1999, subsuming aspects of four previous schemes, and is available to all farmers outside of ESAs. Agreements are normally for 10 years;
- The *Organic Farming Scheme* was introduced in 1999 to replace the former Organic Aid Scheme. It provides a minimum of five years of support to farmers converting to organic production.

10. Other Agri-environment Measures

The Woodland Grant Scheme (WGS) is operated by the Forestry Commission and provides grants to create new woodlands and to encourage the good management and regeneration of existing woodlands.

The Farm Woodland Premium Scheme (FWPS) is run by DEFRA and aims to enhance the environment through the planting of farm woodlands. It supports the creation of farm woodland by providing annual payments to farmers to encourage them to convert agricultural land to woodlands. Payments are made for 10 years (for mainly conifer woodlands) or 15 years (for mainly broadleaved woodlands).

FWPS payments are additional to woodland establishment grants available under the WGS. Entry into the FWPS is conditional upon the land concerned being converted to woodland under the WGS. Until January 2000 the FWPS was governed by EC Regulation 2080/92 on forestry measures in agriculture, since then all approvals are governed by Regulation 1257/99. The ERDP provides for a total expenditure over 7 years of £77m on the FWPS and £139m on the WGS over the 7 years 2000–2006.

The Hill Farm Allowance (HFA) is a compensatory allowance for beef and sheep farmers in the English LFAs in recognition of the role they play in maintaining the landscape and rural communities of the uplands. The budget varies annually and in 2004 it amounted to £34.8 million.

11. Transaction Costs and Management Agreements

Theories of economic organisation developed by Williamson (1985) can be used to guide the design of management agreements aimed at delivering public goods. These suggest that it is helpful to examine the transaction costs (TCs) associated with the delivery of public goods through policies based on voluntary management agreements (Falconer & Whitby 1999a).

In order to increase the efficiency of resource allocation we need to identify the magnitude and type of TCs for schemes using management agreements, these include the cost of information, of negotiating and of policing compliance with contracts (see Box 14.2). Management agreements impose costs under all three headings in Box 14.2, whereas other approaches to public goods provision discussed in earlier chapters such as regulation and public land purchase incurs costs under 1 and 2, with market-based mechanisms mostly incurring costs under 1.

Box 14.2: Categories of administrative costs.

- information and set-up costs (promotion, design, survey, etc.);
- contracting (negotiation and administration);
- policing, monitoring and evaluation.

TCs are often ignored or under-estimated in economic analysis which means that unknown inefficiencies fail to be remedied. The administrative costs of implementing agri-environment policies and the, sometimes substantial, costs incurred by farmers participating in them are also a cost item to be reckoned in the balance (Mathews 1986). Indeed, Falconer (2000) suggests that the potential TCs of entering a scheme, along with the mechanisms of implementation, are a major factor in a farmer's decision to participate.

The increase in resources devoted to agri-environment schemes under RDPs, means that it is now more important than ever to understand the resource implications associated with the implementation of management agreements. TCs should be recognised as a variable element in agri-environment contract arrangements, particularly in the early stages of implementation. Historically the EU can be relied upon to cover the bulk of the financial costs of such mechanisms, with the administration costs falling to the member states. In this situation there could be an incentive for the U.K. to implement schemes with low TCs and high compensation: this would improve the uptake of schemes and have the least impact on the U.K. Exchequer.

In general, to achieve economic efficiency in the supply of public goods our strategy must be to choose a mix of approaches that minimises TCs, while producing the desired level of supply. In an "administrative market" for agri-environmental goods, the state purchases those goods from land managers. This has the advantage of reducing the search costs of buyers (the public) and sellers (the land managers) and facilitates the transaction. This is typified by management agreements.

Typically the Government effectively acts as the negotiator on behalf of society saving some but not all TCs. The Government can use any of the following mechanisms:

- standard payments (homogenous farms producing homogenous goods);
- auctions of entitlements for payments (heterogeneous farms producing homogenous goods); and
- targeted payments (heterogeneous farms producing heterogeneous goods).

Information asymmetry should also guide the policymaker (Williamson 1985). For managers, high TCs reduce participation in the policy. It is crucial to reduce TCs if agri-environment schemes are to achieve objectives. Falconer (2000) suggests that farmers perceive the TCs of many management agreements to be high and suggests that scheme implementation could be rationalised by the creation of a single administering agency for all such schemes. Moves towards this have been made through existing rationalisation of schemes under the RDPs. Such changes in the design and delivery of management agreements may encourage an increasing number of the "potential enrolers" identified by Lobley & Potter (1998) to join.

In general there is a need to reduce TCs for both land managers and the public sector, therefore it may be the optimal strategy to choose options where TCs are a lower proportion of total costs. Agri-environment measures typically have high TCs compared with other measures; however, per unit administration costs are observed to fall over time from implementation (Falconer & Whitby 1999b). Finally, increasing the transparency of schemes may reduce TCs as this could reduce the need for negotiation and monitoring.

12. Comparing the Effectiveness of Different Incentive Mechanisms

Any comparison of the effectiveness of different approaches to delivering public goods is particularly difficult. The most obvious unit for comparison between different instruments is the area of land protected or enhanced by a policy. Clearly, each hectare protected is not equally valuable, in conservation terms, nor is the level of protection equal either within or between mechanisms. Similarly, the costs of management will differ across different activities and in different areas. McInerney (2001) provides an analysis of the maintenance and capital costs of different countryside management activities in England and Wales, suggesting that in 1998 these cost some £250 million, or just under £25 per hectare of all farm land. These activities include the management of field boundaries, non-commercial woodland, ponds, scrub, footpaths and bridleways and traditional and listed farm buildings (not used as dwellings).

The benefits of management depend upon the context within which they are being provided and in particular on the supply of substitute and complementary goods One solution to the appraisal of policies delivering public goods is to use economic approaches to compare costs and benefits of different mechanisms. This has been attempted in a number of studies (e.g. Garrod *et al*. 1994). Such analyses allow decision-makers to make a more systematic comparison of the economic implications of a given policy by taking into account the public goods nature of many of the benefits. This concentration on social costs and benefits rather than merely financial costs (as in McInerney 2001), takes the economic evaluation of such policies a stage further away from that which additionally incorporates TCs.

As already stated, it is appropriate to assess the use of management agreements in terms of resource costs rather than merely financial costs. Such an examination would require evaluation, at the social opportunity cost, of all the resources allocated as a result of each policy instrument (Whitby *et al.* 1998). These are typically closer to the full economic costs of the activity than the financial costs alone, e.g. they include the value of losses in agricultural or forestry output as a result of the mechanisms applied and would also be net of the resource costs of any savings in productive inputs.

Such costs are not only important to the public exchequer but may form part of the barrier that prevents potential participants from joining a scheme. If management agreements are to be a successful mechanism for delivering public policy objectives they must be made as attractive as possible to their target groups. This requires us to understand the motives underlying the adoption of such schemes and to ensure that their design and delivery promote rather than discourage participation.

13. Strategic Implications

In the U.K., providing incentives for countryside management through management agreements has become an accepted means of achieving strategic goals related to biodiversity conservation, landscape management and public access. Such agreements underpin a variety of agri-environment schemes across Europe, encompassing an even broader range of environmental goals.

With EU policies on agricultural support moving away from production-based payments to those which offer increased environmental benefits, incentive-based mechanisms will continue to be important instruments for achieving the objectives of countryside management. The fact that such measures support rural development by enhancing environmental quality and thus supporting economic and social objectives, will ensure that increased funding is available to finance an expansion of agri-environment schemes.

While incentive-based agri-environment schemes continue to proliferate and encompass an ever greater area of land, policy makers must still be aware of the design issues highlighted at the beginning of this chapter. CAP reform seems to pave the way for these schemes to offer increasingly dynamic incentives, though possibly at the expense of higher transaction costs. Though not increasing incentives, the adoption of so-called "broad and shallow" agri-environment schemes will expand the coverage of management agreements and incur relatively low transaction costs. As with all mechanisms aimed at land management, the length of contract is a key issue in agri-environment schemes and if farmers take land out of schemes, possibly in response to changes in market conditions, then any benefits of the agreement will be short lived. Therefore it is important that these schemes are not seen as a short-term measure but as part of a longer-term land management strategy. Such strategies may have to be supported by fundamental changes in the property rights system that would prevent landowners from opting-out of schemes, or at the very least ensure that they incur some form of financial penalty for doing so.

Such changes would be likely to encounter severe opposition but are a logical extension of the decision to decouple agricultural support payments from production and to increase the policy focus on the procurement of environmental benefits. If such benefits are to be a focus of public policy then their provision should be mandatory rather than optional, with support payments reflecting the opportunity costs of the activities foregone to achieve this end. Cross-compliance mechanisms that require a degree of environmental management to be undertaken before support payments can be claimed, provide a step in the right direction.

If land managers wish to exploit their land more intensively then, as well as forgoing their support payments, they could be required to compensate society for the loss of environmental benefits that such activities incur. In certain important landscapes and habitats such activities could be prohibited altogether. While such a change would certainly have an adverse impact on food production it would provide society with many other benefits.

References

Battershill, M. R. J., & Gilg, A. W. (1996). Traditional farming and agro-environmental policy in southwest England: Back to the future. *Geoforum, 27*, 133–147.
Beedell, J., & Rehman, T. (2000). Using social psychology models to understand farmers' conservation behaviour. *Journal of Rural Studies, 16*, 117–127.
Brotherton, I. (1991). What limits participation in ESAs? *Journal of Environmental Management, 32*, 241–249.
Commission of the European Communities (1997). *Agenda 2000. Volume 1. For a stronger and wider union*. Doc/97/6. Brussels, 15 July 1997.
DEFRA (2002). *Facing the future: The strategy for sustainable farming and food*. London: Department of Environment, Food and Rural Affairs.
Falconer, K. E. (2000). Farm-level constraints on agri-environment scheme participation: A national perspective. *Journal of Rural Studies, 16*, 379–394.
Falconer, K. E., & Whitby, M. C. (1999a). The invisible costs of scheme implementation and administration. In: G. Van Huylenbroeck, & M. C. Whitby (Eds), *Countryside stewardship: Farmers, policies and markets*. Oxford: Pergamon.

Falconer, K. E., & Whitby, M. C. (1999b). Administrative costs in agricultural practices: The case of the English environmentally sensitive areas. *Centre for rural economy research report.* Centre for Rural Economy, University of Newcastle upon Tyne.

Garrod, G. D., Willis, K. G., & Saunders, C. M. (1994). The benefits and costs of the Somerset levels and moors ESA. *Journal of Rural Studies, 10,* 131–146.

Green, B. (2002). The farmed landscape: The ecology and conservation of diversity. In: J. Jenkins (Ed.), *Remaking the landscape: The changing face of Britain.* London: Profile Books.

Hanley, N., Whitby, M. C., & Simpson, I. (1999). Assessing the success of agri-environmental policy in the UK. *Land Use Policy, 16,* 67–80.

Ilbery, B., & Bowler, I. (1993). The farm diversification grant scheme: Adoption and non-adoption in England and Wales. *Environment and Planning C: Government and Policy, 11,* 161–170.

Lobley, M., & Potter, C. (1998). Environmental stewardship in UK agriculture: A comparison of the environmentally sensitive area programme and the countryside stewardship scheme in south east England. *Geoforum, 29,* 413–432.

Mathews, R. C. O. (1986). The economics of institutions and the sources of growth. *Economic Journal, 96,* 903–918.

McInerney, J. P. (2001). Countryside management and farming practice. *Journal of the Royal Agricultural Society of England, 162,* 75–88.

Morris, J., Mills, J., & Crawford, I. M. (2000). Promoting farmer uptake of agri-environment schemes: The countryside stewardship arable option scheme. *Land Use Policy, 17,* 241–254.

Morris, C., & Potter, C. (1995). Recruiting the new conservationists: Farmers' adoption of agri-environment schemes in the UK. *Journal of Rural Studies, 11,* 51–63.

Moxey, A., & White, B. (1998). Contracts for regulating environmental damage from farming: A principal-agent approach. *Etudes et Recherches sur les Systèmes Agraires et le Devéloppement, 31,* 205–219.

Ohlmer, B., Olson, K., & Brehmer, B. (1997). Understanding farmers' decision making processes and improving managerial assistance. *Agricultural Economics, 18,* 273–290.

Whitby, M. C. (2000). Challenges and options for the UK agri-environment. *Journal of Agricultural Economics, 51,* 317–332.

Whitby, M., Saunders, C., & Ray, C. (1998). The full cost of Stewardship Policies. In: S. Dabbert, A. Dubgaard, L. Slagen, & M. Whitby (Eds), *The economics of landscape and wildlife policies.* Wallingford: CABI.

Williamson, O. E. (1985). *The economic institution of capitalism: Firms, markets, relational contracting.* New York: Free Press.

Wilson, G. A. (1996). Farmer environmental attitudes and ESA participation. *Geoforum, 27,* 115–131.

Wilson, G. A., & Hart, K. (2001). Financial imperative or conservation concern? EU farmer's motivations for participation in voluntary agri-environmental schemes. *Environment and Planning, A32,* 2161–2185.

Chapter 15

Managing Access to the Countryside

1. Introduction

The issue of public access to the countryside in Great Britain is complex and controversial. Over the years many customary rights of informal access have been lost through development, cultivation or, more commonly, lack of use. At the same time, landowners have been successful in defending the rights of exclusion traditionally attached to private property (Cox *et al.* 1996). New legislation enacted at the beginning of the twenty-first century finally breached some of these defences, although it remains to be seen whether the battle for wider access to the British countryside has finally been won.

The desire to restore lost rights of access to the British countryside has been the ambition of a variety of activists for nearly 150 years. The resulting debates have raised the recurring question of the desirability of some form of "right to roam" over the British countryside and its compatibility with ingrained systems of property rights and cultural values. Such rights have existed for many years in some European countries, particularly in Scandinavia (for example *Allemannsrätt* in Sweden), though not, as some people believe, in Scotland. A number of recent surveys, such as Gallup (1998), have suggested that the public are in favour of more access to the open countryside, whilst authors, such as Pearlman & Pearlman (1996) have argued that media interest in the issue captures the flavour of a strongly perceived need for such access. In spite of these claims there seems to be relatively little hard evidence to support the demand for a public right to roam.

Whitby & Falconer (1999) argue that, rather than seeking a general right of access over open countryside, the public would prefer additional well-defined access rights that are properly sign-posted and way-marked. The 1998 Gallup poll for the Country Landowners Association (CLA), for example, found that 63% of respondents preferred to follow way-marked paths than choose a route of their own through open countryside (Gallup 1998).

This chapter begins with a discussion of some of the more common sources of access to the countryside, before going on to examine the public good characteristics of such access and to review the historical background to the access debate. These sections are followed by a summary of some of the options that have been available to policymakers to increase access provision in the countryside. Recent increases in the provision of access rights achieved through agri-environment schemes, the 2000 Countryside and Rights of Way Act and the Land Reform (Scotland) Act will also be discussed.

2. What do Countryside Managers Mean by Access?

The particular concerns of countryside managers mean that they tend to use a legal rather than a social definition when referring to access. Access can either be *de jure* "in law" or *de facto* "through custom." As Curry (1994) points out, there are a number of ways in which legal rights of access can be achieved. Some rights are based on legislation or on a legally binding access agreement, whilst others have evolved over many years when a particular route has been used by the public without challenge. The most familiar examples of *de jure* access are public rights of way (PROW), such as those recorded on the definitive maps held by local authorities in England and Wales.

PROW are defined by the 1980 Highways Act as routes or minor highways over which the public has a right of access and they include footpaths, bridleways, and byways. The public has the right to pass along the route and use it for other reasonable purposes such as taking photographs or stopping to talk or admire the view. Being legally defined as highways, these routes are covered by the same controls and statutory obligations as roads and motorways and must therefore be kept open and available for public use at all times (Bromley 1990). This has become a common source of conflict in the countryside whenever a PROW has become blocked for any reason. The 2000 Rights of Way Condition Survey estimated that walkers and cyclists could encounter problems on average once every two kilometres travelled.

Other *de jure* access results from land owners giving permission for others to walk or ride on their land for a certain period of time, the so-called permissive or concessionary access. Such access is often linked to an access agreement and cannot result in the automatic creation of a public right of way. An extension of such permissive access was introduced in England, from September 2003. From this time, freeholders, or those who hold a lease in excess of 90 years, are able to dedicate land to be open for the public to access on foot. This dedication is irrevocable and access continues to exist even following a change in ownership. Dedication can also be extended to include horse riders and cyclists. Whilst some individuals may dedicate access land in this way, it is more likely that local authorities, Government Departments and businesses that own or lease land will be encouraged to participate.

Curry (1994) shows that *de facto* access can originate in a number of ways, in particular where the public have access to land to which they have not been specifically invited and where no formal rights of access exist: this may include common and publicly owned land. In some cases, as Curry points out, such access may constitute trespass. In most cases, however, such informal access is tolerated because it is essentially low key, involves local users, or because prevention is too expensive or difficult. Ravenscroft (1996) suggests that "the establishment" has sought to maintain *de facto* rights, both by refusing to criminalise trespass, and by awarding low damages in civil suits. Such behaviour is not necessarily altruistic but can be seen as a way of maintaining the *status quo* by not increasing the pressure for change.

Curry (1997) makes a number of observations on what he defined as "permitted access" in England and Wales. He estimates that permitted access exists, with or without formal written agreement from the land occupier, on approximately 32% of all holdings in England and Wales. Of these, some 17% are through formal agreements (about half of these with specific users or with the local parish or town council) covering approximately 600,000 hectares and some 9,100 km of access. Overall, Curry estimates that more than eight million hectares of informal areal access and over 95,000 km of informal linear access exist in England and Wales: some 13% of this is classified as covering "open country." This access represents a considerable recreational resource for the general public, and Curry estimates that some 400 million trips are made across permitted access each year.

While permitted access may be welcome, it is a poor substitute for properly defined public rights of access. Access agreements are by definition temporary. Informal rights are unreliable over the long term, as they are easy to dispute and vulnerable to closure or "commoditisation" (Curry 1994). The recent Foot and Mouth epidemic illustrated the potential fragility of such permissive access, when following the outbreak some landowners failed to reopen their land to the public, even when adjacent public paths were again open.

Similar temporary loss of access also occurred on land where more formal access arrangements existed, for example those arrangements made in lieu of inheritance tax. Risk-averse behaviour of this sort can lead to inconsistency and public confusion. An example of this was observed in October 2001 at Hulne Park, a large estate near Alnwick owned by the Duke of Northumberland and a popular recreational resource for local people. The gates of the estate were shut, displaying signs bearing the legend "Closed until further notice." Less than 20 metres away a notice from Northumberland County Council informed walkers that the nearby public footpath was open and set out a list of sensible precautions for those who chose to use it.

In view of the potential threat to livestock from Foot and Mouth disease, such caution by a landowner is understandable, especially when public access to the estate is at their discretion and they bear the costs of managing that access. Even so, the decision not to allow public access to an estate when nearby rights of way had been reopened, could serve to revive many old prejudices concerning the insensitive behaviour of landowners with regard to walkers.

Other examples, of the loss of informal access have occurred over recent decades when *de facto* access was lost after land formerly owned by publicly-owned water authorities was moved into private ownership following the 1990 Water Act. Similar depletions occurred following the 1981 Forestry Act which allowed the Forestry Commission to dispose of some of its land into private hands. Concerns over this loss of access, led to arrangements being made in 1991 to enable local authorities to enter into legal agreements to ensure that public access would continue after woodland had been sold. Between 1991 and 1999 approximately 9,800 hectares of woodland in England and 10,400 hectares in Wales were sold, with access agreements made on 19% of the associated land (Countryside Agency 2000a). Furthermore, following the 1994 Government Forestry Review, safeguards were put in place to ensure that forests with high levels of public access could only be sold if future public access could be guaranteed in some fashion (Countryside Agency 2000a). Similarly, the 1990 Water Act requires Water Companies to have regard for public access issues and under the Act an unknown amount of land is now classified as having a statutory right of access (DETR 1998). Clause 7 of the same Act allowed water companies to charge for customary access on their land, though the extent to which this has occurred is unclear. The 1991 Water Resources Act ensured some public access across land owned by water companies by prohibiting them from placing absolute restrictions on access to their land.

3. Countryside Access as a Public Good

Countryside access is a public good in a legal and in an economic sense. Many footpaths and bridleways are statutory rights of way and a landowner over whose property such a route passes cannot legally exclude any rightful user (walkers on footpaths; horse riders, cyclists and walkers along bridleways). This access is by way of a "common property resource." The use of such "rights of way" can be classified as:

- *a public good, with zero opportunity cost of consumption*, where there is no congestion, and no damage to the footpaths through existing levels of use;

or

- *a public good, with non-zero opportunity costs of consumption*, where congestion occurs which reduces the utility of the path to other users, and/or results in erosion of the path surface or damage to the environment through which the path passes (see Chapter 12). In this case, whilst the good continues to be free, after a certain critical level of use its enjoyment by any additional user simultaneously produces a local bad, perhaps congestion or footpath erosion.

Footpaths, thus, have analogies with other open-access resources in that there is a degree of rivalry in consumption of the good (i.e. the use of the resource by one person reduces its availability to others) when congestion occurs (see Chapter 12). However, whilst over-exploitation of footpaths will not reduce the resource to zero (as it can in the case of depletable resources such as sea fisheries), high levels of congestion reduce the practical usefulness of the resource.

Footpaths are a classic example of market failure. The absence of producer rights over access to a PROW raises the question of who pays for the provision and maintenance of these footpaths. The use of footpaths by walkers has kept them open; whilst the maintenance of stiles and gates along their routes has been an external cost imposed on the owner or occupier of the land.

Owners and occupiers have little incentive to create new footpaths: the linear nature of such routes, with many entrance and exit points, renders the collection of any entry fee impractical because of high transaction costs. This lack of "effective" producer rights means that there is generally no economic incentive for landowners to provide footpaths.

The provision of access through voluntary agreements, and financed from general taxation, can be regarded as the provision of a public good. Provision by voluntary agreements where landowners are compensated for their loss of rights and any potential transaction costs, is the only mechanism which potentially ensures that the Pareto criterion (see Chapter 12) is satisfied, so that there are no losers, only winners.

4. Historical Perspective

Historically, the public enjoyed a much greater freedom to roam across the landscape. Shoard (1987, 1999) has described in detail the diminution of the general public's right to walk in the countryside as a result of the Enclosure movement and Game Acts. Even in the twentieth century large areas of accessible countryside, for example in the Pennines, have been closed to the public with paths ploughed up, or closed (see Harrison 1991).

As the enclosure of land increased rapidly in late 18th and early 19th century, customary rights of access to the countryside were severely curtailed. From 1700 to 1874 Parliament approved nearly 5,000 Acts enclosing more than 1.8 million hectares of open fields and common pasture in England and over 0.8 million hectares of wild land and forests. In Wales, in the nineteenth century alone, around 0.4 million hectares of upland were enclosed. At the same time, the urban middle classes began to see the potential of the countryside as a place for recreation. Art and literature had shown these people that the countryside was a desirable place to visit or inhabit and many wished to experience it at first hand.

For many less-fortunate individuals, the population explosion associated with the industrial revolution, coupled with inward migration into towns, caused over-crowding and poverty. These conditions were cited by various contemporary figures to demonstrate the need for greater public access to open spaces for recreation and fresh air. In 1849 the first northern municipal park designed by Joseph Paxton, the architect of the Crystal Palace was opened in Birkenhead. The Recreation Grounds Act of 1859 provided a basis for the provision of urban space for children to play. Increasing access to open space in urban areas was not the only pressing issue, and a number of influential figures began to campaign for the rights of legal public access to open spaces and gave rise to what became known as the Open Space Movement.

Founded as an extra-parliamentary group in 1866 by George John Shaw-Lefevre MP later Lord Eversley, the Commons Preservation Society (CPS) was an important part of this movement. The society's main focus was its members concern over the loss of common land. Shaw-Lefevre had been responsible for the 1866 Metropolitan Commons Act which helped to protect some 10,000 acres of commons around London and was the natural leader for such a group (Shoard 1989). The CPS set its sights outside of London and aimed to make legislators see the public need for lawful access to public spaces. Subsequently in 1866 CPS was involved in the legal battle that followed the Berkhamsted Trespass which was a response to an attempted enclosure. This campaign and subsequent battles won the CPS great public support.

The CPS was, in effect, a middle-class grouping dedicated to the defence of common rights and titles. Its real purpose, however, was the preservation of open spaces and the battle for the commons was only a means to an end. Under the influence of Robert Hunter and Octavia Hill the CPS widened its interests into the defence of public rights of way and the preservation of beautiful countryside.

Meanwhile, in 1884 James Bryce's Access to the Mountains Act (Scotland) sought to ensure that landowners or occupiers could not lawfully exclude people from walking on uncultivated moorland or mountain for the purpose of recreation (Glyptis 1987). This bill stimulated demands for similar levels of access in England and Wales and provoked numerous private members bills (Rubenstein 1982). In 1899 the CPS incorporated the National Footpaths Society and in 1910 was renamed the Commons, Open Spaces and Footpaths Preservation Society. Some of its early members became leading figures in the embryonic National Trust, which in its early days was more concerned with the preservation of fine landscapes than the houses that came with the land.

Reformers took action (through parliament) to prevent many planned enclosures and to preserve open spaces for all citizens Initially public protests and land purchase were used to achieve this and then in 1925, Section 193 of the Law of Property Act was passed, providing rights of access over all urban commons in England and Wales (Shoard 1999). Private member's bills calling for free access to moor and mountain were also introduced to Parliament. The 1939 Access to the Mountains Bill, introduced by Arthur Creech Jones, provided a procedure to establish legal access over specific areas of land, but fell far short of the general rights of access to mountain, moor and heath sought by campaigners (Shoard 1999). The Scott Report on Land Utilisation in Rural Areas (Scott 1942) recognised the need for public access to the countryside that should not interfere with the "proper use of the land." The Report also advocated the creation of a Footpaths Commission, and recommended that local authorities keep maps of footpaths (Curry 1994). The report of the 1947 Hobhouse Committee (Hobhouse 1947a) looked at issues of National Parks and countryside access and paved the way for the increases in access over private land that would soon be achieved.

Whilst the legislators were active in this area, their efforts were being spurred on by a variety of pressure groups. These groups were protesting against substantial gaps in countryside access, for example, in the early 1930s only 1% of open moorland in the Peak District had public access, although half of the population of England lived within 50 miles of it (Shoard 1989). The inter-War years had seen a sharp increase in the demand for informal outdoor sports, and the lack of access in certain areas led to a number of mass trespasses in the 1930s as thousands of walkers asserted their right to roam freely in the hills (a phenomenon satirised in Sir Compton Mackenzie's novel "The Monarch of the Glen"). The most famous of these was the mass trespass on Kinder Scout in 1932 led by the British Workers Sporting Federation as a protest against the Duke of Devonshire's exclusion of the public from his grouse moors (Rubenstein 1982). Following the Second World War the time was ripe for progress and the scene was set for the 1949 National Parks and Access to the Countryside Act.

5. Public Rights of Way and the Definitive Map

The Report of the Special Committee on Footpaths and Access to the Countryside (Hobhouse 1947b) provided the basis of the public access provisions set out in the 1949 National Parks and Access to the Countryside Act. Although the Act designated National Parks (see Chapter 13), it confirmed that public should have "*no right of access to open country, whether in a National Park or not, except by agreement or order.*" The Act permitted local authorities to enter into access agreements with landowners over "open country" defined as "*predominantly mountain, moor, heath, down, cliff or foreshore,*" powers aimed more at the National Parks than the countryside in general. Little was done to promote the access rights of the wider public in the 1949 Act (Harrison 1991). This was in spite the views of powerful advocates such as Lewis Silkin, the then Minister for Town and Country Planning and a prominent supporter of the Ramblers' Association (Blunden & Curry 1990). The terms of the Act were designed to compensate landowners for access to their land, rather than to repay the public for their historic loss of access. This upheld the principal that all access onto private land must be negotiated individually with the landowner and maintained the traditional pattern of property rights in the countryside.

Local authorities had the responsibility of mapping areas of open country within their area and of specifying their plans regarding access provision. They would negotiate with the landowner regarding compensation, provide wardening and, in certain circumstances, were granted powers of compulsory purchase over land. Bromley (1990) recognises the importance of another clause in the Act, which allowed local authorities to contribute towards management expenses incurred by land occupiers.

As well as dealing with open countryside, the Act also had important implications for PROWs through the introduction of the definitive map, a record of existing public rights of way that is kept by local Highways Authorities, most commonly the local county councils. These authorities became responsible for surveying paths and preparing and reviewing definitive maps. These maps were required to ensure that existing customary *de facto* access routes were given the protection of proper legal standing (Curry 1994). In effect the Act replaced *de facto* with *de jure* access and gave the public statutory rights of access over customary routes. To ensure that this protection was maintained it was the intention of the Act that the maps should be comprehensive and regularly updated.

The initial task facing Highways Authorities was to produce draft maps showing all footpaths, bridleways and roads used as public paths (RUPPs) in their areas. These were to form the basis of consultation with landowners, and would represent the first stage in the completion of the definitive map. It is worth noting that though Highways Authorities were responsible for recording access rights, they had no mandate for recreation and even today are only responsible for ensuring that unobstructed access exists.

Slow progress with the preparation of the definitive map, led to the introduction of certain procedural changes in the 1968 Countryside Act. These were designed to help speed up the mapping process through rationalisation of the consultation procedures (basically reducing it from a three-stage to a two-stage process). The 1968 Act also dealt with the powers and duties of the local Highways Authorities to signpost and maintain PROWs and introduced the new classification of "byways open to all traffic" (BOATs) (Curry 1994).

Changes or additions to the existing supply of public rights of way have, until recently, been made through the 1980 Highways Act, which also provides for the diversion or abolition of existing routes. The legal procedure, known as a Public Paths Order (PPO), was undertaken by the local authority. Costs could be reclaimed from those applicants who gained some benefit from the change. Such procedures tend to be time-consuming and expensive, and as a result are used more sparingly than they might otherwise have been (Curry 1997).

Curry (1997) reported on the use of PPOs in England and Wales in the early 1990s. At this time applications were mainly concerned with affecting desirable changes to existing footpaths and bridleways; and it was estimated that 75% of diversion orders were in the interests of the landowner, occupier, or lessee; with less than a tenth being solely in the public interest (see Curry 1997). PPOs involved substantial transaction costs and some local authorities chose not to use them to create public footpaths because of the high costs involved. In the context of budgetary constraints local authorities can recover some if not all administrative costs in making private interest PPOs, whereas they must bear the cost of public interest PPOs themselves. As Curry (1997) argues, this prioritised PPOs towards private, rather than public interests.

The 1981 Wildlife and Countryside Act made provision for the "continuous review" of the definitive map, moving away from the notion that at any one time the map should provide the definitive picture of PROWs in a given area (Bromley 1990). The Act also allowed certain modifications to be made to the map and permitted the Secretary of State for the Environment to apply for the completion or abandonment of the review of objections over the definitive map (Curry 1994). Such decisions were designed to speed up a review process hamstrung by large numbers of unresolved objections.

In 1987 the Countryside 2000 initiative was launched in England by the Countryside Commission in an attempt to ensure that, by the end of the century, the entire rights of way network would be legally defined, properly maintained and well publicised. A national survey of the condition of the PROW network in 1988, found that 39,000 km of public access in England and Wales were blocked. In addition many of the definitive maps were still incomplete and there were still many thousands of outstanding objections to be resolved. Such findings were worrying as many customary routes for local people that were no longer in regular use were in danger of being lost. The 1990 Rights of Way Act sought to address some of these problems and placed restrictions on ploughing and planting on footpaths and made it an offence to obstruct footpaths without lawful cause.

Countryside 2000 had only limited success but by 1991 the Commission estimated that 82% of Highways Authorities were working towards the national target and annual spending on PROWs had increased almost twofold. However, less than half of the Highways Authorities had been able to develop and publish a comprehensive strategic plan of how they would achieve their objectives. As a result the Commission launched the so-called Milestones Approach in 1993 (Countryside Commission 1993). This was designed to help Highways Authorities demonstrate the progress they were making towards the 2000 targets and provide a clearer framework within which to plan and monitor future work. This approach had some positive impacts and, by 1999, the definitive maps for England and Wales documented 163,000 km of footpaths, 35,000 km of bridleways, 3,200 km of BOATs and 6,400 km of RUPPs (DETR 1999).

The Countryside and Rights of Way Act 2000, which is discussed in more detail in Section 8, sets an end point of January 1st 2026 for the recording of certain rights of way on the definitive map in England and Wales. Any rights not claimed by then may be extinguished. The Act also re-designates RUPPs as Restricted Byways having public rights of way for non-motorised users. This removed an existing obligation under the 1981 Act for local authorities to review all RUPPs and, if the necessary rights exist, to reclassify them as BOATs.

While the public in England and Wales enjoy considerable access to public paths, provision in Scotland and Northern Ireland is not so widespread. Neither administration has the equivalent of the definitive map of access that exists in England and Wales. In Northern Ireland local authorities must prepare maps of rights of way, while in Scotland such a duty is discretionary. Shoard (1999) reports that no district in Northern Ireland has more than the 40 public paths found in the 250 square miles of Down District. She also estimates that only 10,202 miles of rights of way exist in Scotland, less than 10% of the total in England and Wales. By the end of the twentieth century, the vast majority of rights of way in Scotland enjoyed no legal status, and Shoard observed that in only a small proportion of these were local authorities able to compel landowners to remove obstructions. Significant improvements to the Scottish situation will result from the Land Reform (Scotland) Act (see Section 10).

6. Long Distance Footpaths and the National Cycle Network

The 1949 Act established the basis for a number of National Trails in England and Wales. These are long distance paths normally over 70 miles in length, which are available to walkers, cyclists and horse riders. There are 13 such National Trails in England (Countryside Agency 2000b), recent additions including the Hadrian's Wall National Trail and the Thames Path a 179 mile route following the Thames from its source in Gloucestershire to its end in London. The first National Trail was the Pennine Way which opened in 1965, and the longest is the 610 mile South West Coast Path which passes through four counties. Three National Trails exist in Wales: the Pembrokeshire Coast Path, the Offa's Dyke Path (which also passes through the border counties of England) and Glyndwr's Way in Powys.

Powers for the creation of Long Distance Routes (LDRs) was obtained in Scotland under the 1967 Countryside (Scotland) Act and, at present, three such paths (the West Highland Way, Southern Upland Way, and the Speyside Way) have been opened. One further LDR, the Great Glen Way, opened in 2002, whilst a six mile section of the Pennine Way terminates at Kirk Yetholm in the Scottish Borders. The circular Ulster Way is currently the only established LDP in Northern Ireland. A number of other longer routes such as the North Down Coastal Path also exist, as do a range of forest walks for those seeking shorter routes.

The National Cycle Network, part-funded by a £43.5 million Millennium Commission (see Chapter 8) grant seeks to provide long-distance routes for cyclists. The network, founded on partnerships involving more than 4,000 individuals and groups, concentrates on routes free of motor vehicles and covers the whole of Britain, which should extend to over 16,000 km by 2005.

7. Increasing Countryside Access

Increasing public access to the countryside has remained high on the agenda of a variety of organisations for a number of years. Any proposals that may lead to an increase in public rights of access to the countryside are of concern to landowners given the possibility of increased insurance premiums and damage to crops, livestock, land and equipment and the erosion of privacy that such changes might bring (CLA 1998). Particular concerns have been voiced about the possibility of damage to grouse moors and other important ecosystems (CLA 1995). Some supporters of the need for additional access rights refute these claims, pointing to the experience in other European countries with more extensive rights of countryside access.

A survey by the National Farmers Union (NFU 1995) estimated that the costs incurred by farmers of having PROWs crossing their land as about £422 per year (1995 prices). Some 30% of this was devoted to clearing litter; 36% to repairing fence damage; 21% to repairing stiles and 13% to compensate for damage to vegetation. Crabtree *et al.* (1993) identified highly variable access costs, with higher costs associated with proximity to urban areas or with sites having desirable recreational characteristics. Scientific studies such as Yalden & Yalden (1988) also suggest that walkers themselves cause limited ecosystem disruption, though greater problems are created by those who are accompanied by dogs.

A number of options exist for increasing access to the countryside (see Box 15.1), each with different implications for the supply of access and the distribution of property rights. The most far reaching involve altering the system of property rights in the countryside to give the public new statutory rights of access over certain areas of land. This would create new *de jure* rights of access, which would relate both to land with no existing access, and to land where *de facto* rights existed. As we shall see, this is the approach that has been adopted in England and Wales by the Government through the 2000 Countryside and Rights of Way Act.

Box 15.1: Approaches to Increasing Countryside Access.

(1) *Statutory access:* use of legislation to grant full or partial public rights of access to defined areas of land, dependent on ownership, use or other factors, such as conservation importance. This approach underpins the access elements of the 2000 Countryside and Rights of Way Act.
(2) *Access orders:* Highways Authorities and Government ministers have powers under various Acts (e.g. Town and Country Planning Act 1990 or the Highways Act 1980) to make public path orders that allow them to create, divert or extinguish footpaths and bridleways: in practice creation orders constitute only a minority of applications;
(3) *Access agreements:* purchasing the rights to public access to land, i.e. under the Wildlife and Countryside Act 1981; and agri-environmental schemes under EC Regulation 2078/92, such as the Countryside Stewardship Scheme, Environmentally Sensitive Areas scheme, Countryside Access Scheme, Tir Gofal (Wales only), and the Countryside Management Scheme (Northern Ireland only).
(4) *The work of charitable trusts and public bodies*, acquisition and management of land through lease or purchase by bodies such as the National Trust, Woodland Trust, Ministry of Defence and the Forestry Commission.
(5) *Voluntary access arrangements:* a system of temporary voluntary access provision without formal access agreements and co-ordinated by a local access forum or body such as the Country Land and Business Association.
(6) *Dedication* use of legislation to allow landowners to dedicate permanent public access to their land in perpetuity.
(7) *Other access provisions:* e.g. through the Water Industry Act 1991 and inheritance taxes legislation.

Adapted from: Countryside Agency (2000a).

A range of voluntary approaches to access provision has also been utilised, notably through the use of formal access agreements where landowners are compensated for giving up their rights to exclude members of the public from their land. Section 7 discusses the introduction of voluntary access agreements as part of agri-environment schemes. These are an addition to the access agreements negotiated under the provisions of the 1949 Act, and only occur on land eligible for entry into one of the agri-environment schemes available in the U.K. The debate surrounding the statutory and voluntary approaches to access is outlined briefly in Section 8, which reports on the provisions of the 2000 Countryside and Rights of Way Act.

In addition to these more far-reaching solutions to access provision, a number of other approaches are available which may be of use in particular circumstances. These include market solutions such as the permanent acquisition of access rights by land purchase on behalf of the general public or by CARTs (see Chapter 12). Such an undertaking would be very expensive if it was to occur on a large scale and the temporary acquisition of rights through access agreements seems more feasible. Other market approaches based on the commoditisation of the countryside are less likely to prove a fruitful supply of access for the purposes of quiet recreation.

An increase in the use of voluntary access arrangements was the system favoured by the CLA and promoted in their document "Access 2000" (CLA 1995). In this document the CLA encouraged landowners to consider positively the benefits of improving the quality and quantity of the access they provide, and recommended the introduction of a properly structured and adequately financed voluntary approach to increasing access provision. Within this framework, landowners and agencies would work in partnership to secure a net gain in the quality and quantity of access.

Such voluntary mechanisms could be effective but much hard work and goodwill would be required before any significant long-term gains in access could be achieved. Such access is fragile and vulnerable to the prevailing economic, social and political forces. If the approach had succeeded, however, it could have been a positive force in the countryside promoting both partnership and understanding, especially if it were underpinned by a careful analysis of the supply and demand for recreational access to the countryside at a local level.

The dedication of land to permanent access, outlined in Section 2, would by contrast provide a robust supply of additional access, but one that may be hampered by a lack of support with landowners unwilling to permanently relinquish rights over their land and possibly reduce its future value. The Countryside Agency (2000a) suggests that this option could be made more feasible if public sector bodies were directed by Government to enter into permanent access arrangements over their holdings. This would then act as a cue for other major landowners, such as the Church of England and the Royal Family, to follow suit.

Whitby (1996) reported that some 58,000 hectares of land had been made available for public access up to 1995 as a condition of inheritance tax relief. Such access has not been well publicised, though matters have improved over recent years following media attention (particularly from the comedian Mark Thomas). Ironically, the rationale for tax relief no longer exists in some cases as the public have gained statutory rights of access to the land in question under the 2000 Countryside and Rights of Way Act.

This section shows that a range of mechanisms are available to provide access. The Countryside Agency (2000a) estimates that of the £2 billion per year directly invested in rural land management in England and Wales through agricultural subsidies, grants, tax-incentives, agri-environment payments and other management agreements only 5% takes any account of whether the land has public access. Such data may lead to suggestions that more effort should be put into redressing this issue and, where appropriate, making access a possible condition of more of these payments. Such an approach could be used in association with an analysis of supply and demand to begin to redress local shortages of access. This would be relatively costly in terms of administration, but would have the advantage of improving the level of social benefits returned from land that is already in receipt of public money.

8. Agri-Environment Access Schemes

A number of agri-environment schemes (e.g. Environmental Stewardship, ESAs) offer options where participants can gain additional payments for allowing access onto land subject to the agreement. While these schemes have many important differences, the access elements tend to be quite similar. All of the schemes aim to provide additional opportunities for public access to the countryside for the purposes of quiet recreation and enjoyment. It is usually preferred for access to be located close to public roads, rights of way or settlements. In many cases, agreements cover sites near to, or incorporating, a feature of landscape that is of historical, recreational or wildlife interest. New access is sometimes targeted to link existing rights of way or to provide a new circular walk. Access for cyclists, horse riders, educational establishments and disabled people may be provided at some sites.

In Wales access agreements are made through Tir Gofal (see Chapter 14). CCW estimate that for every 100 Tir Gofal farm agreements approximately 32 km of new access is gained.

Even with the new provisions of the 2000 Countryside and Rights of Way Act agri-environment access schemes have some value for access provision. The restriction of the proposals to unenclosed land suggests that schemes, such as these, which often deal with enclosed agricultural land, can play an important strategic role in providing additional access. Additional access to enclosed land may be desirable in some areas, particularly close to centres of population, and mechanisms should exist to promote such access. Even so, the prospects for continued payments for the provision of access alone, do not seem encouraging and a more positive development would be to shift payments towards more proactive management of access land, both within and outside the categories specified in any legislation.

9. The Countryside and Rights of Way Act 2000

At the Labour Party Conference in October 1997, Michael Meacher, then Minister of State for the Environment, said: "We will soon be issuing our Right to Roam proposals, for a countryside for the many, not the few, so that nobody any longer is a trespasser in the land of their birth." In February 1998, the Department of the Environment, Transport and the Regions (DETR) and the Welsh Office produced a consultation document entitled "Access to the Open Countryside in England and Wales." In this paper the Government proposed to extend public access to the open countryside either through voluntary means or, failing this, through some form of legislation.

The proposals concerned the 8–12% of open land in England and Wales that could be defined as mountain, moor, heath, down or registered common land. Increased access to other areas of open countryside, such as cliffs and foreshore, woodland and watersides were also considered but were not given the same priority. It was proposed that the Countryside Agency and the CCW should make recommendations on the identification of access land, along with advice on how it should be defined.

The proposals stated that landowners and tenants should not be eligible for general compensation for access to their land. This was based on the presumption that participation in countryside recreation would not immediately increase as a result of the proposals, merely spread across more land, and that recreationalists would cause little additional damage to walls, fences and land and have little effect on agricultural production.

The consultation document acknowledged the scope for increasing access opportunities through agri-environment schemes and stated that the Government was prepared to await the outcomes of any changes to the access arrangements in these schemes before deciding whether the right of access should be extended across other areas of open country beyond those suggested in the consultation document. The document also made it clear that existing publicly-funded access agreements, including those under agri-environment regulations, would be honoured but not necessarily extended. The proposals did, however, suggest a role for management agreements in extending access to open land not included in any legislation and in providing a framework for payments to be made that would improve access on land under legislation, e.g. through capital grants for path creation, stiles, way marks, notices and information boards.

Despite the representations of the CLA and a variety of other organisations in favour of a voluntary approach to increasing access to the open countryside, the Government opted for a statutory solution. Whilst the resulting legislation was designed to greatly increase access provision, it would also provide effective measures to safeguard the needs of land managers and other interests, particularly wildlife. The Government's proposals to introduce a new statutory right of public access on foot over open country in England and Wales were published in March 1999 and implemented through the 2000 Countryside and Rights of Way (CRoW) Act.

Under Part 1 of this Act, areas of "open country" in England and Wales qualify as access land: that is land *"which is wholly or predominantly mountain, moor, heath or down."* Land 600 m above sea level and registered common land immediately qualify under the Act, which does not affect existing access rights. The exact nature and location of the less well-defined areas of open country is decided upon by the various countryside agencies. Cultivated, military and developed land are excluded from the statutory right, and the Act includes specific restrictions about dogs, motor vehicles, cycling and horse riding. The Act does, however, include provision to extend access rights to coastal land, but only following public consultation. Options for increasing access to coast, woodland and waterside were discussed at length in a joint report by the Countryside Agency, CCW, Forestry Commission, English Nature and the Environment Agency (Countryside Agency 2000a).

The new rights of access should not increase the liability of the land owner or occupier — for example, there will be no liability with respect to natural features such as rabbit holes. The Act also includes provisions for landowners to restrict access without needing permission for up to 28 days per year. Landowners are able to apply for further exclusions or restrictions from the relevant agencies. The Act also provides for access authorities to appoint wardens on access land to secure compliance and enforce by-laws.

The Act has specific provisions for people with mobility problems, and requires local authorities to consider the needs of this group when dealing with crossing points and boundaries along rights of way such as gates and stiles. Such issues are now of more general concern to countryside managers seeking to comply with the terms of legislation designed to reduce inequalities in access that exist for people with disabilities. The CRoW Act also includes new powers to divert rights of way for security purposes, or to protect SSSIs and allows landowners to temporarily divert footpaths and bridleways in order to permit certain types of work to be carried out.

The provisions of the Act make it the responsibility of the Countryside Agency and the CCW to interpret the meaning of the terms "mountain, moor, heath and down" and to identify such areas. Working interpretations were drawn up by the Countryside Agency (Countryside Agency 2001) and were refined during the mapping process. Areas of common land were drawn using the boundaries from the statutory registers established following the Commons Registration Act 1965. The restrictions placed on access by the new Act did not meet universal favour and were criticised by Shoard (2000). She argued that the legislation had missed an opportunity to overturn the law of trespass and implement a new general right of access that would be supported by necessary restrictions to protect privacy, crops and other easily defined interests. Even those who disagree with more general rights of access may sympathise with Shoard's more general points about the complexity of the mapping exercise required to implement the Act and the possibilities for confusion about how the Act is interpreted in different areas. Land cover is not a constant and the decision as to whether or not land is "*predominantly*" moor, heath or down at a given time could cause confusion both for those defining open land and for those who subsequently wish to access it.

The mapping exercise that defined where the public can walk began with two pilot areas — the north west and the south east of England. Agencies have discretionary powers to adjust the boundaries of open countryside, to allow them to coincide with physical features such as roads or rivers, that will provide clear boundaries for landowners and users. As part of a public consultation exercise the Countryside Agency issued draft maps at a scale of 1:25,000 at a county or unitary authority scale and made them available to the public through a variety of media. Changes to the draft maps, made as a result of the consultation exercise, were incorporated into provisional maps of open countryside and used as the basis for any subsequent appeals against inclusion. Any changes recommended by the Secretary of State following appeal were included in the conclusive maps which constitute the legal record of open country and registered common land for the purposes of the Act (Countryside Agency 2001), The mapping exercise was scheduled to be completed by 2005 (Countryside Agency 2001).

Press reports concerning the early impacts of the mapping exercises suggested that a variety of errors in mapping occurred. Such errors arise from the fact that not all land identified as open land in the mapping exercise has been visited by those drawing the maps. The consultation process should identify the majority of such errors, though there will inevitably be cases where disputes arise over whether certain areas of land fall under the provisions of the Act. More worrying are unconfirmed reports that some landowners have decided to cultivate certain areas of land in order to ensure that it is excluded from the new access rights. Such actions could degrade important areas of heathland and upland grassland. Of less concern were the well-publicised efforts of some individuals in the public eye to have their land removed from draft maps on the basis that the introduction of access rights would compromise their expensively purchased privacy.

A National Access Forum for England was established in July 1999 to advise the Countryside Agency on the implementation of access legislation and has played an important role in bringing various interested parties together to discuss the practical implications of the new legislation. By autumn 2001 the Forum had already met over a dozen times and discussed a wide range of issues and reviewed progress on matters such as the mapping of open land. The Countryside Agency has also published guidelines on its website for the implementation of Local Community Access Forums which will manage plans for new access provision at a local level. Falconer & Pringle (1999) describe the operation of a similar group in the Yorkshire Dales.

The CRoW Act also attempts to improve rights of way legislation in ways consistent with earlier recommendations by organisations such as the Countryside Commission (Countryside Commission 1998). These were also first outlined by the Government in their Framework for Action in March 1999 and in the Government consultation paper on rights of way (DETR 1999). The latter suggested that local authorities should be required to review and publish plans for improving the rights of way network in their areas.

This will be achieved through Rights of Way Improvement Plans (ROWIPs) which highway authorities will be obliged to produce by November 2007. ROWIPs must cover all non-motorised routes, not just PROWs, and consider the needs of all users including those with impaired mobility or vision. They are expected to assess how well rights of way meet the needs of users and the opportunities that they provide for exercise, recreation and enjoyment.

Guidance on the production of ROWIPs has been provided by DEFRA and Local Access Forums are expected to participate in this process. ROWIPs will eventually be merged with Local Transport Plans, which will be required from each highway authority from August 2005. In order to inform the preparation of ROWIPs, several three-year Integrated Access Demonstration Projects (IADPs) were implemented across England from 2000. These projects sought to capitalise on the links between access, tourism, social inclusion and education and to develop a more integrated approach across these areas that would provide sustainable benefits for local communities. For example, a pilot IADP in Lancashire set out to:

- devise means of implementing county-wide access audits and show how this information will inform ROWIP;
- explore how access networks can be improved;
- show how access can be integrated with conservation and land management on private land;
- examine issues arising from designation of open access land;
- look at new ways of providing information on access, e.g. via the internet; and
- explore new ways of funding access (Countryside Agency 2003).

The project provided a number of tangible outputs including a digitised definitive map of PROWs, the upgrading of some existing routes and the construction of a new bridleway link to the West Pennines Moors area. In addition, the project carried out a county-wide access audit covering all permissive access and researched demand for off-road cycling (Countryside Agency 2003). It also provided some valuable insights into the integration of access with land management and conservation objectives through a project in the Bowland Fells, an area of high conservation value with low levels of access (Environmental Design Consultancy 2003).

10. Land Reform in Scotland

Nearly 60% of the land in Scotland could be classified as open country and over much of this area public access is accepted even though, by some interpretations, it may not be lawful (Reid 2000). Indeed it is a common misconception that legal rights of public access existed over open land in Scotland. In fact, the provision of statutory access rights over countryside in Scotland has for many years been far worse than in England and Wales. Reid (2000) points out that of the estimated 60,000 km of tracks and paths in Scotland less than a quarter are claimed to be rights of way and that, of these, only 150 km carry the full weight of the law. In these circumstances it is not hard to understand why a number of groups, such as the Scottish Rights of Way and Access Society and the Paths for All Partnership, have campaigned vigorously for an improvement in access rights in Scotland.

Following extensive public consultation, the Land Reform (Scotland) Act was published in March 2003. The Act establishes new statutory rights of responsible access in open land across Scotland and improves the ability of people living in rural communities to buy land. As in England and Wales this right will not extend to land under cultivation, or to areas where grass is being grown for hay or silage. Similarly, the new access rights should not affect the duty of care owed by the occupier to another person present on the land. Unlike the CRoW Act this Act does not contain the provision to allow landowners to temporarily suspend access rights, though local authorities do retain the power to exempt land from the access rights that would otherwise apply to it, or to exclude particular activities from the exercise of these rights. SNH have a duty under Section 10 of the Act to draw up a Scottish Outdoor Access Code providing guidance on the rights and responsibilities of access users and land owners.

The Act also clarifies the responsibilities of local authorities in upholding access rights and makes them responsible for planning and establishing networks of core paths that are sufficient for providing reasonable public access through their area for people on foot, bicycle or horseback. The local authority, following a consultation period where draft maps are made available to the general public, will be responsible for drawing up maps of core path networks. Each local authority is also responsible for establishing a local access forum in its area. Members will be appointed by the local authority and when established the forum will advise the local authority about the core path network and other access issues. The forum may also be called upon to offer advice in disputes over access.

11. Strategic Implications

Existing rights of way have evolved over many centuries. As a result of the National Parks and Access to the Countryside Act 1949, rights of way in England and Wales were recorded on definitive maps and the public gained statutory rights of access to them. Anecdotal evidence from some local user groups suggests that some rights of way may have been omitted from the definitive maps, a problem which has been exacerbated by the delays in their completion and review. These losses, and others that have occurred since the Enclosures, are partly being rectified by the increases in access gained through the Countryside and Rights of Way Act 2000 and the Land Reform (Scotland) Act 2003.

Providing society with additional countryside access is costly and can give rise to a potentially inefficient allocation of resources if the access is not used. The rights of access outlined by the Acts are something of a blunt instrument and do nothing to identify or target those areas where residents are in the greatest need of additional access. It may be that the statutory access provisions in the new Acts seem likely to benefit a small minority of walkers, while inconveniencing many landowners.

The analysis of relevant opinion polls (e.g. Gallup 1998) by Whitby & Falconer (1999) suggest that the public would prefer to follow properly way-marked paths rather than make their own way across open fields and hillsides. Indeed, a small survey of walkers in the Yorkshire Dales National Park reported by Mansley (2000), suggested that only 38% of respondents would change their walking habits as a result of the CRoW Act, while 73% preferred to remain on paths rather than stray onto open land. If this pattern was repeated across the population of serious walkers, it would provide little justification of the costs and disruption associated with the new access provisions.

The areas in most need of additional access opportunities are often associated with large urban populations, and are not always adjacent to open countryside. If additional access is required in these areas it must be found from other sources. Here, the 2000 Act could be useful in helping to accelerate existing mechanisms used to create rights of way. These mechanisms have, however, been shown to be drawn-out and costly and are not an effective means of achieving significant increases in access. Agri-environment schemes may offer better potential for targeting access, but these schemes are of limited duration, restricted in extent and focused on other objectives apart from access.

It seems, therefore, that current mechanisms offer little to those who live in urban areas remote from areas of open countryside. New and more imaginative approaches are required if countryside access is to be improved for these individuals. The example of community forests in England is a good one and the scheme has the potential to provide a range of access opportunities across lightly-wooded landscapes. The recent promotion of local access forums is also a positive step, though it remains to be seen how effective these will be, especially in areas largely unaffected by the new statutory rights. New initiatives to improve access to footpaths and National Trails for users with limited mobility are also encouraging. Possible options to improve access include improving the information available to disabled users about access routes (e.g. about gradients, surface, barriers, parking) and the possible redesign of gates and stiles that may not be suitable for some users.

An extensive mapping exercise will determine the land that falls under the new Acts. This exercise is likely to be dogged by controversy and based on the experience of the definitive map, may not be completed on time. Clearly, much of the bureaucratic energy that could be devoted to countryside access will be spent on defining these maps rather than on looking to generate additional access on enclosed land close to urban populations. Thus, though large expanses of countryside may be opened up, the vast majority of the public may experience limited or no benefits. Dedication of land by public bodies and private sector organisations may provide a more strategic means of opening up other areas of countryside of greater interest to the general public, though it remains to be seen whether or not the increased access opportunities provided in the early years of the twenty-first century will lead to significant increases in participation over coming years.

References

Blunden, J., & Curry, N. R. (Eds) (1990). *A people's charter? 40 years of the 1949 National Parks and Access to the Countryside Act*. London: HMSO.
Bromley, P. (1990). *Countryside management*. London: E & F N Spon.
Country Landowners' Association (1995). *Access 2000: Countryside access and recreation into the next millennium: A CLA policy statement*. London: Country Landowners Association.
Country Landowners' Association (1998). *Access to the countryside: The CLA proposal*. London: Country Landowners Association.
Countryside Agency (2000a). *Improving access to woods, watersides and the coast: A joint report to Government on the options for change*, CA 33. Cheltenham: Countryside Agency.
Countryside Agency (2000b). *National trials: An introduction to the national trail routes in England and Wales*, CA 15. Cheltenham: Countryside Agency.
Countryside Agency (2001). *Drawing the boundaries: Mapping and consultation for the new countryside access rights*, CA 66. Cheltenham: Countryside Agency.
Countryside Agency (2003). Partnership work improves rights of way. *Countryside Focus, 28*, 4–5.
Countryside Commission (1993). *National target for rights of way*, CCP436. Cheltenham: Countryside Commission.
Countryside Commission (1998). *Rights of way in the 21st century — Conclusions and recommendations*, CCP550. Cheltenham: Countryside Commission.
Cox, G., Watkins, C., & Winter, M. (1996). Game management and access to the countryside. In: C. Watkins (Ed.), *Rights of way: Policy, culture and management*. London: Pinter.
Crabtree, R., Chalmers, N. A., & Appleton, Z. E. D. (1993). The costs to farmers and estate owners of public access to the countryside. *Journal of Environmental Planning and Management, 37*, 415–429.
Curry, N. (1994). *Countryside recreation, access and land use planning*. London: E & F N Spon.
Curry, N. (1997). Enhancing countryside recreation benefits through the rights of way system in England and Wales. *Town Planning Review, 68*, 449–464.
Department of the Environment, Transport and the Regions and the Welsh Office (1998). *Access to the open countryside in England and Wales*. A Consultation Paper, February 1998. HMSO, London.
Department of the Environment, Transport and the Regions and the Welsh Office (1999). *Improving rights of way in England and Wales*. A Consultation Paper, July 1999. Department of the Environment, Transport and the Regions, London.

Environmental Design Consultancy (2003). *Assessing demand in relation to countryside access.* Cheltenham and Lancashire County Council, Preston: Countryside Agency.

Falconer, K., & Pringle, S. (1999). Sustainable countryside access: The Dales access partnership. *Ecos, 20*(2), 5–13.

Gallup Organisation (1998). Countryside survey 22nd to 28th January 1998. New Malden: Gallup Organisation.

Harrison, C. (1991). *Countryside recreation in a changing society.* London: TMS Partnership.

Hobhouse, A. (Chairman) (1947a). *Report of the National Park Committee (England and Wales).* Cmd 7121, London: HMSO.

Hobhouse, A. (Chairman) (1947b). *Report of the Special Committee on footpaths and access to the countryside.* Cmd 7207, London: HMSO.

Mansley, C. (2000). Managing the 'right to roam'. *Ecos, 21*(3/4), 54–59.

National Farmers' Union (1995). *The NFU rights of way survey, in focus on access to the countryside.* London: National Farmers' Union.

Pearlman, D. H., & Pearlman, J. J. (1996). Is the right to roam attainable? An aspiration or a pragmatic way forward? In: C. Watkins (Ed.), *Rights of way: Policy, culture and management.* London: Pinter.

Ravenscroft, N. (1996). New access initiatives: The extension of recreation opportunities or the diminution of citizen rights? In: C. Watkins (Ed.), *Rights of way: Policy culture and management.*

Reid, R. (2000). Changes in access to Scotland's countryside: "of Bruce, Bryce and Bon Accord." Paper presented at the Town and Country Planning Summer School 2000, University of St Andrews.

Rubenstein, D. (1982). The struggle for ramblers' rights. *New Society*, 15th April.

Scott, Mr Justice (Chairman) (1942). *Report of the committee on land utilisation in rural areas.* Cmd 6378, HMSO, London.

Shoard, M. (1987). *This land is our land.* London: Collins.

Shoard, M. (1999). *A right to roam.* OUP: Oxford.

Shoard, M. (2000). Off the track: Problems looming for the right to roam. *Countryside Recreation, 8*(1), 2–6.

Whitby, M. C. (1996). Losers and gainers from rural policy. In: P. F. Allanson, & M. C. Whitby (Eds), *The rural economy and the British countryside.* London: Earthscan.

Whitby, M. C., & Falconer, K. E. (1999). Reinstatement, renewal or re-creation of access rights. The economics of a right to roam. Centre for Rural Economy Working Paper Centre for Rural Economy, Department of Agricultural Economics and Food Marketing, University of Newcastle upon Tyne.

Yalden, P. E., & Yalden, D. W. (1988). The level of recreational pressure on blanket bog in the Peak District National Park. *Biological Conservation, 44*, 213–227.

Chapter 16

The Demand for Countryside Recreation

1. Introduction

Despite the importance of the countryside in Britain, it is notable that there has been no systematic data collection to document the evolution of countryside use for recreational purposes. Although the agencies concerned have funded surveys of countryside use since the 1950s, these have never been repeated in a way that would allow measurement of the *trend* of recreational use. This is even more remarkable given the concern about over-use of the countryside which has surfaced from time to time. In this chapter we therefore consider the evidence of over or under-use of the countryside first before turning to the issue of use measurement and how it is attempted. The argument then turns to consider demand for recreation using the new rights of access to open countryside in England and Wales as an example. Finally some conclusions are drawn.

2. Over- or Under-Use?

The best known example of the over-use position was stated in an article by Dower (1965) in which he warned of a Fourth Wave of development which threatened to engulf the countryside.[1] Dower predicted a great increase in recreation by the end of the Twentieth Century associated with an expanding population (up to 70 million), more adults in full-time education or in retirement, shorter working weeks (only 30 hours), higher levels of car ownership (30 million cars) and higher *per capita* incomes.

Like many forecasts Dower's were only partially accurate. Thus, while the population in 2004 was 10 million fewer than Dower expected, *per capita* incomes were substantially higher, and cars less common than expected. Similarly, while there are more young people in full-time education there are fewer pensioners than he predicted. This is particularly important in estimating recreational demand because the increased size and longevity of the retired population will particularly contribute to most forms of leisure pursuit. Perhaps the largest discrepancy is in the length of the working week which has proved much more difficult to reduce than expected. One could summarise this set of comparisons by saying that the population is smaller than expected and wealthier. While we are richer and have

---

[1] The preceding three waves after 1800 where the growth of individual towns, the spread of railways and the growth of the suburbs mainly in the inter-war period.

more leisure opportunities, the balance of these factors has not led to the expected increase in countryside recreation.

A possible explanation of this observation may be the proportion of population taking holidays overseas, a figure that has grown steeply since 1970. The share grew from 3% in 1951, through 14% in 1971 to a massive 30% in 1991. Evidently preferences for spending our leisure time have changed markedly over the last half century. Nevertheless Dower's projections are defensible as being as close to the mark as might be expected over a 40 year period. For strategic management purposes we might conclude that it is not sufficient to produce a set of relevant variables. It is also necessary to have a clear view about how they may affect each other and also how they will develop in the future. In this state of the art we would argue for a much simpler model based on economic principles which embodies the key relationships more centrally.

These criticisms are useful for those considering the future of countryside recreation. Such work is at the core of strategic countryside policy making and management. Dower's article is claimed (by Curry 1994) to have been very influential with recreation providers. Curry argues that this has led to undue concern as to the capacity of the countryside to cope with the projected floods of people and hence to the introduction of unnecessarily protective attitudes towards recreation provision.

3. Measuring Use

We can best illustrate the problems of measurement by reference to recent surveys of countryside use. First we consider some findings from the 2002/2003 GB Day Visits Survey (TNS Travel and Tourism 2004). This appeared following previous surveys in 1994 and 1998. It is relevant that these studies are paid for a by a consortium of agencies with an interest in the results. This means that they have to cover an array of issues and the survey is broad rather than deep. Sponsorship from the Forestry Commission and British Waterways means that specific questions are asked about visits to woods and forests and to water (with or without boats).

For the purposes of these surveys, a day visit is defined as a home-based leisure day visit with no minimum duration. In other words visits could be up to twenty-four hours long, although the average length of trip was much shorter than this. The study also includes "tourism day visits" defined as "those trips which lasted three hours or more and which were not taken on a regular basis."

In the 2002/2003, survey, a total of 6,600 people were interviewed in their homes during the survey period (March 2002 to March 2003). The survey covered England (3,188 responses), Wales (1,941) and Scotland (1,471) and provided data on over 21,000 leisure day visits. Respondents were asked a range of questions about the types of trip made during the last fortnight and past year, their duration, destination, party size, distance travelled, amounts spent, as well as calibrating questions about the age of participants, party composition, social class of respondents and so on. Table 16.1 refers to recent leisure visits made in the two weeks preceding the interview.

In 2002/2003, 62% of adults had visited the countryside, compared to 87% visiting towns or cities and 53% the coast or seaside. The survey estimated that a total of 5.2

Table 16.1: Percentage of sampled adults making leisure day visits in the last two weeks: GB, 2002/2003.

Destination	% of Sample
Visit to town or city	50
Visit to countryside	21
Visit to seaside/coast	10
Visit to wood/forest	8

Source: TNS Travel and Tourism (2004).

billion adult day visits were made in 2002/2003, a notable drop from the 5.94 billion visits estimated in the 1998 survey (National Centre for Social Research 1999). Of these, 1.262 billion visits were made to the countryside (compared with 1.427 billion in 1998), with 252 million visits (a sharp decline from 355 million in 1998) made to woods or forests. Plausible explanations have been provided to explain some of the disparity between the 1998 and 2002/2003 figures, but despite these there is still some evidence of systematic differences. Even so, given the snapshot nature of these surveys it remains unclear whether or not there exists any systematic trend away from countryside and other day visits.

The relative importance of different activities undertaken are summarised in Table 16.2. The contrast between activities undertaken at different destinations is consistent with expectations and broadly enhances confidence in the survey. Thus, while eating out and drinking were the most popular activities for visitors to towns and cities, walking and rambling were the most common countryside activities. Overall, the differences in activities undertaken between destinations are perhaps rather small (TNS Travel and Tourism 2004).

When looking at the characteristics of people making leisure day visits in the past two weeks, the proportions of adults visiting either countryside or woodland in 2002/2003 were almost identical for both the over and under 45 age ranges and genders. More significantly, nearly two thirds of countryside and woodland visitors were in social classes ABC1, with over 88% having access to a car. The comparable figures for visits to all U.K. destinations were 51% in classes ABC1 and 74% having personal access to a car. This suggests an uneven pattern of participation in countryside recreation across social classes in Great Britain, an issue which is addressed in Section 5.

The report also details the average distance travelled to destinations, where 13 miles to town or city compares with19 miles on average to the countryside and 30 to the coast. The average duration of all trips was between 3.25 and 3.5 hours and, as in previous years, the countryside visits were slightly shorter than average and substantially longer for trips to the coast, probably reflecting the greater distances travelled to the latter. In terms of transport, 36% of leisure day trips made to the countryside were by foot, compared with 57% by car and only 1% by public transport (bus and train).

The mean amounts spent on day trips were close to £15.60 for visits to towns and cities but only £8.60 for visits to the countryside. For tourism visits these amounts converge slightly, increasing to £30.80 and £20.70 respectively (TNS Travel and Tourism 2004). Worryingly,

Table 16.2: Relative importance of the most important visitor activities by destination: GB. 2002/2003.

	% of Total Trips			
Visits To:	**All Visits**	**Town/City**	**Country-Side**	**Seaside/Coast**
Main activity				
Eat/drink out	18	19	15	13
Walk/hill walk/ramble	15	9	32	20
Visit friends/relatives at their homes	14	16	10	9
To go shopping (not food or regular)	11	15	3	5
Sports or active pursuits	9	8	11	7
Hobby/special interest	8	8	8	6
Entertainment (e.g. cinema, theatre, club?	5	7	1	2
Informal sports & games	4	4	3	2
Visit leisure attraction, place of interest, special event	3	3	5	4

Source: TNS Travel and Tourism (2004).

from a regional development perspective, locally-made products were purchased on only 3% of leisure day visits. Overall, £10.9 billion (£9.7 billion in England) was spent on countryside day visits out of a total leisure day visit spend of £71 billion: thus, while visits to the countryside made up 24% of the total visits they only accounted for 15% of the total expenditure (TNS Travel and Tourism 2004).

A sharp contrast with the Day Visit Survey is provided by the surveys of use of the National Parks in England and Wales. This series of sample surveys were carried out in 1994 with a more specific purpose of assessing the rates of use of National Parks, partly for purposes of budgetary allocation, which concluded that there were a total of 138 million day visits to the National Parks in 1994 (Coulter *et al.* 1996). The methodology here was significantly different from that in the Day Visit Surveys. In particular, with this comparatively small number of visits it would not have been appropriate to base the study on a household survey. This can be seen from the fact that, at the most, only 10% of the visits found in the Day Visit Survey were to the National Parks. Therefore, if the study had been conducted through household interviews, it would have been necessary either to first establish whether those drawn in the sample had been to a National Park recently or to accept a 90% non-response rate to questions regarding the National Parks.

It was therefore decided to proceed with sample surveys of visitors at each National Park and cordon surveys of those entering the Parks were conducted on specific days and the results raised to annual totals from the information obtained. Cordon surveys involve stopping visitors as they enter the Park and asking them questions on the spot. To be effective all visitors should be included on the survey day(s) but this proves difficult where there are many minor roads cutting across Park boundaries thus introducing errors into the sampling procedure and potentially distorting the results. Also, the day chosen for interviews will obviously be one where a number of visitors may reasonably be expected but such visitors may not be representative of the whole population of visitors. In assuming away such problems the loss of the more precise basis of sampling at the household level has to be set against the significant cost-savings offered by the cordon sampling technique. It must also be recognised that there is no perfect basis for sampling and that this is a key practical problem, requiring judgement.

The results of these separate sampling studies were obviously important to individual Parks because they feature in discussions about their level of funding (see Chapter 9). Consequently the Peak District National Park Authority was particularly unhappy with the conclusions of this study, so much so that it commissioned an alternative survey by Touche Ross (1996). A particular point of dispute was over the number of entry points to the Park where entrants had been interviewed. Touche Ross found that the original sample was too small and that sampling errors would have been introduced in raising the results. They argued that the resulting annual visitor estimate of 12.4 million for the Park was much too low and should be increased to 21.9–26.3 million. An assessment of these results (Whitby & Falconer 1999) suggests that their aggregate estimates of day visit number for the national Parks, as a whole, might reasonably be increased from 78 million to 138 million.

Furthermore the nature of visits to National Parks is, as might be expected, qualitatively different from that to the countryside in general. In particular the frequency and repeatability of visits are very high, with over half of respondents visiting the Park at which they were surveyed once a month during the summer. Ninety four percent of respondents had been to the same park before and 73% had been to the same park in previous years. This high level of visitor loyalty to a particular site has obvious implications for visitor management strategies, such as closing areas temporarily in response to fire risks. Fifty-eight percent of visitors go to the parks for scenery and landscape and 29% for peace and quiet. Some 12% considered over-crowding to be a problem and ease of access was particularly important for those near to population centres (the Peak, the Brecon Beacons and the New Forest). Furthermore, a significant proportion of visits were accounted for by those travelling from far afield, perhaps less regularly. Traffic management is an obvious key issue as 91% of visitors come by car and only 6% use public transport.

4. Measuring Demand

Day-visit surveys measure only the use of the countryside and perhaps record the specific activities undertaken. However, for policy purposes, for example when considering changing the amount of countryside access to be supplied, it may be necessary to know how people will respond to the new conditions of supply. Demand is, strictly, the amount of any good that will be taken up by consumers, under known conditions of price. It is an expression of the consumers' enthusiasm to obtain the good. However, we know that most countryside goods are public goods (see Chapter 12) and the demand for them is particularly difficult to assess, first because they are typically not priced and second because those who consume them have an interest in understating their demand for them in the hope that they may reduce any payment that could be extracted from them. In these circumstances it becomes vital to have direct information from people about their attitudes to and enthusiasm for visiting the countryside.

A relevant study of the demand for access to the countryside was commissioned from the Gallup Organisation (1998) by the Country Landowners Association. This survey was based on a random sample of 1,000 households and focussed on their present and prospective usage of the countryside. It found that 80% of respondents would welcome greater access to the countryside and 92% would support restrictions to countryside access to protect and conserve wildlife and the environment. Forty-four percent took short walks in the countryside frequently, with those aged 45–64 being more likely to do so than the younger 16–24 age group. Twenty-five percent of the sample frequently went for longer walks (in excess of two miles). Further questions established comparatively slight expected changes in the frequency of taking countryside walks at local sites (within five miles) if more access were to be provided and little enthusiasm was shown for longer (fifty miles or more) countryside trips for walks.

The probable importance of knowledge of access rights as a determinant of demand suggests that the ignorance of rights exhibited by this survey may have led respondents to overstate their demand for additional recreational access. The ignorance of respondents of the extent of current access rights led them to seriously under-estimate the current extent of existing public footpaths. Other findings from the survey were that 60% of respondents preferred to follow way-marked paths, rather than choose their own route, 53% were concerned for their safety in the remote countryside and 52% were worried about getting lost.

Evidence like this suggests that there is a genuinely bi-modal distribution of the population with a majority feeling somewhat intimidated by open and remote countryside but a significant minority who are very enthusiastic about having access to the wider countryside. This situation poses significant problems for policy-makers dealing with issues of access provision. They must balance expenditure between provision of remote access, for a vociferous minority, against making access more secure for the more cautious majority. If this dichotomy persists, to achieve a rational allocation of resources between the two groups will require considerably more detailed information about the nature of demand for countryside recreation than is at present available.

5. Participation in Countryside Recreation

When reviewing levels of participation in countryside recreation it is not uncommon to observe that participants are not equally distributed across different social groups. Some evidence to support this observation is found in the results of the 2002/2003 GB Leisure Day Visits Survey (see Section 3) which demonstrates that social classes ABC1 make proportionately more countryside visits than other social groups. Using the Office of National Statistics 1991 Standard Occupational Classification, class A is defined as higher managerial, administrative or professional, B is intermediate managerial, administrative or professional, and C1 is supervisory or clerical, junior managerial, administrative or professional (TNS Travel and Tourism 2004). The Leisure Day Visits Survey does not enquire about ethnicity.

Uneven participation in countryside recreation across different social and ethnic groups is a major concern for countryside managers, especially in those cases where recreational opportunities are publicly funded. How managers respond to this problem will depend upon the degree to which non-participation results from a genuine lack of interest in countryside recreation, or from other factors, such as social pressure, lack of information or access problems.

To explore this issue further, we will examine one of the first papers to consider the issue of uneven participation in countryside recreation. Emmett (1970) used the sociological concept of the social filter and applied it to the question of recreational provision and use. Emmett makes a simple but important point in her article:

> recreational participants can usefully be seen as passing through a filter which takes out many possible participants and allows only a small highly selected group to reach the countryside.

Emmett argues that three major factors determine the level of participation in countryside recreation:

(1) knowledge of existing facilities;
(2) access to existing facilities; and
(3) the values of suppliers.

To these, she adds the social dimension, arguing that the physical aspects of the countryside:

> ...are controlled, used and different rights in them owned by a group of people and this group of people acts as a social filter controlling the kinds of other people who use the facilities and affecting the behaviour of those other people.

Emmett identifies various elements of the social filter shown in Box 16.1. Applying this model to countryside recreation emphasises that place is as much a social as a physical entity and that the social filter will be busily at work in the countryside. The social filter is another factor for consumers, along with income, tastes and preferences, which will determines their use of the various recreational facilities on offer.

The legal filter works through assignment of rights to own and control property. People regulate access to the things they own using their direct (e.g. gamekeepers) or indirect employees (e.g. police officers and civil servants). Some property owners may encourage visitors as a means of increasing revenue, while others will discourage recreational use.

Emmett argues we should study the values of these suppliers carefully. She suggests that the suppliers of countryside recreation display three types of value:

- *utilitarian* (providing the greatest good for the greatest number of people);
- *paternalistic* (knowing what is best for others); or
- *exclusive* (maintaining rights for personal benefit).

> **Box 16.1: Elements of the social filter.**
> **The legal filter**: rules and regulations governing entry, property rights that allow holders to choose who enters.
> **The informal filter**: language, style and custom. Adopting a group norm will discourage the "out-group" and encourage the "in-group."
> **The physical filter**: certain places and structures. will not be accessible to particular groups, e.g. the disabled or people who rely on public transport.
> **The information filter**: the existence of relevant information and the knowledge and ability of the individual to access it.
>
> *Source:* Emmett (1970).

We can add the bureaucratic self-seeking values, or the wish to expand agencies and keep them alive as bodies in their own right. The utilitarian motive is probably the most acceptable of these values. Someone has to provide countryside goods and utilitarian motives are likely to provide broad benefits. Paternalist values have shaped many policies on countryside recreation, most notably the original rationale for the provision of country parks. Exclusivity is a commodity valued by most of us, especially when it relates to resources. In the countryside the desire for exclusivity is heard in the howls of protests over new housing developments from those people lucky enough to already live in the area and in the protests of landowners seeking to restrict public access to open land on their properties. In some cases, the desire to exclude others from a resource is motivated by economic concerns, and the desire to exploit a marketable resource such as game or fishing rights. Exclusivity can be maintained by action or by inaction. Potential visitors can be discouraged actively, or merely not provided with any information about the resource. Emmett suggests that public suppliers of countryside recreation are assumed to be in consensus with existing consumers. One of the reasons for this assumed consensus is due to the operation of the filter. Most of the countryside facilities have become the dominant preserve of "like-minded" people.

Emmett argues that private landlords and public recreation providers have limited the provision of recreation to a wider public, often with the intention of limiting use. She agrees that there are technical aspects of providing for large numbers, but there are also exclusive reactions from those in possession. Similarly some providers may attempt to preserve particular resources for certain groups, often under a guise of paternalist concern for the resource in question, for example to protect it from over-use or from damage. Emmett makes a very strong case for paying careful attention to recreational plans to determine who loses and who gains from proposals.

Emmett suggests the following checklist of questions which are highly relevant for new facilities:

(1) How many people, of what kind and indulging in what behaviour, do those who open the facility wish to open it to?

(2) Who already has the rights in the facility: rights to game, grazing or access?
(3) When plans are made to publicise and encourage wider use by the public of a facility, who are the existing users, what will their reaction be, what tools, power and influence have they at their disposal for reserving the facility for "their kind of people?"

Based on Emmett's work we expect to find the middle classes dominating the countryside recreation scene. This can be examined with reference to Curry & Comley's (1986) paper "Who Enjoys the Countryside?" discussed in Curry (1994). This study concluded that:

(1) participation varies across social classes, with lower participation from the lower classes. This is partly attributable to variations in capacity and partly to differences in preferences. It is easier to address the former than the latter;
(2) demand management policies which might improve access to recreation seem beyond the scope of the recreation sector;
(3) supply-led policies are probably more difficult to target and as such constitute blunt instruments in influencing peoples' behaviour;
(4) supply-led policies can influence participation by increasing awareness of rights and opportunities in the countryside;
(5) Ultimately, it may be that countryside recreation policy overall has a limited role to play as a "social" policy influencing people's behaviour patterns. It could be more constructive to accept that these patterns are more likely to be influenced by exogenous social policies, and that the real role of recreation policy lies in the development of land use and land management systems to cater for a predetermined profile of participation.

A number of recent studies have looked at barriers to countryside recreation. In a report for the Countryside Recreation Network Slee *et al.* (2001) identified a range of barriers to countryside recreation (see Box 16.2) that have much in common with Emmett's social filters.

The 1996 U.K. Leisure day Visits Survey (SCPR 1998) that found that 23% of those not visiting the countryside in Great Britain had "no particular reason" for not doing so and for a further 19% it had no appeal. Slee concludes that while barriers may cause some people not to visit the countryside many just choose not to do so. Chesters (1998) suggests that low rates of participation may reflect preferences for urban recreation and may be linked to lifestyle cycles, while a variety of studies have suggested that young adults are perhaps most under-represented in countryside recreation.

Giving up all pretensions to provide countryside recreation for all seems unduly pessimistic. Education may help to develop tastes or interests, while better information and marketing may increase the potential market for countryside recreation. Similarly, a planning system more sympathetic to the needs of recreation could help to encourage access through the provision of more attractive facilities than are often offered.

Curry (1994) examines rural land use policies, asking whether they were likely to promote recreation. He carried out an analysis of 100 Structure Plans in England and Wales and concluded that recreation tends to be encouraged in accessible urban fringe locations and not in the highly productive or environmentally sensitive areas.

> **Box 16.2: Barriers to countryside recreation.**
>
> *OUTER BARRIERS*
>
> **individual** — *income, family, attitudes, perceptions, confidence*
>
> **social** — *relationships, discrimination*
>
> **economic** — *wealth distribution, public expenditure, prices*
>
> **access** — *mobility, signage, design, attitudes*
>
> **facility** — *images, activities*
>
> **management** — *policies, pricing, practice*
>
> *INNER BARRIERS*
>
> **self** — *sense of self, self-esteem, identity*
>
> **mental health disorders**
>
> **hallucinations & medication**
>
> *Source:* Slee et al. (2001).

He analyses the types of facility that will be restricted or encouraged and concludes that more passive recreational activities are more common in Structure Plans and that the public sector tends to permit or promote more active pastimes rather than provide them. This is in contrast to the preferences of the population for what he calls unmanaged countryside recreation, compared with activities in urban areas and the managed countryside.

Curry attributes this lack of enthusiasm for providing open country recreation to two types of motivation: first the fear of a recreation explosion and second to what he calls agricultural fundamentalism. This is code for a rather subservient approach to farming interests on the part of the planners which is only recently diminishing. Such priorities, he tells us lead to three types of problem:

- first, not encouraging recreation in areas of high landscape value steers the visitors away, from the parts of the countryside they would enjoy most;
- second, promoting the misconception that recreation nearly always causes serious damage to such areas;
- third, not encouraging recreation reduces the options for and possible extent of farm diversification.

Originally, responses to these priorities led to the establishment of country parks (see Section 7) and similar peri-urban sites designed as "honeypots" that would attract visitors from the town and deflect them from more sensitive areas. Encouragingly, many of these attitudes have diminished over time as managers and policy makers take a more realistic view of trends in countryside recreation.

6. Country Parks

In the mid-1960s a Government White Paper identified the potential importance of urban fringe land for countryside recreation. While such land was close to urban populations, and therefore attractive as a recreational resource, it contained few of the required amenities to accommodate sustained recreational use (Glyptis 1991). This led to the establishment of country parks under the 1968 Countryside Act, and 1967 Countryside (Scotland) Act. Under Section 6 of the 1968 Act, local authorities in England were empowered to purchase land, lay out, plant and improve sites to establish parks close to urban or built-up areas. Private landowners could also establish these parks and were eligible for grant aid of up to 75% of costs from the Countryside Commission, who would also meet up to 50% of local authority costs (Glyptis 1991). The country park concept was later extended in Scotland with powers to create Regional Parks under the Countryside (Scotland) Act 1981.

The policy for establishing parks was based on two contradictory demands, the first to provide increased opportunities for countryside recreation and the second to provide an alternative recreational resource to other more sensitive sites such as those in national Parks. Country parks were designed to provide urban populations with a "countryside experience" in created or modified areas of land close to the areas where they lived (Curry 1994). As such, they have attracted criticism from a number of commentators, notably Shoard (1987) who described them *as "miniature Red-Indian reservations for the urban underclass."*

Despite these attitudes country parks increased substantially in numbers since the 1960s and now account for an estimated 73 million leisure day visits per year (Countryside Agency 2003). Glyptis (1991) noted that less than half of the new parks represented new access opportunities, with many existing sites, such as Tatton Park in Cheshire, improved and extended using grant aid. Sustained improvements in their management have been supported by studies such as those carried out by the Countryside Commission in Cannock Chase in the early 1980s looking into management planning at such sites (Countryside Commission 1985).

From the late 1980s onwards the objectives of country parks have been modified, and today, country parks are not viewed as a means of keeping urban populations away from the wider countryside but rather as "gateways" between town and country which will encourage visitors to explore areas beyond the managed parks (DETR 2000). The Countryside Agency (2003) sets out its new vision for country parks in England, outlining a much broader set of objectives including the promotion of social inclusion, community engagement, health and sustainability. This represents a considerable step forward from the notions of containment so prevalent in the 1960s and 70s but will need to be supported by considerable investment from local authorities.

7. Strategic Implications

Developments such as the 2000 Countryside and Rights of Way Act and the Land Reform (Scotland) Act (see Chapter 15) will greatly increase the supply of land for recreational access. Yet it seems highly likely that a significant part of it will be unattractive to many individuals and may attract few if any new visitors.

At the same time, we must also take into account any growth or shrinkage in the population of countryside recreationists. Will this source of new users expand or will it contract (as perhaps suggested by the results of the 2002/2003 GB Leisure Day Visits Survey)? More sophisticated version of models such as those developed by Dower could certainly suggest some trends, though may be less successful in predicting shifts in tastes and fashion. Many areas have enjoyed a substantial increase in visitors associated with an association with a popular television programme (e.g. "Heartbeat Country" in the North York Moors) or the development of a popular visitor attraction such as the Eden project in Cornwall.

Economic demand models looking at how the consumption of recreation changes relative to changes in income or price (the so-called elasticity measures) could also provide useful information for those engaged in the strategic management of facilities or in developing strategies to maximise revenue. While common in other sectors, such elasticities are rarely estimated for countryside recreation and it should remain an important goal of the research community to provide some robust demand estimates for outdoor recreation.

Efforts to manage recreational demand in the countryside have been made since the introduction of country parks in the 1960s. More recent initiatives designed to address concerns about uneven participation in countryside recreation may reflect a particular facet of the demand problem. It is important that any such initiatives are based on strong evidence of the existence of barriers to participation. Where such barriers exist it is important that efforts are made to remove them in order to permit equal opportunities for all of the U.K. population to enjoy countryside recreation regardless of age, physical ability, ethnicity or social class. If, however, lack of participation is an artefact of personal tastes or preferences then any attempts to change the status quo might suggest an element of social engineering designed to improve the performance of recreational sites rather than increase the overall well-being of society.

Approaches to increasing participation in countryside recreation must address a number of factors. Take the example of promotional material. This must take account of the interests and attitudes of different user groups and beware of unintended signals given by photographs and other material. For instance, the wording and style of some material may discourage some potential users, while choice of photographs might suggest that only certain types of people visit the site or that some individuals will have little in common with established users. This suggests that promotional material must seek to be as inclusive as possible without falling into the trap of tokenism or merely appealing to the lowest common denominator. Similarly, countryside organisations should encourage a more balanced media portrayal of rural areas, their inhabitants and the issues that concern them. These measures may help potential visitors to realise that the countryside is the not the exclusive domain of particular groups and that it offers something for nearly everyone to enjoy.

References

Chesters, A. (1998). Who's been left out. In: E. Blamey (Ed.), *Making access for all a reality*. Proceedings of the 1997 Annual Conference of the Countryside Recreation Network. Department of City and Regional Planning, University of Cardiff, Cardiff.

Coulter, F., MacGregor C., & Denmand, R. (1996). *Visitors to the National Parks*. Cheltenham: Countryside Commission.
Countryside Agency (2003). *Towards a country park renaissance*. Cheltenham: Countryside Agency.
Countryside Commission (1985). *Cannock Chase 1979–1984: A country parks plan on trial*, CCP181. Cheltenham: Countryside Commission.
Curry, N. (1994). *Countryside recreation, access and land use planning*. London: E & F N Spon.
Curry, N., & Comley, A. (1986). *Who enjoys the countryside?* Strathclyde Papers on Planning, University of Strathclyde, Department of Urban and Regional Planning.
Department of Environment, Transport and the Regions (2000). *Our countryside: The future — A fair deal for rural England*. London: HMSO.
Dower, M. (1965, February). The fourth wave. *Architects Journal*.
Emmett, I. (1970). The social filter in the leisure field. *Recreation News Supplement, 4*.
Glyptis, S. (1991). *Countryside recreation*. London: Longman.
National Centre for Social Research (1999). Leisure day visits: Report of the 1998 UK leisure day visits survey, CAX 14. Cheltenham: Countryside Agency.
Shoard, M. (1987). *This land is our land*. London: Paladin.
Slee, W., Joseph, D., & Curry, N. (2001). Social exclusion in countryside leisure in the UK. A Report for Countryside Recreation Network Department of City and Regional Planning, University of Cardiff, Cardiff.
Social and Community Planning Research (1998). UK leisure day visits: Report of the 1996 survey finding. Cheltenham: Countryside Agency.
Touche Ross (1996). *Peak National Park: Assessment of visitor numbers*. Peak National Park Joint Planning Board.
TNS Travel and Tourism (2004). *GB leisure day visits survey*. Edinburgh: TNS Travel and Tourism.
Whitby, M., & Falconer, K. (1999). Re-instatement, renewal, or re-creation of access rights: The economics of the right to roam. Centre for Rural Economy Working Paper 38.

Chapter 17

Visitor Management

1. Introduction

Many countryside managers spend a significant proportion of their time dealing with the general public. In many cases this will involve managing sites where public access is permitted, while in others the aim may be to provide the public with information or to encourage them to participate in countryside recreation. Visitor management is required both to protect vulnerable areas from damage and to help ensure that those of us who visit the countryside have an enjoyable experience. From the point of view of the provider visitors may also offer a useful opportunity to generate revenue, either to provide income or to be used to fund the management of the site.

Providing information to the public about the countryside either on-site or off-site is a key part of any strategy for visitor management. Information provision helps to promote understanding and encourage participation, this is increasingly important given the large sums of public money currently devoted to its support and management. Similarly, by providing the right kind of information managers can also help visitors to get the most out of their trips to the countryside and may in some cases promote certain kinds of behaviour that contribute to particular management objectives.

This chapter explores a range of issues of strategic importance to those countryside managers who have to deal with the general public. First, we examine the issue of charging for access to the countryside. The price of any good or service is part of something called the marketing mix, and we go on to explore the broader role of marketing in strategic countryside management. We then examine the role of interpretation in countryside management, before looking at the broader issue of how we educate young people about the countryside.

2. Charging for Countryside Access

One of the most direct ways to regulate the flow of visitors to a site is through charging for access. Historically, the idea of regulating countryside access through a price mechanism has received little support from public agencies. This is not surprising. Many countryside sites are open access and the costs of collecting entry fees could easily exceed the revenue generated. Even where it is feasible to charge for access, the existence of cheaper alternative recreational sites and activities may reduce the volume of visitors significantly. As well as such practical concerns, there may also be a feeling that it is in some sense wrong or unreasonable to charge for access to what might otherwise be a public good.

In theory, it would be possible to charge visitors for entry to a range of sites in the countryside. Indeed, we are all familiar with the charges levied by bodies such as the National Trusts and English Heritage for access to their properties. For the manager, the key questions to consider are whether or not charging for access is practical, the appropriate charge for access and the impacts that charging will have on visitors, the site and other sites that might act as substitutes. Where management strategies are aimed at revenue generation or at controlling visitor numbers, then charging for access may be considered. If, on the other hand, strategies emphasise maximising the number and social range of participants then it may not be sensible to charge for access.

In the following section we will review the options currently available to managers in terms of regulating countryside access through a price mechanism. The discussion is in two parts. First we consider the technology available for charging for access and second we review, in some detail, an early Countryside Commission study (Bovaird *et al.* 1984) that assessed the potential for charging for access to countryside sites.

3. Collecting Access Charges

Many areas of open countryside have very long boundaries and to control entry to these and collect fees from users would be prohibitively expensive. Yet this could be achieved if it was known when people entered and left the area. Such information is not usually available, but it could be obtained if it were possible to monitor and record the entry and exit of visitors. The necessary technology to provide this information could become available in the near future if it becomes standard practice to fit motor vehicles with electronic tags to help monitor their use of toll roads and areas where congestion charges are levied. With such tracking devices in place it would be a relatively simple matter for countryside managers to identify and record the location of car users and for suitable charges to be debited from the user's bank account or credit card. As well as generating revenue such mechanisms would have the advantage of encouraging car sharing and the use of alternative modes of transport.

If such a system were introduced it would be easy to modify it to collect revenue from cars, say, as they enter National Parks and to charge them accordingly. Charges could varied to reflect times of peak use in order to reduce congestion and the fees collected could be returned to the park to use in pursuit of its purposes. The use of such a system would be effectively to "privatise" the parks and if this were to be done it would have to be accompanied by careful rules which would ensure that its use was enhanced and did not detract from the success of the Parks in carrying out their functions.

Other more traditional ways of pricing countryside goods internalise their benefits by restricting access to the members of clubs that charge a membership fee. Use of mechanisms such as off-peak memberships can help to spread demand and reduce congestion. Like other forms of charging, the operation of clubs can also encourage the exclusion of certain groups from the countryside and the levels of exclusion would depend on the fees structure (for example, generous discounts could be offered to the unwaged) and the ways in which membership fees were spent. What is important to note, is that the costs and effectiveness of operating such systems are changing continually and that they are likely to be more easily applicable in the future. Sensitively used, the price mechanism may be able to guide people away from congested sites and towards less congested ones. This may require sophisticated technology but this may be available to managers at very low cost if charging for road use is widely adopted.

4. What Level of Price is Appropriate?

This is the question addressed by Bovaird *et al.* (1984). Their study obtained information on admission prices and visitor numbers from two sets of countryside properties, some administered by the National Trust and others by Department of the Environment (and now operated by English Heritage). Bovaird *et al.* suggested that pricing information is important because it indicates the scope for:

- obtaining information on visitor preferences;
- revenue raising;
- demand regulation.

The data gathered were used to investigate the relationship between admission charges and the demand for site visits. The resulting price-demand relationship was estimated and from this the researchers were able to determine whether or not an increase in admission charges would result in an increase or decrease in revenue.

From an economic perspective, the relationship between price increase and revenue generation is expressed through a measure known as the price elasticity of demand (ε_p). This is calculated from a conventional demand equation which models the quantity consumed of a good or service as a function of its price and other factors such as the price or availability of substitutes or complements. Box 17.1 describes the key elasticity measures and their impact on revenue generation.

Box 17.1: Price elasticity of demand and revenue generation.

unit elasticity [$\varepsilon_p = -1$] in this situation total revenue is unaffected by price changes, i.e. impacts on revenue of any changes in the quantity demanded are exactly offset by the impacts of a change in price.

inelasticity [$-1 < \varepsilon_p < 0$] here, an increase in price will result in an increase in revenue.

elasticity [$\varepsilon_p < -1$] where revenue will fall if the price is increased.

In practice, the demand curves for very few goods demonstrate constant elasticity and for most elasticity varies over the length of the demand curve. This begs the question as to where the operators should pitch their price in order to maximise revenue, or obtain some target revenue.

Recreation suppliers are usually "price-fixers" in that they can set the price at whatever level they like as long as they are prepared to suffer the consequences. In contrast, recreation

Table 17.1: Price elasticities of demand for National Trust sites.

Site	Price Elasticity of Demand
Chedworth	−0.36
Hidcote	−0.85 to −1.05
Packwood	−0.8 to −1.0
Sheffield Park	−0.6 to −0.7
Shugborough	−0.35 to −0.5
Wallington	−0.25 to −0.3

Source: Bovaird *et al.* (1984).

consumers are generally "price-takers," in that they have to accept the price determined by the supplier and can only react to it. They cannot determine its level by any other means. Examination of the graphs of demand curves suggests that producers should aim to move consumers to the point where the price elasticity of demand is −1. Such a move is logical because at any other point on the curve they can increase revenue by moving price towards the point of unit elasticity where revenue generation is optimal.

In their case studies, Bovaird *et al.* found that the National Trust tended to charge more than the Department of the Environment and that the price elasticity of demand was higher at National Trust sites than at the Department of the Environment sites (see Tables 17.1 and 17.2). On the basis of these results they inferred that the managers of Department of the Environment properties had more scope for raising prices than those at National Trust properties.

The results of this study are now somewhat dated but still provide an interesting illustration of the potential for economic analysis to help managers determine a pricing policy that

Table 17.2: Price elasticities of demand for Department of Environment sites.

Site	Price Elasticity of Demand
Avebury	−0.15 to −0.23
Carisbrook	−0.33 to −0.3
Dover Castle	−0.2 to −0.3
Goodrich	−0.2 to −0.35
Hampton Court	−0.2 to −0.3
Kenilworth	−0.5
Lullingstone	−0.13 to −0.5
Osborne	−0.55 to −0.7
Richmond	−0.25 to −0.3
Scarborough	−0.25 to −0.36
Walmer	−0.09 to −0.18

Source: Bovaird *et al.* (1984, Table 8.22).

maximises revenue. The analysis is, however, somewhat limited in that it relies on price alone and does not account for other demand shifters such as income levels and substitute goods. Estimates are based on demand behaviour alone and if supply were to change at the same time, it would bring about changes in consumption that are not captured in the model.

5. Pricing Policies

Maximising revenue may not be the only objective that managers wish to pursue when determining pricing policies. Other objectives may address the need to spread demand more equally across different times or to increase participation across different user groups. In pursuing various objectives managers may consider a number of questions.

- *Should separate prices be charged for individual parts of the site (e.g. gardens and house) or should an all-in price be used?*
  The profitability of such a policy will depend on the number of visitors wishing to see the whole site, or only part of it, and the costs of operating such a system.
- *Should the price structure differentiate between on and off-peak periods?*
  Here the price mechanism is used to even out peaks and troughs in demand and to improve the quality of the experience for users as well as reducing management costs.
- *Should managers offer reductions for large parties booking in advance?*
  This makes sense for managers because it may encourage more people to visit the site and at the same time could reduce any associated costs by allowing for any necessary forward planning.
- *Should prices differentiate between categories of visitor?*
  Reduced entry charges for children, retired people or the unwaged are common, but vary in size and on demand. In some cases, for example when children are more prone to damage sites, such reductions may not be defensible. On the other hand, children are the consumers of the future and the educational benefits of visits may make up for the reduction in revenue. It would also be possible to compensate for any loss in revenue by making adults pay more, effectively letting those without children subsidise those who have them. Seasonal price differentials might also be justified in that adults are more likely to take children with them during school holidays. Reduced prices for other groups may reflect social objectives and may be limited to off-peak times to spread demand.
- *When should we charge for access to the countryside?*
  When considering the question of whether or not to charge for access at countryside sites, the question of equity between groups becomes an issue, because admission charges may exclude users from some low income groups. This may be so, but evidence from the Bovaird *et al*. study and others, suggests that many existing visitors to these properties come from the middle classes. This implies that a low price policy may also benefit these better-off groups. Against this, it must be pointed out that the existing pattern of use reflects the response of the whole population. It is not clear that lowering prices would necessarily attract more participants from lower income groups.

300   Strategic Countryside Management

Type of Recreation	Management Cost	Cost of Provision	Charging Probability
Access land	Low	Low	Low
Natural attraction — something to see	Low/ high*	Medium	High (parking charges)
Natural attraction — something to do	Medium/ high*	High	High (admission or facility charges)

*dependent on visitor patterns, especially peak demand.

Figure 17.1: A pricing strategy for countryside recreation. *Source:* Bovaird *et al.* (1984, Figure 11.1).

- *Should season tickets be available for regular visitors?*
  Season ticket and life membership schemes are well-established in the National Trusts and many other organisations. High entry charges to single properties encourage visitors to take up season tickets, though in many cases, especially after the early years of membership, such arrangements may not yield full value to the consumer. Bovaird *et al.* (1984) found that members tended to spread their visits more evenly over years and seasons, thus increasing membership through season tickets may encourage a more even, less congested use of sites. Season tickets are also a good means of controlling and maximising income flows and can help to guarantee finance for long term projects.
- *Pricing as part of the marketing mix*
  In their concluding section Bovaird *et al.* (1984) examined the role of pricing as part of the marketing mix (see Section 6). They concluded that there is much scope for increasing the use of pricing in marketing policy and they imply that monitoring the effects of pricing is essential if the systems used are to be adequately fine tuned. Figure 17.1 illustrates the type of site and associated strategy recommended by Bovaird *et al*. Effectively, this suggests that admission or facility charges are only appropriate where there is a considerable attraction offering both activities and visual pleasure. Such facilities are costly to provide and hence charges might be justified. Notice that they recommend parking charges for the natural attractions where access is more of an issue than facilities. In this case options for charging are currently through honesty boxes, ticket machines or collection at the point of entry.

6. Marketing the Countryside

When the word marketing is used in a business context, it might be assumed that it is referring only to some form of promotion or advertising. However, the many marketing text books available to students cover a much wider range of concerns than merely promotion.

In highlighting the breadth of the discipline, the American Marketing Association (AMA) define marketing as:

> the process of planning and executing the conception, pricing and promotion and distribution of ideas, goods and services to create exchange and satisfy individual and organisational objectives (AMA 1985).

Clearly this encompasses a range of activities relevant to the countryside manager, especially when that manager is engaged in implementing strategies. The definition is also consistent with what many marketing textbooks refer to as the marketing mix, or the "4Ps" (Borden 1964) — that is *price, product, place* and *promotion*. Once the manager has determined the dynamics of the environment within which they operate then the management of these four elements of the marketing plan become crucial.

The notion of price, that is the cost of accessing countryside goods, has already been covered at some length in the previous section. Price tends to be the aspect of the marketing mix most associated with the private sector, though membership fees and admission charges to reserves and other sites are issues that concern a range of charitable organisations and statutory bodies. For countryside managers product and place are often constrained by the very nature of the goods that they deal with. Even so, there are many possibilities for the design of visitor services at countryside sites and an increasing awareness that place does not have to mean physical location but can refer to points of access where prospective users can learn more about the countryside and what it has to offer. This need to make potential users aware of the potential benefits of the countryside gives rise to the need for promotion.

All organisations operate within an environment where they engage in transactions with a group of consumers, exchanging goods or services for money. In some cases the transaction is carried out directly with the consumer, while in others the payment is made on his or her behalf, possibly by some Government agency. Within this context, any marketing task can be categorised as either identifying or satisfying the needs of customers. In the private-sector, these aspects of marketing may be viewed as a necessary step towards profit maximisation, while in the public sector they may relate more to ensuring that public money is being spent efficiently. This may be revealed in the organisational strategy to increase visitor numbers or membership levels, or to improve the satisfaction of visitors and other stakeholders, then a marketing approach may be an appropriate route for an organisation to develop.

Like any other aspect of management, marketing requires careful planning, timely and accurate information, skilled personnel, and adequate resources. Many countryside managers work for organisations whose prime concern is the delivery of countryside goods to the public. Any discipline which can help them to deliver the right type of countryside goods to their stakeholders is clearly worthy of consideration.

Once implemented, a marketing plan requires the same sort of monitoring and evaluation as any other strategy. Clearly, this kind of effort requires considerable commitment from an organisation if it is to be successful. Such commitment is generally worthwhile: it is too easy for an organisation to set short term marketing objectives without the support of a coherent strategy and such practices seldom produce long-term benefits.

In many countryside organisations, the marketing strategy may focus on increasing visitor satisfaction and enjoyment. Similarly, CARTs and other membership-based organisations must ensure that the needs of their members are met. If these objectives are not achieved then visit rates and membership numbers may fall. In these situations there is an element of attempting to supply the product desired by the majority, thereby increasing the chances that either profits or social benefits are being maximised. In the public sector there may be the additional constraint of needing to ensure an equitable distribution of benefits. In this case, it may be desirable to produce a marketing strategy that broadens consumption across different target groups rather than maximising consumption over a more limited range. This need for an equitable distribution of benefits across stakeholders is one of the fundamental differences between marketing in a public and private sector context.

7. Countryside Marketing in Action

Many of the organisations and agencies working in the countryside engage in a range of activities, dealing with a variety of individuals and groups. Charitable organisations such as the National Trusts have a strong identity in heritage tourism, but are also active in other areas such as education, land management and, more recently, rural development. Statutory agencies such as the Countryside Council for Wales and Scottish Natural Heritage have a wide variety of responsibilities covering a range of important economic, social and environmental concerns.

Where an organisation has diverse interests and deals with a range of stakeholder groups, it is vitally important that it has good marketing communication skills at its disposal. Marketing communication is important for disseminating information, helping public understanding and creating awareness of particular issues. Promotion and publicity are key elements in marketing communication and a vital part of marketing strategies of all kinds and are particularly important in the countryside. Awareness of the nature of different market segments can help to identify target groups for a promotional strategy and these can then be approached using techniques specifically aimed at them. Advertising is one possible route for managers wishing to promote their sites to the public, though more cost-effective approaches may seek to involve the broadcast media (e.g. coverage of countryside events in local television news programmes) or features in newspapers and magazines with a local or specialist readership.

The Foot and Mouth outbreak in 2001 provided a good example of the need for countryside organisations to be able to communicate effectively with the general public and other groups. Foot and Mouth disease caused many areas of open countryside to be made off limits to the general public and in particular many thousands of miles of footpaths were closed. Both at the height of the outbreak and in the following summer, there were pressing reasons for keeping the public well informed about which areas of the countryside were accessible to them.

At first the emphasis was on ensuring that members of the public did not risk spreading the disease by entering restricted areas. Later as the outbreak receded and the negative impacts on local tourism were being felt, the emphasis changed as strategies were developed to encourage people back into the countryside. Thus, the initial tactic was to ensure that people were made aware of where they should not go and the reasons behind this prohibition. Later it became more important for people to realise that the countryside was open for business and for them to be able to find out where they could visit safely.

The efforts associated with Foot and Mouth were interesting in that, in addition to trying to reach as many members of the general public as possible, specific organisations targeted particular specialist groups to ensure that they had access to information relevant to their interests. In contacting these target groups different channels of communication were used to increase the effectiveness of the message. Thus, while the national media was used to spread more general messages and information, web-sites, newsletters, fact-sheets and posters were also use to inform particular groups about how the crisis was impacting on their activity.

The use of marketing to communicate particular messages during the Foot and Mouth Crisis contrasts with the more strategic use of the discipline to achieve planned objectives. Such an approach was adopted at Rufford Country Park in Nottinghamshire in a study by the Countryside Commission and Nottinghamshire County Council. Rufford Country Park, situated two miles south of Ollerton and 17 miles north of Nottingham, is one of three country parks in Nottinghamshire. The park was originally part of the estate of a tweflth century Cistercian abbey and after a succession of owners was purchased by the County Council in 1952. The area was designated as a country park in 1969, after which the site was extensively redeveloped.

In 1977 the County Council Countryside Division drafted a strategy for the creation and management of countryside sites with the aim of increasing public access and enjoyment of the countryside (Countryside Commission 1979). As a result of this strategy the county Leisure Services Committee decided to proceed with the development of the Park. Before this development commenced, a full scale marketing strategy for the site was developed. This project broke new ground in its efforts to demonstrate to countryside managers the common misperceptions that many held regarding marketing.

The Rufford Park study attempted to demonstrate how:

> the essentials of a marketing approach are concerned with being clear about what you are trying to achieve: deciding who and how many people you can and should cater for; what should be provided in the way of attractions; how people can be made aware of the attractions and the way they are presented to visitors; the price which they can be expected to pay for services; and finally deciding what information is required to allow each of these to be changed in the light of experience (Countryside Commission 1979).

The study consisted of a number of phases:

- analysis of the market for craft centres and interpretive facilities to complement those at the county's two other country parks;
- analysis of competition from 40 other local sites;
- identification of potential marketing opportunities at Rufford;
- analysis of pricing options;
- development of a promotional strategy.

The study made a number of recommendations, one of the most important of which was the establishment of a Craft Centre in the old stable block, incorporating a gallery, craft and gift shops. This development was identified following an analysis of demand for such facilities. Also mooted were an interpretive resource centre, an auditorium and exhibition area. The study discussed a range of pricing options, particularly in relation to car parking and looked at a range of promotional options, particularly focusing on increasing use at off-peak times.

Since the initial marketing study further developments have taken place including restoration of the Orangery and the opening of a new restaurant. The Craft Centre has expanded and a number of new retail units have opened. Today Rufford attracts some 800,000 visitors per annum.

The success of Rufford's marketing strategy has led to the introduction of a range of similar initiatives at countryside recreation sites across the UK aimed at boosting numbers and improving the visitor experience. A range of other marketing activities exist both at local and national levels, ranging from the mundane to the slightly eccentric. One example is an initiative in rural Wales that assists owners of hotels and holiday cottages whose properties play host to roosting bats. The "Batty Holidays" pilot project encouraged the owners of this holiday accommodation to promote their properties as a particular eco-tourism "niche market" providing information on bats to visitors and organising events such as bat-watching. (Countryside Council for Wales 2000).

8. Countryside Education

In 1999 Ian MacNicol, a leading member of the Country Landowners' Association made an impassioned plea for more space to be found in the National Curriculum for children to learn about farming and the countryside. His argument for promoting a greater understanding of the countryside among children is based on a need to dispel some of the myths and misunderstandings that surround the countryside. Increasingly, children living in urban areas have become remote from the countryside and understand little about how it works or the people who live there. A similar view is expounded by Pretty (1998) who argues that as more and more people become remote from the process of food production the less they understand it, with consequent costs for society.

These days, if you ask a child from an inner city school to name a job that someone living in the country might do, it is a near certainty that the reply would be "farmer." When countryside management students at Newcastle University posed this question to local children studying at key stage 3, more than two thirds were unable to name a second job after "farmer" despite the fact that the vast majority of rural dwellers no longer work in agriculture.

While a lack of knowledge about the broad base of the rural economy is perhaps unsurprising, it is more worrying to realise that many children are poorly informed about other fundamental aspects of farming and the countryside. A survey carried out by MORI in 1999 on behalf of the National Farmers' Union found that many 8–11 year olds were unclear about the source of common products such as ham or margarine, while a more recent survey for Country Life magazine found a similar lack of understanding about a broader range of countryside issues.

In England the National Curriculum for secondary school children makes only limited mention of the countryside. The most relevant curriculum area in terms of countryside education is the environmental education element of the Geography curriculum. In 1990 the National Curriculum Council stated that "Environmental education is the subject of considerable debate and there is no clear consensus about the issues." Little seems to have changed since then and while our children may be becoming better informed about issues such as global warming or sustainable development, fewer are likely to be aware of some of the more local issues facing the British countryside. In 2001 the curriculum for key stage 3 students (pre GCSE, i.e. 13–14 year old students) suggested that they should be taught "the location of places and environments studied, places and environments in the news and other significant places and environments" and be able to "describe and explain the physical and human features that give rise to the distinctive character of places." Students should also be able to "describe and explain patterns of physical and human features and relate these to the character of places and environments . . . and their impact on places and environments." While this could be designed to include rural areas, such matters are left to the discretion of the teacher.

The National Curriculum (see: www.nc.uk.net) offers some scope for local issues to be raised but provides insufficient focus on the countryside. For key stage 3 students doing geography, for example, the Curriculum suggests that investigational skills may be based on gathering views and evidence on appropriate local issues. Similarly all nine "Thematic Studies" at key stage 3 should involve work at a local scale as well as at international, national and regional levels. While this could involve city-based children looking beyond the town at rural issues it seems likely that in many cases lack of resources or enthusiasm may mean that local issues relate exclusively to the urban environment.

While our educational system may be partly to blame for this lack of awareness, we must also recognise that this phenomenon is partly attributable to decades of social change which have taken our children further away from the reality of the countryside. Indeed, in these days of foreign holidays and theme parks, the images of the countryside that are most common to many inner city children come from soap operas such as "Emmerdale" or popular dramas such as "Heartbeat." While the attractive scenery of the North York Moors or the Yorkshire Dales provides a striking backdrop to these entertainments, the local environment tends to play second fiddle in terms of plot development and much of the action revolves around concerns that cross the urban rural divide. Occasionally an agricultural story line or something related to outdoor activities may be introduced to provide verisimilitude but for the most part children are left with a somewhat warped view of what goes on in the countryside.

Such images of rurality are unlikely to prove harmful while children retain sufficient critical abilities to be able to separate fiction from reality. Thus, most children living in inner city areas know that real life is somewhat different from the enhanced realities of "Eastenders" or "Coronation Street." Things may be different, however, when the images concern something less familiar, such as the countryside and it is in these cases that we need to ensure that children are able to assess the validity of the material which they are being exposed to. It is an interesting irony, that while the National Curriculum recognises the potential value of television as an educational tool, that much of the media interpretation has been removed from the English Curriculum (Ferry 2001). Clearly, if children are to rely on the media for information about the countryside then we should at least hope that they are able to make some judgement about the authenticity and significance of what they are exposed to.

Commentators, such as Elliot (1995), accuse the Government of being willing to pay lip service to the notion of environmental education but lacking the commitment to ensure any significant and worthwhile educational outcomes. It can be argued that while the National Curriculum deals with environmental issues, particularly at the global scale, there is insufficient emphasis on ensuring that British children grow up with a firm understanding of that part of their country that extends beyond the urban fringes. Events associated with the Foot and Mouth crisis highlighted the lack of public understanding about the rural economy and led to an increase in calls for a greater proportion of classroom time to be devoted to the countryside.

Until such calls are heeded by policymakers, it is left to individual organisations to attempt to redress the imbalance between town and country in our education system. Statutory bodies such as Scottish Natural Heritage (SNH), the Countryside Council for Wales, the Countryside Agency and the National Park Authorities all participate in a variety of environmental education initiatives. SNH provides a number of examples detailing their environmental education initiatives. One of these is the "Environmental Community Chest," a box full of high quality educational materials such as books, posters and video cassettes designed to help community education worker with no specialist knowledge of the countryside to address environmental projects with children and adults (SNHa 1996). Another innovative SNH project was "Grounds for Learning" which encourages schools and colleges to make better use of their playing fields and other land for environmental studies.

The National Trust provide a good resource for teachers wishing to link countryside activities with the National Curriculum. Many National Trust properties have opportunities for fieldwork and for learning based on first-hand experience and offer education staff and facilities such as study bases and resource. The Trust runs an Education Group Membership scheme which allows educational institutions to make low cost visits to Trust properties. The Trust's educational website provides guidance on National Curriculum links at specific properties. In addition the Trust often runs special projects which focus on particular areas of the Curriculum and its website (www.nt-education.org) suggests that Trust properties are particularly useful for "fieldwork based on geographical features, geomorphological processes, ecosystems, environmental change and issues, locality studies and rural economy and settlement."

The Trust are also engaged in more than 70 coast and countryside Guardianships, long-term partnerships between the Trust and a school. Children from the school can undertake a range of activities in association with their partner site, including site visits, camps, conservation projects, wildlife surveys and workshops (National Trust 2001). The Trust also offers research fellowships for young people wishing to compare methods of heritage management at Trust sites with examples in Europe and runs a number of projects with students from inner-city schools. As well as education projects with young people, the Trust also runs a number of adult education courses and activities, including an "Adult Learners Week" (National Trust 2001). These are supplemented by the Trust's working holiday's programme which in 2000–2001 hosted some 3,400 volunteers (National Trust 2001).

A number of other organisations are also attempting to increase understanding of the countryside through educational initiatives. The Country Trust is a national educational registered charity which works with farmers to provide visits for school children to farms so that they can meet people who live and work in the countryside. The Trust concentrates on introducing children to rural England and offers day or even week long educational expeditions. The Trust estimates that more than 160,000 children have benefited from their work. The Countryside Foundation for Education (CFE) has spent the last eight years attempting to redress the imbalance that they perceive between myth and reality in the way in which the countryside is portrayed in the classroom (Goodfellow 2001). The CFE produce teaching materials about a variety of rural issues and provide training for teachers in their use.

The Chief Executive of the CFE provides some strong arguments for increasing coverage of countryside and rural issues in the National Curriculum (Goodfellow 2001). She highlights a number of missed opportunities in this respect, notably the failure of Government funded programmes, such as Groundwork's "Farmlink Scheme" and the Educational Access element of DEFRA's Countryside Stewardship Scheme to seek guidance from the Department of Education and Employment or the Qualifications and Curriculum Authority (Goodfellow 2001). This has inevitably reduced the relevance of these schemes to the National Curriculum and their uptake by schools.

Goodfellow also points out the very real cost constraints faced by schools who wish their students to experience the countryside and the logistical problems faced when attempting to take a coach full of under-thirteens to a farm or other attraction. There is also the additional problem of Health and Safety Regulations, a particular concern following several highly publicised incidents when students have been killed or injured while on school trips.

Goodfellow offers a number of suggestions to improve the situation, these include:

- encouraging farmers, through appropriate training and appropriate financial incentives, to diversify into public access initiatives;
- broadening the work of countryside agencies in promoting understanding of the countryside in more varied ways to wider target groups;
- using the teaching of sustainable development to promote understanding of the British countryside as a living and working environment;
- ensuring that the curriculum contains specific reference to rural Britain and producing case studies to demonstrate to teachers how this can be achieved across a range of subject areas;
- including a criterion related to consideration of countryside issues into the framework for school inspection.

While some of these measures would prove unpopular in an increasingly overburdened state education system, there are some clear benefits to be gained from ensuring that our children have a better appreciation of the countryside and how it impacts on their lives through the food that they eat and the environment that they live in.

9. Interpretation

Interpretation can be defined as any technique which is used to enhance the visitor experience through explaining the meaning and significance of a recreational site in an interesting and entertaining way. Ham (1992) describes the role of interpretation as being to translate technical or unfamiliar ideas and terms into concepts that are easily understood by lay people. Stewart *et al.* (1998) extend this idea and discuss the influence that interpretation can have in helping visitors to improve their appreciation of the unique sense of place' that can be experienced at many sites.

In terms of its role as specific countryside management activity, the significance of interpretation was first recognised in the United States, particularly in the National Parks early in the twentieth century. Indeed, the American author Freeman Tilden is generally credited with being the father of the modern approach to interpretation and his work still tends to form the basis of most modern studies of interpretation. According to Tilden (1957) interpretation is:

> An educational activity which aims to reveal meanings and relationships through the use of original objects, by firsthand experience, and by illustrative media, rather than simply to communicate factual information.

Tilden's rather high-minded approach to interpretation is revealed when he describes its objective as "the revelation of a larger truth that lies behind any statement of fact" and suggests that it should "capitalise mere curiosity for the enrichment of the human mind and spirit." He goes on to offer six principles for interpretation which can be broadly summarised as follows:

(1) Effective interpretation should connect to something within the personality or experience of the visitor.
(2) Information and interpretation are not the same: the interpreter uses information as the foundations upon which a greater understanding is constructed.
(3) Interpretation is an art, which combines many arts, and as such can be taught.
(4) The main aim of interpretation is not to instruct but to challenge.
(5) Interpretation should embrace the whole site experience rather than any one part and should similarly aim to address its entire audience.
(6) Interpretation addressed to children should not merely be a watered down version of what is offered to adults, but should be designed specially for them.

The need for interpretation is not peculiar to the countryside and can be noted at a range of visitor attractions based around heritage, science or technology. Indeed, many of the earliest examples of interpretation were used at museums and open-air exhibitions (see Phillips 1989 for a useful summary of the history of interpretation).

As authors like Bromley (1990) are at pains to point out, interpretation is not just a form of advertising and it has more than merely an educational function. This does not mean that interpretation cannot function as promotional material or that it does not contain certain educational elements, rather it suggests that the contribution that interpretation can make to countryside management goes beyond either of these important functions.

> **Box 17.2: Commonly used interpretation techniques.**
>
> **Interpretive panels**: display boards using a combination of text, illustration and maps to achieve interpretive objectives.
>
> *Key concerns:* audience, design, location and construction.
>
> **Multi-Media:** interpretation through medium of televison, video, audio, slide-show or other electronic devices.
>
> *Key concerns:* audience, costs, content, design, delivery
>
> **Leaflets:** achieves similar objectives to interpretive panels but in a portable paper format which can be targeted at specific groups or interests.
>
> *Key concerns:* audience, design, distribution, production
>
> **Guided Walks:** combining information with experience as visitors are guided through a site by a specially-trained or experienced individual.
>
> *Key concerns:* audience, personnel, choice of routes
>
> **Live Arts:** putting across a message or idea through story-telling, theatre, song, dance or other performance media.
>
> *Key concerns:* audience, cost, quality.
>
> Partly adapted from Bromley (1990).

Bromley (1990) provides a useful summary and description of a number of commonly used interpretation techniques, some of which are summarised in Box 17.2. Many of these techniques will be familiar to readers, particularly the use of information boards and leaflets, while Bromley provides some examples of the various live arts activities that can be used for interpretive purpose. Bob Jones, of the Design and Interpretive Service of Forest Enterprise, reports their strategy for the design of signs and interpretive panels, quoting the following from their management guidelines:

> Signs are probably the single most visible manifestation of our corporate face, and as such can have a powerful impact on how we are perceived by others. Consistency throughout is all-important (Jones 1998).

Forest Enterprise provides guidance to the location, format and content of panels based on many years of experience. Current strategies revolve round the use of "non-invasive signing" to maintain site integrity. These include sack-signs, waterproof hessian or jute bags, filled with sand, printed with a simple message and left inconspicuously on a roadside or other location (Jones 1998).

Table 17.3: A typology of interpretation use.

Type of User	Behaviour
Seekers	Visitors who actively seek out information and interpretation
Stumblers	Visitors who encounter interpretation by accident rather than design
Shadowers	Those visitors who are introduced to interpretation by the actions of others (e.g. a teacher or a guide)
Shunners	Those visitors who avoid or ignore interpretation

Source: Stewart *et al.* (1998).

Guided walks and multimedia are a more specialist activities but nevertheless can be very effective. It is in the latter area that the most significant opportunities for interpretation currently exist. The introduction of CD-Rom, DVD and the increasing use of the internet have each served to provide opportunities for more innovative and sophisticated interaction with the interpreter's target audience. Bath (1996) uses multimedia to cover all forms of interpretation, not just those based on electronic sources, but it is the latter with which the term is most closely associated in the minds of the public.

Spicer (1996) reviews some early lessons from the use of multimedia in the United States and while acknowledging its potential suggests that care should be taken in ensuring that a fitting medium is chosen to achieve specific interpretive objectives and that multimedia is not used merely because it is new or trendy. In some cases, Spicer argues, a simpler approach is just as or more effective, particularly in cases where access to a multimedia device or display is limited or difficult for particular groups. In Spicer's opinion multimedia approaches which are both simple and enjoyable to use are most effective. Clearly, there are other advantages particularly where young people are concerned or where an interactive approach is the best means of getting a particular message across. These advantages must be set against the cost and durability of the required equipment and software and the interpretive requirements of the site as a whole.

Stewart *et al.* (1998) identify a typology of interpretation users based on their level of involvement with it. Their typology, shown in Table 17.3, is not particularly informative in that it does not address motive, but nevertheless does provide a useful basis for the analysis of visitor behaviour from which the manager may be able to assess the effectiveness of an interpretive strategy.

10. The Role of Interpretation in the Countryside

In the UK, interpretation was first embraced in the 1950s and 1960s in the work of people like Foster and Aldridge in the Peak District National Park (Phillips 1989). Phillips (1989) identifies the creation of the Countryside Commissions for Scotland and England and Wales in the late 1960s as providing a focus for interpretation in the countryside. He reports that the Commissions had a mandate to introduce interpretation into their countryside schemes, an objective that was made more pressing by the introduction of country parks in the Countryside Acts of 1967 and 1968. These country parks were designed to attract large numbers of visitors from urban areas to enjoy and learn about the countryside. Interpretation was a crucial element of this strategy and led the Commissions to develop their own guides to interpretive strategy in the 1970s (Phillips 1989).

Visitor centres have increasingly become the focus of interpretation at many larger sites, and fulfil that role along with providing information and other services, such as shops, toilets and cafes. Many centres also provide space for workshops, classes or exhibitions and are often the starting point for walks, guided tours and other activities. Scottish Natural Heritage have published a useful guide to the planning, design and operation of visitor centres, which provides a useful checklist of considerations such as location, capacity, costs, staff and monitoring (Scottish Natural Heritage 1996b).

In their 1994 report "Delivering Countryside Information" the Countryside Commission place considerable emphasis on the ability of interpretation to enhance people's enjoyment of the countryside. Rather more practically, Curry (1994), and other writers on the subject (e.g. Moscardo 1996) see interpretation as a tool of management that may encourage individuals to alter their behaviour. From this viewpoint, interpretation is to be used not only to help people to enjoy themselves, but also as a tool to manipulate them and persuade them not to damage the site or hinder the enjoyment of others. This function is highlighted by the National Trust (1997), who emphasise the role that interpretation plays in explaining the significance of its sites to those who visit them. Similarly the House of Commons Sub-Committee on the Environment state that information and interpretation are the most cost-effective means of:

> coping with the mass of car-borne visitors, in reducing vandalism and in helping to reconcile recreational activities with the legitimate interests of farmers, landowners and local residents . . .

Such defensive management can go too far. Curry (1994) provides the example of a study of the North York Moors National Park (Prince 1980, Ph.D. thesis University of Hull) which argues that the 1968 Countryside Act provided for interpretation to be introduced in the towns so that it might attract working class people to the countryside. Because this was not done, Prince claims that the concentration of interpretation facilities in the countryside has contributed to the alienation of the working class. He also shows that the concentration of facilities in the countryside ensured that they were mostly used by the more affluent socio-economic groups.

While this view may be extreme, it is difficult to rebut the notion that interpretation offers a means of persuading people to behave in particular ways. While seemingly harmless if used to protect vulnerable areas of a site from damage, interpretation could be viewed in a more sinister light if it were to be used with the aim of excluding certain groups from using particular areas of the countryside.

Such small possibilities for misuse do not alter the potential of interpretation to provide a valuable element within many countryside management strategies. It has a clear potential for enhancing visitor experiences and it can be used as an effective management tool. Interpretation is an interesting issue in that it is seen by practitioners as the means of influencing people in a rather direct way. The Curry position seems to be that this might not be desirable and perhaps even unethical.

It could be argued that there is some merit in using interpretation to influence behaviour. In such cases the manager should be subject to controls, either through policies, explicit constraints, or monitoring. It may be argued that such use of interpretation requires the sort of complex value judgements that are best not left to the individual. If this is the case, is it safe to allow politicians to use interpretation as the vehicle for particular messages (as has been the case in other sectors, for example health promotion)? At present there seems to be little evidence to suggest that interpretation is being misused and while the countryside remains the habitat of so many independent and tolerant individuals it seem likely that we will be spared from the propagandists.

One indicator of the well-being of interpretation in Britain are the activities of the Association of Heritage Interpretation (AHI). This was founded in 1975 to act as a forum for countryside management professionals concerned with environmental and heritage interpretation. The Association publishes its own journal which provides many useful examples of how professionals deal with interpretation issues in the field. It is also responsible for the Interpret Britain/Ireland Award Scheme which honours outstanding examples of interpretation in the UK and Ireland. Among sites commended in recent years have been several operated by the National Trust, various National Park Authorities and the RSPB.

Another sign of the healthy development of interpretation in the UK is the increasing acceptance of community involvement in the design of interpretive strategies. One example of this is the Nethy Bridge Local Interpretation Plan which is part of Scotland's Highland Interpretation Strategy Project. Here a project officer was recruited from the local community and played an important role in involving individuals and groups from the area in the formulation of the plan. A public meeting identified people, places and cultural issues which local people felt to be important and these were mapped. Other members of the community were also visited and the plan refined. A local steering group was established to take forward the plan which consisted of the construction of a footpath network, supported by an interpretive riverside trail and visitor centre (Scottish Natural Heritage 2001).

The development of material to raise awareness of natural heritage helps to fulfil a number of the objectives of a variety of voluntary and statutory organisations operating in the countryside. Support for interpretation initiatives is available from statutory organisations such as Scottish Natural Heritage and the Countryside Agency. The former provides a range of discretionary grants to help support site interpretation, display areas, interpretive centres, exhibitions, campaigns, and educational initiatives. While these grants seldom cover more than 50% of the costs associated with the interpretation, such spending clearly offers SNH good value for money in terms of promoting partnership and raising environmental awareness.

11. Strategic Implications

The approaches discussed in this section provide the manager with a range of options for improving awareness of countryside issues, managing demand and increasing visitor satisfaction. The price mechanism is at present applied in many parts of the countryside and we should not be afraid of embracing developing technology in order to increase its use as a means of generating revenue and controlling local demand. The adoption of new technologies to collect revenues associated with the use of certain public highways may present an opportunity for pricing access to particularly well used parts of the countryside at relatively low costs. Overcoming the opposition of those who regard the countryside as a free good will require diplomacy and persuasion. The case will mainly be one of reducing congestion and the resulting damage to the countryside and the interests of its users. The revenues collected are unlikely to be large although they may provide a useful means of funding initiatives to promote use by those social groups currently less likely to undertake countryside recreation.

A marketing approach to countryside management extends far beyond promotion and advertising and helps the manager to gain a better understanding of the needs of the public and by so doing improve the level of service that they receive. The implementation of a robust marketing strategy can play a crucial role in the successful achievement of a number of countryside management objectives including the sometimes neglected issue of ensuring an equitable distribution of resources across different sections of society.

While marketing is an effective way of increasing awareness and participation environmental education provides a route for countryside managers to increase public understanding of countryside management issues and to broaden the interests of various target groups. At present, some commentators argue that the National Curriculum does not place sufficient emphasis on countryside or environmental issues. To some extent this shortcoming is being addressed by the work of various agencies and voluntary organisations, but even these sterling efforts cannot ensure that all of our students have a basic understanding and appreciation of countryside matters. Upon leaving full-time education. Perhaps one of the legacies of the foot and mouth crisis of 2001, as echoed in the Report of the Policy Commission on Farming and Food (2002), will be that educators begin to understand how important it is for our young people to recognise how the countryside works and its relationship with our towns and cities. This endeavour would be supported by the work of agencies and voluntary organisations who can provide valuable specialist knowledge and practical insights into how the countryside works and is managed.

Once people are encouraged to use the countryside, interpretation can help them to get even more from the experience. Countryside interpretation plays an important role at many countryside sites and has the ability to make a substantial contribution to the visitor experience and even to alter patterns of behaviour. Interpretation at many countryside sites seems to be rather half-hearted or apologetic, and the challenge for managers is to produce interpretation that is both relevant and consistent with the character of the site. Increased community involvement may help with this objective.

From a strategic perspective improved marketing planning offers higher short-term gains to countryside managers than either of the other two approaches discussed in this chapter. Improving environmental education will, however, offer the most significant long-term benefits and it is imperative that we ensure that future generations consistently receive high quality education in this area. The efforts of the voluntary organisations involved in environmental education suggest that they will continue to have an important role in this area, both in developing the National Curriculum and supporting it with their expertise and facilities.

References

American Marketing Association (1985, March). AMA board approves new marketing definition. *Marketing News*, *1*, 1.

Bath, B. (1996). The digital landscape. *Interpretation*, *2*(1).

Borden, N. (1964). The concept of the marketing mix. *Journal of Advertising Research* (June), 2–7.

Bovaird, A. G., Tricker, M. G., & Stoakes, R. (1984). *Recreation management and pricing: The effect off charging policy on demand at countryside recreation sites*. Aldershot: Gower.

Bromley, P. (1990). *Countryside management*. London: E & F N Spon.

Countryside Council for Wales (2000). *Going batty for holidays*. Press Release, 7/12/2000.

Elliot, J. (1995). The politics of environmental education: A case study. *The Curriculum Journal*, *6*, 377–393.

Ferry, T. (2001). Countryside education: A necessity or a forgotten ideal? Unpublished dissertation, Department of Agricultural Economics and Food Marketing, University of Newcastle upon Tyne.

Goodfellow, D. (2001). Bringing the countryside to the town. In: M. Sissons (Ed.), *A countryside for all*. London: Vintage.

Ham, S. (1992). *Environmental interpretation*. Denver: North American Press.

Jones, R. (1998). Rules of engagement: The forest experience. *Interpretation*, *3*(1).

Moscardo, G. (1996). Mindful visitors, heritage and tourism. *Annals of Tourism Research*, *23*, 376–397.

National Trust (2001). *Annual report to members 2000/2001*. London: National Trust.

The Policy Commission on the Future of Farming and Food (2002). *Farming and food: A sustainable future*. London: HMSO.

Pretty, J. (1998). *The living land: Agriculture, food and community regeneration in rural Europe*. London: Earthscan.

Scottish Natural Heritage (1996a). *Visitor centres: A practical guide to planning, design and operation*. Edinburgh: Scottish Natural Heritage.

Scottish Natural Heritage (1996b). *Environmental community chest handbook*. Edinburgh: Scottish Natural Heritage.

Scottish Natural Heritage (2001). *Nethy Bridge local interpretive plan*. www.snh.org.uk.

Spicer, S. (1996). Lessons from America. *Interpretation*, *2*(1).

Stewart, E. J., Hayward, B. M., & Devlin, P. J. (1998). The 'place' of interpretation: A new approach to the evaluation of interpretation. *Tourism Management*, *19*, 257–266.

Chapter 18

A Future for Strategic Countryside Management

1. Introduction

This chapter draws together the themes presented in this book and considers how the role of strategic countryside managers is likely to change. As those now training to be countryside managers have a reasonable prospect of working well into the present century, we take this as the period for consideration.

Exercises looking into the future have been a popular pre-occupation in the years leading up to and beyond the new millennium, and countryside policies have been no exception. Major projects looking into "Rural Futures" have been funded by DEFRA and in England the Countryside Agency have provided their vision for the countryside in 2020 (Countryside Agency 1999).

It can be argued that the needs of the countryside and its population have increased in importance following the economic and social problems that arose after the Foot and Mouth crisis. This is reflected in an increased emphasis on rural development policy such as the formulation of Rural Development Plans (RDPs) for the constituent parts of the U.K. following the implementation of the EU Rural Development Regulation 1257/99. RDPs provide funding for a range of land-based schemes supporting a variety of environmental, economic and social goals in rural areas (see Chapter 14).

At a broader level, an increased awareness of the importance of considering rural areas in policy design has also been demonstrated in recent moves to ensure the "rural proofing" of all relevant Government policies in the U.K. This activity has emerged out of a recognition that generic policies (for example regional, economic, social and industrial policy) affect rural areas, people and businesses just as much, or even more than, policies specifically designed to address the concerns of rural areas. Rural proofing seeks to ensure that generic policies and programmes take due account of their potential impact and uptake in rural areas.

In recognition of the importance of exogenous factors in determining the strategic agenda for management, we begin with a review of some of broad policy issues that must be resolved over coming decades. Among the factors that we highlight are the future course of agricultural and rural policies, the extent and consequences of new housing development, the potential impacts of climate change and the evolution of traffic management strategies. Also important are the techniques available to managers for assessing the impacts of policies and projects in the countryside and approaches to information and financial management.

The penultimate section of this chapter addresses three key strategic questions for countryside management. These questions concern the supply of public goods in the countryside and the demand issues that arise as a consequence. They arise as a result of one the essential conflicts underlying countryside management, in that the majority of those who work or undertake leisure activities in countryside live in urban areas, whereas the owners and providers of countryside goods are mainly rural residents. Significant parts of the countryside are also in "national ownership," for example state-owned forests or the inalienable properties held by the National Trusts. This diversity of ownership, delivery and use is important because it underlines the conclusion that the whole population has a legitimate interest in the countryside and its management.

Finally, we reach some overall conclusions about the future direction of strategic countryside management in the U.K.

2. Key Determinants of the Future of Countryside Management

While an accurate forecast of the future is impossible it is worthwhile speculating on some of the possible consequences of future developments in a number of areas. Many of these will have implications for landscape character, a major concern of countryside managers. In considering these implications managers should remember that they are not museum curators but managers of a dynamic and evolving environment that must serve the needs of a diverse range of stakeholders. If landscapes evolve from what we know today into something different, but no less rich, then such change is to be embraced rather than fought against. The challenge for the strategic manager is to manage change in a sustainable way across a the broad range of landscapes, providing a stream of benefits for both current and future generations.

2.1. Social and Demographic Change

The phenomenon of counterurbanisation, that is the movement of populations from urban to rural areas, has been well documented and remains a significant issue in rural Britain over several decades. In some rural areas this phenomenon may result in a the lack of affordable housing and a shortage of job and training opportunities, outcomes which may encourage some young people to migrate to urban areas. In addition to these potential problems, shifting populations and demographic structures bring with them different cultures, expectations and demands, some of which will impact on the activities of countryside managers as well as the concerns of those working in the field of rural development.

The resulting implications for housing and transport infrastructure are dealt with later in this section but it is worth remembering that changes in the social and demographic composition of the countryside will also result in different demands for countryside recreation and for the management of landscape character. For example, it is unlikely that the recently enhanced provision of access to open land in Great Britain (see Chapter 15) will fully satisfy the developing needs of either rural or urban populations, though the increased emphasis on maintaining countryside character (see Chapter 10) may contribute to maintaining the image of the rural idyll that so much of the population seek in the countryside.

2.2. Agriculture

Recent reforms of agricultural and rural policy in Britain may have a profound impact on the shape of the countryside. The current round of reforms follow a series of official reports over the last decade and the continued attempts at the EU level to adjust the Common Agricultural Policy (CAP) to the changing world in which it must operate. These changes must satisfy the needs of international trade and must increasingly reflect the notion that agriculture provides a variety of private and public good outputs that are of interest to society and also therefore to policymakers.

One potentially important reform is the movement away from production-based subsidy payments to farmers towards flat-rate single-farm payments that are conditional on keeping the land in good environmental and agricultural condition. It is not easy to predict the impacts of such a major shift in policy. Whilst environmental constraints may promote the supply of public goods, it is not clear what will happen if farmers choose to ignore the policy incentives and react to market forces alone, or accept the payments but fail to deliver the intended policy outcomes.

Recent developments in agri-environment policy have seen the evolution of a new generation of schemes that seek further enhancements to the supply of public goods in the countryside. These measures aim to increase the area of land under management agreements through both increasing the number of farms eligible to join such schemes and encouraging farmers to participate. Recent strategies to broadening participation are based on a simplified scheme where a wide range of farmers can earn payments by adopting a certain number of beneficial land management practices (see Chapter 14).

In addition to policy reform, the dramatic enlargement of the EU from fifteen to twenty five member states from 2004 may lead to a shift in agricultural production towards Eastern Europe. This will have long term impacts on the structure of agriculture throughout Europe and could affect the viability of some forms of production in the U.K. This could lead to farmers diversifying into other activities or leaving the industry altogether. Their holdings may then be integrated into larger holdings or taken over by hobby farmers. At the same time rural policy may lead to changes in biodiversity management and landscape character. Such changes may be accelerated by developments in policy such as changes to the Rural Development Regulation 1257/99 which will lead to new Rural Development Plans across the U.K. to be implemented from 2007. These will lead to adjustments in existing agri-environment schemes and the budgets associated with them.

2.3. Forestry

The second primary land use is forestry which differs from agriculture in that it has expanded its coverage over the last century and is likely to continue to expand in future as a result of various national Forest Strategies. The most recent extensions of forestry have emphasised the provision of public goods, particularly biodiversity conservation and recreation, following both the potential demand for these uses and recognising the current poor market conditions for raw timber.

This emphasis is important in countryside terms and has led to expansion of forests in the urban fringe where they are conveniently accessible to major populations. Continuing this trend, particularly through community forest initiatives, will offer scope in the future for increasing countryside use without putting pressure on existing popular sites or increasing the distances travelled by visitors. By expanding the area of countryside within reach of public transport, important new opportunities can be offered to those who live in urban areas. This will require considerable investment, which at present comes from sources such as the National Lottery. Diversification in funding sources and the increased involvement of the private sector and local community groups should help to increase both the area of accessible woodland and the opportunities that it offers for a range of economic, social and environmental activities.

2.4. Housing and Urban Development

While the threats from intensive agriculture are gradually removed from the land, new challenges arise for the countryside manager. Already, changing demographic trends are forecast to lead to substantial increases in the need for housing, a significant proportion of which will be built on green-field sites in rural areas, particularly in the south of England. As well as posing a threat to local landscape character, these developments will have profound implications for rural communities and the infrastructure that serves them.

Some of the potential problems associated with an increase in housing development may be reduced as a result of forthcoming reforms to the planning system which will move it away from its traditional concentration on land use to a more spatial-based approach (see Chapter 13). Reforms include the replacement of current systems of development plans with Local Development Frameworks and a comprehensive review of the Planning and Minerals Policy Guidance systems. Reforms are intended to modernise the planning system and be consistent with Government policies on sustainable development and community involvement. Other guidance, such as the development of "concept statements" by the Countryside Agency may also prove helpful by making new developments places where people really want to live (Countryside Agency 2003a).

The aim of improving the quality of the built environment in the countryside may be harder to achieve when constrained by current Government targets over the approved density of new housing developments. Current guidelines, strongly supported by pressure groups such as the CPRE, advocate high density housing on development sites. Whilst this may protect some green-field sites from development, it does not encourage the creation of the kinds of housing development that most would want to live in. Rather, there is a danger that this kind of restriction, largely designed to protect undeveloped agricultural land, will lead to the creation of a new generation of rural ghettos, with undistinguished houses packed close together and little room for the type of gardens, found in many older properties, that provide a valuable refuge for a diverse range of wildlife.

Clearly the location of new housing will also have impacts on countryside recreation. Urban location of the development will increase recreational demands in particular areas, whilst more rural locations may affect recreational potential in some areas. The potential scale of these developments is sufficient to indicate that major local and regional effects will be felt. Significant new developments in sensitive rural areas will be regulated but urban extensions may be important to countryside managers in particular areas. Whilst they are being planned, strategic countryside managers face the challenge of adjusting the availability of public goods in anticipation of changing populations in their areas.

2.5. Climate Change

Whilst the debate surrounding the potential consequences of climate change on the world continues, the predicted impacts become increasingly serious. The essentially scientific question of whether or not climate change is occurring, and if so at what rate, remains to be resolved and policy makers must take a view about their responses to the probable outcomes of such predictions. Given the major potential impact of climate change, prudence would demand careful consideration of policy options. Until it can be convincingly shown that the climate of the U.K. is not set to alter dramatically over the next 50 to 100 years then some form of insurance against its worst potential is very attractive.

However, since such insurance involves expense now and a very long term future pay-off, it is not attractive to policy-makers who must face their electorates and justify their activities well before any benefits of their policies have appeared. The decision problem is made worse by the fact that this is a genuinely global problem in that many of the benefits of action by one state will be enjoyed by all. Thus European taxpayers are invited to pay for the benefits accruing to low-lying and often distant countries many years in the future. In these circumstances it is not surprising that this issue is difficult to resolve. However, many governments, including that of the U.K., are trying to implement the Kyoto Agreement and this is likely to have increasing impact on the countryside over coming decades.

Many potential effects can be identified. The need to increase the proportion of our energy generated from renewable sources under the Non-Fossil-Fuels Obligation is encouraging the establishment of wind farms and increased investment in other methods of energy production, such as the use of bio-fuels. Coupled with that is the renewal of emphasis on more efficient means of using energy which would include the extension of public transport systems where possible. This, no doubt, will also feature in attempts to design and build more fuel-efficient cars and perhaps in the wider spread of road pricing systems as a means of discouraging car use. Such changes are already apparent in the U.K. and they will spread further.

Other potential issues resulting from climate change include the increased risks of flooding if sea levels rise, where some rural land may be required as a "flood reserve" to protect vulnerable urban areas. This will raise particular concerns about public good provision as well as the safety and livelihood of rural populations. Changes in climate may also shift the range of certain species and alter habitats. This will have fundamental implications for protected areas, farming and land management and will require robust policy responses in terms of the designation of statutory areas. Already threats have been noted to certain populations of sea birds as changes in the marine ecosystem threaten established food sources.

A particular issue for biodiversity management will be the increase of threats to biosecurity, where new exotic species compete with indigenous species in much the same way as the Grey Squirrel has competed with the Red since its introduction. Such threats will increase in the future as the range of species that can be supported by our climate increases and these migrate from other areas of Europe. This will threaten established populations and communities and could fundamentally alter the diversity of our wildlife and require a complete rethink of our policies on biodiversity conservation as established species are no longer so well-adapted to our climate.

2.6. Transport

Cars have become an increasingly important part of rural life in recent decades. Today while 85% of rural households have one or more cars, nationally only 72% of households enjoy the same benefits (Countryside Agency 2003b). While lack of access to transport may be an important issue to the remaining rural households, many are concerned about the potential problems that motor vehicles can cause in rural areas. Such problems may be exacerbated by current trends in the social composition of rural areas, increasingly long journeys to work and the growing volume of freight moved by road. Indeed, in the next few decades traffic is forecast to grow at a faster rate in rural areas than in urban areas (Countryside Agency 2003b). Increase in traffic and transport infrastructure could have implications for both rural recreation and countryside character, so it is important for countryside managers to continue to raise these particular concerns in order to ensure that the development planning process is properly informed.

A range of recent Government documents have addressed issues of transport in rural areas. These include the 1998 Integrated Transport White Paper and the Ten Year Transport Plan. The Countryside Agency (2003b) set out their strategy for transport in the countryside suggesting that better access to services and facilities should be the key strategic goal rather than an increase in car ownership or transport infrastructure. This would require better integration of public and private transport systems supported by the location of key services and facilities close to the populations that require them. This is rather at odds with various strategies that seem to be based on the centralisation of key services at a regional level and on an increasing reliance on out-of-town facilities that are most easily accessible by car, rather than other more sustainable modes of transport.

While the Countryside Agency (2003b) make a good case for a change in the way in which planners deal with rural transport issues, their approach is perhaps not radical enough in providing disincentives to drivers and means of generating revenue to support improvements in public transport infrastructure. The apparent success of congestion charges to limit road use and raise revenues in central London is promoting consideration of this policy more widely in rural areas and for inter-urban travel. This could have impacts on the countryside. Urban road pricing will increase the attractiveness and relative utility of rural motoring and provide further incentives for individuals and businesses to relocate to rural areas and in so doing increase road use there.

In the foreseeable future, rural road pricing is likely to face a variety of practical and political difficulties. In the long term, by increasing the cost of motoring in rural areas, the introduction of such measures may reduce the use of cars, putting more emphasis on public transport. This may lead to a growth in collective access to the countryside through clubs and commercial transport providers and could encourage the relocation of services and facilities closer to their target populations.

The wider use of road pricing systems may also raise revenue and limit congestion but could have the unwelcome side-effect of increasing problems of exclusion within countryside recreation. This could be countered by increased investment in public transport and the associated infrastructure in order to create real choices for those travelling through the countryside. The Countryside Agency (2003b) make various suggestions that would help to make public transport a more viable choice for existing road users, these include the provision of accessible car and cycle hire schemes at rail stations; the need for additional secure car parking associated with park-and-ride schemes; improved and more accessible information about public transport, and dedicated bus-rail links.

2.7. Management of Information

The last century has seen a continuous evolution in out ability to gather, manage, analyse and interpret information. This evolution will undoubtedly progress over coming decades and the urgent need for improved management of public goods will benefit from this development. Improved information will also contribute to better strategic management. Computer based information systems (see Chapter 6) help by increasing the speed with which management information can be obtained from raw data and transmitted to users and by permitting information to be accessed more widely. Strategic management systems may require greater integration of responsible agencies and this, too, will enhance the options available to managers.

In terms of public participation in recreation improved information provision through broadband internet will provide an increasingly important gateway into the countryside. In the future, users will not only be able to access improved information about recreational opportunities but will be exposed to a range of innovative interpretations that will use the electronic media to provide a range of off-site facilities from virtual tours to interactive educational applications. While such developments may disturb traditionalists, such opportunities for virtual access may become an increasingly valuable approach to making the countryside more inclusive and ensuring that the benefits associated with the countryside are available to as wide an audience as possible.

2.8. Financing the Countryside

As was seen in Chapters 7, 8 and 9, the management of the flow of funds to countryside projects of all kinds is at present diverse. An intelligent change recently introduced has been the use of formula funding for the national parks. Assuming this innovation is successful, we may expect a good deal of development of more sensitive forms of funding which will deliver incentives at the appropriate levels in the countryside. Such improvements offer a potent way of enhancing the quality of countryside available in two ways. First, they will help to increase the yield of the funding applied and second, they will encourage more appropriate forms of management at the individual site level. Design of funding systems is thus an area of activity which offers much scope for improvement of the countryside.

2.9. Assessing the Impacts of Projects and Policies

Chapter 10 details a range of techniques currently used to help managers to assess the various impacts of projects and policies in the countryside both before and after implementation. We expect that the future will see an increase in the use of these techniques to support policy development and to monitor the outcomes of a range of management instruments. In the short-term, qualitative approaches such as Quality of Life Assessment may provide a framework for assessing the sustainability of alternative possible approaches to development. While these techniques are attractive in that they offer complete and largely non-technical solutions to the assessment of projects, policies which impact on the broader countryside may require robust and technical approaches such as Strategic Environmental Assessment (SEA) which can account for a wide range of social and environmental impacts including landscape character. Under the recent EU SEA Directive the approach may become increasingly popular and will prove effective provided that it can be supported by robust forecasts of the future consequences that a policy may have for the countryside.

A variety of economic approaches to assessment, which are beyond the scope of this text, are also available to policy makers seeking to assess the costs and benefits of projects and policies both before and after implementation. While these may not always favour sustainable approaches to development they have the advantage of providing a robust economic calculus to inform decision-making. Used as part of a more holistic multiple-criteria based approach to the assessment of projects and policies in the countryside, these techniques may provide us with an increasingly reliable means of assessment.

3. Key Strategic Questions

Following our review of some of the key policy issues facing countryside managers in the first part of the twenty-first century, we go on to examine some of key strategic questions that managers must answer when determining how they will continue to manage the supply of public goods in the countryside. Any answers to the questions that follow must obviously be no more than approximations, but they are useful in as much as they will frame the future evolution of the strategic work of countryside managers. We therefore suggest some initial thoughts, providing an overview of some of the issues that may engage strategic countryside management over the working lives of those now taking up the activity.

3.1. How Much Countryside is There Potentially? And How Much Actually?

In this text we tend to consider land in terms of the public goods (see Chapter 12) that it supplies and in relation to the individuals and institutions who own and manage it (see Chapters 3 and 4). This is not simply a matter of space but of the whole range of characteristics of space which are of value to members of the public. Thus we are talking about much more than land and the private use that is made of it currently (see Chapter 11) but all of the associations it has for people. These may be historic, aesthetic, ecological, emotional and so on, in any combination. The potential limits to the amount of countryside are set by the space it occupies, but also by how it has been used for other purposes, some primary (farming, forestry) and others secondary, (wildlife reserve, green belt but also battlefields and other historic sites) (see Chapter 2). *Use* is determined by ownership and the legal and other constraints which define it. Its *value* as countryside depends on its availability or accessibility to potential users which will reflect the users' rights of access, their opportunities for access and the physical characteristics and use of the land.

The multiple nature of land use and the complex demands that we place upon it, suggest that simple spatial measurements fail to capture the full intimate and diverse realities of the countryside. Techniques such as Geographic Information Systems (see Chapter 6) can provide managers with valuable information about the relationships between land management and the underlying physical characteristics of the land and the public goods that it supplies. Such insights, however, represent only the start of a more complete understanding of the countryside.

Such an understanding requires that we recognise that the countryside is a rich assemblage of individual and inter-related elements which together comprise the whole. These elements are mainly under the control of private individuals whose behaviour as custodians of public goods is imperfectly regulated through a number of mechanisms and incentives (see Chapters 13 and 14). Significant amounts of public money are devoted to promoting and regulating the management of the countryside and encouraging landowners and managers to supply public goods (see Chapters 8 and 9). The question identifies the important difference between potential and actual availability of countryside, reflecting the notion that the full potential is never in use at any given moment and that availability therefore usually greatly exceeds actual use.

3.2. How Much Countryside Do We Want? What is the Demand for Countryside Recreation?

To investigate the overall demand for countryside and the public goods that it provides, we would need to consider a broad range of outputs from the provision of biodiversity to the maintenance of environmental services. The value of goods demanded generally embraces the notion of all that people might be prepared to pay for them. The demand for countryside recreation is a particularly important issue for managers and the one which will be addressed in most detail here.

When visiting a rural area for recreation most people incur some form of cost and this provides a measure of their willingness to pay for the experiences that they hope to gain from their visit. If they do not believe in advance that the trip offers benefits greater than their costs incurred, why would they go? The sum of every individual's maximum willingness to pay for their recreational visits provides a monetary expression of the total demand for countryside recreation. This will usually exceed the amount that they would have to pay in order to ensure that the recreational opportunities they require are provided. Notice that the demand for countryside recreation depends on a range of other variables, including availability of transport, leisure time, expected weather conditions as well as the distance to the sites in question.

Clearly, a question such as this can only be answered very approximately for all situations at all times but might be addressed in more detail for specific sites on particular days in relation to actual recorded behaviour. In the case of countryside recreation the question could, in principle, be answered from an aggregation and modelling of demand data from all available sites, although such arithmetic has never been done for the U.K. Meanwhile we can record, very approximately, how frequently people visit the countryside and how they use it as a very loose indicator of the demand for it (such as in the GB Leisure Day Visit Survey — see Chapter 16).

This question draws attention to the public as consumers of countryside and the way in which their demands on it may evolve over time. Despite the limited data available, there has been a long term fear that there will not be enough countryside to meet the varied demands for the provision of public goods. In the case of recreation, that view has been strongly challenged by those emphasising the rather modest share of the population visiting the countryside on an annual basis and noting the lack of evidence of significant *growth* in this activity (see Chapter 16). In this case, low total use rates do not imply that local congestion is or will be unknown in the countryside. But congestion does tend to be random, occasional and largely local: congestion may arise but tends to concentrate at well known "honeypot" sites rather than becoming a universal problem. Its amelioration may occasionally become a key concern for strategic countryside managers.

User-demand for countryside recreational opportunities probably will increase over time due to rising affluence, the changing age distribution of the population, in particular due to the growing proportion of elderly and retired people, and the increase in leisure time as efficient working allows longer vacations and shorter working weeks. Sustained increases in *per capita* incomes, cheaper travel and the rising tide of internationalism may bring more tourists to the U.K. and some of these will find their way into the countryside. Any rise in the cost of international travel may replace some foreign visitors with locals, whose numbers may even exceed the number of external visitors deterred.

When considering issues such as the appropriate level of public spending on the delivery of public goods, and the question of uneven participation in countryside recreation, managers should be aware of the strategic importance of improved use of marketing and interpretation techniques (see Chapter 17) in increasing the potential of the countryside to deliver benefits to users. To further this aim, managers should continue to collaborate with educationalists and policy makers to ensure that future generations have a better understanding of the diversity and the complexity of the countryside and the range of benefits that it provides to society.

3.3. How Can the Countryside be Made Available Within Accepted Constraints? What is the Actual and Potential Supply of Countryside?

The supply of countryside reflects its ownership and the constraints within which it operates. Thus we have many thousands of landowners, including some institutions (firms, estates, public bodies) as well as private individuals (farmers, householders). But the property rights that follow land are complex and their re-assignment can provide significant scope for countryside managers attempting to increase the supply of public goods (see Chapter 12). Recent reforms of access and land ownership rights in England, Wales and Scotland (see Chapter 15) have, for example, fundamentally changed the balance of rights between the owners and users of land and such devices may be used in future to ensure that society achieves its required supply of public goods from the countryside.

In addition to rights over land, anyone who owns land is also subject to a significant array of laws limiting the uses that may be made of it (see Chapter 13). Farmers may own their farm but they are not allowed to discharge farm wastes into water courses or to burn unwanted straw and so on. Virtually all landowners are subject to quite strict regulation when it comes to certain changes of land use. In particular, building houses on farm land is subject to planning controls as are many other changes of use (see Chapter 13). Some of the constraints on land use arise because some other activity (for example, planting trees) has received public support in the past, others apply where the land has especially valuable aesthetic or ecological characteristics which are protected by statutory designations (see Chapter 13).

The supply of countryside is more difficult to predict over a long period, depending as it mainly does on the pressures of primary uses. We note, however, that land use change between the three major categories of use is inherently slow (see Chapter 2). As indicated in the introduction to this Chapter, the present tendency of agricultural policy is to reduce the emphasis on primary production and place more stress on rural development. This could mean that traditional land users — farmers and foresters — will increasingly look beyond their usual concerns and towards new uses of their land.

While we can feel optimistic that mechanisms are available to ensure the future supply of public goods in the countryside, it is by no means certain that all the opportunities for improving the provision and management of these goods will be exploited. Overall, however, the problems now apparent seem to be those of establishing sensible strategies for public good provision, providing appropriate funding (see Chapter 8) and managing any short term problems that arise.

4. Conclusions

Finally, the countryside that is now available in the U.K. rests on a unique sequence of historical events (see Chapter 1) and is offered in comparative freedom, with the collaboration of many thousands of private owners and public officials and depends on the continued responsible behaviour of users. It is a major national asset and one that will continue to rely on the constructive behaviour of the many thousands who provide it and the millions who use it. Whilst avoiding change in the countryside is not an option worth considering, steering change in preferred directions that will allow and enhance continued use into the future is a key objective for strategic countryside management. Recognition of all the possible responses of providers, owners and users of the countryside, to management strategies, is a prerequisite for effective strategic countryside management.

The role of strategic countryside managers in steering that change is crucial. Their effectiveness will have a major impact on the enjoyment of future generations of countryside users who will access the countryside in a range of different ways. They will play some part in the formation of appropriate policies and will have a central role in policy implementation at various levels throughout the countryside. This book is offered as a first attempt to explore the relevant issues but it is certain that many more issues will arise for managers to resolve as their careers unfold.

Meanwhile the main impediment to enjoyment will continue to be the incompatibility of the diverse activities people choose to pursue in the countryside. Major clashes can be dealt with by legislation or management. There is also a role for education in encouraging the recognition of the public recreationists' potential role in the countryside. This goes beyond mere congestion management into the way in which the behaviour of one group can affect the enjoyment of others. Countryside managers can encourage appropriate behaviour by example and by recognising their role in generating an appropriate countryside ethos in which "good" rather than "bad" behaviour will predominate. By unobtrusively encouraging users to bear in mind the preferences of others, whilst pursuing their own interests, managers will continue to enhance the enjoyment of all.

References

Countryside Agency (1999). *Tomorrow's countryside — 2020 vision*. Cheltenham: Countryside Agency.

Countryside Agency (2003a). *Concept statements and local development documents — Practical guidance for local planning authorities*. Cheltenham: Countryside Agency.

Countryside Agency (2003b). *Transport in tomorrow's countryside*. Cheltenham: Countryside Agency.

Author Index

Adams, W. M., 33, 126
Adger, N., 104
Aebischer, N., 187
Aicheson, J., 29
Albon, S. D., 190
Alder, J., 45, 46, 167, 214, 215, 230,
American Marketing Association, 301
Anderson, S. J., 108, 109
Andrews, K. R., 77
Ansoff, H. I., 87, 88
Aspinall, R., 113

Baker, P. J., 185
Bateson, P., 184
Bath, B., 310
Bator, F. M., 200
Battershill, M. R. J., 243
Beardwell, I., 54
Bedford Franklin, T., 4
Beedell, J., 244
Best, R., 21, 22, 31
Bishop, K., 139, 140, 142–144
Blunden, J., 266
Borden, N., 301
Bovaird, A. G., 296–298, 300
Bowler, I., 243
Box, J., 60, 79
Bradshaw, E., 184
Briggs, D., 107, 112
Bromley, D., 203
Bromley, P., 262, 267, 268, 308, 309
Brotherton, I., 243
Brown, A., 55
Budge, I., 37, 47
Burns, Lord J., 184, 185
Butterfield, J., 157–159

Cabinet Office, 29
Cadw, 178
Callander, R. F., 4, 5

Capstick, E. J., 29
Cavaliero, G., 11
Central Statistical Office, 7
Chadwick, L., 122
Chesters, A., 289
Clarke, R., 228
Clutton-Brock, M., 190
Cobham Resource Consultants, 187–189
Cole, G. A., 52, 62, 63, 65–67, 79, 81, 86
Comley, A., 289
Commission of the European
    Communities, 251
Common Land Forum, 29
Coulter, F., 284
Country Landowners' Association, 269,
    271
Countryside Agency, 26, 124, 141, 143,
    172, 177, 218, 219, 221, 222, 228,
    263, 269–271, 273–276, 291, 315,
    318, 320, 321
Countryside Commission for Scotland,
    175, 177, 226
Countryside Commission, 26, 29, 156, 170,
    175, 176, 228, 268, 275, 291, 303
Countryside Council for Wales, 304
Cox, G., 186, 261
Crabtree, R., 270
Cullingworth, B., 34, 35, 218, 221, 235
Cullingworth, J. B., 14, 17
Curran, J., 48, 49, 282, 289, 291, 311
Curry, N. R., 226, 266
Curry, N., 222–224, 262, 263, 266–268,
    282, 289, 291, 311

Dahlman, C., 2, 3
Dalton, A., 139, 144
Danziger, J. N., 153
Davies, N., 12
Deane, P., 7
DEFRA, 29, 179, 187, 216, 231–235, 253

Department of the Environment, 167, 170, 225, 236
Department of the Environment, Transport and the Regions, 27, 234, 263, 268, 275, 291
Dillon, J., 16
Dower, J., 223
Dower, M., 281
Downs, A., 67, 68
Drucker, P., 79
Dunleavy, P., 67, 69, 71
Dwyer, J. C., 45, 207–211

Elliot, J., 306
Emmett, I., 287, 288
English Heritage, 235
English Nature, 229, 231
Environmental Design Consultancy, 276

Falconer, K. E., 136, 183, 256, 257, 261, 277
Falconer, K., 275, 285
Ferry, T., 305
Forestry Commission, 25, 27
Foulds, R., 29

Gadesden, G., 29
Gaebler, T., 54, 125
Gallup Organisation, 261, 277
Game Conservancy Trust, 186
Garrod, G. D., 198, 202, 206, 216, 258
Gay, H., 139, 140, 143, 145, 174, 177
Gilfoyle, I., 110
Gilg, A. W., 26, 218, 219, 223–226, 243
Glasson, J., 165, 166, 168
Glyptis, S., 265, 291
Goodfellow, D., 307
Gouldner, A. W., 67
Goyder, J., 43
Green, B., 243, 245
Green, M., 96

Haines-Young, R., 113
Haldane, A. R. B., 5
Hall, D., 1
Ham, S., 55–57, 61, 67, 308
Handy, C. B., 55–57, 61, 67, 99

Hanley, N., 163, 214, 244
Harmon, J. E., 108, 109
Harrison, C., 265, 266
Harvey, D. R., 33, 48
Haskins, C., 35, 38, 41, 72
Heydon, M. J., 183
Hill, D., 186
HLF, 139, 140
Hm Government, 94
Hobbsbawm, E., 12
Hobhouse, A., 224, 266
Hodge, I. D., 45, 203–211,
Hodge, I., 203
Holden, L., 54
Holloway, S., 100
Hooper, S., 190
Hopkins, H., 182
Hoskins, W. G., 5
House of Commons Environment Committee, 14, 15
Humble, A., 113

Ilbery, B., 243

James, 181
James, N. D. G., 3
Jenkins, S., 138, 147
Johnson, C. A., 114
Johnson, S. P., 94
Jones, R., 150, 309
Joseph, D., 289, 290

Keirle, I., 101, 103
Knightbridge, R., 96

Lawrence, D. P., 164,
Leay, M. J., 79
Leonard, R., 221
Lobley, M., 243, 244, 257
Lowe, P., 43, 48, 155, 217, 218
Ludolph, I. C., 186

MAFF, 122, 227
Mansley, C., 277
Mantle, G., 139
Marren, P., 96
Martin, J., 177
Mathews, R. C. O., 256

McHarg, I. L., 111
McInerney, J. P., 258
Miles, R. E., 59
Mintzberg, H., 61, 62, 64
Morris, C., 243, 244
Morris, J., 243
Moscardo, G., 311
Mosely, M. J., 33
Mowl, T., 10
Moxey, A., 243

Nadin, V., 14, 17, 34, 35, 218, 221, 235
National Audit Office, (NAO), 133
National Farmers' Union, 269
National Forest, 26
National Heritage Committee, 138
National Lottery Commission, 144
National Trust for Scotland, (NTS) 130, 131
National Trust, 80, 128, 129, 131, 306, 307, 311
Newbould, P., 143
Nix, J., 122

Ohlmer, B., 243
Oldcorn, R., 81, 82, 88, 89
O'Riordan, T., 115
Orr, W., 6
Orwin, C. S., 205
Osborne, D., 54, 125
Ousby, I., 10

Parker, S., 45
Pavis, S., 15
Pearce, D., 32, 94
Pearlman, D. H., 261
Pearlman, J. J., 261
Peel, W. R., 205
Pendlebury, M., 150
Pennington, M., 231
Peterken, G. F., 24
Phillips, A., 139, 174, 177, 308, 310, 311
Postan, M. M., 2
Policy Commission on Farming and Food, 313
Potter, C., 243, 244, 257
Potts, G. R., 186,
Powe, N. A., 109

Pretty, J., 304
Pringle, S., 275

Rackham, O., 4, 181
Ravenscroft, N., 262
Rawcliffe, P., 44
Rawnsley, A., 49
Rehman, T., 244
Reid, R., 276
Reynolds, J. C., 183
Roberts, L. N., 1
Robertson, P. A., 186
Robinson, T., 158
Rosen, R., 55, 56, 82–86, 88–90
Rubenstein, D., 265, 266

Sandforel, Lord, 225
Schein, E. H., 55, 56, 59
Scottish Executive, 91, 92, 231
Scottish Natural Heritage, 177, 306, 311, 312
Scott, Mr Justice, 266
Serjeant, 96
Seaton, J., 48, 49
Shoard, M., 264–266, 268, 274
Shucksmith, M., 15
SNH, 126, 127, 226, 234
Snow, C. C., 59
Social and Community Planning Research, 289
Spash, C., 163
Stephenson, T., 190
Stewart, E. J., 157, 159, 308, 310
Stoate, C., 186
Strickland, A. J., 82, 83
Strong, R., 11
Swanwick, C., 175, 177

Tantram, D., 107, 112
Tapper, S., 187
Taylor, H., 11, 12
Taylor, M., 123
Thomas, K., 9
Thompson, A., 82, 83
TNS Travel and Tourism, 1, 144, 282–284, 287
Touche Ross, 285
Turner, J., 123, 215, 216

Valentine, G., 100
Vera, F. W. M., 24

Ward, N., 136, 185, 218
Ward, S., 48
Weitzman, M. L., 94
Weston, J., 168
Whitby, M. C., 183, 190, 256, 257, 261, 271, 277
Whitby, M., 243, 258, 285

White, B., 243
Wilkinson, D., 45, 46, 167, 214, 215, 230
Williamson, O. E., 256, 257
Willis, K. G., 198, 202, 216
Wilson, G. A., 243, 244
Winch, D. M., 196
Winter, M., 43
Wong, C., 110
Wood, C., 171
Wordsworth, W., 10

Subject Index

Access orders, 270
Access to the Mountains Act (Scotland) (1884), 223, 265
Access to the Mountains Bill, 266
Accompanying measures, 248, 255
Addison Committee, 222, 233
Additionality, 134, 138
Agenda 2000, 251
Agricultural Census, 28, 102, 103
Agriculture Act (1986), 24, 43, 224, 230, 233, 244, 245, 247, 266, 267, 277, 311
Agri-environment schemes, 317
Ancient Monuments and Archaeological Areas Act (1979), 236
Angling, 89, 182, 189, 191
Arable stewardship, 249
The Archers, 11
ArcInfo, 108
ArcView, 108, 114, 115
Areas of Outstanding Natural Beauty (AONBs), 34, 223, 228, 248
Association of Heritage Interpretation (AHI), 312

Balance sheet, 119, 120, 124, 125, 129, 130
BATNEEC criteria, 215
Beetle banks, 186
Berkhamsted Trespass, 265
Bienn Eighe, 233
Big Lottery Fund, 87, 134, 138, 139, 143–145
Biodiversity, 76, 77, 82, 84, 87, 91–96, 116, 143, 144, 170, 173, 177, 187, 202, 205, 221, 249, 251, 254, 258, 317, 318, 320, 323
Biodiversity Action Plans (BAPs), 92–94, 116, 251
Bio-fuels, 319
Biosphere Reserves, 34, 234
Black Country Urban Forest, 142

Black Environment Network, 140
Brecon Beacons, 112, 113, 225, 285
British Association for Shooting and Conservation (BASC), 186
British Trust for Conservation Volunteers (BTCV), 140, 142
British Waterways, 282
British Workers Sporting Federation, 266
Budget-maximisation, 68, 69, 71
Budgets, 64, 66, 68–71, 123, 149–153, 155, 157, 160, 226, 231, 251, 253, 317
Bureau-shaping, 69, 71
Burns Committee, 184
Butterfly Conservation, 207
Byways Open to All Traffic (BOATs), 267

Cadw (Welsh Historic Monuments), 177, 178, 236
Cairngorms, 178, 227
Campaign to Protect Rural England (CPRE), 220
Camphill Trust, 207
Capital budgeting, 150, 156
Charging for access, 295, 296
Cobham Resource Consultants, 187–189
Common grazing, 29, 190, 203
Commons, 26, 265
Commons Preservation Society (CPS), 265
Commons Registration Act (1965), 274
Community Access Forums, 275
Community forests, 26, 27, 277
Community Fund, 138, 142, 143
Congestion, 145, 196, 207, 264, 296, 313, 320, 321, 324, 326
Conservation areas, 142, 158, 224, 236
Conservation headlands, 186, 187, 249
Contaminated Land (England) Regulations (2000), 217
Convention on International Trade and Endangered Species (CITES), 48, 77

Subject Index

Convention on Biological Diversity, 77, 94, 144
Co-operatives, 59
Coppicing, 186
Corporate strategy, 77
Cost-Benefit Analysis (CBA), 168
Council for National Parks, 140, 224, 225
Counterurbanisation, 316
Country Land and Business Association (CLBA), 43, 186
Country Life, 304
Country parks, 89, 136, 151, 152, 197, 221, 288, 290–292, 303, 311
Country sports, 181, 182, 187
Countryside 2000, 268
Countryside Access Scheme, 249
Countryside Act (1968), 224, 230, 245, 267, 291, 311
Countryside Agency (CA), 62, 77, 81, 133, 144, 145, 149, 169, 237, 273, 307
Countryside Amenity And Recreation Trusts (CARTs), 206
Countryside and Rights of Way (CRoW) Act (2000), 29, 183, 228–231, 238, 261, 268, 270–273, 277, 291
Countryside Character Programme, 35, 116, 176, 177, 236, 316, 320
Countryside Commission (CC), 26, 29, 41, 65, 91, 125, 156, 170, 175–177, 179, 224, 226–228, 248, 268, 275, 291, 296, 303, 310, 311
Countryside Council for Wales (CCW), 178, 230, 249, 250, 272–274
Countryside Foundation for Education (CFE), 307
Countryside Information Service (CIS), 115
Countryside Management Scheme (CMS), 255
Countryside Premium Scheme, 255
Countryside Recreation Network (CRN), 289
Countryside (Scotland) Act (1967), 291, 311
Countryside Stewardship, 135, 187, 243, 246, 248, 270, 307
Countryside Survey, 105, 184
Covenants, 146, 204

Creating Common Ground, 143
Creech-Jones, Arthur, 266
Cross compliance, 136, 205, 259
Curry Report (Policy Commission on the Future of Farming and Food), 29
Cycling, 12, 35, 60, 273, 276

Dalton, Hugh, 224
Dartmoor, 159, 225, 248
Dedication (of land for public access on foot), 262, 278
Deer
  Commission, 94
  Park, 4
  Stalking, 6, 181, 188, 189
Definitive map, 262, 266–268, 276–278
Department of Environment, Food and Rural Affairs (DEFRA), 29, 30, 39–42, 66, 70, 80, 81, 124, 136, 149, 153, 156, 157, 170, 177, 187, 216, 231–235, 246, 252, 253, 256, 275, 307, 315
Development control, 13, 112, 116, 218, 222, 224
Devolution, 24, 35, 38–40, 62, 65, 91, 227, 251
Digital Terrain Models (DTM), 111, 114
Discounting, 150
Diversification, 58, 89, 90, 290, 318
Doorstep Greens, 142
Dower, John, 233
Drag hunting, 184, 185

EC Directive on the Conservation of Wild Birds (79/409), 234
EC Directive 85/337, 165–168
EC Habitat and Species Directive (92/43), 34, 234
EC Nitrate Directive, 217
ECOS, 17
Education, 10, 18, 39, 53, 54, 56, 64, 95, 116, 127, 142, 173, 209, 234, 244, 275, 281, 289, 302, 304–307, 313
Edwards Report, 156, 226
Enclosure Movement, 265
Enfys Partnership, 143
England Rural Development Plan (ERDP), 252, 253, 256
English Heritage, 10, 80, 91, 167, 169, 171, 177, 235–237, 246, 296, 297

Subject Index   333

English Nature (EN), 60, 230, 231, 245
Entry-Level Stewardship (ELS), 253, 254
Environment Act (1995), 41, 42, 156, 215–217, 226
Environment Agency, 41, 42, 70, 106, 142, 171, 177, 216, 218, 273
Environment and Heritage Service (EHS), 42, 236
Environmental education, 305, 306, 313
Environmental Impact Assessment (EIA), 164
Environmental Protection Act (1990), 215, 216, 227
Environmentally Sensitive Areas (ESAs), 106, 135, 159, 243, 247, 248, 250, 253, 255, 272
EU Bathing Waters Directive, 217
EU Directive 97/11, 165
EU Rural Development Regulation (RDR) (1257/99), 47, 251
EU Structural Funds, 47
EU Water Framework Directive, 217
Excludability, 145, 198
Exmoor, 112, 159, 183, 225, 245, 248
Externalities, 195–197, 200, 203–205, 211

Falconry, 181, 188, 189
Fallow deer, 4
Farmers' and Smallholders' Association, 43
Farming and Rural Conservation Agency (FRCA), 70
Farming and Wildlife Advisory Group (FWAG), 244
Farm Woodland Premium Scheme (FWPS), 256
Fayol, Henri, 52
Finance, 16, 63, 64, 68, 119, 123, 133, 134, 145, 147, 149, 151–155, 160, 244, 258, 300
Financial-flow analysis, 120
Flood protection, 197, 198
Fontainebleau Convention, 135
Foot and Mouth disease, 28, 30, 39, 263, 302
Footpath surveys, 101, 102
Forests
    Forest Design Plans, 114

Forest Enterprise, 24, 40, 309
Forest of Burnley, 142
FORESTER, 114
Forestry Act (1985), 24, 32, 263
Forestry Commission (FC), 24–27, 31, 36, 40, 41, 77, 78, 91, 99, 114, 142, 147, 170, 187, 205, 255, 263, 270, 273, 282
Formula-based budgeting, 154
Funding, 18, 26, 47, 69, 70, 84, 85, 87, 88, 96, 119, 131, 133, 135, 137–148, 153, 155, 156, 158, 187, 210, 221, 228, 238, 249, 251–253, 258, 275, 285, 313, 315, 318, 321, 322, 325

Game Acts, 265
Game Conservancy Trust (GCT), 186, 187
Game management, 43, 186, 187
GB Leisure Day Visits Survey, 144, 286, 292, 324
General Agreement on Tariffs and Trade (GATT), 33, 48
Geographic Information Systems (GIS), 99, 108–116, 236
Global warming, 1, 305
Grant aid, 83, 204, 208, 291
Great Britain Leisure Day Visits Survey, 1
Great Glen Way, 269
Green belt, 31, 34, 35, 204, 218, 323
Greenpeace, 44
Green Spaces and Sustainable Communities Project, 142
Grey partridge, 186, 187
Gross margins (GMs), 122
Groundwork, 140, 207, 307
Guided walks, 307, 310

Habitat condition, 232
Hadrian's Wall, 80, 235, 269
Hedgerow Incentive Scheme (HIS), 248, 249
Heritage Lottery Fund (HLF), 139, 140, 143, 145
Higher-Level Stewardship (HLS), 253, 254
Highways Act (1980), 270
Hill, Octavia, 265
Historic Landscape Characterisation, 177
Historic Scotland, 177, 178, 236
Hobby farming, 28

Subject Index

Housing, 23, 31, 147, 166, 218, 221, 288, 315, 316, 318, 319
Hunting, 3, 4, 43, 113, 181–191, 208
Hadrian's Wall National Trail, 269
Haskins Report (Rural Delivery Review), 41, 72
Highland Clearances, 5
Hill Farm Allowance (HFA), 256
Hobhouse Committee, 224, 233, 266
"Honeypot" sites, 324
House of Commons Agriculture Committee, 250
House of Commons Environment Committee, 14, 15, 214, 217
Hypothecation, 134

Incentive measures, 33, 95, 213, 247, 248, 250, 257–259, 307, 317, 321, 323
Information systems, 115
Inheritance tax relief, 271
Institute of Terrestrial Ecology (ITE), 63, 104, 105
Integrated Access Demonstration Projects (IADPs), 275
Integrated pollution control, 215
Interpretation, 15, 18, 53, 54, 101, 104, 106, 107, 121, 131, 141, 151, 215, 219, 224, 295, 305, 308–313, 314
Irish potato famine, 7

John Muir Trust, 78

Kinder Scout, 190, 266

Lake District, 10, 80, 112, 140, 222, 225, 248
Landfill Tax, 134, 144
LAND-LINE, 114
Land Management Initiative, 81
Land Reform (Scotland) Act (2003), 5, 261, 276, 277
Landsat, 106
Landscape Area Special Development Orders (LASDOs), 225
Landscape character assessment, 164, 170, 175, 177, 178
Law of Property Act (1925), 266
Leaflets, 309
Less Favoured Areas (LFAs), 136, 251, 252

Light Direction and Ranging (LiDAR), 106
Line-item budgeting, 151
Listed buildings, 158, 236, 237
Local Agenda, 21, 221
Local Development Documents (LDDs), 219
Local Development Frameworks (LDFs), 219
Local Development Scheme, 219
Local Government Act (1972), 226
Local Government Act (1974), 125, 226
Local Government Act (2000), 219
Local Heritage Initiative (LHI), 140
Local Plans, 80, 112, 218, 219
Loch Lomand and the Trossachs National Park, 78, 227
Loddington Estate, 187
Long Distance Routes (LDRs), 269
Lottery Act (1998), 142

Management agreements, 18, 83, 100, 122, 143, 199, 204, 206, 213, 229, 230, 235, 241–246, 253, 256–259, 272, 273, 317
Management by objectives, 79
Management plans, 76, 79, 95, 112, 116, 171, 174, 183, 228, 229
Manorial system, 3, 4
MapInfo, 108
Marine Nature Reserves, 34, 246
Market failure, 195, 197–200, 211, 215, 264
Marketing, 18, 53, 54, 63–66, 88, 187, 227, 235, 289, 295, 300–304, 313, 324
Marketing mix, 88, 295, 300, 301
Meacher, Michael, 272
Metropolitan Commons Act (1866), 265
Mid-Term Review, 136
Millennium Awards, 140
Millennium Commission, 140, 141, 269
Millennium Forest for Scotland, 140, 141, 144
Millennium Greens, 65, 141, 144
Minerals and Waste Development Frameworks, 219
Ministry of Agriculture, Fisheries and Food (MAFF), 39, 247
Ministry of Defence, 205, 270
Modulation, 136, 155, 251–253, 255

Subject Index   335

Moorland Scheme, 136, 248
Multiple land use, 202

National Access Forum, 275
National Curriculum, 304–307, 313
National Cycle Network, 141, 269
National Farmers' Union (NFU), 42, 269
National Forest, 26, 317
National Heritage Act (1997), 139
National Heritage (Scotland) Act (1991), 226
National Heritage Memorial Fund (NHMF), 139
National Lottery, 137, 138, 144, 145, 205, 318
National Lottery Commission, 138, 144
National Nature Reserve (NNR), 233
National Parks, 14, 34, 38, 41, 80, 99, 140, 149, 153, 156, 158, 159, 171, 173, 178, 183, 204, 218, 220, 222–228, 233, 238, 244–246, 248, 266, 277, 284, 285, 296, 308, 310, 311, 321
National Park Authorities, 80, 142, 157, 204, 205, 219, 226, 227, 285, 306, 312
National Parks and Access to the Countryside Act (1949), 14, 224, 228, 229, 230, 233, 244, 266, 269, 271, 277
National Parks Commission, 14, 223, 224, 228
National Parks (Scotland) Act (2000), 227
National Rivers Authority (NRA), 42, 218
National Scenic Areas, 34, 224, 226, 227
National Trails, 269, 277
National Trust (NT), 10, 45, 66, 80, 89, 126–130, 133, 142, 145, 146, 153, 159, 183, 206–208, 210, 221, 235, 265, 270, 296–298, 300, 302, 306, 307, 311, 312, 316
National Trust for Scotland (NTS), 126, 130
Natura 2000, 235
Nature Conservancy, 14, 44, 60, 62, 126, 229, 233, 234
Nature Conservancy Council (NCC), 60, 62, 123, 224, 229, 234

New Forest, 25, 226, 227, 285
New Opportunities Fund (NOF), 138, 142
Nitrate Sensitive Areas (NSAs), 217, 226, 228, 243
Nitrate Vulnerable Zones (NVZs), 111, 217, 248
Non-Fossil Fuels Obligation (NFFO), 319
Norfolk and Suffolk Broads Act (1988), 226
North Down Coast Path, 269
North Pennines, 80, 175, 218, 228
North York Moors, 112, 140, 159, 225, 292, 298, 311
Nottinghamshire Wildlife Trust, 90

Office of the National Lottery (OFLOT), 138
Open access, 173, 197, 198, 203, 264, 275, 295
Open Space Movement, 265
Ordnance Survey (OS), 105
Organic Farming Scheme, 253, 255
Organisational culture, 51, 55–57, 59–63, 65, 67, 72, 80, 83
Organisational structure, 55, 61, 62
Orkney Islands, 113
Otter Trust, 207
Overlay, 111–113, 168, 203

PANORAMA, 114
Pareto criterion, 197, 264
Partial budgeting, 122
Participation in countryside recreation, 15, 18, 273, 283, 286, 287, 292, 324
Paths for all Partnership, 276
Paxton, Joseph, 265
Peak District, 11, 80, 112, 159, 183, 225, 266, 285, 310
Pembrokeshire Coast Path, 269
Pembrokeshire National Park, 225
Pennine Way, 269
Permissive access, 250, 262, 263, 276
PEST analysis, 83–85, 100
Pesticides, 30, 186, 216, 249
Pheasant, 182, 186, 189
Planning and Compensation Act (1991), 221
Planning control, 204, 220, 325
'Planning gain', 221

336 Subject Index

The 'planning gap', 82, 83
Planning (Listed Buildings and Conservation Areas) Act (1990), 236
Planning (Listed Buildings and Conservation Areas) (Scotland) Act (1997), 236
Planning Policy Guidance Notes (PPGs), 219, 220
Planning Policy Guidance Note 15 (PPG 15) "Planning and the Historic Environment", 220
Planning Policy Guidance Note 16 (PPG 16) "Archaeology and Planning", 220
Policy Commission on Farming and Food (see Curry Report), 29, 313
Polluter Pays Principle (PPP), 214, 215, 217
Population Census, 8, 105
Precautionary principle, 214, 215
Preventative principle, 214, 215
Price elasticity of demand, 297, 298
Pricing, 200, 217, 290, 296–301, 303, 304, 313, 319–321
Private goods, 15, 181, 182, 190, 196
Programme budgeting, 151
Property rights, 9, 29, 191, 195–198, 200–203, 206, 209, 211, 213, 218, 259, 261, 267, 270, 288, 325
Public Expenditure Survey (PES), 123, 151
Public goods, 3, 10, 15, 16, 29, 30, 33, 76, 83, 87, 118, 133, 136, 145, 181, 182, 192, 194, 197–201, 203–207, 209—211, 241, 242, 256–258, 285, 316–319, 321–325
Public Paths Order (PPO), 267
Public Rights of Way (PROW), 158, 262, 265–268
Public sector accounts, 123, 124
Public transport, 12, 283, 285, 288, 318–321

Quality of Life Assessment (QLA), 164, 168, 171, 178, 222, 322
Questionnaires, 60, 101–103

Ramblers Association, 12
Ramsar sites, 34, 234

Recreation Grounds Act (1859), 265
Red deer, 183, 185, 190
Red grouse, 186, 189
Regional Assemblies, 40
Regional Development Agencies (RDAs), 38, 228
Regional Parks, 291
Regional Planning Guidance Notes (RPGs), 219
Regional Spatial Strategies (RSS), 219, 221
Restriction on Ribbon Development Act (1935), 220
Rights of Way Act (1990), 29, 183, 228–231, 238, 261, 268, 270–272, 277, 291
Rights of Way Improvement Plans (ROWIPs), 275
"Right to roam", 261, 266, 272
Rivalry in consumption, 198, 264
Roads Used as Public Paths (RUPPs), 267
Royal Society for the Protection of Birds (RSPB), 44
Rufford Park, 303
Rural Delivery Service (RDS), 41
Rural development, 33, 41, 47, 55, 80, 84, 89, 91, 92, 116, 136, 155, 227, 251–253, 258, 302, 315–317, 325
Rural Development Commission (RDC), 41, 91
Rural Development Plans, 251, 315, 317
Rural Development Regulation (RDR), 47, 92, 251, 253, 315, 317
"Rural proofing", 315
Rural Stewardship Scheme (RSS), 255

Sampling, 100, 102, 103, 285
"Sandford Principle", 225, 227
Scheduled Ancient Monuments (SAMs), 185, 236, 246
Scott Report on Land Utilisation in Rural Areas (1942), 266
Scottish Council for National Parks, 224
Scottish Environmental Protection Agency (SEPA), 41, 94
Scottish Forestry Strategy, 91
Scottish Land Fund, 143
Scottish Natural Heritage (SNH), 41, 63, 94, 125, 177, 227, 241, 302, 306, 311, 312

Subject Index 337

Scottish Rights of Way and Access Society, 276
Section 9 Grants, 125
Set-aside, 135, 248
Severely Disadvantaged Area (SDA), 136
Shaw-Lefevre, George John, 265
Shooting, 6, 11, 15, 181, 183, 186, 187, 188–191
Silkin, Lewis, 224, 266
Single Farm Payment, 136, 317
Site of Special Scientific Interest (SSSI), 34, 139, 201, 217, 229, 232
Snowdonia, 225
Social exclusion, 15, 146
Social filter, 287, 289
Social inclusion, 20, 144, 275, 291
Socialism, 12, 68
South Downs, 224, 227, 248
Southern Upland Way, 269
South West Coast Path, 269
Special Area of Conservation (SAC), 34, 234, 235, 248
Special Protection Area (SPA), 34, 217, 234, 236, 248
Speyside Way, 269
Stakeholder analysis, 83, 85, 86
Standing Committee on National Parks, 222, 223
Statutory Management Plans (SMPs), 228, 229
Strategic Environmental Assessment, 171, 178, 322
Strategic planning, 53, 74, 76, 78, 79, 81–84, 99–101, 109, 114, 174
Structure Plans, 80, 218, 219, 289, 290
Sustainability, 80, 92, 144, 162, 172, 174, 214, 221, 252, 291, 322
Sustainable development, 82, 143, 162, 164, 171, 178, 214, 215, 219, 222, 234, 238, 305, 307, 318
SWOT analysis, 83, 85–87, 90, 101

Tax breaks, 137
Tenant Farmers' Association, 43
Tilden, Freeman, 308
Tir Cymen, 249
Tir Gofal, 249, 250, 255, 270, 272
Town and Country Planning Act (1932), 190, 220, 222, 266

Town and Country Planning Act (1947), 13, 43, 104, 201, 218, 224, 229, 233, 266
Town and Country Planning Act (1968), 5, 219, 224, 230, 245, 267, 291, 311
Town and Country Planning Act (1990), 10, 12, 13, 60, 82, 83, 90, 106, 111, 126, 155, 166, 167, 175, 176, 187, 188, 203, 209, 211, 215, 216, 221, 227, 231, 236, 245, 262, 263, 266–268, 270, 305, 308, 309
Town Planning and Compulsory Purchase Act (2004), 26, 27, 45–47, 95, 144, 177, 219, 225, 227, 229, 233, 235, 249, 256, 280, 282–284, 287, 317
Traffic, 48, 141, 151, 158, 267, 285, 315, 320
Transaction Costs (TCs), 145, 201, 203, 206, 207, 210, 256, 259, 264, 267
Trans-Pennine Trail, 141
Treasury, 39, 70, 123, 124, 134, 135, 137, 149, 153, 155, 156
Trading account, 118, 120, 121
Tree Preservation Orders, 113, 218

U.K. Biodiversity Action Plan (BAP), 92–94, 251
Ulster Way, 269
UNESCO, 34, 234, 235
Unitary Development Plans, 218, 219
Upland Experiment, 81

Virement, 152, 156
Virtual Reality Modelling Language (VRML), 115

Water Act (1990), 263
Water Industry Act (1991), 270
Water Resources Act (1991), 215, 263
West Highland Way, 269
Wildlife trusts, 139, 145, 146, 206–209
Wildlife and Countryside Act (1981), 33, 197, 201, 230, 233, 247, 268, 270
Wildlife and Countryside (Amendment) Act (1986), 230
Wildlife Enhancement Scheme (WES), 245
Wildlife Trusts Partnership, 209
Wildspace, 142

Wind farms, 319
Wiltshire Widlife Trust, 139
Woodland Grant Scheme, 27, 142, 187, 255
Woodland Trust, 142, 206, 270
Woods on Your Doorstep, 141
World Heritage Site (WHS), 34, 235

World Trade Organisation (WTO), 48
World Wide Fund for Nature (WWFN), 145
Wordsworth, William, 5, 10

Yorkshire Dales, 142, 159, 218, 225, 245, 275, 277, 305